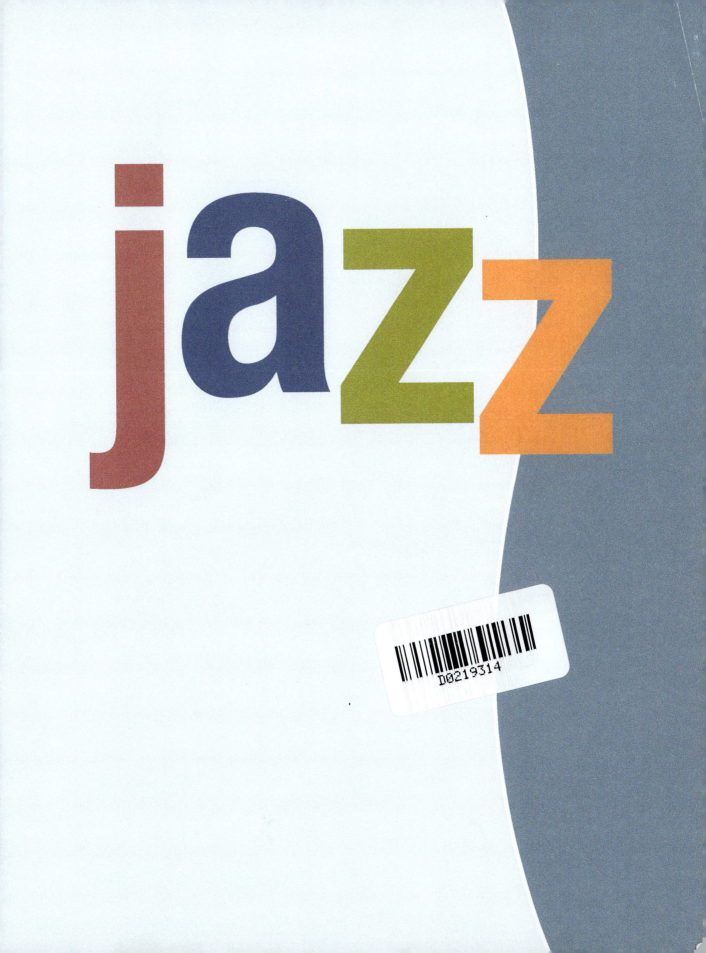

jazz

Twelfth
Edition

Paul O. W. Tanner
University of California
Los Angeles

David W. Megill
MiraCosta College

Connect
Learn
Succeed™

JAZZ, TWELFTH EDITION

Published by McGraw-Hill, a business unit of The McGraw-Hill Companies, Inc., 1221 Avenue of the Americas, New York, NY 10020. Copyright © 2013 by The McGraw-Hill Companies, Inc. All rights reserved. Printed in the United States of America. Previous editions © 2009, 2005, and 2001. No part of this publication may be reproduced or distributed in any form or by any means, or stored in a database or retrieval system, without the prior written consent of The McGraw-Hill Companies, Inc., including, but not limited to, in any network or other electronic storage or transmission, or broadcast for distance learning.

Some ancillaries, including electronic and print components, may not be available to customers outside the United States.

This book is printed on acid-free paper.

2 3 4 5 6 7 QVS/QVS 19 18 17 16 15

ISBN: 978-0-07-802511-2
MHID: 0-07-802511-7

Vice President & Editor in Chief: *Michael Ryan*
Vice President of Specialized Publishing: *Janice M. Roerig-Blong*
Sponsoring Editor: *Jessica Cannavo*
Marketing Coordinator: *Angela R. FitzPatrick*
Project Manager: *Melissa M. Leick*
Design Coordinator: *Margarite Reynolds*
Cover Designer: *Mary-Presley Adams*
Cover Image: *Darren Hopes/Getty Images*
Buyer: *Sandy Ludovissy*
Media Project Manager: *Sridevi Palani*
Compositor: *MPS Limited, a Macmillan Company.*
Typeface: *10/12 Meridien LT Std*
Printer: *Quad/Graphics*

All credits appearing on page or at the end of the book are considered to be an extension of the copyright page.

Library of Congress Cataloging-in-Publication Data

Tanner, Paul, 1917-
  Jazz / Paul O. W. Tanner, David W. Megill, Maurice Gerow. — Twelfth ed.
    p. cm.
  ISBN 978-0-07-802511-2 (alk. paper)
  1. Jazz—History and criticism. I. Megill, David W. II. Gerow, Maurice. III. Title.
ML3506.T36 2012
781.6509--dc23

                                                                        2011047648

preface

We designed this new edition of *Jazz* to offer students a listening-based approach to the evolutionary development of America's unique art form. We have increased the number of musical selections to offer a more comprehensive overview of important musical performances that anchor our historical overview. This edition is also meant to support instructors in their individual approaches to the jazz experience. Comprehensive citations to additional listening are given throughout the text. An Online Learning Center provides numerous enrichment activities to accompany the readings in addition to stylistic musical examples. Jazz is a history of individuals connected to their culture through their musical art. Jazz is a wonderful reflector of the cultural crosscurrents at work in America. When we study jazz, we also study our own cultural development. As we unfold the rich history of jazz, we hope that we will also connect you to the vitality of the American voice heard so clearly in the performances presented here.

CHANGES IN THE TWELFTH EDITION

- A new chapter devoted to John Coltrane.
- The Jazz Heritages chapter (Chapter 2) has been reorganized to clarify the timeline of early jazz influences.
- An expanded recording package features new recordings by Miles Davis, Ella Fitzgerald, Glenn Miller, Dizzy Gillespie's Latin Big Band, Stan Getz and João Gilberto, Poncho Sanchez, Dave Brubeck, and Thelonious Monk, as well as extended recordings by Davis, Michael Brecker, and the Yellowjackets.
- Features found in previous editions on the CD-ROM can now be found at the Online Learning Center, including the following:
  - Interactive Guides illustrating jazz styles
  - Matching quizzes

SPECIAL FEATURES

- **Witness to Jazz:** A series of essays featuring the images of renowned journalist/photographer William Gottlieb conveys personal anecdotes about musicians such as Dizzy Gillespie, Mary Lou Williams, and Louis Armstrong.
- **Profiles in Jazz:** Biographical sketches highlight key figures from the jazz community.
- **Vamping:** Interesting asides interspersed throughout the text add color to the presentation and enhance student understanding of the world of jazz.
- **Effective Learning Tools:** Summaries, suggestions for further study/listening/reading, and listening guides provide students with extensive support to master the material and enhance their knowledge of jazz.
- For those students with some musical training, we offer **optional material in the appendices** that includes notated musical examples and more advanced theoretical discussions.
- The text-specific **Online Learning Center** provides a wealth of additional resources such as listening software for use with the audio CDs, multiple-choice quizzes, enhanced coverage of jazz around the world, and links to useful websites.

We offer additional listening guides in the text for selections found on the *Smithsonian Collection of Classic Jazz.*

The primary author of the text, Paul Tanner, who was the lead trombonist for the Glenn Miller band and the first educator to introduce jazz studies in higher education at U.C.L.A., offers some personal insights throughout the volume. You may also correspond directly with the author on the Internet at *dwmegill@miracosta.edu.*

RECORDINGS

Four audio CDs are now available. All of the selections on each audio CD have a companion listening guide in the text.

SUPPORT FOR INSTRUCTORS

For the instructor, we offer an Instructor's website that includes the following elements:

- Instructor's manual
- PowerPoint slides prepared by Richard Condit

SUPPORT FOR STUDENTS

A text-specific Online Learning Center at **www .mhhe.com/jazz12** is available for students, which offers learning materials to help underpin the reading as well as supplemental activities for personal and classroom use. These activities include multiple-choice quizzes, links to useful websites, and many additional resources. Interactive listening software is available from this site that guides listeners through the musical selections referenced in the text and found on the audio CDs. You might also like to explore the author's web site at http://www.miracosta.edu/home/dwmegill/.

ACKNOWLEDGMENTS

This book could not have been written without the careful manuscript reviews by a number of professors. I would like to thank the following:

Michael Dana, Fresno City College

Robert Grabowski, Florida International University

Keith Hall, Western Michigan University

Maureen Horgan, Georgia College and State University

Greg McLean, Georgia Perimeter College

Jennifer Shank, University of Southern Mississippi

contents

7 DUKE ELLINGTON   151

8 BOP   171

9 COOL/THIRD STREAM   199

10 MILES DAVIS   227

11 HARD BOP, FUNKY, GOSPEL JAZZ   241

Interactive Guides to Jazz Styles

All Interactive Guides can be found at the Online Learning Center and at the interactive listening site: www.emegill.com/listening

1

Listening to Jazz

Jazz is considered by many to be America's greatest contribution to music. Its impact on American society has been enormous and its influence on world culture has been far reaching. Its message has been direct, vital, and immediate, enabling it to hurdle cultural, linguistic, and political barriers.[1]

Robert Hickok

AN OVERVIEW

Jazz is both indigenous to this country and the most democratic music ever to evolve. Performers in an improvised jazz ensemble are equal partners in the developing musical expression. As the music unfolds, the musical leadership may shift several times as the players contribute their expressive ideas. Jazz is defined by this balance between the individual voices that constitute an ensemble and the collective expression unique to that ensemble.

In its early development, all music not clearly classical was generally considered jazz, thereby putting jazz, country and western, and all popular and other types of music into one category. As jazz developed, the lines between it and the other musics in America became much clearer. In fact, even the distinction between "good" and "bad" jazz seems to have settled into a general consensus, but this consensus has seldom developed free of controversy.

The music of America has many faces. Few of these musical expressions survive a temporary popularity, but jazz ultimately matured in a way that wove it into the American fabric itself. It is often called "America's classical music," and it has proven to be an appropriate subject of study in colleges and universities around the world. Although there was other musical activity during this time—such as country and western, blues, rhythm and blues, and the popular songs of musical theater—jazz was the first to claim a dominant foothold in the American identity.

This musical and cultural phenomenon was not to be replicated until the advent of rock and roll, which now appears to have an equal amount of cultural energy to etch itself, as jazz did, into the American identity. Jazz embodies the irony of how a music can move from such lowly origins as the heartfelt expressions of American slaves, the music of the church, and the dance hall to the American academy and the concert stage.

When jazz first took shape, players did not foresee its acceptance as an art form. If this fact had been known, perhaps better records would have been kept of just how the transformation occurred. Jazz coalesced out of the many diverse musical influences present at the turn of the century. It is a music that could have developed only in the United States. It required all the elements, good and bad. It needed the rich African oral tradition of the Negro

Birdland, 1949: Max Kaminsky, Lester Young, George Wettling, Hot Lips Page, and Charlie Parker

slave culture and the formal schooling practices inherited from the Western European musical tradition. It needed the urban and rural folk music as well as the white and black church music practices. It needed the songs of **Tin Pan Alley,** the "Roaring Twenties," the marching bands, the jug bands, the tenderloins, the blues, the religious fervor of the Great Awakening, the hopelessness of slavery. Without all of these elements, the recipe for jazz would have been incomplete and not the American expression it is today.

HISTORICAL FRAME OF REFERENCE

Trying to re-create the actual blend of musical cultures from which jazz emerged leaves a great deal to speculation. The musical examples we do have are limited by the recording capabilities of the time, and these examples often stand stripped of the cultural associations that they reflected. To describe the music, the written accounts tend to use a theoretical system that is tailored to European classical music, a literate system that is significantly limited when applied to music that developed from an oral tradition. Consequently, we cannot notate the expressive singing style typical of the musically nonliterate practice at that time.

Without appropriate notation and audio recordings, only written descriptions are available. Like all historical accounts, these documentations tend to reflect the dominant cultural view. The language of the descriptions often reflects a frame of reference external to the musical culture being described. Such a report from the outside would tend to overlook potentially important nonmusical associations significant to the inside participants. What did the expressive church music mean to the enslaved black? How was jazz influenced by the strong emotional crosscurrents of the Civil Rights movement? From a distance, such cultural forces may unfortunately lose much of their significance. As we look at the substance of the music, we must also strive to place it in a framework that reveals its meaning.

UNDERSTANDING JAZZ

Understanding jazz requires an understanding of the jazz performer. Unlike music of the Western European tradition, which traces the history of musical composition, jazz traces its history through the performance of individuals. Jazz is about personal, unique expressions, and those performers most remembered by history have always stood above others in the power of their personal expressions. These expressions have always depended on the unique balance of the technical and aesthetic prowess of the performers themselves.

Because jazz is defined by the personal voices of its performers and only secondarily by its composers, it is misleading to force the musical styles used to define jazz into overly rigid categories. The stylistic similarities among players of a particular era are useful in understanding the evolution of jazz, but they are only a shadow of the individual creative voices that propelled jazz's evolution.

WITNESS TO jazz

mary lou's salon

Photo and text Courtesy William P. Gottlieb/Library of Congress. Bill Gottlieb stopped taking jazz photos in 1948; but, in 1979, after retiring, he began an intensive involvement with those old, now classic, images. Several of these images are featured in this text accompanied by his personal comments. Gottlieb received the jazz photography "Oscar" of 1999 at the Bell Atlantic Festival in New York. In 1997 he received the annual *Down Beat* Magazine Lifetime Achievement Award, the first given to a photographer.

"The all-time greatest woman jazz musician!" That's a typical description of Mary Lou Williams. Mary Lou was, beyond dispute, a fabulous pianist, as well as a noted arranger and composer.

She also had another role of distinction: that of a sort of "mother spirit" for musicians. Her spacious Harlem apartment was a "salon" where, in the 1940s, many prominent jazz people hung out, especially—though not exclusively—those musicians whose style was at the cutting edge.

I was a friend of Mary Lou and particularly remember when, in 1947, she had me show up at her place for an evening gathering. The turnout was small but choice. Among the group that appeared were three disparate geniuses who were, or became, members of the *Down Beat* magazine

"Hall of Fame": Dizzy Gillespie, the trumpeter and bebop icon; Jack Teagarden, the premier trombonist of the era; and Mary Lou, herself. To top it off, there were two of the most prominent boppers: pianist–arranger Tadd Dameron, and pianist Hank Jones.

It was a serious social gathering. No jamming. Just serious talk, mostly *about* music . . . with some attention to recordings played on Mary Lou's small phonograph and occasional moments at a piano by one or another of the guests to illustrate a point. As for the usually flamboyant Dizzy, he had no horn but smoked a pipe, looking on as if he were an elder statesman. The hostess, for her part, was all dressed up, with a corsage pinned to her dress.

A memorable evening!

An important first step to understanding jazz is recognizing that jazz is not static within its own tradition. This must be established before trying to distinguish it from the other musical traditions in America, a task that at first seems obvious but that ultimately proves more elusive than one would expect. What characteristics are common to almost all jazz and are not typical of other musical traditions? It is much easier to recognize something as jazz than to state how one knows it is jazz and not something else. The more technical musical activities understood only by the practitioners of music somehow signal to even the untrained listener that it is jazz rather than some other musical style. Actually, the musical elements of jazz are similar to those used in other musical styles. Also, most of the musical forms (or structures) of jazz are not new to American music. However, jazz is still recognizably different, its most distinctive attribute being the manner in which all these elements and forms are performed and the improvised context in which this jazz interpretation is carried out.

The interpretation of music in the jazz style originally came about when African Americans attempted to express themselves on European musical instruments. These early instrumentalists tended to think of their musical lines in terms of how they would be treated vocally. Eventually, the attitude developed that *what* was played was not as important as *how* it was played.

In jazz interpretation, the player restricts interpretative ideas to his or her conception of the melody, coloring it with the use of rhythmic effects, dynamics, and any other slight alterations that occur to him or her while performing. The player remains enough within such melodic restrictions to allow a listener to recognize the melody easily, regardless of the player's interpretation. Almost any kind of melodic line can be performed with jazz interpretation. Most jazz musicians will agree that to write down an exact jazz interpretation is next to impossible, and all will agree that only a musician who has played jazz can even approximate the notation.

WHAT TO LISTEN FOR IN JAZZ

"There need be no mystery about jazz, but each listener has a right, even a duty, to be discriminating."[2]

To appreciate music, the listener must be actively involved, and understanding and enjoyment go hand in hand. Passive listening will not bring intelligent musical enjoyment. Rather, such enjoyment is fostered through active participation that includes understanding, careful listening, and emotional response. The thrust of all musical learning should be to develop a sensitized awareness of those expressive elements of music that will foster a wide range of musical interests and activities and a variety of musical pleasures.

The primary aim in listening to a composition is to focus attention on the various musical events as they unfold—not an easy task. Mental concentration of a high order is needed. The mind is so conditioned to hearing music as a background **accompaniment** to daily activities—in the dentist's office or at the supermarket—that it is difficult to devote full attention to listening to music.

In daily living, one encounters many spatial relationships—high walls and low walls, houses and garages, sidewalks and streets, country and urban vistas—that are immediately visual and easily identified. In listening to music, one must forget the visual and learn to concentrate on the nonvisual elements.

Another difference is that music moves in time, and time relationships are less obvious in daily living. For example, a painting can be viewed at leisure and its parts observed in relationship to the whole, but not so when listening to a musical composition, when memory becomes important. The mind must remember at one point what has transpired so that one part of a piece of music can be compared or contrasted with another part.

Finally, if one is to learn more about the structure of music, it is important to develop the ability to separate juxtaposed musical sounds and to focus attention on a single musical element. For example, when identifying the **ostinato** bass employed in boogie-woogie playing, one must be able to shut out the right-hand piano sounds to recognize what the left hand is realizing at the keyboard.

Sounds Associated with Jazz

In classical music, each instrument has an "ideal" sound or tone, or at least there is a consensus as to what the ideal sound is. The jazz musician, though, finds such conformity of little importance. As long as the sound communicates well with peers and listeners, the jazz musician appreciates the individuality of personal sounds. This situation, in which personal expression is more important than aesthetic conformity, often causes listeners not accustomed to jazz to question the sounds that they hear.

Certain sounds peculiar to jazz have their origins in oral tradition and are the result of instrumentalists attempting to imitate vocal techniques. Jazz singers and instrumentalists use all the tone qualities employed in other music and even increase the emotional range through the use of growls, bends, slurs, and varying shades of **vibrato,** employing any device they can to assist their personal interpretation of the music. Jazz musicians have always had a great affinity with good singers, especially those whose interpretation closely resembles their own. Such singers include the early great blues singers (to be discussed later) and other talented performers such as Bing Crosby, Ella Fitzgerald, Billie Holiday, Frank Sinatra, Sarah Vaughan, Billy Eckstine, and Betty Carter.

Distinctive jazz **instrumentation** produces unique sounds. For example, a featured saxophone section or a **rhythm section** is seldom found in other types of music. Although it is a mistake to claim that trumpet or trombone mutes are indigenous to jazz (mutes were used in the 1600s), it is true that a larger variety of mutes are used in jazz.

To many listeners, the sounds of jazz are personified and identified through the musical interpretation of specific artists. Listeners who have not heard much jazz are often surprised that the well-initiated can recognize a soloist after hearing only a few notes—at least within the listener's preferred style. Talented jazz musicians seem to have their own personal vibrato, attack, type of melodic line, choice of notes in the **chord**—indeed, their own sound. Comparatively, few classical connoisseurs can say for sure who is conducting a standard work, let alone identify the individual soloists or section leaders.

Go to the Online Learning Center and listen to the Interactive Guide to Jazz Styles to hear how a classically played melody (Click on the links to Jazz Interpretation. See Appendix A for notational examples.) can be given a jazz interpretation then hear a possible improvisation of that same melody.

Improvisation and Composition

Sarah Vaughan

What is the jazz *idiom*? Classical music and jazz music differ primarily in idiom. A classical musician plays the notes, but the playing lacks the idiomatic execution usually found in jazz. The European system of musical notation cannot represent this kind of expression. "The conventional symbols could, in other words, indicate in a general way *what* should be played, but could not indicate *how* it should be played."[3] Idiomatic expression in jazz is the result of African American musicians interjecting African music into European music.

The Western European musical tradition is a history of literate composition. We study it through whatever written music remains from early musical periods. Without recordings, all that remains is the notation itself or descriptions of musical practice. This shortcoming no doubt influences the way we study Western classical music. The African American oral tradition is a history of performers and performances. How the music is played is more important than how the music was composed. Fortunately, jazz history is relatively recent and there are recordings to help us understand the true musical practice of most styles.

Within the Euro-American culture, literacy was always held in high regard and aural traditions were considered more primitive and less valuable. This perception gave jazz a racially charged context that would play out throughout its entire history. Jazz was often criticized as illegitimate and in some cases even dangerous. So the two cultural streams did not meet on even terms. It should be remembered that literacy was illegal among slaves. As jazz matured, it also had to find legitimacy and establish the oral tradition as a valid musical tradition.

A jazz composition can strike any number of balances between improvisation and composition:

1. The most composed composition is completely notated and the performer is expected to play exactly what is written. An example might be the way a member of the trumpet section of a big swing band would be expected to play his part.
2. The performer may play a melody that is an accurate reflection of the notation but do so in a distinctive interpretive style by bending notes, adding vibrato, altering the rhythm, and so on. An example might be the way a blues singer interprets a familiar melody.
3. The performer may make so many changes in the melody that it is barely recognizable. Swing soloists often made use of this type of improvisation. This type of improvisation would not be written by the composer but rather created by the performer.

4. The performer may play over the chords of a song but not try to include any of the given melody at all. In this case, there would be no written melody—it would be created entirely by the performer.
5. The performer may create the entire musical performance without any reference to a known musical melody or composition. The free jazz players often improvise everything with no previously known chords or melody.
6. Performers can improvise collectively to create new musical performances. All the players in a group make up their own parts, and little or no notation is needed. All the levels of improvisation mentioned above can be used to improvise collectively. For example, the Early New Orleans ensembles created their music by improvising all the parts, while arrangements written for the big bands, like those of Benny Goodman or Glenn Miller, might be completely composed in advance, expecting only the drummer and guitarist to improvise their parts.

The development of jazz can be viewed as a balancing act between the literate tradition of composition and the oral tradition of **improvisation.** These two dominant forces in jazz emanate from the musical cultures that have contributed to the developing art form, in particular, the African Americans and the Western Europeans. Each of these large groups carries sensitivities and preferences that play themselves out in the way each approaches the writing and performing of jazz. Depending on which influence is dominant at any one time, jazz has changed to reflect that influence. This balance is quite unstable and has shifted dramatically from the inception of jazz to the present.

If forced to reduce the contrast between the artistic approaches of the African American and Western European cultures to a single theme, one might consider the African American influence to be one of an oral tradition that expresses itself in the improvisatory actions of performance as contrasted to the literate tradition of Western European compositional practice. The exceptions to this general statement are many and obvious. However, this distinction proves to be quite useful for tracing an evolutionary line through jazz that describes the influence of these two cultures.

It may be useful as you study the musical jazz periods to identify the balance between these musical forces. Some jazz styles tip the scales strongly in one direction while others show a careful balance. Of course, even within a stylistic period different performers strike a different balance. The Western European contributions to jazz often emerge most clearly in those stylistic periods where composition is stressed (cool, third stream, early jazz/rock, the theoretical side of avant-garde, and fusion). These styles form an identifiable evolutionary thread that is interwoven with a parallel thread that is more typical of the African American oral tradition that stresses improvisation (Early New Orleans, bop, hard bop, the free side of avant-garde, and mainstream).

As you will see in later chapters, it was Duke Ellington who best controlled the balance between improvisation and composition. His compositions exhibited a complexity that an edited compositional approach affords while maintaining room within the architecture of the composition for the rich and individual improvisational voices of the members of his ensembles.

Paul Desmond

Rhythm—Syncopation

"Rhythm is the most magnetic irresistible force among all the elements of music."[4]

An emphasis on rhythm has always been an integral part of jazz, one reason being that for many years jazz was considered primarily dance music. Jazz players have found that a steady, unbroken beat is necessary not only for dancing but also for developing the emotional pitch identified with jazz, even though in some cases the pulse is merely implied rather than obvious.

The jazz player does not always play exactly in rhythm with the pulse. He or she sometimes feels the need to be slightly ahead of (on top of) the beat and sometimes to be slightly behind the beat **(lay back).** This is more a feeling than something that can be measured accurately, and it varies from one style and from one individual to another. Throughout the development of most jazz, performers have felt that they needed this pulse to play what they considered jazz. However, recent experiments in jazz have not used a steady beat. For years it was thought that all jazz must be played with a steady beat, but this attitude changed when new, uneven-beat groups **(meters)** began to be used in performing well-accepted jazz works. Pianist Dave Brubeck first brought newer meters to public notice with an extremely popular recording of Paul Desmond's "Take Five."[5] Most jazz, however, still uses even meters.

vamping

Degrees of Swing

Actually, it is quite natural to swing a melody. One only has to listen to children on a playground tease one another to hear a common and natural swing. For example, the tease you might hear is "Suzie has a boyfriend," which is sung in a melody most everyone knows. Children naturally swing this melody. You can experiment with this melody to create different degrees of swing. First tap your foot while you sing Su-zie has a boy friend. The syllables not underscored fall between the beats and are the notes that create the swing.

1. First sing the melody with the notes exactly in the middle between the beats. This should feel stiff with little or no swing. Even children swing it more than this.
2. Keep the notes exactly in the middle between the beats, but now put an accent on them so that "zie" and "a" are louder than the surrounding syllables. You should begin to feel a swing develop. This is the type of swing found most in jazz ballads.
3. Now delay the notes in the middle so they come just before the next beat, keeping the accents. This should create a stronger sense of swing that is more typical of faster swing or bop performances.
4. Experiment with the placement and accent of the middle notes to create different amounts of swing.

As you can see, how much swing a performer uses can be personal and quite individual. It is interesting that the amount of swing used can vary geographically. Often, the more relaxed West Coast Swing is compared to the harder-driving East Coast Swing. But even within these broad categories, individual performers or ensembles are characterized by the way they swing.

Jazz also makes use of a specific type of rhythmic treatment called **syncopation,** which places accents between the basic beats in the music. Jazz uses this so much that it has become one of its identifying characteristics. Syncopation is responsible to a great extent for the "swing feel" most often associated with jazz.

Syncopation and Swing

Tap your foot as you listen to a jazz selection and listen for notes that fall between the taps. These notes in jazz are often accented for emphasis. When the notes between the beats are accented more than the notes on the beat, a syncopated style is created. These syncopated notes also determine how much swing the music has. As you listen you may notice that the notes do not always fall exactly between each of the beats. Often the notes in the middle of the beats are moved back in time toward the beat that follows them. The combination of the delayed notes and their **accents** give the performance its swing. Some styles, like bop, swing more (or harder) than others, like cool. This swing is considered by many to be an essential ingredient in jazz, although we will find that some jazz styles have little swing while others are characterized by it.

Form

The word **form** in music describes the overall structure of a musical composition or performance. Perceiving and understanding the elements of form present a greater challenge in listening to music than in considering visual art. In music, the various parts of a composition are presented in time, and a listener can compare them by memory only. Many jazz pieces have relatively simple forms, such as the blues, which have a single musical section made up of three smaller **phrases.** During the entire performance, this musical section is repeated many times.

Repetition is the presentation of the same musical material in two or more parts of a composition. **Contrast** is the introduction of different musical material. From earliest times, repetition of a melody has played a vital role in prolonging a game, dance, or story. A similar reason for repetition is found in work songs, in which repetition of the melody depends on the amount of work to be done by those singing the song. When contrasting musical ideas are introduced, a new section of the form begins. The repetitions and contrasts tend not only to build the performance but also to give a feeling of balance and symmetry to the composition as a whole. If you understand the principles of repetition and contrast, you can sharpen your listening focus by anticipating the parts that are repeated and those that are contrasted and thus will have a much better idea of what to listen to and for. Consequently, you will enjoy the music more as it unfolds.

LISTENING GUIDELINES

As you continue your study of jazz, we suggest that you concentrate on some specific points while you listen, remembering that any jazz performance can have a blend of any of the following:

1. What are the general stylistic characteristics that make the style identifiable? For example, is the music fast? Does it have a swing feel, or does it have a rock-and-roll feel? Does it seem agitated or subdued?
2. What instruments are used, and how do the instrumentalists interact? Do they work closely together in a way that would require a previously written arrangement, or do they interact spontaneously?
3. What makes the performance a personal one? Does the singer or instrumentalist use any unique tone or inflections? Are there melodic or rhythmic clues that would distinguish this performer from another? Does the performance focus more on virtuoso technique or expressive content?
4. How do the bass player, drummer, and rhythm player (guitar, piano, etc.) interact? Which has the more dominant role? How do their balance and their roles differ from other styles? How does the drummer (if present) use the drum set differently for this style?
5. What other types of music possibly influence what you are hearing? Are there any classical, rock, country, gospel, rhythm and blues, or world music influences? From what jazz style is the performance derived?
6. Is there any obvious musical form (e.g., standard song form), or are the performers also improvising the form?

7. Is the melody singable, or is it designed more appropriately for the instrument playing it? Do the melodies played or sung overlap, or are they harmonized?
8. What is the musical focus of the performance? The performer? The composition? The group as a whole?
9. What is the social context for this style? Is it a reaction to previous musical styles? Is there a social message?

For a more technical approach to listening to jazz, see Appendix A.

listening guide form

Artist _____ **Title** _____
Key Personnel (musicians and arrangers/composers)
_____

The following characteristics are only suggestions. You may have other descriptors that better describe this selection. More than one characteristic in each category may be appropriate.

Melody
Parts with jazz interpretation
Parts improvised
All parts improvised
Uses blue tones
Ornamented melody

Tempo
Slow
Moderate speed
Fast
Extremely fast

Meter
$\frac{2}{4}$
$\frac{3}{4}$
$\frac{4}{4}$ (with backbeat)
$\frac{4}{4}$ (flat four)
Other (identify)

Rhythm/style
Ballad
Medium swing
Fast swing
Latin
Bossa nova
Shuffle swing

Harmony
Relaxed (not complex)
Slow moving
Uses IV to I (funky)
Tense (complex)
Fast chord progressions
Modal

Texture
Vertical (homophonic, harmonic)
Horizontal (polyphonic, melodic)
Both

(continued)

(continued)

Instrumental color

Solo spots played by:

Banjo

Clarinet

Cornet (trumpet)

Guitar

Percussion

Piano

Saxophone

String bass

Trombone

Other (identify)

Form

Twelve-bar blues

AABA

ABAB

Free

Other (identify)

Size/type of group

Small (one to two players with a
rhythm section)

Chamber ensemble (three or more
with no doubling)

Large, with sections

Mood or feeling

Frantic, driving

Happy

Low key, understatement

Rough, aggressive

Soulful

Sweet, calm, smooth

Detached

Other (identify)

Jazz style

Dixieland

Swing

Bop

Cool

Hard bop

Third stream

Free

Fusion (jazz/rock)

Latin

Neoclassical

Other (identify)

Piano techniques

Left hand (bass part in $\frac{2}{4}$ rhythm)

Left hand (walking bass)

Left hand (chordal, "comping")

Stride

Boogie-woogie

Other (identify)

Bass techniques

Two beat

Four beat with repeated notes

Walking bass

Free

Drum techniques

Backbeat

Flat four

"Bombs"

Rides the cymbal

Syncopated accents

Other jazz influences

Classical

Contemporary large band

Electronic

Free form

Liturgical

Rock

Popular

Latin

The following is an example, using Interactive Guide 2, of Early New Orleans.

Melody

Parts with jazz interpretation

Parts improvised

Uses blue tones

Tempo

Moderate speed

Meter

$\frac{4}{4}$ (flat four)

Rhythm

Syncopated but not fast

Harmony

Relaxed (not complex)

Uses IV to I

Blues chord progression

Texture

Horizontal (polyphonic)

Tone color

Solo spots played by clarinet

Form

AABA

Size of group

Small

Mood or feeling tone

Happy

Era or style

Early New Orleans

Piano style

No piano

Other jazz influences

Early New Orleans

summary

As we have seen, listening to jazz is an active endeavor that benefits from knowing the historical context of this developing art form as well as the identifying characteristics that set it aside from other styles of music. The characteristics outlined here are not present in every jazz performance. They are really only tendencies more likely to occur in a jazz performance than in other musical styles.

1. Jazz evolution is a history of performers more than composers, although both improvisation and composition are important parts of jazz.
2. Most jazz performances have some degree of improvisation. At one extreme it may only be a freely interpreted melody, and at the other so free that no precomposed music or compositional intentions are used at all.
3. Jazz has an interpretive style that makes use of vocal and instrumental inflections or idioms less common in other styles of music.
4. Jazz performances are usually very rhythmic and syncopated and have varying amounts of swing.
5. What is played is often less important than how it is played. Performers are expected to integrate something of their personality and background into the performance.

These are, of course, broad in scope and it is easy to find jazz performances that may clearly avoid most traditional jazz characteristics.

FOR FURTHER STUDY

1. If you were asked to describe why you prefer a particular type of music, what would you say?

2. Listen to "Silver" from the album *Collaboration* by the Modern Jazz Quartet with Laurindo Almeida and answer the following:
   a. Is the ensemble a large group or a small combo?
   b. See how many of the following instruments you can identify in the tune: violin, vibraphone, saxophone, oboe, piano, percussion (drums and others), string bass, and amplified guitar.

3. Listen to the Modern Jazz Quartet's rendition of the familiar carol "God Rest Ye Merry Gentlemen." Describe as many of the jazz ingredients as you can, including specific instrumental sounds.

4. The Benny Goodman Trio and Coleman Hawkins on saxophone use jazz interpretation and jazz improvisation in the same composition. Listen to "Body and Soul" and identify the places where you find interpretation and improvisation. Do the same with the music of Coleman Hawkins.

NOTES

1. Robert Hickok, *Exploring Music* (Dubuque, Iowa: Wm. C. Brown, 1989), 22.
2. Dom Cerulli, Burt Korall, and Mort Nasatir, *The Jazz Word* (New York: Ballantine Books, 1960), 36.
3. From Henry Pleasants, *Serious Music and All That Jazz;* 1969. Reprinted by permission of Simon & Schuster, 51.

4. Gunther Schuller, *The Swing Era* (London: Oxford University Press, 1989), 223.
5. Dave Brubeck Quartet, *Time Out*, Columbia Records, CL-1397, and *Time Further Out*, Columbia Records, CS-8490; Don Ellis Orchestra, *Live at Monterey*, Pacific Jazz Records, PJ-10112, and *Live in 3/4 Time*, Pacific Jazz Records, PJ-10123; Elvin Jones Quartet, "That Five-Four Bag," *The Definitive Jazz Scene*, vol. 3.

2

Jazz Heritages

Jazz is the big brother of the blues. If a guy's playing blues like we play, he's in high school. When he starts playing jazz it's like going on to college, to a school of higher learning.[1]*

B. B. King

AFRICAN AND EUROPEAN INFLUENCES

The initial contributions to the development of jazz as an art form are basically undocumented because their importance was not recognized. The country had recently finished a revolution that freed part of the population to practice religion independently of the mother country while the other part of the population was just finding its independence from within the first. These two populations, one white and the other black, put in place the balance of forces that were to shape the jazz expression. Their separate traditions, both musical and cultural, were to establish a musical genre that would be unique in the world. However, the disparity between the two also set up a constantly shifting balance between the dominant expressions of each culture, one from Western Europe, the other from Africa. Both brought different values and needs to the musical fusion that continues to define jazz: One tradition is predominantly literate and reflects that interest in its performance practice, while the other works through an expressive language typical of the oral tradition. As these traditions met, a balance of compositional concern and spontaneous expression was set in motion that ultimately shaped jazz.

INTERPRETATION AND CONTENT

All musical styles and traditions have an interpretive system of presentation that cannot always be fully described in terms of the musical elements that make up a performance. Consider the theatrical nature of a classical music concert and compare it to the performance elements of a rock concert. The manner in which each presents its musical ingredients—harmony, rhythm, and melody—is quite different. The musical elements of both are certainly arrayed differently but remain essentially the same: Both use similar scales, harmonies, and even rhythmic structures, yet the outcome of the performances is so different. These musical ingredients alone do not necessarily describe the meaning inherent in each style, much like describing the

W. C. Handy

parts of a butterfly fails to reveal the beauty of the creature. As the European and African cultures interacted to create a new music, they offered different resources that generated a new way of arranging the musical elements and expressively performing them.

Jazz, as a hybrid of musical traditions, reflects a blend of musical interpretations as well as a blend of musical elements. When looking at musical style, one is tempted to deal with the describable elements of the music and overlook the more elusive but essential expressive delivery. The problem of finding the beauty in a jazz statement is compounded by the tool set we traditionally have used to describe this beauty. This tool set is inherited from the Western European musical tradition and best describes music from that tradition. For example, the European notation system does not allow for the small pitch variations employed by jazz performers, nor does it address the subtle rhythmic delivery typical of jazz. Writing music down is useful as a compositional device but is not as important in a spontaneous improvisation. Therefore, when we try to notate an expressive oral performance, we are again pulling apart the butterfly.

Outside of the musical elements themselves, there is also the expressive context in which the elements are presented. Currently, no real language exists for describing the expressive meaning of any music, let alone that of jazz. To make matters worse, the expressive context rather than the musical substance may carry the most meaning to the average listener. Certainly, the majority of listeners do not know the complex musical jargon wielded by aficionados; but their interest in the music is still genuine. We must keep this context in mind as we examine the influences that shaped the early jazz expression.

We will also see that the balance of musical content and interpretive expression did not remain static during jazz's development. It is not uncommon in jazz for the meaningful content to reside more in the expressive nature of the music than in the describable substance of the music, particularly when the majority of earlier jazz's repertoire was borrowed from other musical streams. Interpretive expressions also shift constantly as jazz responds to the needs of the day. It is this changing balance between the various social and cultural attitudes on the one hand and their relationship to the musical contents on the other that generates the continuing evolution of jazz. The fact that several cultural groups are also working with the jazz expression means that simultaneous interpretive voices may be at work in any one jazz period. Compare, for instance, the white and black bands working in the swing era or the cool and hard bop styles that existed together under the same umbrella of the jazz definition.

The scattered origins of jazz—with their companion oral and literate traditions—tend to obscure any clear lines of development toward a jazz definition because that definition is one of a shifting balance and cannot be frozen for all time. Oral traditions are messy but prove to be a definite advantage for a growing and evolving art form. They have no rational guiding force or conscious theoretical systems that keep them historically neat. They develop through practice, not theoretical planning. To impose, in retrospect, a neat historical explanation on the happenings of early jazz music in America would be misleading. Oral traditions stress the expressive delivery of their musical substance rather than the compositional integrity on which they are based. Fascination with the theoretical underpinnings of the jazz expression was a much later development.

AFRICAN INFLUENCES

Western Africa is within itself both culturally and linguistically diverse. The music of each group would naturally be distinct. However, we might look for some overarching similarities that could help us understand the connection between American jazz and these African cultures. Music was by far the most vital and demonstrative form of expression in the life of Africans. From morning until night, from the cradle to the grave, everything was done to the rhythm of their music. The art form was passed down by word of mouth from one generation to the next and was a means of preserving tribal traditions, ambitions, and lore.

Music performed a vital role in maintaining the unity of the social group. Singing the same songs in the same way at the same time bound individuals together and established a strong group feeling. Whether religious or secular, improvised or traditional, the music of Africans was a powerful influence in their lives.

In Africa, music was for a whole community, and everyone from youngest to oldest participated. Music was so interwoven with work, play, and social and religious activities that to isolate one phase from its role in the total life of the people is difficult.

The Western European traditional notion of an *art music* tends to place it outside the functional daily workings of a society. For example, classical music is isolated from the lives of average Americans, except in the form of highly structured, well-planned performances. The Africans did not have such a notion of art music—their music was expressively tied to the everyday workings in their lives.

Many of the daily activities within a West African tribe were accompanied by the pulse and beating of a drum. It was a part of religious ceremonies and special occasions such as births, deaths, and weddings. Drums, ranging in size from small hand drums to great tree drums (sometimes fifteen feet high) were common. The drum served as one fundamental means of coordinating the movements of the wonderful rhythmic native dances, aided hunting parties, and played an important part in sport and physical exhibitions.

African slaves brought these traditions to the United States and nurtured them in the woe and hardship of slavery. The music that the African slaves brought to America drew on their African musical styles and traditions, which were subject to the crosscurrent of their new cultural context.

African Rhythms

One common misconception about the origins of jazz is that its rhythms came from Africa. Actually, it is only the *emphasis* on rhythm that can truly be designated African, not the direct influence of any specific rhythmic pattern.[2] Three important points to keep in mind concerning Africans and rhythmic sounds are that (1) religion, very important in the cultures of Africans, is a daily way of life, not just a Sunday activity; (2) African religions are greatly oriented toward ritual—their sincerest form of expression; and (3) African rituals have always involved a great deal of dancing, so rhythmic sounds have always been pervasive in the lives of Africans.

At the time when the chief exponents of jazz were generically closest to their African ancestry, the rhythms used by these jazz performers were simple, far removed from the complex pattern combinations used by native Africans. The rhythm used by these early jazz players generally consisted of quarter notes evenly spaced in the measure of music without syncopation or accent. At this time, the complex African rhythms should have been most influential on their performance!

However, emphasis on rhythm is such a natural element in African life that even African languages are rhythmically oriented. Because of their rhythmic cultures, Africans were interested in Spanish music. Some researchers even state that Spanish music is so rhythmical mainly because Spain was once conquered by the Moors from North Africa. Thus, it is conceivable that slaves in America heard something from their past in this particular branch of European music. In a pamphlet titled *Afro-American Music,* William Tallmadge writes of African penetration into Spain.

> This penetration occurred during the Mohammedan conquest [758–1492], and accounts for much of the highly individualistic and non-European rhythmic character of Spanish music. Spanish fandangos, tangos, habaneras, etc., were derived from African antecedents. This Spanish music readily amalgamated with the music of the African slaves who were shipped to Latin American countries as early as 1510. Afro-Spanish music influenced the music in North America in two ways: through Spanish possessions in America and through the importation of slaves into America from Spanish colonies. Since New Orleans played such an important part in the early development of jazz, it should be mentioned that Spain controlled that city from 1763 to 1803.
>
> It was soon discovered that slaves adjusted themselves to conditions in North America much better if they were first shipped to the West Indies and acclimatized there before being sent on. Latin American influences have, therefore, been a factor in Afro-American music from earliest times. "Jelly Roll" Morton, a jazz pioneer, once stated that Spanish rhythms were a part of jazz. In connection with that statement one might point out that the traditional bass pattern of [one strain of] the "St. Louis Blues" is a tango. Latin American rhythms continue to exert an influence on the progress of jazz, as these rhythmic patterns are employed in many contemporary styles.[3]

There is no doubt that the Moorish conquest considerably changed the music of Spain, Portugal, and southern France. Therefore, European music brought to the United States had already been influenced by Africa. Many slaves who were brought to America were first kept on the Caribbean Islands (which were French or Spanish possessions before they became British) for months and sometimes for years and thus were heavily exposed to French or Spanish music before ever arriving in the United States.

Call and Response

The **call-and-response pattern** heard recurrently in jazz can be traced directly to African tribal traditions. In its original form, the call and response was a ritual in which a leader shouted a cry to which the group responded.[4] A common, present-day form is a congregation's response to a minister or another leader. One hears the influence of the call-and-response pattern constantly in jazz. One example is the musical instance called **trading fours,** in which two improvising instrumentalists play solo parts on alternating four bars. In short, they are responding to each other's musical thoughts.[5] This interplay can be heard on many jazz recordings. Listen to Stanley Turrentine on tenor saxophone and Kenny Burrell on guitar as they use a minor blues tune to go so far as to alternate single measures of improvisation.[6] At one spot in "Casa Loma Stomp," the complete brass and saxophone sections alternate with one measure apiece.[7]

Another example is when a solo instrument "calls" and is then responded to by the background melodic and/or percussive figures of the other members of the band or of a specific section of the band. Listen to the entire band responding to Count Basie's piano in "Queer Street."[8] On the swing part of the Online Learning Center for this book, the clarinet solo is answered by the trombone section; later, the saxophone section is answered by the brass section. In Manny Albam's "Blues Company," Oliver Nelson and Phil Woods on saxophones are answered by trombones.[9] In Benny Goodman's "King Porter Stomp," Goodman's clarinet has the brass section as a background, whereas the saxophone section is the background for Harry James's trumpet solo. Later in the same selection, the brass and saxes alternate measures.[10]

EUROPEAN INFLUENCES

The melodic feature of jazz is inherited directly from European music. The **diatonic** and **chromatic** scales used in jazz are the same as those used for centuries by European composers.

The harmonic sonorities also derive from European sources: polkas, **quadrilles,** hymns, and marches. This does not dispute the fact that Africans had varying pitches in their drums, reeds, and logs, but the sense of harmony absorbed by jazz is strictly that of the European school.

The African Americans who first sang gospel music, work songs, and so on, satisfied the desire to imitate rich European melody and harmony. On the other hand, nothing in European music could compare with their oral sonority and the rhythmic vitality of their music.

The musical forms of Europe became standard in jazz works. The twelve-bar strains, such as those found in the blues, are directly traceable to early European music. Most jazz is constructed in a theme-and-variations form that is symmetrical. Africans, however, were not concerned with symmetry of form. In fact, if their music resulted in a symmetrical construction, they considered it crude and unimaginative.

AFRICAN AMERICANS
IN THE EARLY COLONIES

The evolution of African music in the colonies depended greatly on the particular colony to which the slaves were brought. In the Latin-Catholic colonies, their musical life was allowed more latitude. Latin planters were not too concerned with the activities of slaves as long as the work was done. Thus, slaves were allowed to play their drums, sing, and dance when not working. The British Protestants, on the other hand, tried to convert the slaves to Christianity. The slaves in these colonies were required to conceal their "pagan" musical inheritance. (It is interesting to speculate on how the resulting music would have sounded if the slaves from Africa had been taken to some part of Asia. For example, if African and Japanese music had influenced each other centuries ago, what would have been the result? Would it resemble any music we know today?)

Field Hollers (Cries)

West Africa had no art music by European standards, only functional music used for work, love, war, ceremonies, or communication. American slaves were often not allowed to talk to one another in the fields while working, but garbled singing was permitted. They established communication between themselves by **field hollers,** or *field cries,* that whites could not understand. The outstanding element of the field cry that is constantly used in jazz is the bending of a tone,[11] which is simply the overexaggerated use of a slide or slur. A tone is bent (slurred) upward to a different tone or pitch, downward to another pitch, upward to no specific tone, or downward to no specific tone. Examples of the four typical ways of employing this feature in jazz follow (see Appendix B for the notation of these examples and visit the Online Learning Center (http://emegill.com/listening/) for the Interactive Guide to Jazz Styles, click on the Jazz Expressions link.):

1. Example 6A (in Appendix B) demonstrates the bending of a note upward to a specific pitch.
2. Example 6B uses a blues cliché to show the bending of a note downward to a specific pitch.
3. Example 6C illustrates the bending of a note upward to no specific pitch.
4. Example 6D illustrates the bending of a note downward to no specific pitch. As it is demonstrated here, this is called a *fall-off.* Every jazz fan has heard ensemble endings with this type of bending.

The adaptation of these effects allowed the musician a freedom of embellishment not available in European music.

Work Songs

Some African American songs were born on the banks of the Mississippi to the accompaniment of work tasks associated with the riverboats. Others were born in the mines of Virginia, in the cotton fields of the South, and in the labor gangs of prison camps in Texas and Georgia.

The singing of these songs had one thing in common: They were sung without instrumental accompaniment and were associated with a monotonous, regularly recurring physical task. Also, the singing was sprinkled with grunts and groans inspired by the physical effort of straining muscular activity. Many years later, these sounds became a distinguishing feature of both vocal and instrumental jazz.

listening guide

🎧 (CD 1, track 1)
Huddie Ledbetter (Leadbelly)—Work Song (Axe Cutting Song)
"Juliana Johnson"

This song has a two-part phrase structure for each verse. Listen for the accent vocalization on the third beat of each **measure.** This signals when the coordinated work activity would take place.

:00   Verse one, line one. Notice the accent grunt at the end of each phrase.

:07   Second line responds to the first line. The grunts continue on the third beat of each measure, which signals where the axe would fall.

:14   Second verse is a repeat of the first verse.

:25   Third verse. New words: Gonna leave you, (grunt), oh may (grunt) . . .

:36   Fourth verse. Look out Juli, (grunt), oh may (grunt) . . .

:47   Fifth verse. What's a matter with Juli, (grunt), oh may (grunt) . . .

:58   Sixth verse is a repeat of the second verse.

1:07   Ledbetter explains that the singing will continue to show that the rhythm is still maintained, but you won't hear the axes again until later.

1:23   Seventh verse. The singing continues without the accented beats where the axe falls.

1:32   Eighth verse is a repeat of the third verse. Notice that the tempo increases slightly at the end of this verse.

1:41   Ninth verse. I'm gonna get married, oh lord . . .

1:50   Tenth verse. Gonna marry Martha, oh lord . . .

1:58   Eleventh verse. At the end of this verse he says, "Axes are coming back now."

2:10   Twelfth verse. Return to verse one with the grunts on beat three.

2:18   Thirteenth verse. Drop them axes, (grunt), oh lord, (grunt) . . .

2:27   Fourteenth verse. Dropping together, (grunt), oh lord, (grunt) . . .

2:35   Return to first verse as the song begins to close.

2:44   Final verse is a repeat of verse three.

2:52   Ends with a final grunt.

Jazz historian Rex Harris has described work songs as "tribal songs which started life in West Africa."[12] In addition, he stated that they were used "to ease the monotony of a regular task and to synchronize a word or exclamation with a regularly repeated action."[13] An example of this type of work song is the "Song of the Volga Boatman," probably the best known of all work songs. The grunt indicates the exact time when concerted action is to take place—in this case, when pulling on the oars. (Circus workers standing in a circle hammering huge tent stakes are another example of accomplishing a difficult task through rhythmic coordination; for notation example 7, see Appendix B.)

A good work-song leader was essential in coordinating the workers. He not only caused the work to be more efficiently done but also helped to make time pass. Huddie Ledbetter (Leadbelly) is reputed to have been one of the best leadmen ever, and recordings are available to prove it.[14]

Though work songs varied according to their use, the main contribution of the work song to jazz was the emphasis on rhythm and meter.

Minstrels

In 1843 Dan Emmett formed a group of four white actors called Dan Emmett's Virginia Minstrels. They began as a spoof of a popular touring group, the Tyrolese Minstrel Family, who performed mittel-European folk songs. Emmett's group was the first to perform in blackface and created cartoonish Negro caricatures. Minstrelsy was to become the most popular form of American stage music. The subject of these shows was often the lost world of plantation slavery. Eventually, African Americans began to perform minstrelsy themselves, wearing blackface and making fun of their race to entertain the white audiences.

At the beginning of the twentieth century, traveling minstrel shows were the main form of entertainment for both races. The shows featured the top blues singers of the day such as Bessie Smith, Ma Rainey, and others. The performances were accompanied by small jazz bands, which helped to spread the popularity of the new music.

The cakewalk, a popular dance at the turn of the century, was often a feature of minstrel shows. It was originally called the Chalk Line Walk, in which dancers would walk solemnly along a straight line with buckets of water on their heads. It eventually became an exaggerated parody of white ballroom dancers. It was the first dance to cross over from African American culture to mainstream white society. Contests for cakewalking and ragtime playing became intensely popular and a great moneymaker for Tin Pan Alley.

Creole Music

A segregation movement was initiated about ten years after the end of the Civil War. The **Creoles**—people with Negro and French or Spanish ancestry—were ostracized from white society and joined the ranks of the African Americans. Prior to the segregation movement, the Creoles had the rights and privileges of whites, which included conservatory training for musicians. The combination of the musical talents of conservatory-trained Creoles and the improvised oral tradition of African Americans resulted in an interchange of musical expression, and the music that evolved from this interchange was an early form of jazz.

Most jazz historians leave a considerable gap between the activities at Congo Square and the first known jazz band led by Buddy Bolden at the turn of the twentieth century. Actually, there was no gap because this period was filled by the Creole music in New Orleans. It was natural that this music was mainly French and Spanish and much more advanced (at least by European standards) than the music of the first jazz bands.

There were performances of French and American folk songs, society dances, parades, church music of varying types, and a great plethora of blues singing and playing. French culture was more predominant in the New Orleans area than it seemed to be in any other part of the country. With French culture came the European musical influences heard throughout the territory. In fact, Jelly Roll Morton added a jazz flavor to much music from the French culture such as operatic excerpts and French quadrilles, one of which he claimed to have transformed into "Tiger Rag."

Social discrimination, as it was practiced in post–Civil War segregation, placed the educated Creoles of French-black heritage into the true American Negro slave society. In 1894, Code 111 forced the Creoles to move to the undesirable uptown section of the city. In 1896, "separate-but-equal" status resulted in a closer association of musicians with different backgrounds. Code 111 essentially recognized the distinction between the Creole and Negro but legally declared them equal. This intra-ethnic cohesion reduced status anxiety, and, in turn, helped fuse the disparate cultural influences into a single jazz expression. The Creoles, with their French background, contributed harmonic and formal structures to this early music. Without any directions from the more educated musicians, it would have been impossible for the loosely organized blues or slave music to have congealed enough for Dixieland ensembles to have performed with the great success that was the beginning of this art. A blend of the oral tradition and the European

vamping

Congo Square

Congo Square is frequently mentioned in many accounts of jazz. Congo Square was a large field in New Orleans where slaves were allowed to gather on Sunday to sing, dance, and play their drums in their traditional native manner. (The name was changed to Beauregard Square in 1893. In 1974, plans were finalized for the area to be part of the impressive Louis Armstrong Park.) The principal significance of Congo Square to the history of jazz is that it gave this original African music a place to be heard, where it "could influence and be influenced by European music."[15] When the famous dances of Congo Square began around 1817, the backgrounds of the participants produced a music that was often a cross between French and Spanish with African rhythms.

musical tradition was necessary for a successful assimilation by the cross-cultural listening audience of the New Orleans urban society.

> But the repressive segregation laws passed at the turn of the century forced the "light people" into a closer social and economic relationship with the black culture. And it was the connections engendered by this forced merger that produced jazz. The black rhythmic and vocal tradition was translated into an instrumental music which utilized some of the formal techniques of European dance and march music.[16]

Marching Bands

At first, African American music in the United States was vocal, being accompanied by a rhythm of clapping, stomping, and beating on virtually anything available. Then gradually, after the Civil War, African Americans were able to make some instruments and to buy pawned and war surplus instruments. Marching bands began to influence their music. (Military bands, important in all French settlements, also influenced the development of jazz.)

There were many other bands in the New Orleans area as well. Every secret society or fraternity, for example, had a band, and there were bands for hire that were not affiliated with any organization. Most of the early jazz players started their careers in such bands, playing marches, polkas, quadrilles, and so on.

At the turn of the twentieth century, the most publicized use of marching bands was for funerals. These bands were used not only in New Orleans but also in the Southeast and as far west as Oklahoma. Such bands, usually composed of five or six players, should be considered a separate type of musical aggregation in contrast to large modern bands. Nonetheless, these small marching bands played an important part in the early development of jazz.

For a funeral procession, the African American band would drone a traditional funeral march on the way to the cemetery. After the burial ceremony, the band would march two or three blocks from the cemetery with only a conservative drumbeat. The band would then break into a jazz type of march, such as "Didn't He Ramble" or "When the Saints Go Marching In." The reasoning

vamping

First and Second Lines

When the bands marched down the street, their enthusiasm was enhanced by their *second lines,* found in every band. *The first line,* or **front line** (not an actual line), was composed of the players of instruments. Those composing the second line were young people who danced and clapped and generally encouraged their heroes in the first line. One of the second line's duties was to carry the instrument cases.

Another, more unusual, obligation was to protect the first line from competitive agitators from other bands. Of course, the goal of each member of the second line was to move up to the first line someday.

**Marching band
in New Orleans**

behind this established plan was that the traditional funeral music elicited mourning, whereas the later use of the more rhythmic music signified that the departed was going to a happier place—a cause for rejoicing.

When the band began to play a livelier version of the march, its followers would gradually respond more to the music. Their responses were often in the form of clapping, stomping, or any physical rhythmic movement leading toward dancing. In those early days, a band often marched directly from the street into a hall, where the same music accompanied dancing.[17]

The most common instrumentation used by these bands consisted of cornet, trombone, clarinet, tuba, banjo, and drums. One of the first leaders of a jazz marching band is thought to have been Buddy Bolden, who is usually credited with establishing the set instrumentation for these bands. Bolden combined brass-band music with ragtime, quadrilles, and blues in the first stages of jazz. The small size of these marching bands made the groups adaptable for various functions such as advertising campaigns, weddings, serenades, and so on. A group might also perform in a horse-drawn wagon, an activity that generated the name **tailgate trombone** to describe how the trombone player sat at the end of the wagon in order to have sufficient room for the trombone slide.

Because this music lent itself so well to dancing, much of the early jazz repertoire developed from marches.

> The transformation of straightforward marches into jazz may be compared with the process which took place when hymns were changed into spirituals. . . . This jazzing of marches was achieved partly by the trick of shifting the accent from the strong to the weak beat and partly by allowing solo players to "decorate" the melody they

were playing—solo improvisation; or several players to indulge in their extemporization simultaneously—**collective improvisation**.[18] [Boldface added.]

The regularity of march music could have easily influenced early jazz; today, people often "swing" as they march. The integration of the playing of the conservatory-trained Creoles with the self-taught African Americans produced well-played marches with the freedom of an oral tradition.

Most important to jazz are the emphasis on rhythm taken from African music, the harmonies taken from European music, and the melodies added by the improvisations from American culture. All these elements fuse to make jazz an American music rather than the music solely of the African Americans, who were (and remain) its pioneers and innovators.

RELIGIOUS MUSIC

Among the many places from which the jazz expression can be traced, the church is a central contributor. The expressive voices heard there were reflective of those heard in the field, but the subject and much of the musical content are taken from the white spiritual tradition. After the American Revolution, a religious fervor spread throughout this country and expressed itself in revival services and camp meetings. The services offered a marriage of preaching and singing. Most of these meetings were shared, but the congregants were segregated by race. The religious expressions commonly associated with the African American church today grew out of that interaction. The hymns used in these services were of Scottish and English origins as was much of the singing practice. Although much of the musical material was shared, a distinct manner of singing was maintained. The call-and-response technique of African musical groups had a counterpart in the Scottish singing tradition of *lining out*. The leader sings a line of the hymn and is then joined by the congregation. The resultant sound comprises a number of individual and overlapping melodies—individual expressions within the congregation.

This melodic singing style is actually quite similar to that of the African tradition. It is not controlled by the vertical musical structures, meter and harmony, most often associated with Western European music. The rhythm used is freely generated, and whatever harmony results is a by-product of the melodic singing style. Such a singing style was accessible to the African Americans who attended the camp meetings. However, the theatrical delivery of the two groups, white and black, did differ. Listen to the Reverend J. M. Gates's sermon "Dry Bones" for both the type of inflection he uses and the manner in which the congregation interacts with him. The call and response used here is spontaneous, and the vocalizations suggest later singing styles.

George Pullen Jackson, who authored a great deal of research on the folk music in America after the revolution, suggests that the later, and better-known, black spirituals must be completely attributed to the white spirituals typically used during the Great Awakening. This is certainly an extreme point of view that is generally not supported by other musicologists (see Eileen Southern's *History of Black Music in America*). However, the reciprocal relationship between the two musical expressions and the fact that they shared the same musical context in a common arena is significant.

listening guide

(CD 1, track 2)
The Reverend J. M. Gates
"Dry Bones" sermon

:00   Sermon begins.

:09   Spoken responses from the congregation.

:32   Short sung phrases from the congregation.

:45   Hymnlike sung lines in the congregation. This continues off and on throughout the sermon.

:59   Shouted responses to the short phrases in the sermon.

1:06   Gates begins to intone the sermon as the energy of the sermon mounts.

1:27   Shouts from the congregation.

1:33   Gates begins to sing some of the phrases.

1:50   Shouted call and response.

2:13   Gates sings a phrase.

2:32   The sermon's intonation here is very similar to that of a holler.

2:40   Gates begins the main point of the sermon as he continues to sing the sermon. The vocalizations are similar to those also heard in early blues. The congregation continues to respond spontaneously.

3:41   End of the recording.

Spirituals

"The impact of Christianity on the African Americans was, of course, the origin of the spiritual; owing to the fact that practically all of the missionary work was done by nonconformist ministers, their evangelical hymns set the style and flavour of the spiritual as we know it today."[19] Around 1800 there occurred in America a religious mass movement known as the Great Awakening. **Spirituals** and revival **hymns** that carried a great amount of emotion were sung at camp meetings. Spirituals, often called "hymns with a beat," were the first original songs created by Protestant African American slaves on American soil.

Spirituals are an excellent example of the blend of African and European cultures and can be easily traced back to 1780, but most seem to have originated between 1790 and 1883. The slaves added a rhythmic emphasis to any music taught to them, **liturgical** or otherwise. The better-known spirituals of today are the type that were generally heard in large concert halls. Examples are the familiar "Swing Low, Sweet Chariot" and "Nobody Knows the Trouble I've

Seen." The European influence of more emphasis on melody and harmony than on rhythm is obvious in these songs.

The greatest number of spirituals performed in the 1800s employed a call-and-response pattern[20] in which there was great emphasis on rhythm, with hand clapping and foot stomping—an example of the West African influence on European liturgy—in a set pattern of emphasis on the second and fourth beats. As Ernest Borneman states, "The accent was shifted from the strong to the weak beat."[21] Piano players executed this rhythmic accentuation with the left hand and brought it to ragtime music.

There are many similarities between popular songs and rhythms and religious music in African American church services today. Methodist John Wesley once defended such similarities: "Why should the devil be the only one to make pleasing music?"[22]

> The fervent participation in their "syncopated hymns" is something very remote from the Western conception of reverent quietude as an expression of worship, but hymns without beat are to the Negro religion without God. It is as natural, and no more naive, for them to sing hymns in this style as it was for Renaissance painters to portray Christ in Italian dress and environment.[23]

Early African American church music can be divided into three categories:

1. Many of the selections were improvised, made up at the moment by the preacher and his congregation; they would be remembered and eventually notated. Many of these were based on the blues chord progression because of its simplicity and because it seemed natural and flowing.
2. Some African American congregations would adopt European church music and add not only their own rhythmic concepts but also their own variations.
3. In many cases, African ritual music was altered so that it could be used in these services in America.

The spiritual, besides being a type of folk song, made its contribution to the development of the popular song and to vocal jazz. Although the singing of African Americans attracted little attention in the period before the Civil War, their singing of spirituals began to arouse interest and widespread attention after the war. It is interesting to note that the first collection of American spirituals, *Slave Songs of the United States*,[24] was published in 1867. The collection contains many errors in notation because, in the words of the editors, "their notations could only approximate, not accurately reproduce, the characteristic traits of the music in actual performance."[25]

The singing of spirituals was primarily a group activity performed in a religious setting or on a plantation. There is evidence that spirituals were used in work situations as well. A good example is "Michael, Row the Boat Ashore," one of the songs found in the 1867 collection. Often the song leader would be joined by the chorus singing the refrain (call-and-response pattern).

African Americans also participated in camp meetings, singing the same hymns and revival songs as the whites. In addition, however, they practiced a ceremony after religious services that had a direct influence on the preservation of the spiritual in its traditional performance style. This ceremony—called the *shout*, or "holy dance"—included a group of singers and shouters who would stand to one side singing the spiritual and clapping hands with great fervor while another group would shuffle and dance in a circle with a monotonous thumping of their feet. The swing element in the spiritual was kept alive through this rhythmic intensity of performance.

It is important to recognize the two trends that occurred in the development of spirituals in the middle 1800s. One movement adopted the forms and techniques of European art music, whereas the other conserved the traditional folk character by retaining the characteristics of the African tribal influences. The former spread rapidly through harmonized arrangements sung by choirs and concert performances by trained soloists. The latter, a style much like the shout or holy dance, was cultivated in rural areas or small communities, attracting little attention from outsiders. This type of African American vocal singing used traits that are fundamentally of African origin.

Gospel

In 1921, at a convention of African American Baptists, Thomas A. Dorsey was so inspired by the leading gospel singers that he decided to devote his life to the composition and singing of gospel music. His five-hundred-odd songs became so popular that in 1973 he was designated "The Father of Gospel Music" by the publication *Black World*.[26] His composition "There Will Be Peace in the Valley" was written for Mahalia Jackson. He also composed the most popular gospel song of all time, "Precious Lord, Take My Hand."

By 1940, gospel music became so popular in the Holiness churches that these singers were prompted to become professionals and to go on tours. By 1948, Sister Rosetta Tharpe was singing before as many as thirty thousand people in stadiums and parks. She had an unusual ability to raise audiences to new emotional heights through her moaning techniques and shaking head.

In 1950, Mahalia Jackson recorded "Move On Up a Little Higher," and the Ward Singers recorded "Surely, God Is Able." Both sold over a million copies, thus establishing gospel music in the mainstream of American music.

Gospel music, to be better understood, has to be experienced in person. By tradition, when gospel music is performed in African American churches, it is important that the audience respond. In fact, the performer's skill is measured by the amount of active support, or *talking back,* that comes from the listeners. Often a singer becomes so caught up in the intensity of the moment that he or she begins to improvise and embellish the melodic lines by bending, sliding, or adding tones, all enhancing the intense feeling generated by mutual emotional release.

Some gospel ensembles consist of groups of men who sing unaccompanied and supply the rhythm by slapping their thighs or hands in time to the music. Other ensembles are composed of women who sing with piano accompaniment and clap their hands for rhythmic accentuation.

The melody of a **gospel song** can be embellished in several ways. These techniques are used mostly by individual soloists or a soloist backed by a vocal ensemble. One of the most popular techniques is to use a passing tone, that is, one inserted between two tones that are a third apart. Another technique is to add one tone either above or below the last tone of the phrase, and yet another is to use several extra tones sung in rapid succession either stepwise or by skips.

Church choir

Gospel singing has been freely adapted by performers of other types of music and is, in a sense, a synthesis of many American vocal styles dating back at least to the Fisk Jubilee Singers. It must be remembered that spirituals and gospel songs are not necessarily musical works of yesterday, as the thoughts and lyrics contained in them are often contemporary. A fine set of recordings (four sides) includes a collection of gospel songs recorded between 1926 and 1968.[27] In fact, gospel and jazz are still partners in vocal groups such as Take 6.[28]

Spirituals sometimes contained symbolic references to the railways or rivers that led to freedom or to heaven, and sometimes the songs gave directions for escaping from slavery. Most spirituals and gospel songs refer to biblical characters such as Daniel, Moses, Joshua, and Gabriel. Many are well-known choral and nonjazz instrumental melodies (e.g., "Nobody Knows the Trouble I've Seen" and "Swing Low, Sweet Chariot"), and others are standard Dixieland and other jazz pieces (e.g., "When the Saints Go Marching In" and "A Closer Walk with Thee").

Gospel songs and spirituals are often considered religious forms of the blues. Blues singer T-Bone Walker agrees:

Of course, the blues comes a lot from the church, too. The first time I ever heard a boogie-woogie piano was the first time I went to church. That was the Holy Ghost Church in Dallas, Texas. That boogie-woogie was a kind of blues, I guess. Then the preachers used to preach in a bluesy tone sometimes. . . . Lots of people think I'm going to be a preacher when I quit this business because of the way I sing the blues. They say that it sounds like a sermon.

The visitor to a church in Harlem, or on Chicago's South Side, will not find a great contrast to the ecstatic atmosphere that might be found at a jazz concert or in a jazz club. He will find the identical rhythms, the same beat, and the same swing in the music. Frequently, he will find jazz instruments—saxophones, trombones, drums; he will hear boogie-woogie bass lines and blues structures and see enraptured people who beat time with their hands and sometimes even begin to dance.[29]

In the early Catholic churches, participation in the services by even the most faithful worshipers was limited. In the Latin-Catholic colonies, slaves often worshiped a combination of Catholic saints and voodoo deities:

> On the English and Protestant side, the question is as diverse as are the numerous sects of the reformed churches. The Protestant churches are less rigid than the Catholic church; one listens to the sermon and then freely sings hymns. It is this freedom which allows one to celebrate God according to one's own conscience which was to encourage a host of Negroes into the Protestant religions. Furthermore, God, among the Protestants, is praised in everyday language and not in the dead language, Latin. This permitted the Negroes to sing to God according to their hearts and according to some of their own traditions. The ancestral rhythm was reborn, transfiguring a religion.[30]

Methodist hymns were the most emotional, but even these were too somber for the slaves; therefore, improvisation gradually began to creep into hymn singing. "The hymn book of the day stressed part-singing which harmonized only by accident."[31] This accidental vocal harmonization indicates that the voice lines were invented independently of each other. In music, this is known as **polyphonic** (horizontal) construction, and this approach to the creation of musical line was carried over into Dixieland music and was later employed in more contemporary jazz styles. Polyphonic music makes use of two or more melodies that work well together but that also seem independent of one another. In contrast, **homophonic** music is more like singing a harmonizing melody to an existing melody. Both melodies are essentially the same only at different pitches. (For notational examples of polyphonic and homophonic music, see Appendix B.)

Often, some confusion arises regarding the difference between spirituals and gospel songs. Although the two terms are often used interchangeably, gospel songs are usually considered religious songs that recount passages from the scriptures, whereas spirituals are considered hymns.[32]

In 1867, a choral group from Fisk University in Nashville, Tennessee, left school to do a series of concerts to raise money for their college. This group, called the Fisk Jubilee Singers (*jubilee* is another name for a spirited, joyful hymn), traveled all over the United States, England, and Europe, carrying spirituals, gospel songs, and work songs to an international audience. Examples of this type of singing today are heard in the records of Mahalia Jackson.[33] Generally, most gospel music is simple in melody and harmony, and the excitement comes from the jazz type of rhythmic pulse.

Mahalia Jackson and The African American Church

Gospel music as an art form was all but ignored until the recognition—or, rather, the great triumphs—of Mahalia Jackson. Jackson never performed in a jazz situation, and she sang only songs that she believed served her religious

**Mahalia Jackson
with Louis
Armstrong**

feelings. She believed so profoundly in her religious convictions that she felt entirely free to expose her emotions as sincerely as any singer had ever done.

Francis Ward, writing about Jackson in the *Los Angeles Times,* said, "The earliest important musical influence in her life was blues singer Bessie Smith whose recording of 'Careless Love' was a favorite of Miss Jackson's and from which she learned much about the phrasing of African American folk music. Despite Bessie Smith's influence, Miss Jackson never sang blues or any kind of jazz, only gospel."[34]

For many years, Jackson's singing was not accepted in middle-class African American churches, as her music was a reminder of a lifestyle that parishioners seemed to want to forget. However, record sales grew, and she primed the world for the many gospel singers who eventually followed. Jackson went on to become one of the most stirring, most sought-after singers in the world. She died of heart disease in Chicago on January 27, 1972.

> When a gospel group gets up on stage before an audience, two things become important to them. They want to sing well and to express some religious convictions so that they can reach the souls of the listeners. When the soul of an audience is reached, you will very often see the people shouting, crying, screaming, clapping as a genuine response to the music.
>
> Although many Gospel groups write some of their own material, most of the songs making up the repertoires of these singers are old spirituals and religious songs that date back to slavery. These songs have been passed down from generation to generation and the people have sung them in church since early childhood. There are about fifteen or twenty "Gospel standards" that are sung by hundreds of choirs, quartets and groups throughout the country. It is therefore important for a group or singer to create his own sound.[35]

The worldwide penchant for spiritual music has not dampened since the early tours of the Fisk Jubilee Singers, a fact aptly demonstrated by Albert McNeil's

Jubilee Singers, who have given concerts to standing ovations in twenty-five countries. Some African American churches today still believe that association with jazz is wicked, an attitude that may account for the lack of African American jazz critics. However, because of the sacred works of Duke Ellington and many other fine jazz composers, this attitude has moderated considerably.[36] In an interview with jazz critic Leonard Feather, singer Vi Redd explained that

> the church was people's only hope in the midst of all the discrimination and oppression, so their ties to it remained very close and they felt obliged to go along with whatever precepts it dictated.
>
> I was brought up in this environment, but not as strictly as some of the other children, perhaps because my father was a musician. Some of the kids I associated with were not even allowed to have a record player in the house. They used to come over to my place to listen to Nat King Cole Trio records. That was their only opportunity to listen to jazz.
>
> Her [Mahalia Jackson's] music has the same harmonic structure, the same feeling, in many of those gospel songs. By the same token, Milt Jackson is a product of the sanctified church. Sarah Vaughan, Dinah Washington and a lot of the greatest jazz artists came directly out of a church background; yet the people in the church, in all sincerity, still refuse to accept it when it's known as jazz.[37]

summary

Jazz began with a blending of African and European musical cultures. From Africa came

1. emphasis on rhythm,
2. call-and-response patterns,
3. expressive interpretive style based on a close relationship between music and daily living, and
4. improvisational spontaneity typical of oral traditions.

From Western Europe came

1. the kinds of melodies, harmonies, and musical forms, and
2. compositional approaches typical of literate traditions.

The musical interaction between these cultures can be found in

1. plantation work songs,
2. church singing (and preaching) styles,
3. minstrel shows,
4. marching bands, and
5. the rich cross-cultural musics of the Creoles in New Orleans.

The balance that jazz strikes between these cultural offerings shifts continuously throughout its march toward art form status. As you will see in future chapters, new styles often emerge whenever the balance shifts dramatically.

FOR FURTHER STUDY

1. American jazz came about through a blend of the musical cultures of Africa and Europe. Discuss the influences on early jazz made by Africans and those made by Europeans.

2. Explain why it is incorrect to say that jazz rhythms came from Africa.

3. Explain the importance of Congo Square and other, similar, places in the South to the development of jazz.

4. Compare and contrast spiritual songs to gospel songs and to modern liturgical jazz.

5. Describe the following and discuss their contributions to early jazz:
   a. Field hollers
   b. Work songs
   c. Spirituals
   d. Marching bands

6. Give the instrumentation most commonly used in the early marching bands.

7. What is the difference between the construction of homophonic (vertical) harmony and polyphonic (horizontal) harmony?

8. Pretend that you are pounding railroad spikes as you sing the work song "I Got to Roll." Notice the places in the music where the singers give a half-shout or grunt. (This song is found on page 544 of Alan Lomax's *The Folk Songs of North America* [Doubleday], a splendid resource for background material on spirituals, work songs, ballads, and blues.)

ADDITIONAL READING RESOURCES

Brooks, Tilford. *America's Black Musical Heritage.*
Haskins, Jim. *Black Music in America.*
Roach, Hildred. *Black American Music: Past and Present.*
Roberts, John Storm. *Black Music of Two Worlds.*

Note: Complete information, including name of publisher and date of publication, is provided in this book's bibliography.

NOTES

1. B. B. King (b. 1925), U.S. blues guitarist. *Sunday Times* (London, Nov. 4, 1984).
2. "Royal Drums of the Abatusi," *History of Classic Jazz.*
3. William Tallmadge, *Afro-American Music* (Washington, D.C.: Music Educators National Conference, 1957).
4. Ethnic Folkways Library, 01482B, vol. 1, Secular.
5. Santos Brothers, "Beat the Devil," *Jazz for Two Trumpets,* Metro Jazz Records, E1015.

6. Kenny Burrell, "Chittlins Con Carne," *Three Decades of Jazz,* vol. 1.
7. Glen Gray, "Casa Loma Stomp," *The Jazz Story,* vol. 4.
8. Count Basie, "Queer Street," Columbia Records, 36889.
9. Manny Albam, "Blues Company," *The Definitive Jazz Scene,* vol. 2.
10. Benny Goodman, "King Porter Stomp," *The Great Benny Goodman,* Columbia Records, CL-820; *Big Band Jazz,* Smithsonian Collection of Recordings, cassette 3, band 2.
11. "Field Cries or Hollers," Album 8, Library of Congress Recording.
12. Rex Harris, *Jazz* (Baltimore: Penguin Books, 1956), 34.
13. Ibid., 30.
14. *Leadbelly,* Columbia Records, C-30035.
15. Marshall Stearns, *The Story of Jazz* (London: Oxford University Press, 1958), 38.
16. LeRoi Jones, *Blues People* (New York: William Morrow, 1963), 139.
17. Olympia Brass Band of New Orleans, *New Orleans Street Parade,* BASF Recordings, 20678.
18. Harris, *Jazz,* 57.
19. Harris, *Jazz,* 47.
20. Stearns, *Story of Jazz,* 93.
21. Ernest Borneman, "The Roots of Jazz," in *Jazz,* ed. Nat Hentoff and Albert J. McCarthy (New York: Holt, Rinehart & Winston, 1959), 17.
22. André Francis, *Jazz* (New York: Grove Press, 1960), 20.
23. Avril Dankworth, *Jazz: An Introduction to Its Musical Basis* (London: Oxford University Press, 1968), 49.
24. William Francis Allan, Charles Pickard Ware, and Lucy McKim Garrison, *Slave Songs of the United States* (New York: Peter Smith, 1867).
25. Gilbert Chase, *America's Music from the Pilgrims to the Present* (New York: McGraw-Hill, 1955), 243.
26. Horace Clarence Boyer, "An Overview: Gospel Music Comes of Age," *Black World* 23, no. 1 (November 1973).
27. *The Gospel Sound,* Columbia Records, KG-31086/KG-31595.
28. Take 6, *Take 6,* Reprise Records, 9 25670-2.
29. Joachim Berendt, *Jazz Book: From New Orleans to Rock and Free Jazz,* trans. Dan Morgenstern (Westport, Conn.: Lawrence Hill, 1975).
30. Francis, *Jazz,* 20.
31. Stearns, *The Story of Jazz,* 63.
32. Francis, *Jazz,* 20.
33. Mahalia Jackson, "If We Ever Needed the Lord Before," *Come On Children, Let's Sing,* Columbia Records, CS8225; *Mahalia Jackson,* Columbia Records, CL 644.
34. Francis Ward, "Mahalia Jackson, Renowned Gospel Singer, Dies at 60," *Los Angeles Times,* 28 January 1972.
35. Charles Hobson, "Gospel," *Sounds and Fury* 1, no. 4 (February 1966): 30.
36. Dave Brubeck, *The Light in the Wilderness,* Decca Records, DX3A-7202; Duke Ellington, *Concert of Sacred Music,* RCA Victor Records, LSP-3582; Duke Ellington, *Third Sacred Concert,* RCA Victor Records, APL 1-0785; Lalo Schifrin and Paul Horn, *Jazz Suite on the Mass Texts,* RCA Victor Records, LSP-3414.
37. Leonard Feather, "End of the Brainwash Era," *Down Beat* 36, no. 16 (August 1969): 71.

3

The Blues

As Ray Charles says, everybody can understand the blues, regardless of whether they've had them, or were born with them or born without. It doesn't matter.[1]

B. B. King

Before we discuss the blues, go to the Online Learning Center (http://emegill .com/listening/) and listen to the recording of the hymnlike melody on (click on the blues interpretation link, notational example 9A in Appendix B), which uses the blues harmonic construction. Notice how this same hymnlike melody (notational example 9B in Appendix B) is given a jazz interpretation. Let us analyze the blues construction.

The blues is neither an era in the chronological development of jazz nor a particular style of playing or singing jazz. Because of the great variety of individual styles used by those who are referred to as blues singers, it can be said that there is no single set manner of interpreting this type of jazz that should be labeled a blues style. General research has pictured the blues as something sung by old people accompanied by guitar; yet, from the mid-1920s through the 1930s, young energetic singers in Kansas City were accompanied by complete jazz bands.

The blues has been played and sung in every era in the development of jazz and can be performed with many interpretations. Any recorded anthology of jazz in general, or of blues in particular, shows this great variety of styles.[2] Blues can be slow and sad like a dirge, or it can be happy and rollicking. Blues is as important today in jazz as it ever was. Many modern jazz selections still use the basic blues progression with expanded harmonies. Charlie Parker's "Another Hair Do" is a good example of blues in bop, and Milt Jackson's "Bags' Groove" is played in both cool and funky styles, showing minor blues to be apropos in a contemporary setting.[3] Notice at the Online Learning Center the blues melody that progresses through Interactive Guides of each era. The same blues tune is used in each case, showing the flexibility of this form. Note that no matter how frantic sounding the music may become (e.g., the bop), the same blues structure is apropos.

THE ORIGIN

When African and European music first began to merge, the slaves sang sad songs about their extreme suffering. The singing was in unison, no chords were determined, and no specific form was designated. At this time, the name *blues* was not in popular use. During Reconstruction, however, African Americans could perform their music more openly, and, as it entered the American popular mainstream

Bessie Smith © Institute of Jazz Studies, Rutgers University as a published music, the blues began to take on a specific musical form. At first this form consisted of the three vocal phrases (AAB) and eight musical measures (each measure had four pulses, or beats; see example 3.2A on p. 44). The number of musical measures varied between eight, twelve, and sixteen, the most popular being twelve. The chords or harmonies that supported the vocal line also became standardized, and these harmonies supported the three sung phrases. (For a more detailed discussion of the blues form, see Appendix B.)

Slight variations and embellishments may be used to alter this form. If, however, the basic construction does not use the chord progression, the music is *not technically in the blues format.* Therefore, many melodies that have the word *blues* in the title and that are often spoken of as being the blues are not the blues because they lack the blues harmonic construction. The well-known "Bye, Bye Blues," "Limehouse Blues," and "Wabash Blues" are examples. Regardless of their titles and the fact that they are often placed in the blues category, the harmonic progressions of these songs are not constructed in the blues pattern. One of the most famous melodies with a blues title is "The St. Louis Blues," but of the three strains found in this music only two are constructed in the blues pattern. However, the blues is bigger than the technical form that normally defines it, and it also has an affective definition that comes more from the manner in which the music is performed than from the form, notes, or harmonies that are sung or played. Let us first look at the music itself and then follow it with the performers who made the blues come alive.

BLUE NOTES

One characteristic associated with the blues is the **blue tonalities,** which, in the authors' opinion, resulted from the West Africans' search for comparative tones not in the Western European or **pentatonic** scales.[4] The easiest way to explain blue tonalities without the use of a piano is to use a diagram such as the one in example 3.1.

Example 3.1

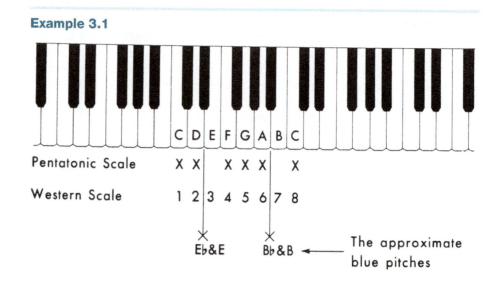

Western diatonic and chromatic music includes all the tones indicated on the piano keyboard. If the tonal center (C) is arbitrarily used as the basis for discussion, the tones marked with an X are included in a pentatonic scale more typical of the West Africans. As is noted, this West African scale has neither the third or seventh tone nor the flat third or flat seventh. Therefore, imitating either of these tones requires that the pitch be sounded about midway between the tone E-flat and E-natural and between B-flat and B-natural, causing what is called a blue tonality. Because no keys on the piano correspond to these blue tonalities or blue notes, pianists must obtain the blues effect by striking these two keys at the same time.

Blue notes, or blue areas, cannot be designated as concretely as stated in this explanation. Jazz players have always had a tendency to bend and twist notes as an additional means of self-expression. Long ago, lowering the fifth note of the chord became a standard device comparable to other blue notes. The use of the **flatted fifth** can be traced back to early players such as Bubber Miley in the 1920s. Musicians have always compromised normal musical practice in an effort to find personal expression.

One possible reason a blues tune does not feel as melancholy when performed at a faster tempo is that there is less time to bend the blue notes around in a dramatic fashion. The blues players used these blue areas so much that the scale used by these players permanently included these new blue notes.

FIELD AND PRISON HOLLERS

The work song often sung collectively by plantation workers evolved into solo *hollers* or *cries* that were free in form and used to make calls across open fields. This practice can be traced to West African groups that cultivated in open fields. The holler might be echoed across a field as a means of social interaction. It has been described as a "long, loud, musical shout, rising and falling and breaking into falsetto." Some hollers are actually wordless but full of expression and feeling. These cries might be compared to later street cries typical of street vendors in urban centers.

The holler was also associated with songs sung by prison inmates. A good example of a prison holler is Doc Reese's "Ol' Hannah" on the Folkways collection (FJ 2801). Although prison and field hollers developed later than the first references to the blues, they often are assumed to have contributed to the type of vocalizations now associated with blues singing.

Before the field cry, with its bending of notes, musicians had not considered exploring the area of the blue tonalities on instruments. Blue tonalities and note bending can be heard on many records by early jazz brass bands (FJ, "Didn't He Ramble," vol. 3). In fact, blue notes are heard in work songs, spirituals, and all styles of jazz. Tin Pan Alley (the popular music publishing industry) has used this element excessively. One can also find the use of blue notes in the works of many twentieth-century classical composers. Blue notes as performed in the blues were of melodic origin and reflected the oral tradition. The European developments placed blue notes in their harmonic structures within their compositions.

Example 3.2A The Usual Format Showing Fill-in Areas

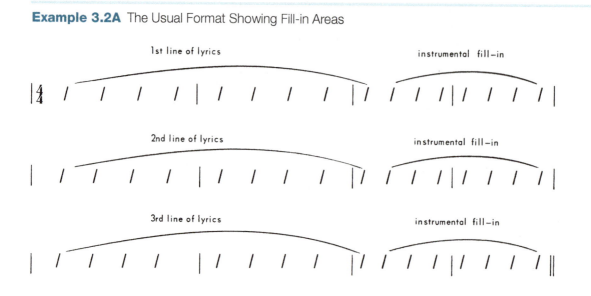

Both wind and string instruments offered an opportunity to use blue notes. The string player could pull on the string with the left hand to make a note slightly higher in pitch, whereas the wind player could move the pitch slightly by making changes in the **embouchure** (mouth position). These slight adjustments would create a pitch that falls between two notes on the piano. This out-of-tuneness helped create that blue-note feeling.

BLUES LYRICS

The meter of the blues lyrics is generally written in **iambic pentameter.**[5] Each line of the lyrics has five (penta) accented syllables that alternate with unaccented syllables (iambic). There are usually three lines of text in each verse, the first two of which are the same (AAB). For example, in "I hate to see the ev'nin' sun go down," the first line is generally repeated (a throwback to the African call and response) and then followed by an original third line. The repetition of the first line gives the singer the necessary time to improvise a third line. Often the lyrics of the blues do not seem to fit the music, but good blues singers "would stress certain syllables and almost eliminate others so that everything falls into place neatly and surely."[6] Each line of the lyrics consists of four measures of music. Because the lyrics seldom use the four measures completely, the remainder of each four-measure segment of the strain is completed by an instrumentalist. These areas within the strain are known as **fill-ins** (see examples 3.2A and 3.2B). Listen to the saxophone fill-ins for Billie Holiday on "Fine and Mellow" (CD 1, track 5), the trombone performing the same function for Bessie Smith on "Empty Bed Blues," and Louis Armstrong playing the fill-ins on Bessie Smith's "St. Louis Blues" and "Lost Your Head Blues."

Fill-ins were the first means by which some jazz instrumentalists were heard on records. In this way, some of the more talented players, such as

Example 3.2B

*Iambic pentameter markings.

Louis Armstrong, began to build a broader reputation. The fill-ins gradually developed in importance and interest to the point where they often were called **breaks.** Their importance was emphasized by the fact that the entire musical organization often stopped playing to feature the solo instrument filling in the break.

The blues, as they are sung, use lyrics that usually are concerned with unhappy situations: being out of work, hungry, broke, away from home, lonely, or brokenhearted because of an unfaithful lover. Consequently, their melancholy lyrics usually describe the blues emotion: "I'm laughin' to keep from cryin'," "Nobody knows you when you're down and out," "I've got the blues so bad, it's hard to keep from cryin'," and so on.

"By their very etymology the blues are songs of abandon, despair, or lyric sadness. However, content soon goes beyond form, and in the same mold all kinds of sentiments have been cast. Today, given blues are gay, ironic, sarcastic, vengeful. They were slow; they may now be fast (as in boogie-woogie) and even, in modern jazz, very fast."[7] Most people recognize the blues only by melancholy lyrics; and, as a consequence, many jazz listeners do not know that the blues can also be happy, swinging tunes. The great variety in this one form allows some entertainers to base their entire repertoire on blues.

Interpretation of the blues by instrumentalists and singers varied all over the United States as early as the latter part of the nineteenth century,[8] a fact that helps support those who contend that jazz did not originate in any one area of the country.

The word *blue* has been associated with melancholia as far back as Elizabethan times. Washington Irving is credited with first using the term *the blues*, as it is now defined, in 1807. By 1910, the word *blues* was in fairly wide use.

W. C. Handy, an Alabaman who was called the Father of the Blues, wrote "The Memphis Blues" in 1909 as a political campaign song. His two most

listening guide

Bessie Smith
"Lost Your Head Blues"*

Bessie Smith singing "Lost Your Head Blues" with Louis Armstrong playing fill-ins on trumpet:

:00   Four-bar introduction. Open trumpet solo by Louis Armstrong.

:11   First chorus, sung by Bessie Smith, backed by muted trumpet. The first vocal phrase, "I was with you baby when you didn't have a dime," is followed by trumpet fill-in.

:21   The second vocal phrase of the blues chorus, which repeats the same lyric phrase.

:30   The third and final vocal phrase, which has a new lyric phrase that responds to the first two phrases: "And since you got plenty money you threw your good gal down."

:44   Second blues chorus. The structure is the same in both harmonies and lyric phrases, but the lyrics are new.

1:17 Third blues chorus. This and the remaining choruses follow the same pattern established in the first two choruses.

1:50 Fourth blues chorus.

2:22 Fifth blues chorus with a more lyrical phrasing used by Smith.

2:54 End.

*Smithsonian Collection, CD 1, track 4.

famous songs with "Blues" in the title are "The Memphis Blues" and "St. Louis Blues." Handy proved that money could be made from writing and publishing blues tunes. Around 1917, blues became more popular as ragtime began to fade. White artists had recorded blues songs as early as 1910. An early blues recording by an African American artist was Mamie Smith's "Crazy Blues" in 1920; it sold seventy-five thousand copies in the first month and a million copies in the first six months.

A common misconception is that the blues originated with work songs. Actually, work songs were functional, whereas blues songs were usually quite emotional and had no specific function. The consensus among authorities who write about jazz is that the blues was important in the development of jazz. This musical form has never lost its importance, and it is heard as frequently today as it was in all the previous eras of jazz. Blues performances in general are filled with subtleties. Recent adaptations, such as rhythm and blues in 1945 and rock and roll in 1955, show the durability of the form as it continues to survive through all adaptations.

listening guide

Jelly Roll Morton
"Dead Man Blues"*

:00 Introduction: A funeral march with trombone lead.

:14 Ensemble: Listen for the standard blues chord sequence over the established Dixieland instrumental format. Listen for the loose interweaving instrumental lines that make up the polyphonic Dixieland style.

:35 Clarinet solo for a blues chorus.

:57 Trumpet solo for two blues choruses.

1:20 Second chorus of trumpet solo.

1:41 Clarinet trio: Accents by the rest of the band on the fourth beat of every other measure that anticipate the riffing that will become important in later big bands.

2:02 Clarinet trio with trombone playing a solo legato line.

2:23 Ensemble in the Dixieland polyphonic style.

2:45 Tag played by the clarinet trio.

2:49 End.

*Smithsonian Collection, CD 1, track 7.

The period from 1930 on is divided primarily between singers and instrumentalists. The singers include such talented artists as Joe Turner, Jimmy Rushing, Joe Williams, and Jimmy Witherspoon. The problem with listing the best blues instrumentalists is that they were also singers (e.g., Louis Armstrong, Jack Teagarden, and Ray Charles). It is an oddity that in the beginnings of jazz, instrumentalists copied vocal techniques but that later some of the best jazz singers imitated instrumental jazz. Consequently, some of the best jazz singers were also instrumentalists.

COUNTRY AND URBAN BLUES

"I guess all songs is folk songs. I never heard no horse sing 'em."[9] Big Bill Broonzy

During the early 1930s, the blues more typical of the South had migrated to cities like Chicago, where it reflected in its more extroverted style the hard times of urban life. One of the most important figures of late country blues is guitarist-singer Robert Johnson. Listen to "Hellhound on My Trail" for his unique vocalizations.

vamping

Big Bill Broonzy

A transition figure in the development of urban, or city, blues is "Big Bill" (William Lee Conley) Broonzy. He was originally a fiddle player who learned the guitar. His "Big Bill Blues" and "Keep Your Hands off Her" show the range of his personal style.

Big Bill Broonzy's recordings span a thirty-one-year period. Broonzy, who directly influenced Josh White and many others, composed about three hundred songs. One of the most famous of his records, "Troubled in Mind" (Folkways Records), has lyrics in the eight-bar blues construction that have inspired many downtrodden persons to have hope:

> *Troubled in mind, I'm blue.*
> *But I won't be blue always.*
> *The sun's gonna shine*
> *In my back do' someday.*[10]

Huddie Ledbetter

vamping

Tin Pan Alley

Before continuing a discussion of the genre that produced vocal jazz, a brief description should be made of the printed outlet for such music, namely, the sheet music publishing industry.

Before 1880, the most important song publishers were located in such cities as New York City, Chicago, Pittsburgh, Detroit, Milwaukee, and San Francisco. By the middle of the 1890s, however, Union Square of New York City became the center of the largest concentration of song publishers in the country.

The method of selling their songs to the public was unique even for those days. The song pluggers would do almost anything to get an audience. They would visit the shops selling sheet music and play the tunes on the piano all day long. Others would travel by truck through the city streets singing their songs through megaphones to attract the people.

By 1900 the "Street of Song" moved from Union Square to 28th Street between Fifth and Sixth Avenues. This location of the music publishing industry was baptized Tin Pan Alley by a journalist who heard a piano being played with strips of paper stuffed between the piano strings producing a tinny effect. It was in Tin Pan Alley where the song plugger was king, demonstrating newly published songs on the piano, and where the million-copy sale of sheet music became a common event.

About 1930 with the advent of recordings, radio, and talking motion pictures, Tin Pan Alley with its techniques of writing and selling songs became obsolete.

City blues seems to be more rhythmic, more crisp, than country blues. Most country blues singers accompanied themselves on guitar, whereas urban blues performers often used fairly elaborate accompaniment, including that of jazz musicians like Louis Armstrong.

Huddie Ledbetter, known as Leadbelly, was discovered on a prison farm in Louisiana by John and Alan Lomax. He has been quoted as saying that he was born in 1885 in Louisiana and raised in Texas. He became a guide for Blind Lemon Jefferson and learned twelve-string guitar technique from him. Ledbetter spent a considerable amount of time in prison and became known as a valuable leadman for work songs. The Library of Congress contains 144 songs recorded by Ledbetter between 1933 and 1940 under the supervision of the Lomaxes. Some recordings can be heard today on Folkways Records and some on Columbia Records. Ledbetter seldom played softly, as he felt that blues tunes were meant to be danced to or worked to. His blues and folk songs gained him much popularity and led to many tours and concerts. Huddie Ledbetter died in 1949 in New York. His "Good Night, Irene" became extremely popular even among people who knew nothing about him.

SINGING THE BLUES
Blues Singers

The history of the blues and the story of blues singers are complete studies in themselves, deserving of the fine volumes written about them. Students of the blues and blues singers will be aided greatly by the historically important Library of Congress recordings. The aim of this book, however, is to point out a few singers who were important in this field.

All types of blues, from the early to the present-day forms, have greatly influenced how jazz players perform, but certain singers have been heard more than others and thus have had more influence. "The great blues singers of the twenties and the early thirties bred the jazz men, but they also bred a line of itinerant musicians who sang and played only the blues."[11] Today, in retrospect, it is impossible to separate blues from jazz as performed in the past or the present.

After World War I, America saw the largest population movement in U.S. history: the Great Migration. This migration carried a large number of the African American population to large northern cities and proved to be a key modernizing moment in African American history. These people wanted the type of entertainment they were accustomed to, and so there was a demand for blues singers. Because recordings of African American singers were bought and heard only by African Americans, a collection of what were called *race records* developed. When whites eventually began to hear them, the fragile 78 rpm records became collector's items, sometimes selling for over $100 each.

Two blues periods can be discerned, the first from the latter part of the nineteenth century to about 1930 and the second from about 1930 to the present. The early period is usually divided between performers who sang *country,* or *rural, blues* and those who sang *city,* or *urban, blues.* The best-known early rural blues singers were Big Bill Broonzy, Robert Johnson, Josh White, Blind Lemon Jefferson, Huddie Ledbetter ("Juliana Johnson"), Son House, and Lightnin' Hopkins, who were followed by Albert King, T-Bone Walker, B. B. King, and others. The early urban blues singers were mostly women: Ma Rainey, Chippie Hill, Mamie Smith, Trixie Smith, and, most famous of all, Bessie Smith.

Early rural blues was created by African American singers in solo form accompanied by guitar, harmonica, or both. These itinerant singers converged on the cities of the South and Midwest in the 1890s in search of work. Eventually, the influence of female blues singers in the cities made its impact on Tin Pan Alley as another type of American popular song: the blues.

The blues became popular in the performances of such singers as Gertrude "Ma" Rainey, who recorded fifty records,[12] and her pupil Bessie Smith. W. C. Handy, a composer of early published blues, later introduced this type of rural folk song as the blues.

Both Ma Rainey and Bessie Smith were professional vaudeville singers who took great pride in their ability to sing popular songs (vaudeville blues was popular music composed by Tin Pan Alley professionals). These singers used a song style that was smooth; the words were well enunciated and the overall delivery was somewhat dramatic.

Usually, the women who sang vaudeville blues were accompanied not by a guitar or another instrument but by a small jazz **combo** in which the piano played the underlying beat and a solo horn improvised on the fill-ins during a

listening guide

(CD 1, track 3)
Robert Johnson
"Hellhound on My Trail"

:00	Guitar introduction.	I got to keep movin'
:09	(A) First verse. This is the first blues phrase. The phrasing is very loose as the song gets under way.	I got to keep movin' blues fallin' down like hail blues fallin' down like hail
:23	(A) (humming in place of repeating the first line) The second blues phrase. Notice the guitar fill before the next verse begins.	Umm mmm mmm mmm blues fallin' down like hail blues fallin' down like hail
:36	(B) Second blues phrase with an underpinning chord change. Notice how text lines are repeated to fill up the harmonic phrase.	And the days keeps on worryin' me there's a hellhound on my trail hellhound on my trail hellhound on my trail
:51	(A) Second verse. Notice how he bends the guitar notes here.	If today was Christmas Eve If today was Christmas Eve and tomorrow was Christmas Day
1:03	(A) Spoken line used to fill the phrase.	If today was Christmas Eve and tomorrow was Christmas Day spoken: Aow, wouldn't we have a time, baby?
1:13	(B) Vocal repeat used to fill the phrase.	All I would need my little sweet rider just to pass the time away, huh huh to pass the time away
1:25	(A) Third verse. Notice throughout how the melody notes are expressively altered (bent, scooped, etc.).	You sprinkled hot foot powder, mmm mmm, around my door all around my door
1:35	(A)	You sprinkled hot foot powder all around your daddy's door, hmm hmm hmm
1:45	(B)	It keep me with ramblin' mind, rider every old place I go every old place I go
1:58	(A)	I can tell the wind is risin' the leaves tremblin' on the tree Tremblin' on the tree
2:10	(A)	I can tell the wind is risin' leaves tremblin' on the tree hmm hmm hmm mmm
2:21	(B)	All I need's my little sweet woman and to keep my company, hey hey hey hey my company
2:38	End.	

pause in the vocal line. If a solo pianist provided the accompaniment, the style of playing consisted of a stride bass line with improvised fill-ins.

Bessie Smith

Bessie Smith was born in Tennessee in 1894. She made her first recording, "Downhearted Blues," in 1923, selling eight hundred thousand copies to an almost exclusively African American public and becoming the best-known blues singer of the 1920s. Smith had a large voice and showed a wonderful talent for interpreting lyrics personally. Even today, when one listens to her recordings, it is easy to feel the deep emotion that she communicated to her contemporaries. Her repertoire was varied, and her personal feelings show on her recordings—sometimes sad, other times happy and full of humor.

Smith would interpret any given song by reshaping it to her special vocal style and to her feelings about the text. She would infuse the melodic line by embellishment, that is, melodic and rhythmic changes with a special type of word emphasis. Through her unique style of singing, she not only became known as the Empress of the Blues but also served as a model for the blues and jazz singers who followed.

By the end of her first recording year (1923), Smith had sold over two million records and by 1927 four million. She recorded 160 songs and literally saved Columbia Records from bankruptcy at that time. Smith also made a movie short—quite a breakthrough for an African American singer whose market was primarily ethnic. She earned a great deal of money and spent as much. By 1930, public interest in her began to wane, some say because she would not adjust to more modern song material. But listening to Bessie Smith

listening guide

(CD 1, track 4)
Bessie Smith (singing)
Charlie Green, trombone
"Empty Bed Blues"

:00   Four-measure introduction by trombone and piano; the trombone plays a tailgate style.

:11   First vocal chorus: 12 measures of fill-ins by trombone throughout the recording. First lyric phrase, "I woke up this moning with a awful achy head."

:23   Second phrase of blues chorus with repeat of first lyric phrase.

:34   Third lyric phrase responds to the repeated first phrase, "My new man had left me just a room and an empty bed." This completes the standard 12-bar blues chorus.

:45   Second vocal chorus. This chorus, like the rest to follow, is also a standard 12-bar chorus.

1:18   Third vocal chorus. Listen for the trombone growls and the different accompaniment patterns used by the piano: 12 measures.

1:24   Trombone growls continue.

1:53   Fourth vocal chorus. Continued variation in the piano accompaniment: 12 measures.

2:26   Fifth vocal chorus. Piano uses ragtime feel as accompaniment: 12 measures.

3:01   End.

records, one can feel that the blues was very personal to her and that she sang these songs with great sincerity.[13]

Smith was always selective in choosing her accompanying musicians, among whom were Clarence Williams, Fletcher Henderson, Louis Armstrong, Don Redman, Coleman Hawkins, James P. Johnson, Jack Teagarden, Benny Goodman, Charlie Green, and Buster Bailey.

She died penniless in 1937 in an automobile accident. At the time of her death, about ten million of her records had been sold. With her great gift of communication, Bessie Smith set the standard for all future singing of the blues.

Ma Rainey, Bessie Smith, and other singers trained on the minstrel circuits. Sadly, many black minstrels were copies of white minstrels—truly imitations of imitations—and their performances often did not reveal the artistry they were capable of. Ma Rainey, called the Mother of the Blues, was born in 1886, yet recordings of her work are still available on the Document label. Reissues of Bessie Smith's work are now available on the Columbia label.

listening guide

Bessie Smith (singing)
"St. Louis Blues"*

:00   Chord on reed organ and muted trumpet.

:03   First strain: vocal (Bessie Smith) accompanied by fill-ins on the muted trumpet (Louis Armstrong); listen for the standard blues chord sequence that is repeated.

:18   Repeat of first vocal phrase "I hate to see the evening sun go down."

:32   Third responding phrase of the blues chorus.

:48   Repeat of the first chorus with new lyrics: vocal with trumpet fill-ins; this section breaks the 12-bar blues pattern with 16 measures that set up the return to the next section

1:31   Middle section: vocal with trumpet fill-ins; leaves the standard blues chord sequence—16 measures.

2:26   Last section: Returns to the blues structure with trumpet fill-ins.

3:07   End.

*Smithsonian Collection, CD 1, track 3.

Technical mastery on these recordings is very good, and they are quite important for historical documentation. They are also fine recordings for mere listening pleasure.

Ethel Waters

Ethel Waters made a name for herself in the early 1920s by making records and appearing in black nightclubs. Her repertoire broadened from blues to jazz styles of singing and then to pop. She made records with swing bands such as Benny Goodman and the Dorsey Brothers. In addition, she starred in successful Broadway musicals and appeared in films and television shows.

Waters was born an illegitimate child and married for the first time when she was fourteen. Starting as a cleaning lady, she managed to work her way up as a singer in Harlem nightclubs and in vaudeville. Her singing style influenced singers such as Mildred Bailey, Connee Boswell, Ella Fitzgerald, Pearl Bailey, Lena Horne, and Sarah Vaughan. Waters died in 1977.

Listen to her famous recording of "Stormy Weather" and you will feel deeply the mood she projects of a woman who has lost her man. This recording is a good example of how her singing emphasizes the consonants *n, m,* and *l.*

Waters was different from most blues singers. She noted herself that she was not a shouter. Her singing style was smoother than most blues singers, and her tones and vibrato were unique.

CONTEMPORARY BLUES

The blues is a tradition all its own. It is not merely a precursor to jazz but a musical stream that is still undergoing development independent of jazz or any other musical style that has borrowed from it. There are contemporary blues singers who, like B. B. King and Robert Cray, might be easily included in the jazz tradition but better represent the contemporary vitality of the blues tradition. B. B. King considers the blues a contemporary experience, a living music rather than a folk art. He plays electric guitar, as did T-Bone Walker. King's album *Live and Well* on ABC Records shows the great freedom that was typical of early blues performers.[14] Many rock superstars have acknowledged their debt to King's lyrical guitar virtuosity.

The blues continues to export its influence on other music styles while maintaining its identity. You can find blues references in the work of the late Miles Davis, John Scofield, Mike Stern, Michael Brecker, and others in the jazz tradition, and you can also see its influence in the development of rock and roll.

Austin, Texas, and Nashville, Tennessee, continue to be important locations for the blues. Stevie Ray Vaughan moved to Austin from Dallas and played a very high-energy blues until his death in 1990. He often crafted extended guitar solos that charted exciting emotional curves. On the other hand, Keb' Mo' of Nashville often played a more relaxed, blues-inspired repertoire. His first album in 1994 featured two Robert Johnson covers connecting him clearly to the blues tradition. Keb' Mo' also portrayed Robert Johnson in a documentary film, *Can't You Hear the Wind Howl?* He has performed with Eric Clapton and Robert Craft, both important to the ongoing blues tradition.

Keb' Mo'

summary

There is no era designated as a blues era, and there are many individual blues styles. Over the years, the blues performances settled into a twelve-measure construction with a specific chord progression.

The so-called blue notes originally resulted from the West Africans' search for comparative tones not included in Western European or pentatonic scales. Blues lyrics, although flexible, were ideally composed in iambic pentameter. Three lines of lyrics, the first two being similar, are traditional.

There has always been a great interchange of ideas among blues singers and instrumentalists.

The two easily determined periods of blues are from the latter part of the nineteenth century to about 1930 and from 1930 to the present. Most of the early urban blues singers were women, whereas most of the rural blues singers were men.

Blues feelings, blue stylings, and the blues construction are all as important today as they have ever been.

FOR FURTHER STUDY

1. Select a blues melody, such as the first twelve measures of "St. Louis Blues," and adapt a sonnet or original poem to the melody.

2. Sing the spiritual "Lord, Lord, Lord," shown in Appendix B, example 11. What melodic characteristics in this spiritual suggest a blues melody?

3. Give some titles of blues melodies that do not follow the usual harmonic construction but have the word *blues* in their titles.

4. Describe the *blue tonality*. How does a pianist obtain the effect of blue tonality at the keyboard?

5. Listen to "In the House Blues" as sung by Bessie Smith and answer the following questions:
   a. Is there an introduction?
   b. Do the lyrics follow the iambic pentameter and AAB form (i.e., the first line repeats, whereas the third line is original)?
   c. How many times does she sing the blues song?
   d. What instrument accompanies her? What instruments play the fill-ins?
   e. When you hear the melody sung, do you hear the singer interpolate the blue notes?

6. The twelve-bar blues became standard with instrumental ensemble musicians during the 1920s. No further instruction was necessary once an experienced jazz musician was told "blues in B-flat." This structure, with its set harmonic pattern, became the norm. Listen to "Dippermouth Blues." After the four-measure introduction, answer the following: How many ensemble-improvised choruses (twelve measures each) are there?

How many choruses did the clarinet and cornet play? Do you hear the stop-time device used by the ensemble?

7. Describe the differences between a folk song and a popular song.

8. Select a blues melody with text. Individually or as a class, learn to sing the blues song; then, with each repetition, add some new element of either the melody or the rhythm. Ask all the other students to listen actively and critically to those additions. A tape recorder can be a good aid for the participants.

9. Select three or four different recordings of jazz singers. Listen for the specific techniques used by each artist to achieve her or his effects. Copy the jazz phrases on paper or reproduce them vocally.

10. Feel the excitement of a gospel selection by responding physically while listening. This may be accomplished through syncopated hand clapping, which is an integral part of gospel performance. Respond to the music by tapping the foot on beats 1 and 3 and clapping the hands on beats 2 and 4.

11. After listening to Ella Fitzgerald's "One Note Samba" on the album *Fitzgerald and Pass,* select a familiar song, such as "De Lovely" or "Great Feelin'" by Scott Fredrickson, and make up your own scat rendition. Try to select a variety of vowels and consonants that do not follow the familiar "shoo-bee-doo-bee-doo-bee-doo." Create a musical line with form and sense to it. After the scat syllables have been created, repeat the song and start to make creative alterations by changing the rhythmic patterns. Next, alter the melody. Perhaps a portion of melody can be sung as written and another portion altered.

SUGGESTED ADDITIONAL LISTENING

Bailey, Mildred, *Greatest Performances 1929–1946.* Columbia Records, C31-22.
The Blues: Folkways of Jazz, vol. 2.
The Blues: History of Classic Jazz, vol. 3.
Carmen McRae and the Great American Music Hall. Blue Note Records, LA-709-H2.
The Essential Jimmy Rushing. Vanguard Records, 65/66.
Jazz Singers: Folkways Jazz, vol. 4.
Mean Mothers/Independent Women's Blues. Rosetta Records, RR1300.
Negro Folk Songs for Young People. Folkways, SC 7533.
The Roots of the Blues. New World Records, 252.
Singers and Soloists of the Swing Bands, Smithsonian Collection of Recordings.
Sorry But I Can't Take You/Woman's Railroad Blues. Rosetta Records, RR1301.
Washington, Dinah. *Dinah Jams.* Trip Records, TLP-5500.
When Malindy Sings—Jazz Vocalists 1938–1961. New World Records, 295.

ADDITIONAL READING RESOURCES

Albertson, Chris. *Bessie.*
Balliett, Whitney. "Miss Holiday." In *Dinosaurs in the Morning,* 74–80.
Bernstein, Leonard. *The Joy of Music,* 95–111.

Broonzy, William, and Bruynogle, Yannick. *Big Bill Blues.*

Charters, Samuel B. *The Country Blues.*

Chilton, John. *Billie's Blues.*

Harris, Rex. *Jazz,* 34–42.

Hentoff, Nat, and McCarthy, Albert. *Jazz: New Perspectives on the History of Jazz.*

Holiday, Billie, and Duffy, William. *Lady Sings the Blues.*

Jones, LeRoi. *Blues People.*

Keil, Charles. *Urban Blues.*

Oliver, Paul. *Bessie Smith* (King of Jazz Series).

———. *The Meaning of the Blues.*

Pleasants, Henry. *The Great American Popular Singers.*

Smith, Charles Edward. "Billie Holiday." In *The Jazz Makers,* 276–95.

Stearns, Marshall. *The Story of Jazz,* 14, 75–81, 196–98.

Ulanov, Barry. *Handbook of Jazz,* chap. 1.

Note: Complete information, including name of publisher and date of publication, is provided in this book's bibliography.

NOTES

1. Mike Toombs (quoting B. B. King), *San Diego Union,* 11 August 1989, D-4.
2. *Many Faces of the Blues,* Savoy Records, MG12125; Bessie Smith, *Empty Bed Blues,* Columbia Records, G39450; *The Story of the Blues: Jazz Odyssey,* vols. 1–3; Port of Harlem Jazzmen, "Port of Harlem Blues," Albert Ammons, "Boogie Woogie Stomp," Meade Lux Lewis, "Honky Tonk Train Blues," Ed Hall, "Profoundly Blue," Josh White, "Milk Cow Blues," Sidney de Paris, "The Call of the Blues," and Sidney Bechet, "Blue Horizon," *Three Decades of Jazz (1939–1949).*
3. Charlie Parker, "Another Hair Do," *Charlie Parker Memorial/Album,* vol. 1, Savoy Records, MG-12000; Milt Jackson, "Bags' Groove," Horace Silver, "Senior Blues," and Lou Donaldson, "Blues Walk," *Three Decades of Jazz (1949–1959);* Jimmy Smith, "Back at the Chicken Shack," Kenny Burrell, "Chittlins Con Carne," Lee Morgan, "The Sidewinder," and Stanley Turrentine, "River's Invitation," *Three Decades of Jazz (1959–1969);* McCoy Tyner, "Flapstick Blues," *The Definitive Jazz Scene,* vol. 1.
4. Marshall Stearns, *The Story of Jazz* (London: Oxford University Press, 1958), 15.
5. Leonard Bernstein, *The Joy of Music* (New York: Simon & Schuster, 1959), 109.
6. Rex Harris, *Jazz* (Baltimore: Penguin Books, 1956), 39.
7. André Francis, *Jazz* (New York: Grove Press, 1960), 17.
8. Marshall Stearns, "Sonny Terry and His Blues," in *The Art of Jazz,* ed. Martin T. Williams (London: Oxford University Press, 1959), 9.
9. Charles Keil (quoting Big Bill Broonzy), *Urban Blues* (Chicago: University of Chicago Press, 1966), 37.
10. "Troubled in Mind," words and music by Richard M. Jones. © 1926, 1937 by MCA Music, a division of MCA, Inc. © renewed 1953 and assigned to MCA Music, a division of MCA, Inc. © 1971 by MCA Music,

a division of MCA, Inc., 445 Park Ave., New York, N.Y. 10022. Used by permission. All rights reserved.

11. Ralph J. Gleason, "Records," *Rolling Stone* (May 1971), 45.

12. *Ma Rainey,* Milestone Records, M-47021.

13. Bessie Smith, *Empty Bed Blues,* Columbia Records, G39450; *The Empress,* Columbia Records, G30818; *The Bessie Smith Story,* Columbia Records, C1855.

14. B. B. King, *Live and Well,* ABC Records, S-6031; *Best of B. B. King,* ABC Recordings, 767.

4

Piano Styles: Ragtime to Boogie-Woogie

THE BIRTH OF RAGTIME

Ragtime music has been considered by some to be outside the jazz tradition because it is completely composed before it is performed. But, as was pointed out in Chapter 1, if jazz must be improvised to be considered jazz, then most of the music generally conceded to be jazz could not be classified as such. Even without being improvised, ragtime has the improvisatory feel that seems so essential to jazz. In fact, some consider ragtime to be another name for early jazz.[2] (For an introduction to ragtime, click on the Ragtime link at the Interactive Listening site: http://emegill.com/listening/ at the Online Learning Center.)

Ragtime is often said to have originated in Sedalia, Missouri, because a large number of such players performed there. However, a great deal of ragtime was played before these performers migrated to Sedalia in the late nineteenth century. (When reform government came to Sedalia in 1901, however, all ragtime activity there ceased.) Ragtime, then, predated jazz if Buddy Bolden is considered the one who brought the elements of jazz, or at least of Dixieland jazz, together.

Ragtime had a direct impact on the development of jazz, but because of its juxtaposition chronologically to Early New Orleans Dixieland, ragtime can best be considered a performance style that developed as a result of special conditions.

Because pianists were not used in the first Dixieland bands (which evolved from marching bands), the pianists developed a solo style of playing. A piano player was hired in place of a six- or seven-piece band, forcing the player to develop a technique that provided a full sound. The left hand had to play both the bass notes and the chords, leaving the right hand free for highly syncopated melodic lines. This playing was much more difficult than merely accompanying a vocalist or instrumentalist, in which case a pianist was responsible only for the bass notes with the left hand and the chords with the right. In fact, the extreme difficulty of the technique caused many academic piano players to completely oppose the unusual style of ragtime.

Eubie Blake

listening guide

Interactive Guide 1
Ragtime

:00   The first phrase of two choruses of piano solo with tuba, banjo, and drums playing a $\frac{2}{4}$ rhythm accompaniment.

:05   Second 4-measure phrase. Notice the strong upbeat feel on the second and fourth beat of each measure, which is accentuated by the banjo player.

:10   Third 4-measure phrase.

:14   Second chorus. Listen for each phrase and compare the steady rhythm of the accompaniment to the syncopated melodic work.

:28   End.

The accompaniment consists of the bass part confined to the first and third beats and the chords played on the second and fourth beats, or **offbeats.** Because of the physical action of the left hand, it became the practice for pianists to accent these offbeats, a technique that led to the new rhythmic style of the following era.

The intricate syncopation used in ragtime could well have been the reason this music was called *ragtime*, or *ragged time*. This is only one of many versions of the origin of the name *ragtime*, and, as in the case of the name *jazz*, it is impossible to say which explanation is correct.

Ragtime began as a manner of playing. Originally there was no ragtime repertoire, only preexisting songs and dance tunes played in a ragged manner. Ragtime became more compositional when rags were later published for others to play. Ragtime was a refreshing change from the usual songs that often had commonplace melodies and predictable rhythmic feeling. Unlike many of the blues tunes and some of the spirituals, the mood of ragtime is happy. The country welcomed this happy music because it had just experienced the long depression of the 1890s.

The general public first became aware of ragtime during a series of world's fairs held in Chicago, Omaha, Buffalo, St. Louis, and other cities where peripatetic piano players from the Midwest and the South found employment along the midways, where the amusement rides, entertainment, and food outlets were located. Ragtime flourished for over twenty years. When the music publishing industry (Tin Pan Alley) began to sell rags, the music was too difficult for uninitiated pianists to play; it had to be considerably simplified if it were to sell. Ragtime players frequently earned substantial income teaching ragtime style.

The ragtime players then began to migrate to Sedalia, Missouri. Though it was later said that ragtime was born in Sedalia, these players merely drifted into the town because of employment opportunities. One player, Tom "Million" Turpin, owned a series of clubs in Sedalia and sponsored many ragtime players.

Turpin's "Harlem Rag" (1897) is reputed to be the first rag ever published (although some say William Krell's "Mississippi Rag," also published in 1897, was first). When reform came to Sedalia in 1901, many ragtime players moved to St. Louis, which then became the ragtime center.

Much controversy exists about who composed what rag. Possibly, some rags were a compilation of ideas "borrowed" from many players, and the player who had the knowledge to notate the rag on music manuscript received credit for the composition. It is interesting that typical ragtime selections were composed in a definite format that showed a European influence in its concern for balance and form. Each selection included four themes (or strains), and each theme had equal stress, or equal importance, within the composition. Examples are "Tiger Rag" and "Maple Leaf Rag." This fairly rigid form was probably borrowed from the construction of marches. Ragtime players, both black and white, were expected to be good readers, and sheet music was one of the principal means of disseminating ragtime music.

Scott Joplin

The most prolific composer of ragtime music was Scott Joplin, a schooled musician who published about fifty rags (some say he composed about six hundred). The most famous, "Maple Leaf Rag" (1899), sold hundreds of thousands

listening guide

(CD 1, track 9)
Scott Joplin (piano)
"Maple Leaf Rag"

:00   A: Establishes the main recognizable theme.

:22   A: Repeat of A forecasts Joplin's involvement with form.

:45   B: New theme demonstrates further attraction to syncopation.

1:06   B: Repeat of the second theme.

1:28   A: Reiteration of the A theme helps the ear hold the form together.

1:50   C: Playing in a higher register causes the third theme to seem brighter in spite of the fact that the tempo stays firm.

2:12   C: Repeat of the third theme.

2:33   D: Syncopation becomes even more daring.

2:54   D: Repeat sounds like improvisation, which of course it is not.

3:17   End.

of copies in the first ten years of publication. Many jazz critics are not aware that Joplin wrote a symphony and two operas, one of which, *Treemonisha*, is still performed today.

A monument in honor of Joplin was erected in Sedalia at the site of the old Maple Leaf Club. When the movie *The Sting* was released in 1973, some of the citizens of Sedalia expressed concern about the popularity of ragtime. They were worried that Joplin's tunes would be associated only with the film and that the composer and the city itself would be lost to obscurity. (In hindsight, more recognition could have been given Joplin and his music when he was living there instead of sixty years later.)

Jelly Roll Morton

The best-known ragtime piano player was Jelly Roll Morton (born Ferdinand de Menthe). In his Library of Congress recordings and on his calling card, Morton claims that he originated jazz in 1902 as well as ragtime, swing, and just about everything else in this area of music. He may not have been *that* important, but he was surely at the top among ragtime players. Morton had no peer as a soloist,[3] and he also performed successfully with a variety of bands.[4]

As soon as their finances permitted, some ragtime pianists formed their own orchestras: Jelly Roll Morton formed Jelly Roll Morton and His Red Hot Peppers, Jelly Roll Morton's Stomp Kings, and Jelly Roll Morton's Jazz Band. Some already established jazz bands then added piano players: Lil' Hardin, later to be Lil' Armstrong, joined King Oliver's orchestra. As the ragtime bands had

listening guide

(CD 1, track 10)
Jelly Roll Morton
"Maple Leaf Rag"

:00   Introduction: driving very hard, influencing a future era (swing).

:11   The A strain shows Morton to be a master of syncopation.

:27   Introduction reenters, helping to hold framework together.

:33   B strain as a relief from A, usually called a bridge.

:52   The A strain again but with noticeable additions in both hands.

1:13   Interestingly contrasting section (C).

1:34   Repeat of the C section with new variations.

1:53   New strain (D) vacillates between a tango and a swing feeling.

2:12   Repeat of the D strain, this time in most acceptable stride style.

2:32   End.

Jelly Roll Morton

to have piano players as leaders, this trend carried over to bands not so involved with ragtime. This was especially true in the Southwest, where Bennie Moten, Count Basie, Jay McShann, and many other piano players were leaders.

Morton was an ideal ragtime bandleader. He was an excellent piano player, a creative and knowledgeable **arranger,** and a fair singer. He had an extremely attractive, outgoing personality. In fact, Morton was the first jazz musician who is thought to have precisely planned what each musician was to play on his recordings, thus opening the way for recorded **arrangements** of jazz. The recordings on which he plays piano and talks with folklorist Alan Lomax are important in the history of jazz to the 1930s.[5] "In Jelly Roll Morton, we recognize for the first time in jazz that the personality of the performing musician is more important than the material contributed by the composer."[6] Because ragtime players were becoming bandleaders, the need for players to be more schooled in music became obvious.

RAGTIME AND DIXIELAND MERGE

When the piano players began to play with other instrumentalists, the two music styles, Dixieland and ragtime, began to merge. There are many recorded examples of bands playing rag tunes that were primarily meant to be played on a piano. Listen, for example, to Paul Mares's recording of "Maple Leaf Rag," the New Orleans Rhythm Kings' recording of "Tiger Rag," and others[7] (FJ, vols. 3 and 6).

Two important changes resulted from the merging of Dixieland and ragtime. First, the basic melodic concept of the rags was changed and, second, the rhythmic accentuation indigenous to the rags was carried over into Dixieland jazz. As a consequence, a new repertoire was added to the music of the jazz bands, which began to play the rags but altered the form. The first strain became a **verse,** the second and third strains were omitted completely, and the fourth became a repeated chorus and the basis for improvisation.[8]

The rhythm of the bands changed from a flat four (four equal pulsations in each measure) to a two-four ($\frac{2}{4}$) rhythm (four beats to a measure with accents on beats 2 and 4). These measured offbeats correspond to the action of the left hand of the ragtime pianists.

RAGTIME LIVES ON

Ragtime, then, was a style of playing that coexisted with Early New Orleans Dixieland jazz. It influenced the interpretation of jazz by shifting the rhythm from a flat $\frac{4}{4}$ to $\frac{2}{4}$ interpretation and by additions to the jazz repertoire, such as "Maple Leaf Rag" and "Tiger Rag." While ragtime may have been most frequently heard on the piano, it was also a band music employing brass, strings, and woodwinds in pit orchestras.

Ragtime is still played today, and recordings are available from several sources. One source consists of recordings of ragtime played on a **tack piano,** which is a piano that is altered to sound much older than it is so that the ragtime sounds more authentic. This is accomplished in various ways. One way is to put thumbtacks in all the felts of the piano hammers. Other ways include laying a light chain across the strings or putting newspaper, aluminum foil, or something similar over the strings.[9] Most of these adjustments, however, are harmful to the piano felts.

Another good ragtime source is the re-pressing of old master recordings by such players as Morton, Joplin, and others[10] (S, "Grandpa's Spells," CD 1, track 8; "Dead

Man's Blues;" "Black Bottom Stomp"). Many good ragtime and stride players made piano rolls that can be purchased, and recordings made from rolls are satisfactory[11] ("Maple Leaf Rag").

Another important source consists of recordings of old-timers, such as *The Eighty-Six Years of Eubie Blake*, played by Eubie Blake.[12] Blake, at age ninety-eight, received the Medal of Freedom from President Reagan in October 1981. After charming the nation as a composer and performer for over seventy-five years, James Hubert Blake died on February 12, 1983, at age one hundred.

Interest in authentic ragtime began to wane because some players played the style so fast and aggressively that the original relaxed feeling dissipated. As a result, stride playing became more popular. Also, the Dixieland players had destroyed the important ragtime form. Since 1920, however, revivals of this style continue to bring talented composers and players to public notice.

The public was more aware of ragtime in 1973 than during any time since 1920 because of the popular motion picture *The Sting*. Throughout the movie, Scott Joplin's rags established the mood for the period in which the movie was set, and the composer's name once again became a household word. Marvin Hamlisch, the musician who adapted the Joplin rags for the movie, received an Academy Award for the best movie score of the year. As he accepted the award, Hamlisch acknowledged his absolute indebtedness and gratitude to Scott Joplin and his genius. Joplin (who died frustrated and penniless in 1917) was given screen credits as well.

It is interesting to note that although *The Sting* was set in 1936, ragtime had not been popular since 1920 and that, although ragtime had not been played at all in 1936, the music was still apropos for the movie. It is also interesting that a quiet revival of ragtime had preceded the movie. It was common during 1971 and 1972 to hear students in college practice rooms working on the intricacies of "Maple Leaf Rag." After the release of the film in 1974, students turned their efforts to "The Entertainer," a piece used extensively in the movie. The revival may have preceded the movie, but the film, in turn, strengthened the revival. The important point is that ragtime was once again popular, to the delight of its present-day practitioners.

Ragtime again emerged as the underpinning for the film *Ragtime* in 1981. Both the film and musical are based on E. L. Doctorow's novel by the same title. The score, composed by Randy Newman, features a full orchestral setting of several rags, waltzes, and polkas. In 1998, yet another Broadway musical, *Ragtime*, brought ragtime to the forefront of popular entertainment. The music for this production was composed by Stephen Flaherty. Unlike the movie, *The Sting*, which featured a ragtime title song, much of the music of *Ragtime* reflects the syncopation and melodic idioms of the ragtime style, although modernized considerably ("Getting Ready Rag").

At the beginning of this chapter it was mentioned that some authorities do not consider ragtime to be jazz. To illustrate this point, in 1974 the Academy of Recording Arts and Sciences gave an award to a ragtime record without placing it in any specific award category. *The Red Back Book* won a Grammy Award for being the best **chamber music** record of 1973. Its competition included string quartets, classical piano duos, and woodwind trios.

Listen once again to the musical example of ragtime (Ragtime link at the Interactive Listening site: http://emegill.com/listening/, example 12A in Appendix B is the basis of an interpretation showing ragtime style).

listening guide

OLC

Interactive Guide 2
Boogie-Woogie

:00   First chorus on solo piano (note the left hand is playing 8 beats to the bar while utilizing what is known as the *wagon-wheels pattern*); drums play $\frac{8}{8}$ rhythm.

:18   Second chorus.

:36   End.

Art Tatum
© Institute of Jazz Studies,
Rutgers University

BOOGIE-WOOGIE

Boogie-woogie is another stage in the evolution of jazz and, like ragtime, is a piano style that was important in the development of jazz. The term *boogie-woogie* itself is very descriptive. Although historically the term is used by Rousas Rushdoony in reference to ancient rites in Morocco,[13] the musical association

vamping

Rent Parties

Rent parties were actually all-night jam sessions. The word was passed around that a musician, or sometimes a friend, could not come up with the rent payment. A piano would be rolled into the apartment, and musicians would drop in and play. On a table would be a hat that acted as a pot for contributions. Much more often than not, when dawn's early light made its appearance, the necessary rent money had accrued. For the musicians, these sessions were often learning experiences, but at times **cutting contests** developed, much to the audiences' approval.

is the feeling created by playing eight beats to the bar. This style of piano playing came into prominence during an economic crisis—the Great Depression of the early 1930s. Jazz again faced a situation in which a full style of piano playing was needed as a substitute for hiring a band. (For an introduction to boogie-woogie, listen to the Boogie Woogie link at the Interactive Listening site: http://emegill.com/listening/)

Ostinato Bass

The most identifying feature of boogie-woogie is the eight beats to a measure that are played as an *ostinato*, the term for a melodic figure that recurs throughout the music. The ostinato is a structural device that helps hold a piece together.

In boogie-woogie piano playing, the ostinato phrase is always in the bass. It is possible, however, to hear boogie-woogie played by a big band when the ostinato is not present; there will still be eight beats to the bar. Distinguished from jazz played in the even $\frac{4}{4}$ rhythm of Early New Orleans Dixieland or the $\frac{2}{4}$ rhythm of ragtime and Chicago Style Dixieland, boogie-woogie employs eight beats to the bar in the ostinato.

There are two distinct methods of boogie-woogie playing. In both, the right hand is kept free for melodic interpretation or improvisation. The difference between the two methods occurs in the use of the left hand. In one the left hand plays full, moving chords, and in the other a **walking bass** line outlines the chords in a melodic fashion. (For notational examples of these two methods of playing boogie-woogie bass, see example 13 in Appendix B.)

Boogie-woogie has also been called "8 over 4," a description that comes from the eight notes that the left hand of the piano plays in the normal four-beat measure. Although the music might be written in the usual four-beat time signature, the feel of the music emphasizes the eight faster beats. (For notational examples of 8-over-4 playing, see example 14 in Appendix B.)

Although the right hand can play an interesting melodic line, the main feature of this style is rhythmic virtuosity. The left hand and the right hand operate so independently that boogie-woogie often sounds as if it is being performed by two pianists instead of one. The style is extremely taxing physically, as it is usually played loudly with tensed muscles, a most tiring means of performing. The **riff** emphasis, typical of Kansas City (to be discussed in Chapter 6), is often heard in the right hand of the boogie-woogie player as the left hand busies itself with the ostinato. Boogie-woogie is generally, but not always, played in the blues form.

The Players

Boogie-woogie was usually played by untrained pianists. Ragtime had incorporated European influences, but it appears as though boogie-woogie piano players worked out their style without any thought of European concert tradition. Many could not read music, so they simply listened and developed this full style of playing. Most of the time, boogie-woogie players were comfortable playing only this one style of jazz. However, Pete Johnson, who was surely the number one boogie-woogie pianist in Kansas City, was also a fine stride player. He really showed his versatility when he accompanied blues singer Joe Turner hour after hour.[14]

Meade Lux Lewis

listening guide

(CD 1, track 5)
Meade Lux Lewis (playing)
"Honky Tonk Train Blues"

:00   Piano solo throughout; trill for short introduction.

:02   Chorus 1: left hand playing *full, moving chords pattern*, right hand playing melodically and independently.

:19   Chorus 2: Lewis shows his control by playing 6 beats with the right hand while playing 8 beats with the left (this occurs often on this record).

:36   Chorus 3.

:53   Chorus 4: picks up last small idea from previous chorus and expands on it.

1:10   Chorus 5: uses trills and shows extreme independence of hands.

1:27   Chorus 6: shows a small thought, then develops a technical display.

1:44   Chorus 7: many full chords and use of the "6 against 8" as in chorus 2.

2:02   Chorus 8: similar to chorus 7.

2:19   Chorus 9.

2:36   Chorus 10: getting softer, seems to be tapering down, preparing to stop.

2:57   End.

Although it is true that boogie-woogie reached its peak of popularity during the early 1930s, the style surely was not invented then. The first time that the word *boogie* appears to have been used on a record was in 1928 by Chicago's Pine Top Smith as he recorded "Pine Top's Boogie."[15] Huddie Ledbetter claimed that he first heard this type of playing in 1899, Bunk Johnson (an early New Orleans trumpeter) said 1904, Jelly Roll Morton said 1904, and W. C. Handy said 1909. This music has also been called *Western rolling, fast Western,* and *Texas style*, indicating that its origin was in the western part of the country, although Florida has also been named as a birthplace.

There were three fairly defined generations of boogie-woogie players. The earlier pianists were active primarily in the 1920s: Jimmy Yancey, Cow Cow Davenport, and Pine Top Smith[16] (Jimmy Yancey, "The Mellow Blues," "Yancey Stomp"). The middle group, popular during the early 1930s, consisted of Meade Lux Lewis, Albert Ammons, Joe Sullivan, Clarence Lofton, and Pete Johnson[17] ("Honky Tonk Train"). The last group, popular during the late 1930s and the 1940s, included such players as Freddie Slack, Cleo Brown, and Bob Zurke.

Origin

Max Harrison states that this style of piano playing developed from a guitar technique used in mining, logging, and turpentine camps.[18] When three guitar players performed together, one picked out an improvised melody, the second played rhythmic chords, and the third played a bass line. To imitate three guitars at one time, piano players had to develop a very full style by having the right hand play the melodic improvisation and the left hand substitute for the other two guitars. By playing the eight faster notes in the left hand, the piano player can give the impression that the three guitar parts are all there. The result is that both a bass line and the chords are outlined by the left hand, leaving the right hand free to play an improvisation. (For notational examples of how the harmonies are outlined with the left hand, see example 14 in Appendix B.)

Although boogie-woogie is considered a definite piano style, it has been successfully adapted by large bands such as those of Will Bradley, Lionel Hampton, Tommy Dorsey, Count Basie, Harry James, Glenn Miller, and others.[19] The eight beats to the bar created by the ostinato bass is considered its most important feature. This rhythmic component exemplifies the fact that jazz players are always searching for new means of expression. However, having been created within a fairly limited set of circumstances (the guitar origin), regardless of the rhythmic interest, this style's range of expression is rather narrow.

Boogie-woogie has never really disappeared, although it is not prominent today. The boogie-woogie revival around 1938 was so popular that almost all performing groups had at least one number in their repertoire. Some boogie-woogie pianists toured and even played in such notable concert venues as Carnegie Hall. Pete Johnson, Meade Lux Lewis, and Albert Ammons perform a boogie-woogie trio on the *Spirituals to Swing* album, which was recorded live at Carnegie Hall.[20] It seems that, when three of these stylistic players perform at the same time, they almost try to outshout one another. In their exuberance, they even lose the eight-to-the-bar feeling. The revival was a boon to these players but did not help the style evolve further.

Later Developments

Boogie-woogie laid the groundwork for some later musical styles both inside and outside of jazz. The left-hand rhythm of boogie-woogie is similar to what later was called *shuffle rhythm*. Shuffle rhythm was used later by swing groups and imports both the energy and eight-beats-to-the-bar feel of boogie-woogie. The shuffle rhythm was also used by rhythm and blues artists and early rock songwriters like Jim Croce ("Bad, Bad, Leroy Brown").

An even later reemergence of boogie-woogie can be found in the swing revival of the late 1990s, which makes heavy use of the shuffle beat mixed with some rock elements like a heavy backbeat (strong accents on 2 and 4 of the measure). This revival, like the music of the original swing period, was dance centered, featuring the same dances used in the swing period (jitterbug, lindy). Although most of the new swing compositions are original, some revitalized arrangements from the swing period like Glenn Miller's "In the Mood" can be heard at the frequent dance engagements, but these arrangements have a *shuffle rock* underpinning.

Brian Setzer's CD *The Dirty Boogie* is an example of music typical of this swing revival. Although the *jump swing* style of the swing revival often uses some instrumentalists like those in the earlier swing bands, the music reflects its close association with the later rhythm and blues and shuffle rock styles in its dominant use of electric guitar in its arrangements.

STRIDE PIANO

As we have seen, jazz bands were not bound by the original construction of the rags. Piano players were no longer compelled to play alone; consequently, the piano was considered a part of the jazz band's instrumentation. Also, as tempos were increased, the relaxed feeling of the early ragtime gave way to virtuoso displays, and improvisation, not present in early ragtime, began to gain importance in piano music. The culmination of these developments resulted in what is known as *stride piano*, an extension of ragtime. There are three basic differences between stride piano playing and ragtime:

1. Stride players did not maintain the ragtime form. They played popular tunes of the day and any other kind of music that appealed to them.
2. The original ragged style placed on pre-existing song-and-dance tunes gave way to a more improvised style of playing.
3. The feeling of stride music was intense because, in general, stride pianists played faster and with much more drive than the more relaxed players of ragtime.

James P. Johnson and "Fats" Waller

James P. Johnson, composer of the famous tune "Charleston" (among many others), is considered to be the father of stride piano. There are many fine recorded examples of his performances[21] ("Carolina Shout," "Snowy Morning Blues"). Closely akin to Johnson, and usually discussed in superlatives, is Willie "The Lion" Smith. However, perhaps the most entertaining and exciting stride piano player was Thomas "Fats" Waller, a student of Johnson. Waller mugged and clowned incessantly; and, if a purist found this disturbing, he merely had to concentrate on the piano playing to hear true artistry and a most energetic rhythmic pulse[22] ("I Ain't Got Nobody," "Handful of Keys," "Squeeze Me"). Waller

"Fats" Waller

listening guide

(CD 1, track 6)
James P. Johnson
"Carolina Shout"

Entire selection is a piano solo.

:00   Introduction: 4 bars.

:05   Section A: first chorus—16 bars.

:25   Section A: repeat of first chorus.

:45   Section B: starts out with a vamplike part but develops—16 bars.

1:04   Section C: third type of chorus—16 bars.

1:24   Section C: repeat of section C.

1:45   Section B: improvisation of section B theme—16 bars.

2:01   Section D: new theme—16 bars.

2:20   Repeat of section D theme.

2:39   Coda: 4 bars.

2:46   End.

began to accompany blues singers on recordings in 1922. He was Bessie Smith's accompanist on tour and worked for a short time in Fletcher Henderson's orchestra. In 1927 he formed a solo act. His records sold well, and he even performed in motion pictures.

Art Tatum

Art Tatum was possibly the best—surely the most versatile—piano player in the history of jazz. It is impossible (thankfully) to put Tatum in a stylistic category, but stride was certainly one of his favorites. Tatum worked occasionally with a small group, but he felt this was confining, so he usually played alone. He seemed so far ahead of other players technically and harmonically that he was merely listened to in awe. Tatum was instrumental in bringing advanced harmonies into jazz. He was almost completely blind, but some maintain that his only handicap was his virtuosic technique—Tatum could not possibly harness his rapid flow of thoughts in order to play with simplicity. Of course, he often proved this wrong. His followers would be Bud Powell, Oscar Peterson, and Paul Smith.

Art Tatum's recordings include some of the best stride piano on record[23] ("Willow Weep for Me"). Some musicians never have the opportunity to record their achievements for posterity, but this cannot be said of Tatum. He was hired by Norman Granz for two days of recording in December 1953 and for two days in April 1954. The result was a set of thirteen long-playing records (twenty-six

listening guide

(CD 1, track 7)
Willow Weep For Me
Art Tatum

The form of the song is AABA. The performance includes two choruses.

:01   Intro vamp with a rolling chord in the left hand.

:10 (A)   Melody begins with quick notes ornamenting the melody and many of the chords rolled as in the introduction.

:16   The ornamentation increases to fill in the areas between the major melodic notes.

:22   The ornamentation increases even more.

:26   Return to the opening introduction pattern in preparation for the next chorus.

:30 (A)   Next chorus very similar to the first chorus.

:46   The melody gives way to extended melodic flights but notice that the basic rhythm of the melody is never lost.

:51 (B)   Tatum breaks into a relaxed stride type section. Notice the left hand alternating between bass note and chord.

1:04   The melodic flights reappear to fill in between melody notes but now take over the primary melodic structure.

1:13   Second chorus. Tatum falls back into the original melodic statement as in the first chorus.

1:32   A light swing feel is introduced which develops into a more blues feel.

1:51   Blues feel gives way to extended melodic flights.

2:00   Notice how Tatum comes out of the the ornamented melodic activity at exactly the right place in the chorus.

2:06   Tatum begins to work his way into a faster stride style which doesn't fully develop.

2:11   Return to the relaxed style of the first chorus.

2:18   Another melodic flight to close the phrase ending in the high piano note.

2:25 (B)   Begins with the melody and hints at a ragtime feel. From here to the end Tatum shifts quickly through a variety of stylistic areas, some heavily ornamented others with smooth chord changes and others closer to a stride feel.

2:47 (A)   Develops into a short lived stride section.

2:59   Tatum closes with the same vamp that opened the performance.

3:09   End.

sides) that was released to the public in 1974 on Pablo Records, truly a historic event for Tatum followers in particular and for jazz fans in general.[24]

Another collection of previously unreleased recordings of Tatum received a Grammy Award from the National Academy of Recording Arts and Sciences as the best solo album of 1973.[25] The collection was recorded on a portable home-recording device by a young friend of Tatum's. Some songs were recorded in an apartment and others in various after-hours clubs. The title of the album, *God Is in the House*, was taken from a remark made by Fats Waller when Tatum entered a club where Waller was playing. The remark reveals a respect for Tatum that is common among musicians.

Later Stride Pianists

Oscar Peterson, though also difficult to label stylistically, often ventured into some of the best stride piano on record. He was a talented and versatile musician. Basie and Ellington, too, often went into authentic stride piano during improvisation. Stride can also be heard in an interesting manner in the $\frac{5}{4}$ excursions of Johnny Guarnieri.[26]

summary

Ragtime is a style of music played within certain accepted forms that resemble those used in traditional marches. This is not to say that some exponents of this style were not capable of excellent improvisation.

Ragtime displayed a definite separation of the hands at the piano: The left hand played both bass and chords and the right hand the melodic parts. The syncopation in ragtime compositions was advanced for the time, making the music difficult for less proficient pianists.

Stride piano developed directly from ragtime, and it was more aggressive, more improvisational, and less formal.

It appeared for a few years that ragtime was to be relegated to history; however, it is accepted today not only for its nostalgic value but also as regular concert fare.

Boogie-woogie music has not evolved further because, if it were to change rhythmically, it would no longer be considered boogie-woogie. It could progress harmonically, but, because of the very mechanics of performing this style, most players are comfortable only with quite simple harmonies. In fact, since the beginnings of this style, the standard chord sequence has been the blues chord progression, and this is still true today.

FOR FURTHER STUDY

1. Compare the musical role of a ragtime pianist with that of a pianist in an instrumental ensemble.
2. How did the techniques of the pianist's left hand (playing alternately bass parts and chords) influence the flat-four rhythm played in early Dixieland music?

3. Listen to "Grandpa's Spells" as played by Jelly Roll Morton (S, CD 1, track 8) and discover the offbeat accents in the left hand. Is this left-hand technique continuous, or does it change at times? If there are changes, what are they?

4. Now listen to "Kansas City Stomp" by Jelly Roll Morton and compare the ragtime rhythm that Morton used in his piano playing with that used in his instrumental rendition of "Kansas City Stomp."

5. Usually, how many different themes or melodies are there in ragtime compositions?

6. As a result of the merging of ragtime and Dixieland, what happened to ragtime's melodic design and Dixieland's rhythm?

7. What is stride piano?

8. Listen to "Carolina Shout" (CD 1, track 6). Is the tempo of the music like a stately march, or is it faster? Listen to the left hand. Is it the "oompah" of the earlier ragtime pianists, or is it broken up with irregular, shifting beat patterns?

9. Define the term *boogie-woogie* as applied to piano technique.

10. In this style of piano technique, how many beats are in each measure?

11. Describe two methods of boogie-woogie playing.

12. Listen to "Yancey Stomp" by pianist Jimmy Yancey.

13. Listen to "Honky Tonk Train" and decide whether the left-hand ostinato bass is in the walking bass style or the chordal bass style.

SUGGESTED ADDITIONAL LISTENING

Boogie-Woogie. Folkways Jazz, vol. 10.

Boogie-Woogie. History of Classic Jazz, vol. 5.

Boogie-Woogie Piano: Original Recordings 1938–40. Columbia Records, KC-32708.

Boogie-Woogie Rarities.

Classic Jazz Piano Styles.

Cuttin' the Boogie. New World Records, 259.

Johnson, James P. *Father of Stride Piano.* Columbia Records, CL 1780.

———. *1917–1921: Rare Piano Rolls,* vol. 1. Biograph Records, 1003Q.

Joplin, Scott. *Joplin.* Biograph Records, 1013/4Q.

Kansas City Piano. Decca Records, DL-9226.

Maple Leaf Rag: Ragtime in Rural America. New World Records.

Morton, Jelly Roll. *The Immortal Jelly Roll Morton.* Milestone Records, MLP 2003.

———. *New Orleans Memories.* Atlantic Records, 2-308.

———. *Stomps and Joys.* RCA Victor Records, LPV-508.

New England Conservatory Ragtime Ensemble. *The Red Back Book,* by Gunther Schuller and the New England Conservatory Ragtime Ensemble (playing Scott Joplin music), Angel Records, S-36060.

Pitchin' Boogie. Milestone Records, MLP-2018.

Waller, Fats. *African Ripples.* RCA Victor Records, LPV-562.

———. *1934–1935.* RCA Victor Records, LPV-516.

ADDITIONAL READING RESOURCES

Blesh, Rudi, *Classic Piano Rags*.
Blesh, Rudi, and Janis, Harriet. *They All Played Ragtime*.
Dance, Stanley. *The World of Earl Hines*.
Gammond, Peter. *Scott Joplin and the Ragtime Era*.
Harris, Rex. *Jazz*, 60–72.
Hentoff, Nat, and McCarthy, Albert. *Jazz*.
Hodeir, André. *Jazz: Its Evolution and Essence*.
Kimball, Bob, and Bolcum, Bill. *Reminiscing with Sissle and Blake*.
Kirkeby, Ed. *Ain't Misbehavin': The Story of Fats Waller*.
Rose, Al. *Eubie Blake*.
Shapiro, Nat, and Hentoff, Nat, eds. *The Jazz Makers*, 3–17.
Stearns, Marshall. *The Story of Jazz*.
Ulanov, Barry. *Handbook of Jazz*.
Williams, Martin T., ed. *The Art of Jazz*, 95–108.

Note: Complete information, including name of publisher and date of publication, is provided in this book's bibliography.

NOTES

1. "Maple Leaf Rag" (1903). Music by Scott Joplin, words by Sydney Brown.
2. Guy Waterman, "Ragtime," in *Jazz*, ed. Nat Hentoff and Albert J. McCarthy (New York: Holt, Rinehart & Winston, 1959), 107.
3. *Jelly Roll Morton*, Mainstream Records, S/6020.
4. Jelly Roll Morton, *The King of New Orleans Jazz*, RCA Victor Records, LPM-1649.
5. Jelly Roll Morton, *The Saga of Jelly Roll Morton*, Riverside Records, 9001–9012; *Smithsonian Collection of Classic Jazz*.
6. Joachim Berendt, *Jazz Book: From New Orleans to Rock and Free Jazz*, trans. Dan Morgenstern (Westport, Conn.: Lawrence Hill, 1975).
7. Paul Mares, "Maple Leaf Rag," *Folkways Jazz*, vol. 6; New Orleans Rhythm Kings, "Tiger Rag," *Folkways Jazz*, vol. 3; Joe King Oliver, "Snake Rag," *Folkways Jazz*, vol. 3; New Orleans Feetwarmers, "Maple Leaf Rag," *Folkways Jazz*, vol. 11; Papa Celestin, "Original Tuxedo Rag," *Jazz Odyssey*, vol. 1.
8. Waterman, "Ragtime," *Jazz*, 7.
9. Phil Moody, *Razz-Ma-Tazz*, Urania Records, UR 9009; Joshua Rifkin, *Scott Joplin Ragtime*, Nonesuch Records, H-71248.
10. Jelly Roll Morton, "Grandpa's Spells," *Piano Roll Hall of Fame*; "Perfect Rag," *History of Classic Jazz*, vol. 2; "Big Fat Ham" and "Black Bottom Stomp," *Folkways Jazz*, vol. 5; "Tom Cat Blues" and "Wolverine Blues," *Folkways Jazz*, vol. 9; "Kansas City Stomps," *Folkways Jazz*, vol. 11; "London Blues," *Jazz Odyssey*, vol. 1; "Someday Sweetheart," *Jazz Odyssey*, vol. 2; Scott Joplin, "The Cascades," *History of Classic Jazz*, vol. 2; "Original Rags," *Folkways Jazz*, vol. 11; *History of Classic Jazz*, vol. 2; *The Jazz Story*, vol. 2; *Reunion in Ragtime*, Stereoddities Records, S/1900.

11. *Piano Roll Hall of Fame* and *Piano Roll Ragtime,* Sounds Records, 1201; Jelly Roll Morton, *Rare Piano Rolls,* Biograph Records, 1004Q; Fats Waller, *Rare Piano Rolls,* vols. 1 and 2, Biograph Records, 1002Q, 1005Q.

12. Eubie Blake, *The Eighty-Six Years of Eubie Blake,* Columbia Records, C2S-847.

13. Rousas J. Rushdoony, *The Politics of Pornography* (Sandtron City, Sandtron, South Africa: Valiant Publishers, 1975), 98.

14. Joe Turner and Pete Johnson, "Roll 'Em Pete," Columbia Records 35959; "Johnson and Turner Blues," *Jazz of Two Decades,* EmArcy Records, DEM-2.

15. Pine Top Smith, "Pine Top's Boogie," *Encyclopedia of Jazz on Records,* vol. 1.

16. Jimmy Yancey, "The Fives," *History of Classic Jazz,* vol. 5.

17. Meade Lux Lewis, "Far Ago Blues," *History of Classic Jazz,* vol. 5; Albert Ammons, "St. Louis Blues," *Folkways Jazz,* vol. 10; Joe Sullivan, "Little Rock Getaway," *Folkways Jazz,* vol. 9; Clarence Lofton, "Brown Skin Gal," *Folkways Jazz,* vol. 10; "Blue Boogie," *History of Classic Jazz,* vol. 5; Pete Johnson, "Let 'Em Jump," *Folkways Jazz,* vol. 10; "Lone Star Blues," *History of Classic Jazz,* vol. 5.

18. Max Harrison, "Boogie Woogie," in *Jazz,* ed. Nat Hentoff and Albert McCarthy (New York: Holt, Rinehart & Winston, 1959), 107.

19. Will Bradley, "Beat Me Daddy, Eight to the Bar," Columbia Records, 35530; Lionel Hampton, "Hamp's Boogie Woogie," Decca Records, 71828; Tommy Dorsey, "Boogie-Woogie," RCA Victor Records, 26054; Count Basie, "Boogie-Woogie," *The Best of Basie,* Roulette Records, RE118; Harry James, "Boo Woo," Columbia Records, 35958; Glenn Miller, "Bugle Woogie," *The Glenn Miller Chesterfield Shows,* RCA Victor Records, LSP-3981 (e).

20. Pete Johnson, Albert Ammons, and Meade Lux Lewis, "Cavalcade of Boogie," *From Spirituals to Swing,* Vanguard Records, VRS-8523/4.

21. James P. Johnson, "Keep off the Grass," *Jazz Odyssey,* vol. 3; "Black Bottom Dance" and "Mr. Freddie Blues," *Piano Roll Hall of Fame.*

22. Fats Waller, *Ain't Misbehavin',* RCA Victor Records, LPM-1246; "Mama's Got the Blues," *History of Classic Jazz,* vol. 8; "Handful of Keys," *Folkways Jazz,* vol. 11; "Draggin' My Poor Heart Around," *Jazz Odyssey,* vol. 11; "Do It Mr. So-and-So" and "If I Could Be with You," *Piano Roll Hall of Fame;* "The Flat Foot Floogie," *The Jazz Story,* vol. 3; *The Complete Fats Waller,* Bluebird Records, 2AXM-5511.

23. Art Tatum, *The Art of Tatum,* Decca Records, DL 8715; *Piano Discoveries,* vols. 1 and 2, 20th Century Fox Records, Fox 3032/3; "Too Marvelous for Words," *Smithsonian Collection of Classic Jazz.*

24. *The Tatum Solo Masterpieces,* Pablo Recordings, 2625 703.

25. Art Tatum, *God Is in the House,* Onyx Recordings, ORI 205.

26. Johnny Guarnieri, *Breakthrough in 5/4,* Bet Records, BLPS-1000.

Early New Orleans and Chicago Style Jazz

The life span of a musical masterpiece may encompass a number of generations, but music, being a reflection of society, is subject, like any other art, to social obsolescence. It may endure, metaphorically speaking, in libraries, on records and in the occasional archeological revival, but it will not satisfy a changing society's changing musical requirements.[1]

Henry Pleasants

EARLY NEW ORLEANS STYLE

The transition between jazz eras is gradual and thus eras overlap. In some cases, a new era arises as a reaction to a previous one. In others, the transition may be slow and not immediately recognizable. We have chosen to designate each era of jazz by its most commonly used name, and the dates given for each era are approximate because no style of jazz started or stopped at a given point. (For an introduction to Early New Orleans style jazz, listen to Interactive Guide 2 at the Online Learning Center.)

Throughout the history of jazz, labels of various kinds have been used to make distinctions between the different styles. Sometimes a new label is used by the players to identify a new emerging way of playing. At other times, critics and listeners develop a label for a new style of jazz. And ultimately historians settle on a term that shares general consensus that may not be at all the same as the label used when that style was popular.

Dixieland is such a term. Players of early music of New Orleans did not use the term *jazz*. The Creole bands played a ragtime style of music not yet referred to as Dixieland. Ironically, it was a white band, The Original Dixieland Jazz Band, that popularized the label of Dixieland. In fact, the term was used to some extent to distinguish between the white and Creole bands. It was not until the players had moved to Chicago and then to New York that the term began to extend backward to include all the early New Orleans bands.

As we will see in later chapters, the transition from one style of jazz to another is not always merely a matter of changing a label. There are often attitudes, preferences, and even a sense of insecurity that accompanies dramatic changes in the style of jazz. Dixieland, as it moved from New Orleans to Chicago, was not a dramatic transition when compared to later stylistic changes like swing to bop or cool to avant garde.

Also, as we continue to study a history like that of jazz, we are sometimes inclined to change labels to better reflect our growing understanding of the time and cultural forces at work in a given stylistic period. The term *Dixieland*

Louis Armstrong

listening guide

Interactive Guide 2
Early New Orleans Style

:00   Ensemble chorus (trumpet, clarinet, trombone); tuba, banjo, and drums keep $\frac{4}{4}$ (flat-four) rhythm. You can hear that the roots of this kind of ensemble came from the early marching bands that populated New Orleans.

:08   Second phrase.

:16   Third phrase.

:23   Clarinet solo (one chorus) in the low register.

:47   Ensemble chorus (same as first chorus). Listen for the different roles of the horn players. The clarinet plays responding phrases that overlap the melody of the trumpet, while the trombone plays countermelodies that reinforce the changing harmonies. The tuba, banjo, and drums maintain the steady flat-four rhythm.

:56   Second phrase.

1:05   Third phrase.

1:15   End.

better reflects the musical style of the Chicago bands in the 1920s and less so the musical practice of their predecessors, the Creole bands of New Orleans.

In fact, the labels used to describe most eras are somewhat misleading and tend to encourage an oversimplification of the diversity within that era. As we use these labels throughout this book, we encourage you to view them as general descriptors rather than totally inclusive of all the musical activity during that era. Most musicians do not restrict themselves to one era or style of jazz; their style may even vary within a given improvised chorus. However, the various styles do have certain characteristics that differentiate them, and the use of labels can help focus the discussion.

New Orleans

The era of jazz discussed in this chapter is called Early New Orleans style jazz not because New Orleans was the only geographical origin of this type of music but because, at the beginning of the twentieth century, New Orleans bred more jazz and more notable jazz musicians than in any other era. However, when considering New Orleans as the birthplace of jazz, we must keep two facts in mind: (1) Slaves were brought first to Virginia in 1619, and they brought with them their musical traditions, thereby producing, through the merging of their music with European music and the music of the Caribbean, the first faint

vamping

1890s–1910, LATIN JAZZ IN EARLY NEW ORLEANS

From the earliest records Latin music was a part of the New Orleans musical mix and contributed to the Creole musical vocabulary. Buddy Bolden, often cited as the first jazz trumpeter, grew up in this New Orleans time frame and may well have played early Mexican dance-form compositions first made popular by the "Mexican Band" in 1884 at the New Orleans World's Industrial and Cotton Centennial. This band played many *danzas*, like schottisches, mazurkas, waltzes, and polkas, that left an impression on the area that was clearly felt by Bolden several years later.

Certainly Cuban and Haitian music, like French music, were prevalent influences in the early, prejazz music of New Orleans. As early as the 1890s, ragtime pianist Benjamin R. Harney states specifically that ragtime was derived initially from Mexican music compositions like the habanera, the danza, and the seguidilla. It could be easily argued that several of the Joplin rags contain rhythms typical of the habanera. And Joplin himself claimed that jazz could not be jazz without a "Spanish tinge."

As we saw in the chapter on jazz heritages, Spanish music was a significant influence in early New Orleans; and, although much of the music at this time was attributed to Mexican origin, many of the dances were derived originally from Spain.

Some people believe that Latin rhythm was an element added to jazz in the 1940s by the orchestras of Dizzy Gillespie, Stan Kenton, and others or in the 1960s, when the bossa nova became popular. Actually, the addition of Latin rhythm can be traced to the beginnings of jazz. One example of Latin rhythm in early jazz is the tango section of "St. Louis Blues," written by W. C. Handy in 1914.

beginning of jazz; and (2) the first instrumental jazz was recorded in New York about three hundred years later (1917).

The more in-depth the research, the more difficult it becomes to claim one city as the origin of this art form. W. C. Handy said that music that was later called jazz was played in Memphis around 1905 but that the performers did not know until about 1917 that New Orleans had the same kind of music.[2] However, jazz critic Dan Morgenstern writes, "Jazz: one of the great and wonderful mysteries of our age. New Orleans: the cradle of this mystery. You don't agree? Have you a better myth? Have you Louis Armstrong?"[3] The word *early* is included in this label to differentiate the Dixieland music played from approximately 1890 to 1920 from the jazz developed in Chicago after 1920. The Dixieland music performed in New Orleans today, however, often includes elements of all the jazz eras since 1920.

The historical background of New Orleans, an exciting city that keeps alive many of its early customs and traditions, provided a receptive environment for jazz to develop and grow. For the first forty-six years, New Orleans was a French possession. It was then ceded to Spain in 1764 and remained a Spanish possession for the next thirty-six years, when it once again came under French rule. In 1803 it came to the United States as part of the Louisiana Purchase. This heterogeneous atmosphere was tolerant of all races and was a natural setting for the music of West Africa, Europe, and the Caribbean to meet and to merge. New Orleans was and is an exciting city with great activity of all sorts, both business and pleasure.

Oddly enough, recognition of jazz players in New Orleans by the New Orleans press has been quite poor ever since the art form took shape at the turn of the twentieth century. The New Orleans musicians "testify that it is easier to get national and international recognition of their talents than it is to get the attention of the *Times-Picayune* and the *States & Items*. . . . When their talents are adequately fossilized, their instruments museum pieces, and the musical forms they are creating safely a part of jazz history, they probably will show up on the cover of the *Picayune* Sunday supplement."[4]

The Oral Tradition

It was said in Chapter 2 that early jazz combined the techniques of formally trained Creole musicians with the techniques of African Americans whose playing was based on oral tradition. There is no better example of playing based on the oral tradition than that heard on any Louis Armstrong record when he sings first and then plays the melody. His phrasing in each instance is identical. This is an example of how the instrument is used as an extension of the voice.

Charles "Buddy" Bolden, who led one of the earliest marching bands, is usually credited with establishing the fixed instrumental combination used in this era.[5] The first jazz instrumentation was a logical outgrowth of that used in the marching bands and in the music halls—the same instruments were used. In its beginnings, this music was generally a creation of African Americans, with the exception of a few whites such as drummer Jack "Papa" Laine, who led a band as early as 1891. But soon the music was being created by both African Americans and whites. It should be noted, however, that the African American musicians did much more to foster these beginnings and to continue their development. Bolden was a cornet player in his brass band and was a member of a *shouting congregation* in his church. Obviously, he was heir to many of the early influences leading to jazz. His band played ragtime melodies, marches, quadrilles, and a great amount of the blues. Bolden stopped playing entirely in 1907, a fact that points out the diversity of this music at an early date. Unfortunately, there are no recordings of Bolden performing.

Small bands playing Dixieland music developed concurrently with ragtime. Dixieland and ragtime influenced each other and were influenced a great deal by the same sources. The same players were often involved in both, and ultimately the two styles merged.

Although ragtime and Dixieland share some characteristics, they offer two quite different jazz expressions. Ragtime is predominately a solo piano music, whereas Dixieland is an ensemble music. Both have syncopated textures, but they use the syncopation in different ways. Ragtime uses the left hand to alternate between the bass and chord punctuations. Together these two elements create the steady harmonic rhythm against which the right hand can play syncopations. Dixieland syncopation occurs within a polyphonic texture. The frontline instruments weave syncopated lines against the steady flat-four rhythm created by the rhythm section.

Ragtime was also based on a specific form and represented the literate musical tradition in its harmonic and formal structures. As we saw earlier in the Jelly Roll Morton version of "Maple Leaf Rag," a great deal of freedom was taken by players as they performed a written rag. The variations on the original notation were improvised rather than planned out in advance. Even with the improvised variations, rags were still predominantly a written form. In contrast, Dixieland was a predominantly improvised activity. The only fixed musical element was the melody; everything else was improvised during the performance.

The developing Dixieland ensembles were premised on the interactive interplay that was more typical of the oral tradition. They also shared different musical functions. Ragtime was most prevalent at social gatherings, theaters, and bars; Dixieland was used more for dancing, parades, and funerals.

All Early New Orleans bands did not sound the same. In New Orleans there were at least thirty well-known bands in just the first decade of the twentieth century. It was only natural that the bands varied according to personnel, just as jazz groups do today.

Another important point is that a given jazz band altered its style according to each job. The music played in some African American clubs was considered far too "rough" for the white dances, where the musicians would have to adjust to a more "sweet" style.

Storyville

In any discussion of New Orleans at the turn of the century, the name **Storyville** figures prominently. In 1896 a New Orleans alderman, Sidney Story, sponsored a civic ordinance confining the red-light district to a thirty-eight-block section adjoining Canal Street. Undoubtedly, Mr. Story was humiliated when the area came to be called Storyville. Some of the larger night spots in this section hired small bands, but mainly solo piano players were employed. However, there was much activity for street bands. Before the Navy closed Storyville in 1917, the district made important contributions to the beginnings of jazz.

Instrumental Obligations

There is a certain amount of solo work in Dixieland music, but from its very beginnings each of the frontline players (cornet, clarinet, and trombone) had a definite obligation to fulfill in ensemble playing.

Because by usual standards it is the loudest instrument in the orchestra, the cornet (or trumpet) played the melody. The cornet player was allowed to decorate the melody according to individual interpretation. The melody, however, was usually not altered to the point where it became unrecognizable to the lay listener. The clarinet player had a dual role: to play a harmony part, a countermelody above the melodic line carried by the trumpet (a natural task for the clarinet because it can be played at a higher pitch than the trumpet), and to create momentum (because the clarinet can be played with more agility than can the two other melodic instruments).

The role delegated to the trombone was to play the most important note in the chord to help clarify the change in harmonies.[6] The banjo, tuba, and drums played straight rhythm parts as they had in the marching bands. No piano was used in these first Dixieland groups because they were often the same groups that played in the street marches, where a piano could not be used.

listening guide

(CD 1, track 8)
King Oliver's Creole Jazz Band (playing)
"Dippermouth Blues" (also called "Sugarfoot Stomp")

:00 Introduction: ensemble.

:05 Two ensemble choruses: two cornets, clarinet, trombone; rhythm played by piano, bass, banjo, and drums—$\frac{4}{4}$ rhythm. True collective improvisation with Oliver on lead cornet. Trombone slides into each chorus.

:37 Two choruses of clarinet solo (Johnny Dodds). The rest of the band plays what is called *stop time;* it seems to make the solo more dominant.

1:09 Ensemble chorus, same pattern as first chorus. The solo in the background is played by the second cornet player, Louis Armstrong.

1:26 Three choruses of cornet solo by Oliver; note his use of the plunger as a mute for his instrument. The clarinet and trombone also play as in an ensemble chorus, except now they are very soft.

2:12 Vocal break ("Oh play that thing!").

2:14 Ensemble chorus similar to the first chorus, but a short tag is added on the end.

2:32 End.

For this reason the tuba rather than the string bass was used. (For a notational example of Early New Orleans Dixieland, see Appendix B.)

Another identifying feature of the music of this era was that the rhythm section played in a flat four, that is, with no accents—four even beats to a measure (or bar).[7] This is contrary to the belief of many Dixieland advocates who believe that all Dixieland music uses a $\frac{2}{4}$ rhythm with accented afterbeats. One need only listen to recordings of the King Oliver band (typical of this era) for confirmation that these rhythm sections played with no regularly accented beats[8] ("Dippermouth Blues").

Another important aspect was that the frontline players conceived their parts polyphonically (horizontally), as shown in example 17 in Appendix B. It should be noted that the direct roots of the counterpoint in modern jazz are from the music of the Dixieland bands and early classical music, as both used the polyphonic approach in construction.

The customary structure of a Dixieland format consists of an ensemble **chorus,** the solo choruses, and a return to the ensemble. The case is often stated that all Dixieland music is composed of collective improvisational playing. But it can be pointed out that during ensemble playing that included improvisation, patterns were often established in which a player repeated the same part on the last chorus of the arrangement that was played on the opening chorus.

Thus, these choruses were played from memory rather than by strict improvisation. In spite of this, Dixieland music has a feeling of spontaneity.

One of the most interesting aspects of Dixieland music is the rhythmic complexity caused by collective improvisation, in which conventional **chord changes** become secondary to creative interaction and instrumental independence. (For a notational example of this syncopated type of interaction, see Appendix B, example 18.)

It should be kept in mind that even though there were solos during most of the selections, the ensemble playing was truly the most important aspect of the Early New Orleans style jazz. Later, the emphasis shifted more to the soloists, due much to the virtuosity of Louis Armstrong in the 1920s. An example for comparison will show Oliver's "Sweet Lovin' Man" opening with the ensemble, going next into solos, then returning to ensemble again. Armstrong's record of "Sweethearts on Parade" starts with a trumpet solo, then Armstrong sings a chorus, then he goes back into a solo for the third chorus, demonstrating that he most emphatically was to be the main attraction. On his record of "I Gotta Right to Sing the Blues," Armstrong sings the first chorus, the ensemble plays the second, then he plays the third chorus as a solo.

The King

In this phase of jazz, one musician was designated by his peers to be the "king." He was always a trumpet player. For example, Freddie Keppard succeeded Bolden as king ("Stock Yard Strut"). Keppard left New Orleans in 1912 and played in Los Angeles in 1914, Coney Island (New York) in 1915, and Philadelphia in 1918. These facts surely dispute the "up-the-river" legend, perpetuated by many jazz writers, that jazz came up the river by steamboat directly to Chicago from New Orleans. (Other famous New Orleans players, e.g., trombonist Kid Ory, went to Los Angeles before going to Chicago.)

The last trumpeter to be called king was Joe "King" Oliver. The type of jazz played by Oliver exemplifies that performed before and during World War I. It is extremely difficult, however, to obtain recordings that have the exact instrumentation and approach to performance that was popular before 1920 (no instrumental jazz was recorded before 1917). By the time Oliver went into recording studios, his style had been somewhat influenced by the activity in Chicago. He was using two trumpets (Louis Armstrong on a second trumpet) and a piano (Lil' Hardin Armstrong). Nevertheless, his recording output around 1923 (thirty-seven numbers in all) is considered a cornerstone in traditional jazz.

The Early New Orleans Dixieland bands relied more on ensemble than on solo improvisation, certainly less improvisation than Chicago Style Dixieland. Still, every member of a band like Oliver's was a star and capable of good solo improvisation. Yet everyone's solos were considerably shorter than those by Oliver himself. Oliver was the leader and hence the featured attraction. Proof of the esteem in which present-day musicians hold Oliver is that whenever the tune "Dippermouth Blues" is played, the trumpet player must always play Oliver's choruses, note for note, or he is not considered to be even playing the right number. Interestingly, Oliver was actually improvising when he recorded the tune.[9]

Sidney Bechet

Sidney Bechet was the first jazz artist to achieve fame through the use of the soprano saxophone. His music was Sidney Bechet himself; he lived for it, going wherever it dictated. He played in various parts of the world, making his audiences acutely aware of his roots just through his playing of the soprano saxophone and the clarinet. His rich tone and heavy vibrato enhanced his forceful melodic creations to the point that he influenced all who followed him on these instruments.

Bechet rivaled Armstrong as one of the most important solo improvisors to come out of New Orleans. He was born on May 15, 1897, in New Orleans and began playing professionally in 1903. He worked with Joe "King" Oliver and moved to New York in 1919. Bechet carried Jazz to Europe with Will Marion Cook's Syncopated Orchestra and then moved to Paris in 1920. He returned to New York City in 1921 and recorded with the Clarence Williams Blue Five. In 1924 he worked with Duke Ellington and then returned to Europe. He joined Noble Sissle in Paris in 1928 and played with him intermittently for ten years. On his return to New York in 1938, Bechet left the music business and opened a tailoring shop. He only stayed away from performing for two years, after which he continued to play clubs and concerts and make recordings in New York City and Paris. Bechet's travels gave him a sophistication that few musicians had at that time, but it also

listening guide

(CD 1, track 11)
The New Orleans Footwarmers featuring Sidney Bechet
"Maple Leaf Rag"

Tommy Ladnier, trumpet; Teddy Nixon, trombone; Henry "Hank" Duncan, piano;
Morris Morand, drums; William "Serious" Myers, bass

:00   Drum intro.

:02   Section A: Bechet enters with the melody on soprano saxophone—4 measures.

:05   Horns all play together—2 bars.

:07   Melodic "break" with Bechet alone to introduce the next phrase—2 measures.

:09   Everyone enters with the first of two 4-bar phrases to end the chorus.

:12   Final 4-bar phrase starts with a trill on the saxophone. Notice that all the parts are being freely improvised while the harmonic phrase structure stays the same.

:16   Section A repeats: begins with melodic interplay between the trumpet and saxophone.

:21   Another solo break for Bechet.

:23   First of two 4-bar phrases to end this section.

:26   Second 4-bar phrase with increased improvisation by the horn players.

:30   Section B: 16 bars of a saxophone solo for Bechet. Notice how the other horn players play a rhythmic riff behind the solo. Listen for the left hand in the piano, which alternates between bass notes on the first and third beats of the measure and the chords on the second and fourth beats.

:44   Second chorus of Bechet's solo. Notice how parts of the original melody can sometimes be heard in the syncopated improvisation.

:59   Section C: 16 bars of a piano solo. Notice the stride style played by the pianist using a syncopated melodic style against the rapid left-hand pattern.

1:13   Second chorus of the piano solo.

1:27   Section A returns.

1:32   Solo break. Notice that it is different from the early ones.

1:33   Other players join for the two final 4-bar phrases.

1:41   Section D: All the horn players improvise collectively. Notice how they exchange melodic leadership. Bechet is most prominent in this chorus.

1:55   Second chorus; the leadership moves more toward the trumpet player.

2:09   Third chorus as the collective improvisation continues. Notice how the overall harmonic texture is created by the individual melodies of the players.

2:23   Fourth chorus. Notice the riff by the other horn players behind the high long notes played by Bechet.

2:38   Final chorus of improvisation begins with a new riff that features Bechet.

2:52   End.

Sidney Bechet

vamping

Early Recording Process

Early jazz recordings were made under rather difficult conditions. The musicians played toward a large megaphone that was reduced at one end to a stylus on a wax disk. The players were placed around the room according to how their individual sounds would affect the stylus. For example, the clarinet was the closest because its sound did not carry as well as the trumpet's did. (Young Louis Armstrong was proud that he was stationed much farther away than anyone else, so "big" was his sound on the cornet.) Cymbals on the drums were hard to record, as were sticks on the snare drum. And it was not until the early 1940s, because of pressure by Duke Ellington to record Jimmy Blanton, that the recording industry solved the problems of recording basses. From today's perspective, it is truly a wonder that there was any kind of respectable blend or balance on those early recordings, as the players stood or sat in some strange configuration unlike that to which they were accustomed in a club or ballroom.

Original Dixieland Jazz Band. Left to right: Tony Spargo, Eddie Edwards, Harry Barth, Larry Shields, Nick La Rocca, and Russell Robinson

pulled him out of the center of jazz as it was developing in New York. He died in Paris on May 1, 1959.

Out of New Orleans

Jazz seemed to become more permanent as it became less localized. Oliver moved to Chicago, as did many other well-known musicians and bands. The Original Dixieland Jazz Band went to Chicago in 1916, then on to New York in 1917. In fact, the Original Dixieland Jazz Band was the first band to record instrumental jazz instead of merely playing background for blues singers (1917). This was also the first group to perform in New York, where they opened at Reisenweber's Cafe (near Columbus Circle) in 1917, and the first jazz band to go to Europe (1919).

The band consisted of a group of young white musicians who listened very intently to and absorbed what the black bands in the New Orleans area were playing. They copied these bands until their own style began to develop.[10] Some jazz critics imply that this band's music and that of the New Orleans Rhythm Kings was more toward barnyard sounds and clowning. It should be kept in mind, however, that the imitation of barnyard animals was as much hip at that time as electronic distortion would be years later as rock developed. The Original Dixieland Jazz Band even recorded a piece called "Barnyard Blues." However, from a more distant historical perspective, the clowning and barnyard sounds may be viewed as parallel to the cartooning in minstrelsy, which reflected prevalent attitudes toward black music as less sophisticated.[11] No matter what a listener's stylistic preferences, it would be impossible to deny the great energy and exuberance of the Original Dixieland Jazz Band.

LOUIS ARMSTRONG (1901–1971)

If the one most influential musician in the entire span of jazz had to be chosen, the choice might be Louis Armstrong. "His heritage permeates all of jazz to this day . . . all that we may hear today has been touched by his genius."[12]

The myth has always been that Daniel Louis Armstrong was born on July 4, 1900. However, extensive research has uncovered his baptism papers at the Sacred Heart of Jesus Church in New Orleans stating that he was actually born on August 4, 1901. Armstrong was born in a poor neighborhood in New Orleans, and his parents were separated when he was very young. His father worked in a factory, and his mother was a cleaning woman. Armstrong was placed in the Colored Waifs Home for boys at age thirteen (because he playfully fired a revolver in the air while celebrating New Year's Eve), and he remained there for eighteen months. At the Waifs Home, Peter Davis taught him to play the bugle and then the cornet. He joined the band and the chorus and played for social affairs outside the home.

After leaving the Waifs Home, he first played with an orchestra of youngsters under Joe Lindsay. Joe Oliver, the king of New Orleans trumpet players around 1917, took an interest in Armstrong and made him his protégé. When Oliver left for Chicago in 1918, he placed Armstrong in his chair with a band directed by trombonist Kid Ory. Armstrong stayed with Ory for eighteen months and then joined Fate Marable's orchestra on a Mississippi steamboat in 1920. He was briefly married when he was eighteen years old.

In 1922 Oliver sent for Armstrong to join him in Chicago at the Lincoln Gardens. Armstrong married Lil' Hardin (the second of four wives) in 1924. She was the pianist with Oliver, but she encouraged Armstrong to organize his own band. However, Armstrong always remained grateful to Oliver and considered him his idol. Another of Armstrong's early idols was B. A. Rolfe, a white virtuoso trumpeter who later conducted a Paul Whiteman–type radio orchestra and who was never associated with the mainstream of jazz. Armstrong heard in Rolfe a good tone and sensible control of melodic thoughts. (In Armstrong's opinion, both of these elements were missing in the performance of more contemporary jazz players.) One of Armstrong's greatest thrills was at his first recording session, when the engineer placed him twenty feet behind the other musicians (including King Oliver) because Armstrong's tone was so powerful.

Armstrong left the Oliver band in 1924, and the band declined. Oliver did make some good recordings in 1926 and 1927. Armstrong joined Fletcher Henderson at the Roseland Ballroom in New York in 1924. At this time he recorded frequently with Clarence Williams's Blue Five accompanying singers. With Henderson, he accompanied Bessie Smith and Ma Rainey. He was a remarkable influence in the Fletcher Henderson band. Because of his spirit and inspiration, he was a true catalyst.

In 1925 he returned to Chicago and was billed as the World's Greatest Trumpet Player. Also in 1925, he started to record under his name. The next four years are notable for the Hot Five and Hot Seven records. With these records (classics in this music), jazz was turning from ensemble-oriented to solo-oriented music.

By 1926 Armstrong was considered the greatest trumpet player who had ever lived. His tone, stamina, range, creativeness, and technique were

listening guide

Louis Armstrong
"Hotter Than That"*

:00   Introduction by the ensemble.

:09   Trumpet solo (Louis Armstrong).

:25   Trumpet break.

:27   Trumpet solo.

:41   Clarinet break into solo.

:43   Clarinet solo.

:59   Clarinet break.

1:01   Clarinet solo.

1:17   Scat singing backed by guitar only.

1:31   Vocal break.

1:33   Scat singing—note rhythmic complexity.

1:49   Guitar and voice alternate short breaks.

2:07   Piano interlude.

2:12   Trombone solo.

2:27   Trumpet break.

2:29   Ensemble (standard established Dixieland format).

2:35   Trumpet break.

2:40   Ensemble.

2:42   Guitar break.

2:44   Trumpet break.

2:46   Guitar break.

2:50   End.

*Smithsonian Collection, CD 1, track 16.

envied by all jazz performers. At that early age, he became the ideal, the model of how to play jazz improvisation. In 1929 he headed for New York again—this time with his own band. Here he continued to record and play nightly on radio as well, which helped to spread his fame. In 1930 he was in Hollywood, and in 1931 he returned to Chicago. Then he went to England and Europe, where he was, of course, a tremendous success. Armstrong was the first jazz player to achieve international fame. His career remained solid

WITNESS TO jazz   louis armstrong

Photo and text by William P. Gottlieb

Louis Armstrong was not only a genius but also a sweet and generous man. Millions loved him. Fortunately, he liked to talk with people and said that he had no trouble remembering names—he simply called everyone "Pops."

Things came easily to Armstrong, but I was aware of at least one of his problems: his weight. He liked to eat and easily became heavy. Often, he was on a diet. The key to his weight-reduction regimen was one or another laxative. When I best knew Satch, his favorite was Pluto Water, a kind of liquid dynamite.

Another of his problems was his teeth—a most important feature for a horn man. Significantly, I last saw Louis when we were both in a dentist's waiting room. We had the same specialist, a fellow named

Gottlieb (no relative). After small talk, Satchmo looked me over, deciding that I had been gaining weight. He reached into his jacket pocket, pulled out a printed diet (that he kept for friends-in-need), and handed me a copy. "Pops," he said, "try this." I quickly noted that it featured Pluto Water. I thanked him, anyway.

Later that week, I had reasons to check out my Armstrong photos. One of them had been taken in a theater dressing room. There, on the counter, were a variety of objects, including a stack of white handkerchiefs (he sweated a lot and always carried a bunch on stage). There, too, just on the edge of the counter and almost out of the picture, was . . . a bottle of Pluto Water. Apparently, Louis's weight problem was under control.

throughout the swing era and even included several motion pictures. He had a large swing band that was usually led by someone else—Louis Russell, for example. The band was usually only a showcase for the talents of Armstrong himself. His big-band phase was neither as productive nor as creative as the earlier and later small-band phases. He seemed to be most comfortable with small bands.

Armstrong's career hit a new high in 1947. He returned to using a combo, which included at one time or another Jack Teagarden, Earl Hines, Cozy Cole, Barney Bigard, Sid Catlett, Arvell Shaw, Dick Cary, Billy Kyle, Joe Darrensbourg, Tyree Glenn, and Trummie Young. With his All Stars, Armstrong toured the world in the 1950s and 1960s and became known as the Ambassador of Good Will. As late as 1964, he had his biggest record success, "Hello Dolly." He had lived to be both wealthy and famous. He died on July 6, 1971.

Armstrong was the first great jazz soloist. Here is Martin Williams's assessment of Armstrong (with which most other writers agree):

> Armstrong's music has affected all our music, top to bottom, concert hall to barroom. No concert composers here or abroad write for brass instruments the way they used to, simply because Armstrong has shown that brass instruments, and the trumpet in particular, are capable of things that no one thought them capable of before he came along. Our symphonists play trumpet with a slight, usually unconscious vibrato that is inappropriate to Beethoven or Schubert because Armstrong has had one. "Louis changed our whole idea of the band," said Henderson's chief arranger at the time, Don Redman. So did he change everyone's idea of every band, and every soloist's idea of himself. From that, the era and the style took its name: swing. From the Henderson band itself came the Benny Goodman style, and, directly or indirectly, most of the popular big bands of the Swing Era. American music was not the same after it became swing, and what made it different was the influence of Armstrong.[13]

In the 1920s, playing high C on the trumpet was considered quite extraordinary, unlike today. Armstrong, however, often amazed his audiences by playing one hundred high Cs (with the band shouting out the count on each one). Then Armstrong would soar upward to a high F. In the 1920s and 1930s, that alone was an incredible feat, but Armstrong would follow this display with an outstanding version of a blues tune of the day. The moment was one to be remembered.

Armstrong was also considered one of the best jazz singers. He was concerned with pleasing his audiences, and he became a great showman and even a comedian. Too often, praise for Armstrong is divided between Armstrong the artist and Armstrong the entertainer, as if artists do not entertain. It is almost inconceivable that the man who was probably America's greatest natural musician, the man who was so personally responsible for a way of playing and listening to music, should be remembered as an affable clown. Is it possible that without Armstrong there would have been no jazz? There may have been jazz, but it truly would have developed in an entirely different way than it did. Armstrong always felt that even if music was one's whole life, it was meaningless if it could not be presented to and appreciated by the public. Armstrong was criticized later by both players (including Miles Davis) and critics for pandering to racist stereotypes, which was still necessary to gain widespread acclaim.

Armstrong was undoubtedly one of the best-known and most highly respected musical personalities in the world. He was probably the first to be recognized as an artist (around 1925) in a music that was at that time considered merely entertainment. Today's researchers benefit greatly from the fact that Armstrong's recordings are a real documentation of his career and his permanent worth. The most mentioned solos are "West End Blues," "Savoy Blues," "Potato Head Blues," "Hotter Than That," "Weather Bird," "Muggles," "Beau Koo Jack," "I'm Not Rough," "Cornet Chop Suey," "Struttin' with Some Barbecue," "Heebie Jeebies," and "Mahogany Hall Stomp."

In Armstrong were combined well-developed technique, rhythmic feel, intuition, good tone, and high register as well as personal warmth and an ability to communicate. Each solo, no matter how deep into improvisation, sounds cohesive and well planned but still spontaneous. In spite of being a great improviser, Armstrong's chief talent was his ability to inject rhythmic feeling into a melodic line, whether that melodic line was improvised or written. The tunes that he recorded were often quite banal until he transformed them into a worthwhile listening experience.

He was a genius at improvisation, and his improvisations showed more than anything else that simplicity leads directly to communication. As great as his trumpet playing was, Armstrong's chief asset was his ability to communicate.

Although he often seemed gregarious and extroverted, Armstrong could play a blues that was lovely and sad at the same time. Almost every player who improvises plays phrases that can be traced back to Armstrong and his influence, and the whole world has benefited. Somehow, he almost single-handedly set the stage for the jazz soloist, maybe the stage for jazz itself. Most musicians agree that Armstrong was the leader that all other jazz players followed: "Daniel Louis Armstrong, the man from whom has flowed so much good music and so much good-will that the world will never fully realize just how deeply it is in his debt."[14] Armstrong's approach to jazz and to life has never been out of style. Somehow Armstrong made everybody happy!

CHICAGO STYLE (THE 1920s)

In 1917 the closing of Storyville, the district in New Orleans where a great number of musicians were employed, contributed to the shift of the heart of the jazz scene to Chicago. By 1918 many musicians had left New Orleans; and, when Congress passed the Volstead Act in 1919 that prohibited the sale and consumption of alcoholic beverages, employment for jazz musicians in New Orleans came to a real halt. Quite a few jazz players drifted to Chicago, where demand for their music and a still-active nightclub atmosphere fostered the further development of jazz.

The Roaring Twenties

There was a growing demand for jazz in Chicago during the Roaring Twenties. Chicago was a prosperous city with many opportunities for employment because

vamping

1910s–1920s, THE TANGO CRAZE

The **tango**, which is a fast habanera, became a very popular musical dance rhythm during the 1910s and found its way into many jazz compositions. When the tango hit its peak, ragtime was also at its peak and a number of ragtime tangos began to appear. The tango could be found in the repertoire of such early composers as James Reese Europe and W. H. Tyers. Club shows, like those by Europe at the Castle club, began to feature the tango and other popular Latin dance rhythms. At the same time, there was a significant migration of musicians from Cuba and Puerto Rico. These immigrant musicians joined club bands as well as many of the vaudeville bands. This early membership was an important requirement for carrying Latin music back into the prejazz musical arena. We will find that this type of musician crossover occurred at each of the intersections of Latin and jazz streams.

of the railroads, stockyards, and mills. Many workers in Chicago had migrated from the South and wanted the type of entertainment they had left behind. King Oliver came to Chicago in 1918 and went to work immediately at the Royal Gardens with Johnson's Creoles from 8 P.M. to 1 A.M., and then went to the Dreamland Cafe and worked until 6 A.M. (For an introduction to Chicago Style Dixieland, listen to Interactive Guide 3.)

In 1920 the nation's leading entertainer was Al Jolson; Bessie Smith was a big success in the Atlanta, Georgia, area. In September of that year, the first radio broadcast took place. Radio soon became a part of many households and did much to popularize jazz in general and some jazz artists in particular. In the 1920s recordings were as important as they are today. Although jazz could be heard in several cities, most of the recording was done in New York (with blues singers) or on the outskirts of Chicago.

In Los Angeles in 1921, New Orleans trombonist Kid Ory recorded what most historians feel were the first instrumental jazz records by an African American band. In 1923 Ory scored another first with his radio broadcasts. Kid Ory trombone solos may sound rough and dated today, but at the time his playing was so modern that he is credited with freeing the trombone from playing glorified tuba parts and allowing the instrument such choices as long flowing lines and even improvisation with the aid of a plunger mute[15] ("Ory's Creole Trombone," "Society Blues"). Kid Ory was also a recognized jazz composer. His most famous work became a Dixieland standard, "Muskrat Ramble."

In New York around 1924, Fletcher Henderson was organizing recording sessions and accompanying blues singers. Chicago Style Dixieland seeped into New York, too. Trumpeter Red Nichols, trombonist Miff Mole, and saxophone-clarinet player Jimmy Dorsey each recorded records that have become jazz classics[16] ("Original Dixieland One Step").

In Detroit around 1927, a band named McKinney's Cotton Pickers featured a fine young saxophonist/arranger, Don Redman. And in Los Angeles, a former New Orleans Rhythm Kings drummer, Ben Pollack, organized a Chicago Style Dixieland band. Pollack used mainly Chicago musicians like Benny Goodman plus a Texas clique like the Teagardens.

(The jazz activity in Kansas City in the 1920s is discussed in Chapter 6 because it was more truly swing jazz.)

To appreciate Chicago Style Dixieland, one must have a sense of the times. It was the Roaring Twenties, what F. Scott Fitzgerald called "the Jazz Age." There were straw hats and arm bands, Model T and Model A Fords and Stutz Bearcats, raccoon coats, and **speakeasies.** Gangsters ruled Chicago during this period; and, with the musicians playing in the saloons, there is no question that these same racketeers had a great deal to say about the careers of the musicians.

In spite of the fact that Chicago was almost entirely in the hands of gangsters, these were happy times for the general public. The emphasis was on having fun. In fact, musicians today call Dixieland music "happy music." World War I was over, and the big stock market crash of 1929 was unforeseen. Life seemed to be a party. New dances such as the **Charleston** and Black Bottom were invented to suit the new energetic music.

The New Orleans and Chicago Styles

Both Chicago Style Dixieland and New Orleans Dixieland used cornet, trombone, clarinet, and drums. The piano was now used in both styles, and the **string bass** had replaced the tuba. The last two changes occurred because the bands that played for dancing no longer played for marching.

Distinguishing between the two styles is based somewhat on conjecture because there are no truly authentic recordings of Early New Orleans jazz. Players who lived during that time in New Orleans have recorded since then but only after the Chicago style had become the dominant Dixieland style. There are several technical features that distinguish the Chicago style:

1. A saxophone (usually a tenor saxophone) was added.
2. The guitar replaced the banjo.
3. Fairly elaborate (by comparison) introductions and endings were common.
4. Ease and relaxation in playing style gave way to tension and drive.
5. Individual solos became more important than the collective improvisation of ensemble sections.
6. Rhythm changed from $\frac{4}{4}$ to $\frac{2}{4}$.

Listen to and compare the two different ways of performing Dixieland jazz. Interactive Guide 2 is Early New Orleans Dixieland and Interactive Guide 3, Chicago Style Dixieland at the interactive listening site, http://www.emegill .com/listening.

The players of the Chicago era preferred the guitar to the banjo. Banjo players made the shift to guitar quite easily, mainly because the type of guitars first played in bands were four-stringed instruments and tuned like banjos. The addition of the tenor saxophone gave more body to ensemble playing and added solo color. When one more player is added to an ensemble of twenty or so, the change could

vamping

Chicago in the Gangster Period

Chicago of the gangster period, the Golden Era, saw the first Vitaphone talkie movie, Al Jolson's *The Jazz Singer,* from Warner Brothers opening in November 1926. Thirteen months later, the Negro weekly *The Chicago Defender* commented on a new-fangled "Amplivox" in a South Side restaurant. It was a machine that reproduced Louis Armstrong's scatting vocal of "Heebie Jeebies." Few musicians recognized the potential popularity of the primitive juke box. And even fewer anticipated the eventual sale of $600 million in records annually, and the millions in fees and royalties payable to the musicians and singers for their services on records.[17]

go unnoticed. But in early Dixieland the front line was only three players; adding another musician to these three made a decided difference.

The Original Dixieland Jazz Band added a baritone saxophone and an alto sax in 1920. The role of the saxophone in ensemble playing was comparable to that of the clarinet, except that its harmony line (or countermelody) was directly under the melodic line of the cornet.

As mentioned before, the rhythmic feel in Early New Orleans Dixieland—four even beats in each measure—was changed in Chicago Style Dixieland to measures with accents on the second and fourth beats (or the offbeats) and was called $\frac{2}{4}$ rhythm in jazz. The reason for the change was that the bands, no longer used for marching, could hire piano players who had been playing ragtime with its accented offbeats. The jazz drummer was now influenced by the addition of the piano, and he began to accent beats 2 and 4. Listen to young drummer Gene Krupa toward the end of the Chicagoans' record of "Nobody's Sweetheart." Krupa, playing in the Chicago style at that time, plays **rim shots** on beats 2 and 4. He is accenting these beats as loudly as he can without putting a hole in his drum ("Nobody's Sweetheart"). The bass player followed the left hand of the piano and played only on beats 1 and 3. The guitar player played on 2 and 4 or, at least, accented beats 2 and 4 to adjust to the piano. (For notational examples showing the difference between the rhythm sections in both styles, see Appendix B.)

This shift of the accents to beats 2 and 4 has held throughout most jazz eras. It has even become a signature of the swing feel of jazz. In fact, jazz-oriented people even now clap their hands or snap their fingers on beats 2 and 4 instead of on 1 and 3.

Chicago

During the 1920s Louis Armstrong and Earl "Fatha" Hines began a long association, indicating that Armstrong influenced not only all wind players but also piano players[18] ("Weather Bird"). Earl "Fatha" Hines developed what was called *trumpet style* piano playing because he played with a melodic style similar to that of his friend Louis Armstrong, instead of that of ragtime or boogie-woogie. This

listening guide

OLC

Interactive Guide 3
Chicago Style Dixieland

:00   Introduction (trombone glissando leading into the following chorus).

:04   Ensemble chorus (trumpet, clarinet, trombone, tenor sax); string bass, guitar, piano, and drums keep $\frac{2}{4}$ rhythm. Notice that the string bass plays only on the first and third beats, leaving the guitar and piano to offer the upbeats that give the $\frac{2}{4}$ meter the swing.

:09   Second phrase.

:14   Third phrase.

:19   Trumpet solo (one chorus).

:34   Trombone solo (one chorus).

:48   Ensemble chorus (same as first chorus). Notice the roles of each of the players on the front line. The trombone connects the chords as it plays a countermelody, and the clarinet plays a higher countermelody that connects the phrases played by the trumpet.

:53   Second phrase.

:58   Third phrase.

1:03   End.

trumpet-style piano had also been used by Jelly Roll Morton and others. But Hines, with his fantastic technique, made great use of octaves and tremolos in the right hand. His fast double time foreshadowed the coming of Charlie Parker and Dizzy Gillespie.

Hines opened the Grand Terrace on Chicago's South Side in 1928 when he was only twenty-three years old. After 1939 his band became a proving ground for young players, as did Stan Kenton's band a few years later. After all the young bop-oriented players began to leave him, he did not record for a short time. When he did record in 1945, there was no bop influence in his band at all. Hines tried a large band (twenty-four musicians) for a while, then disbanded entirely in 1948. He performed for three years with Armstrong's All Stars and then went out on his own again with small groups in the 1950s and early 1960s.

Armstrong was considerably involved in Chicago jazz during the 1920s, and his recordings with the Hot Five and Hot Seven are truly jazz classics[19] ("Sweethearts on Parade," "I Gotta Right to Sing the Blues," "Potato Head Blues," "Struttin' with Some Barbecue"). But Armstrong is a good example of a musician who cannot and should not be categorized so narrowly. He had been a member of King Oliver's band earlier and then later had a famous swing band. His last band was a Dixieland group, one of the most enjoyable in the history of jazz.[20]

Earl Hines

The 1920s brought many professionally trained instrumentalists into jazz. Until this time, jazz had been mainly an African American art form. The only formally trained African American musicians, with the exception of a few piano players, were the Creole performers. With the advent of Chicago Style Dixieland, large numbers of white players with formal musical training entered the jazz field.

As is the case with every new style of jazz, Chicago Style Dixieland brought into jazz many youngsters who were avid fans of the jazz groups that had moved into Chicago. A high school clique called the "Austin High Gang" formed an important nucleus in the development of this style. Among these young players were Pee Wee Russell, Dave Tough, Bud Freeman, Gene Krupa, Eddie Condon, Mezz Mezzrow, and their friends Benny Goodman, Bix Beiderbecke, Muggsy Spanier, and Bunny Berigan—a group of talented young players for the jazz roster. A jazz historian could never find more enthusiasm than these young Chicago players had for their brand of music. However, in comparison with other styles of jazz, the recordings of these musicians simply do not exemplify either their energetic feeling or their musical technique.

As Benny Goodman grew up in the hurried pace of Chicago in the 1920s, he patterned his early efforts after Jimmy Noone of New Orleans and Frank Teschemacher of Chicago's Austin High Gang, but he soon surpassed his models and went on to become the "King" of the swing era.

One of the best and most popular groups in the Chicago era was the New Orleans Rhythm Kings (though they never played in New Orleans).[21] This group

listening guide

(CD 1, track 12)
Louis Armstrong (playing) and His Hot Five
"West End Blues"

:00   Armstrong on solo trumpet cadenza as introduction.

:15   Ensemble chorus. Trumpet plays melody; clarinet and trombone mainly play sustained notes as harmony. Rhythm plays $\frac{4}{4}$ with piano, banjo, bass, and drums.

:50   Trombone solo by Fred Robinson. Rhythm section plays $\frac{4}{4}$ except drummer, who attains special effects by hitting blocks and other various items.

1:24   Voice (Armstrong) and low-register clarinet (Johnny Strong) alternate measures; rhythm in $\frac{4}{4}$.

1:58   Earl Hines plays a piano solo.

2:11   Hines (on piano) goes into his recognizable style of octaves in the right hand, mainly double time.

2:33   Ensemble chorus: Trumpet, clarinet, and trombone all play long sustained notes; $\frac{4}{4}$ rhythm.

2:45   Trumpet goes into more of a solo while others continue their sustained notes.

2:56   Hines plays a short solo piano interlude.

3:05   Trumpet, then other ensemble instruments join in.

3:16   End.

influenced and inspired many young musicians in the Chicago area. It should be noted that combos such as this one and the members from Austin High School played in downtown Chicago, whereas Armstrong and Oliver reigned on the South Side. The Original Dixieland Jazz Band denied (falsely) being influenced by African American musicians; the New Orleans Rhythm Kings stated that they did whatever they could to sound like Oliver and others. It also appears that the New Orleans Rhythm Kings were a link between the New Orleans players and the roster of players entering jazz in the Chicago days. They were actually more important as an influence than as individual players; in other words, those players they influenced often surpassed them.[22]

Bix Beiderbecke

Leon "Bix" Beiderbecke was born in 1903 and lived for only twenty-eight years. His talent was such that his name alone on a record makes it a col-

Bix Beiderbecke with his pickup band Rhythm Jugglers. Left to right: Howdy Quicksell, Tommy Gargano, Paul Mertz, Don Murray, Bix Beiderbecke, and Tommy Dorsey

lector's item. It is said that his style was fairly well formed from listening to records of the Original Dixieland Jazz Band and others before he had heard Armstrong. In Chicago he listened to Oliver, Armstrong, and the New Orleans Rhythm Kings. Some historians state that Beiderbecke developed his style from listening to Emmet Hardy, who played on the riverboats that stopped at Beiderbecke's hometown, Davenport, Iowa. Beiderbecke's first employment was with a group called the Wolverines, whose first recordings were made in 1924[23] ("Jazz Me Blues").

Until Bix Beiderbecke came to Chicago, the best white trumpet player was Francis Spanier, a youngster who followed Armstrong every hour possible. Armstrong nicknamed him "Muggsy." His recordings are some of the best examples of the way these young players attempted to play. The music has great vitality and creativeness, and yet it was meant to be and truly is fun listening.[24]

Beiderbecke worked for a while with his close friend, saxophonist Frankie "Tram" Trumbauer. Trumbauer soon became dedicated to looking after Beiderbecke's welfare, guiding him to the big bands of Jean Goldkette and Paul Whiteman, where top salaries were to be had. Some of Beiderbecke's best records were done with small combos outside his regular job with Whiteman. Especially notable are those with Trumbauer.[25] Debussy's influence can be heard in some of Beiderbecke's piano compositions, the best known of which is "In a Mist." On the cornet, Beiderbecke never seemed to let his style become as dramatic or sensual as Armstrong's. Instead, his cornet music is usually described as poetic, fluid, moving, and sensitive—if words can ever truly describe music ("Somebody Stole My Gal," "Margie").

listening guide

(CD 1, track 13)
Frank Trumbauer and His Orchestra featuring Bix Beiderbecke
"Singin' the Blues"

:00   Four measures: introduction with cornet and sax in thirds.

:06   Trumbauer on C melody sax playing solo for 14 measures—a combination of interpretation and improvisation.

:31   Two-measure break on sax.

:35   Sax solo continues for 14 measures.

1:01   Two-measure break on sax.

1:05   Beiderbecke plays his solo on cornet for 14 measures.

1:30   Two-measure break; Beiderbecke goes into double time for the first measure.

1:33   Beiderbecke continues his solo for 16 measures.

2:03   Third chorus ensemble for 8 measures.

2:18   Clarinet solo for 6 measures.

2:29   Two measures of clarinet break.

2:33   Ensemble on the second half of the tune for 9 measures.

2:50   Guitar takes a 1-measure break (Eddie Lang).

2:52   Ensemble on out to end; Beiderbecke pushes the ensemble harder.

3:03   End.

Many writers refer to Beiderbecke as the first cool artist. (For a discussion of cool jazz, see Chapter 9.) It is true that even though he could move an ensemble almost by himself, he usually did not play with the frenzy of most of the Chicago Style trumpets. This situation could be compared to that of Miles Davis during the bop era, when Dizzy Gillespie's virtuosic style was in vogue.

LATER DEVELOPMENTS

Even though the type of jazz known as Dixieland started one hundred years ago, mainly in New Orleans, it is still with us. As a played-by-ear combination of European melodies, African rhythms, and European brass marching band sounds, it was, and is, colorful, exciting, and carefree. Dixieland is still being played and listened to. The members of Dixieland bands perform their music as if the music itself is fun. Maybe that is why it is still so popular.

vamping

Trad Jazz

Although jazz has undergone many changes since its inception, some bands today play jazz almost as it was played at the turn of the twentieth century. The Early New Orleans Dixieland style had a great revival in the early 1940s. Prominent in this movement was Lu Watters and his Yerba Buena Jazz Band (based in Oakland, California). This band, like others in the movement, did everything possible to re-create King Oliver's style. The advocates of this style of jazz refer to their music as the "real" or "trad" jazz.

To this day, Chicago Style Dixieland music has not lost its appeal, primarily because of its rhythmic concept. When Dixieland is played today, it is almost always Chicago Style. Many musicians are not even aware of the fact that there is more than one style of Dixieland.

Though there are clubs and societies dedicated to the preservation of Dixieland music, it is seldom played exactly as it was in the 1920s. The musicians have lived through other jazz eras, all of which have become part of their musical personalities. Of course, jazz musicians have always been more concerned about playing with good expression than about playing authentically. However, many seventeen- and eighteen-year-old musicians accept the Chicago Style as the best way to express themselves and play it well.[26] This tradition was carried on most admirably by such groups as The World's Greatest Jazz Band and The Dukes of Dixieland and by individuals such as Bobby Hackett.[27]

The Chicago Style was perpetuated by large orchestras such as the Dorsey Brothers and Bob Crosby, the latter of whom built a reputation on a big-band version of this small-band style.[28] In larger orchestras, complete sections play written parts based on lines originally invented for one instrument. This is an example of one style of jazz influencing the styles that followed.

Although Armstrong certainly did not exemplify Chicago Style Dixieland trumpet players, he was extremely important to jazz in this time span. His association with Earl Hines began in Chicago in the 1920s, and he recorded many classics with his Hot Five and Hot Seven groups.

Recording companies have not reproduced Chicago Style Dixieland records with nearly the same enthusiasm that they have Early New Orleans Dixieland, blues singers, and swing bands. Of the records that are available, there is more to be said for the soloists than for the ensemble passages.[29] This seems incongruous when one hears the excellence of ensembles on exceptional records like those of Muggsy Spanier.

Some historians feel that the jazz age ended about 1927. Although jazz did continue, the large bands began to absorb the better jazz players (e.g., Beiderbecke joined the famous Paul Whiteman Orchestra). By the end of the 1920s, the heart of the jazz scene had again moved, this time from Chicago to New York.

summary

The Creole bands of New Orleans made use of a collective improvisational style that became the standard for later Dixieland bands. The Early New Orleans style grew out of the musical practice of the marching bands that adopted the ragtime syncopation. After the close of Storyville, the musical activity for these bands moved primarily to Chicago. The move to the North was accompanied by a shift in the group improvisational style. Over this time the emphasis moved from a predominantly ensemble style of playing to one that centered on the soloists, which was due largely to the influence of the singular voice and melodic invention of Louis Armstrong.

FOR FURTHER STUDY

1. Discuss why New Orleans was important in the development of jazz at the beginning of the twentieth century.
2. At first, early Dixieland music used no piano. What was the instrumentation of these bands?
3. Discuss the influence of Storyville on jazz.
4. Discuss the role each instrument assumed in the overall sound of Early New Orleans Dixieland ensembles.
5. What was the overall plan or design of the music?
6. Listen to the recorded example of the original melody played in Early New Orleans style (Interactive Guide 2) and answer the following:
   a. Do you hear the steady pulse of the flat-four rhythm? Which instruments realize this musical characteristic?
   b. In this Dixieland arrangement, which instrument is realizing the solo chorus part?
   c. In the return section, which instrument is playing the melody?
7. Who recorded the first instrumental jazz music by a black band?
8. Describe Chicago during the Roaring Twenties.
9. Musically, in what ways did Chicago Style Dixieland music differ from Early New Orleans Dixieland?
10. In what ways did ragtime piano playing influence the rhythm of Chicago Style Dixieland music?
11. In this era, what instruments were added and what instruments replaced instruments used in Early New Orleans Dixieland ensembles? Why did these changes take place?
12. Gradually, short solo spots crept into jazz ensembles. Listen to "Maple Leaf Rag" by Paul Mares and his Friars' Society Orchestra. Identify the

instruments that you hear in brief solo spots. Does the piano have an opportunity to play solo? Is there a string bass?

13. Listen to Bix Beiderbecke and His Gang play "Margie." In the opening statement of the melody, which instrument is featured? Is this a good example of the $\frac{2}{4}$ rag rhythm? Notice that a bass sax is used in place of a tenor sax.

SUGGESTED ADDITIONAL LISTENING

Bechet, Sidney, *Master Musician*. Bluebird Records, 2 AXM-5516.
Beiderbecke, Bix. *Bix Beiderbecke and the Chicago Cornets* (4 sides).
————. *The Bix Beiderbecke Legend*. RCA Victor Records, LMP-2323.
Chicagoans (1928–1930).
Chicago Ramblers. *Jazz of the 1920's*.
Crosby, Bob. *Stomp Off, Let's Go*. Ace of Hearts Records, AH-29.
Dukes of Dixieland. *At the Jazz Band Ball*. RCA Victor Records, LSP-2097.
Encyclopedia of Jazz on Records, vols. 1 and 2.
Folkways Jazz, vols. 5–7.
Hackett, Bobby. *The Hackett Horn*. Epic Records, EE 22004.
History of Classic Jazz, vols. 4, 6, 7, and 9.
Jazz at Preservation Hall, vol. 2.
Jazz Odyssey, vol. 2.
The Jazz Story, vols. 1 and 2.
King Oliver's Jazz Band, Smithsonian Collection of Classical Jazz, R-001.
The Original Dixieland Jazz Band. RCA Victor Records, LPU-547.
Ruedebusch, Dick. *Mister Trumpet*. Jubilee Records, 5015.
————. *Meet Mr. Trumpet*. Jubilee Records, 5008.

Louis Armstrong

Autobiography. Decca Records, DX-155.
Best of Louis Armstrong. Audio Fidelity Records, 6132.
Essential Louis Armstrong. Verve Records, V-8569.
Folkways Jazz, vols. 2, 4, 5, and 7.
Hello Dolly. Kapp Records, 3364.
Louis Armstrong. Audio Fidelity Records, 6241.
Louis Armstrong. RCA Victor Records, VPM-6044.
Louis Armstrong and Earl Hines. Columbia Records, CL 853.
Louis Armstrong in Memoriam. Everest Records, 3312.
Louis Armstrong in the Thirties and Forties. RCA Victor Records, LSP 2971.
Louis Armstrong Jazz Classics. Decca Records, 8284.
Louis Armstrong Plays W. C. Handy. Columbia Records, CL 591.
Louis Armstrong Story, vols. 1–4. Columbia Records, CL 851–52–53–54.
Louis Armstrong, V.S.O.P. Columbia Special Products, JEE-20019.
Rare Batch of Satch. RCA Victor Records, LPM 2322.
Rare Items. Decca Records, 79225.
Satchmo at Pasadena. Decca Records, 8041.

Satchmo at Symphony Hall. Decca Records, DXS 7195.
Satchmo on Stage. Decca Records, 8330.
Smithsonian Collection of Classic Jazz, vols. 2 and 3.
Young Louis Armstrong: The Sideman. Decca Records, 79233.

ADDITIONAL READING RESOURCES

Allen, Walter C., and Rust, Brian. *King Joe Oliver.*
Berendt, Joachim. *The New Jazz Book*, 4–12, 32–35.
Berton, Ralph. *Remembering Bix: A Memoir of the Jazz Age.*
Buerkle, Jack V., and Barker, Danny. *Bourbon Street Black.*
Dexter, Dave. *The Jazz Story*, 6–19, 30–55.
Feather, Leonard. *The Book of Jazz*, 30–38.
Francis, André. *Jazz*, 27–34.
Harris, Rex. *Jazz*, 77–93, 189–96.
Hentoff, Nat, and McCarthy, Albert. *Jazz: New Perspectives on the History of Jazz*, 21–43, 139–69.
Schuller, Gunther. *Early Jazz: Its Roots and Musical Development*, 63–88, 175–94.
Stearns, Marshall. *The Story of Jazz*, 33–60.
Sudhalter, Richard M., and Evans, Phillip R. *Bix: Man and Legend.*
Williams, Martin T., ed. *The Art of Jazz*, 59–73.

Note: Complete information, including name of publisher and date of publication, is provided in this book's bibliography.

NOTES

1. From Henry Pleasants, *Serious Music and All That Jazz*, 1969. Reprinted by permission of Simon & Schuster, Inc.
2. Joachim Berendt, *Jazz Book: From New Orleans to Rock and Free Jazz*, trans. Dan Morgenstern (Westport, Conn.: Lawrence Hill, 1975).
3. Dan Morgenstern, "The Meaning of New Orleans," *Down Beat* 36, no. 12 (June 1969): 13.
4. Charles Suhor, "Jazz and the New Orleans Press," *Down Beat* 36, no. 12 (June 1969): 19.
5. Barry Ulanov, *Handbook of Jazz* (New York: Viking Press, 1959), 8.
6. One example is in the tune "Indiana." The first chord is composed of the notes F, A, C, and D, and the second chord moves to F-sharp, A, C, and D. The natural resolution for the trombone player is from F to F-sharp, pointing out to the other players that the chord has changed and that this is the change that has occurred.
7. Larry Gushee, "King Oliver's Creole Jazz Band," *The Art of Jazz*, ed. Martin Williams (London: Oxford University Press, 1959), 45.
8. King Oliver's Savannah Syncopaters, "Snag It," *Introduction to Jazz*, ed. Rev. A. L. Kershaw, Decca Records, DL8244.

9. King Oliver, *King Oliver*, Epic Records, LA16003; "Jazzin' Babies Blues," *Jazz Odyssey*, vol. 1; "New Orleans Stomp" and "Where Did You Stay Last Night?" *Jazz Odyssey*, vol. 2; "Working Man's Blues," *Folkways Jazz*, vol. 2, "Snake Dance," "Dippermouth Blues," and "High Society," *Folkways Jazz*, vol. 3; "Sugarfoot Stomp," *Folkways Jazz*, vol. 5; "Sweet Lovin' Man," *Folkways Jazz*, vol. 6; "Froggie Moore," *History of Classic Jazz*.

10. Original Dixieland Jazz Band, "At the Darktown Strutters' Ball," *Jazz Odyssey*, vol. 1; *The Original Dixieland Jazz Band*, RCA Victor Records, LPV-547.

11. Original Dixieland Jazz Band, "Barnyard Blues," *Jazz Odyssey*, vol. 1.

12. Gunther Schuller, *The Swing Era* (London: Oxford University Press, 1989), 196.

13. Martin T. Williams, "For Louis Armstrong at 70," *Down Beat* 37, no. 13 (July 1970): 22.

14. Leonard Feather, "The Real Louis Armstrong," *Down Beat* 29, no. 5 (March 1962): 23.

15. Kid Ory, "Weary Blues," *History of Classic Jazz*, vol. 10.

16. Red Nichols, "Ida," *The Jazz Story*, vol. 2.

17. Dave Dexter, *The Jazz Story: From the Nineties to the Sixties*, 1964. By permission of Prentice-Hall, Inc., Englewood Cliffs, N.J.

18. *Louis Armstrong and Earl Hines*, Columbia Records, CL 853; Earl Hines, *The Father Jumps*, Bluebird Records, AXM 2-5508; "Piano Man," *Singers and Soloists of the Big Bands*, Smithsonian Collection of Recordings; *Big Band Jazz*, Smithsonian Collection of Recordings.

19. *Louis Armstrong and His Hot Five*, Columbia Records, CL 851; *Singers and Soloists of the Swing Bands*, Smithsonian Collection of Recordings.

20. *Louis Armstrong Plays W. C. Handy*, Columbia Records, CL 391.

21. New Orleans Rhythm Kings, "Livery Stable Blues," *History of Classic Jazz*, vol. 4; Dave Dexter, *The Jazz Story*, 34.

22. New Orleans Rhythm Kings, "Tin Roof Blues," *Introduction to Jazz*, Della Records, DL 8244.

23. The Wolverines, "Royal Garden Blues," *History of Classic Jazz*, vol. 7; *Bix Beiderbecke and the Wolverines*, Riverside Records, RLP 12-133.

24. Muggsy Spanier, "Muskrat Ramble," *History of Classic Jazz*, vol. 9.

25. *The Bix Beiderbecke Story*, vols. 1–3, Columbia Records, CL 844 6.

26. The Windjammers, *Jammin' with the Windjammers*, Argo Records, LP-4047.

27. *The World's Greatest Jazz Band*, Atlantic Records, 1570; *The Dukes of Dixieland*, Audio Fidelity Records, 5962, 5976; Harmony Music Records, 11149; Bobby Hackett, "Struttin' with Some Barbecue," *The Jazz Story*, vol. 2.

28. Bob Crosby, *Stomp It Off, Let's Go*, Mono Records, AH 29; *Greatest Hits*, Decca Records, 74856; "Maryland, My Maryland," *The Jazz Story*, vol. 4; *Mardi Gras Parade*, Monmouth-Evergreen Records, 7026.

29. *The Best of Dixieland*.

6

Swing

Swing is the name given to the era following boogie-woogie in the development of jazz. In general, *swing* refers to the music of large dance bands that played written arrangements, occasionally using improvised solos. Most noteworthy jazz has a rhythmic drive, or swing. Still, the era of jazz in the 1930s and early 1940s is called the swing era.

Some jazz terms can become quite confusing, and swing is one of them. The confusion comes from the fact that some of the most popular swing music did not swing; rather, it involved jazz players doing a jazz interpretation of pretty **ballads.** One unusual aspect of swing jazz is that, though most people remember the **up-tempo** tunes, the swing bands actually played more ballads than anything else. But it should be remembered that those ballads were performed by players who were jazz oriented. Listen, for example, to Benny Goodman, the King of Swing, play his theme, a pretty ballad called "Good-bye"; jazz trumpeter Harry James plays an **obligato** in the background.[2]

Some listeners today feel that all swing bands sound alike. The swing era saw literally hundreds of name attractions, and so one of the biggest concerns for the leaders was identification. They wanted the fans to be able to distinguish their band from all others after hearing just a few measures of music. Therefore, most bands attempted to have an identifying trademark. For example, Tommy Dorsey probably played with a more beautiful tone and control on the trombone than anyone else, so he played solos on just about every arrangement, and the fans recognized his sound.[3] Glenn Miller used a clarinet to play lead over his saxophone section, a most identifying feature.[4] (For an introduction to swing, listen to Interactive Guide 5 at the interactive listening site, http://www.emegill.com/listening.

BEGINNINGS OF THE SWING ERA

Fletcher Henderson, an influential figure in the swing era, is credited with having created, with his brother Horace and with Don Redman, the pattern for swing arrangements.[5] This pattern was successful, being copied by almost every popular dance band of the era. Henderson is said to have established the

Fletcher Henderson © Institute of Jazz Studies, Rutgers University

listening guide

Interactive Guide 5
Swing

:00   Introduction on solo drums using tom-toms.

:04   Ensemble chorus (saxes on melody, brass on riff); full rhythm section keeps $\frac{4}{4}$ (flat-four) rhythm.

:08   Second phrase.

:13   Third phrase.

:17   Drum solo on tom-toms.

:20   Clarinet solo (one chorus backed by trombone riff).

:34   Ensemble chorus (same as first chorus except a tone higher). Notice that in arrangements such as this, entire sections like the saxes or trumpets now play equivalent parts that earlier Dixieland players covered in the front line. What may be lost in spontaneity is compensated for in the complexity offered by written arrangements.

:39   Second phrase.

:43   Third phrase.

:48   Ensemble chorus (same except for another half tone higher for still more intensity).

:53   Second phrase.

:57   Ensemble tag.

1:00   Clarinet solo break.

1:02   End.

independent use of trumpet, trombone, saxophone, and rhythm sections, with the use of soloists. (This exact format is used today by most of the thousands of college and high school jazz bands in the United States. The attitude, also fostered by music publishers, seems to be that this is the easiest avenue for today's jazz education.)

In New York in 1924, Henderson had Louis Armstrong, Coleman Hawkins, and Don Redman among his exclusive personnel. In 1924 in Kansas City, Bennie Moten put together his first saxophone section as such; the idea was simply to create more sonority. Moten added more brass as early as 1931, using three trumpets and two trombones. Henderson had done the same thing in 1929. Some say that the first jazz orchestra to play written arrangements in New York was the Billy Paige Band, with Don Redman as arranger and lead alto sax, in 1922. Redman then joined Fletcher Henderson, stayed with him until 1927, joined McKinney's Cotton Pickers in 1931, and eventually organized his own band. Henderson, Redman, and others took the parts that were generally conceived to be for one trumpet, for example, and harmonized them to be played by three trumpets. (For notational examples, see examples 21A and 21B, Appendix B.)

The swing bands ultimately adopted a consistent instrumentation that has remained fairly stable to the present. There were four sections, each with similar instruments:

1. Saxophone section—two alto saxophones, two tenor saxophones, and one baritone saxophone.
2. Trumpet section—four trumpets; the first was responsible for the highest notes and eventually the second player for most of the jazz solos.
3. Trombone section—four trombones; later a fifth bass trombone was often added.
4. Rhythm section—one drummer, one bass player (string bass), one piano player, and one guitar player.

Although there was a duplication of several instruments in the horn sections, each player usually had a unique part written for him. In the riffing bands of Kansas City, players in the same section often played the same melodic line or riff for energy and volume.

JAZZ ARRANGEMENTS

The general procedure in the creation of a swing jazz arrangement is to write a score that has specific notes for each instrument to play in every measure. (For a notational example, see example 22, Appendix B.) In jazz, the music arranger indicates measures for solo improvisation. After the arranger has decided which musical notations will result in the desired sounds, the score is given to a music copyist who extracts from the score the individual parts for the various instruments. This then becomes a blueprint for each instrumentalist, showing exactly what is to be played while the other instrumentalists play their parts.

Short, repeated refrains or phrases (which are quite typical in African music), or riffs, are common in jazz. Sometimes riffs are used in an ostinato fashion as catalysts that hold the music together. Repeated riffs, which cause great momentum and impetus, were used extensively by Kansas City musicians such as Bennie Moten (later Count Basie's band) in the 1920s and by New York musicians such as Fletcher Henderson, who was scoring arrangements for blues singers Bessie Smith, Ma Rainey, and others. The use of riffs became standard in the more jazz-oriented big bands, sometimes backing up a soloist and sometimes composing entire selections. Listen to Interactive Guide 5 for the swing excerpt in which the brass section plays a riff behind the saxophones. The trombones also play a riff under the clarinet solo. (For notational examples, see examples 23A and 23B, Appendix B.)

Fletcher Henderson

Fletcher Henderson, a schooled piano player from Georgia, came to New York in 1920 originally to do postgraduate study at Columbia University as a chemistry major. Henderson became so involved in music, however, that his other

**Fletcher Henderson
and his orchestra.**

goals were forsaken. Henderson was a pianist, but his most notable talent was his arranging. He wrote most of the library of music that launched the career of the Benny Goodman orchestra.

The personnel of Henderson's orchestra was most impressive. At one time or another, almost all the important black musicians of the day played in his band: Louis Armstrong, Roy Eldridge, Don Redman, Coleman Hawkins, and Lester Young. Many members from the Henderson band went on either to have bands of their own or to become featured solo attractions.[6]

There always seem to be many controversies concerning jazz. Henderson became deeply involved in one: the split between the advocates of small Dixieland bands and those favoring the big bands heading in the direction of swing. Many thought that the rise of the big bands meant the fall of jazz completely. The small-band advocates considered these large ensembles top heavy because of the unusually large number of horn players. Not only was the rhythm section now outnumbered, but, as the ensembles grew in size, the arrangements tended to become more detailed to provide a tighter ensemble sound. With the larger number of musicians, the Dixieland texture, which granted each player much individual expression, was no longer possible. The solo areas in a swing band composition offered chances for individual expression, but they were only a small part of the whole composition.

At first, Henderson toyed with sort of an enlarged Dixieland group. But with the addition of Redman, who had studied at the Boston and Detroit music conservatories, tighter harmonic control became a major interest. Henderson

listening guide

(CD 1, track 14)
Fletcher Henderson and His Orchestra
"Wrappin' It Up"

The structure for each chorus is ABAC.

:00   Introduction: brass has the theme and saxes respond.

:09   First chorus: saxes state the main theme, and each phrase is a variation of the previous one; this is structural phrase A.

:19   Structural phrase B.

:28   Structural phrase A as trumpets join the saxes.

:37   Structural phrase C.

:48   Second chorus: Hilton Jefferson plays an alto sax solo backed up by muted trumpets; same ABAC structure for this chorus.

1:25   Third chorus: Red Allen plays a trumpet solo backed up by saxes.

1:34   Whole brass section plays lead.

1:44   Trumpet solo resumes.

2:03   Fourth chorus: theme is tossed back and forth between brass and reeds (now on clarinets).

2:13   Clarinet solo.

2:22   Saxes take lead.

2:31   Brass join in.

2:39   Ending phrase, which later becomes a big-band cliché.

2:42   End.

thought that too much improvisation was almost dreary unless the improvisers were really exceptional. He also thought that the polyphony established in the Dixieland styles was too risky and that there should be more control.

NEW YORK

During the 1920s, when Chicago Style Dixieland was the most popular jazz expression, New York and Kansas City were the most important geographic areas for developments leading toward the swing style of jazz. In the mid-1920s, Duke Ellington was becoming a name attraction, King Oliver was playing in the Savoy Ballroom in New York's Harlem, and Fletcher Henderson was at the Roseland

Ballroom in Times Square. New York City's network radio programs, booking offices, and recording studios began to draw musicians from all over the country. One of the most swinging bands to invade New York was William McKinney's Cotton Pickers. This band, with many ex-Henderson personnel, recorded more than fifty tunes between 1928 and 1933 ("Four or Five Times").

Chick Webb

The band of Chick Webb was one of the new bands that kept appearing in New York around 1929 or 1930[7] ("Heebie Jeebies"). This band could swing while playing lightly and never exploited showmanship at the expense of musical integrity. In the mid-1930s, the teenager Ella Fitzgerald raised that band to prominence. (One of the authors, while participating often in the famous Battle of Bands at the Savoy Ballroom in New York's Harlem, where Chick Webb's band was usually considered to be a house band, was always glad that the Webb band was not one of his adversaries.)

Jimmie Lunceford

On November 8, 1940, there was a charity affair, a Battle of Bands, at New York City's Manhattan Center. There were thirty bands, each scheduled to play fifteen minutes. These bands included Benny Goodman, Glenn Miller, Count Basie, Glen Gray, Les Brown, Guy Lombardo, Will Bradley, Sammy Kaye, and twenty others. The show lasted from 8 P.M. to 4 A.M. with each band playing its allotted fifteen minutes—except for one. The six thousand enthusiastic fans refused to let the Jimmy Lunceford band leave the bandstand. It was as if they had just discovered this talented organization.

The band was first formed by a group of college students who approached their performance with unusual discipline that stressed correct technique and accurate playing. The result of their dedication was a body of arrangements and recordings that manifest a complex performance skill, setting it apart from other bands of the day. It is interesting to compare their arrangement of "Mood Indigo" with that of Ellington to hear how a highly accomplished band can rework a famous composition.

Musicians knew about the band; it ranked as high as any other swing band. Sadly, lack of exposure and failure to record the popular tunes of the day kept this talented band from being at the top of the public's popularity polls.

Duke Ellington

Just as Armstrong crystallized and popularized the solo aspect of jazz, Duke Ellington, more than any other single musician, proved that orchestrating jazz was an art of the highest level. However, it should be pointed out that Ellington's music was always a combination of solo and ensemble playing. He, like Basie, drew the thoughts of his soloists together into the orchestral whole, accomplishing the feat from the piano. "He was a born orchestral pianist . . . to lead the orchestra, in other words, from the piano, to galvanize it rhythmically, to inspire it creatively, and to complement it pianistically when needed."[8]

On the other hand, the musicians playing for Ellington did not lose their identity. The Ellington orchestra was always made up of the *individual* talents of his players. It cannot be emphasized enough that listeners are always aware of the personalities of the players (Johnny Hodges, Lawrence Brown, Rex Stewart, Harry Carney, and so on). Yet the band always sounded like Ellington regardless of changes in personnel over the years. This is one of the most important aspects of the band: allowing individuals to retain their identities and to expand and explore their own directions. Ellington's band always sounded like a well-knit unit expressing the feelings and personalities of Ellington while achieving a wonderful relationship between compositions and the orchestra. (Ellington is discussed in greater detail in Chapter 7.)

For proof of why Fletcher Henderson and Duke Ellington remain the best-known performers who developed swing in New York in the 1920s, listen to "Wrappin' It Up," "Concerto for Cootie," and "Ko-Ko."[9]

Generally, the New York bands had heavily structured arrangements. But really, no New York school existed as had been the case in New Orleans, Chicago, and Kansas City. There were many important performers in New York in the 1920s, but their styles did not seem to coincide. Regardless, the direction of most was at least toward swing.

KANSAS CITY

"Jazz was literally exploding in myriad new directions—not only musically and stylistically, but geographically as well."[10]

Kansas City was bustling with activity from the early 1920s to about 1938. A political organization known as the Pendergast Machine did much more than encourage the nightclub atmosphere, and so an abundance of employment opportunities for jazz musicians arose. The influx demonstrated that Kansas City had become a jazz mecca: there was Bill Basie from Red Bank, New Jersey; Ben Webster from Tulsa; Lester Young from Mississippi; and Andy Kirk from Dallas.

The Bennie Moten band was considered to be the top band in the Kansas City area from about 1926 to 1935[11] ("Moten Swing," "Toby," "Kansas City Breakdown"), but the competition was extremely keen from the bands of Andy Kirk (piano and arrangements by Mary Lou Williams), Walter Page, Alphonso Trent, and others. The Kansas City bands were looser in musical setting and relied heavily on blues-based riffs.

Mary Lou Williams

One of the greatest performers to come out of the Kansas City area was undoubtedly the multitalented Mary Lou Williams. She was the first woman in jazz history to compose and arrange for a large jazz band, and she dominated the performances of the great Andy Kirk band with her skillful piano playing.[12] Her eclecticism held her in great stead, and she is considered one of the great jazz pianists. Her compositions were in the libraries of a dozen leading swing bands. During the last years of her life (she died in 1981), she received many

honors, including having a street in Kansas City named after her. Mary Lou Williams was a perennial innovator.[13]

Count Basie

Count Basie was in New York in the early 1920s when he joined a road show, the Bennie Moten band, that became stranded in Kansas City. He then started his own band, and most of Moten's better players went with Basie. It is therefore natural that some historians believe that Basie took over Moten's band, especially as all these events happened around the time of Moten's death.

When Moten died, Basie became the leading figure in the Kansas City style of swing. He gave the audiences what they wanted while maintaining a true jazz orchestra with extremely high standards for over forty years.

Basie's players used all of the musical advances developed in the Kansas City territory to good advantage. For example, Basie anticipated bop by freeing the piano from merely keeping time, and his drummer, Jo Jones, added interesting accents to his very moving rhythm. Basie's economic piano style demonstrated the old adage that less is more. The band, with its relaxed swing, was lauded more for its performances than for the compositions it performed. Members were also admired for their consistent ability to swing; hence, the band was often called "the swing machine." Economics forced Basie to go to a small group for two years (1950–52). But "Basie himself is reported to have said in 1950, if he could just have that old band once again before he died, he would leave this earth a happy man."[14]

Basie died in June 1984. However, the Basie band continued to be led by the talented woodwind player Frank Foster[15] ("Doggin' Around," "Taxi War Dance").

Count Basie and his rhythm section. Bass: Walter Page; guitar: Freddy Green; drums: Jo Jones.

SOUTHWEST BANDS—EARLY BASIE

The Southwest bands offered a different solution to big-band improvisational structures. Rather than crafted arrangements that were realized by individual arrangers, the players themselves contributed to the shaping of the final form. In fact, the actual compositional idea would operate like a melodic catalyst around which other melodic lines offered by the players would collect. Basie's signature song, "One O'clock Jump," is essentially that. Basie's name is attached to the arrangement, but, outside of the initial motive, the arrangement belongs as much to the band that developed the final form.

Because of the looser compositional structure, the arrangement's focal point shifted away from the arranger and toward the improvising performer. Particular to Basie in the late 1930s were the solo strengths of players like Lester Young and Herschel Evans on tenor, Harry Edison and Buck Clayton on trumpet, and Benny Morton and Dickie Wells on trombone. It can be noted that Fletcher Henderson also had solo voices that helped identify his band; however, it was how these solo voices worked within the ensemble that differentiated the Harlem bands from those in the Southwest. The riff-style bands depended much more heavily on the solo strengths of the players. Riffing energized the solo work, providing structural definition. Many of the blues-based riffs were transportable from one piece to another. The soloists were in many cases the glue that welded the riff patterns into a structural whole.

The dominant voice among those in the Basie band was that of Lester Young. Like Coleman Hawkins for Henderson, Young is the signature of the late 1930s Basie band. The difference in the sounds of Hawkins and Young was a sense of melody. Hawkins worked more in the hot fashion of Harlem bands, while Young presaged the cool sounds of the late 1940s and 1950s. It is interesting to note

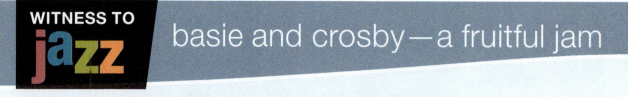

basie and crosby—a fruitful jam

Count Basie, piano; Ray Bauduc, drums; Bob Haggart, bass; Herschel Evans, tenor sax.
Photo and text Courtesy William P. Gottlieb/Library of Congress

Before World War II, when I went to work at the *Washington Post,* our capital city was strictly a southern town. (I had black friends, but the only place where we could have dinner together in public was at the restaurant in Union Station.)

In addition to a customary job at the paper, I had a Sunday jazz column, plus regular programs on WRC (NBC) and WINX (a local station). One week, the Count Basie orchestra was at the Howard, a black theater, while the Bob Crosby orchestra was at the whites-only Earle. (Bob was Bing's brother.)

Wouldn't it be great, I thought, if some of the Basie and Crosby musicians could get together to jam. The Howard manager "owed me." He agreed to let me have the Howard stage after hours. Basie then said he'd show up with key men.

The Crosby part was stickier. His was older-style music, Dixieland. It was the opposite of the hard-driving, Kansas City jazz of the Basie band.

Furthermore, the Crosbyites were white, largely southern, and the proposed session was to be at the Howard, in Washington's "Harlem." Finally, Basie's group included two of jazz's greatest tenor saxes, Lester Young and Herschel Evans. Playing next to these giants could be uncomfortable. But Bob, with a little hesitation, said OK.

Crosby's contingent included bassist Bob Haggart and drummer Ray Bauduc, a duo that, on its own, had just had a huge hit record, "Big Noise from Winnetka." Also attending was Eddie Miller, a top white tenor sax, and clarinetist Matty Matlock. The Count served as pianist.

Listening to this rare session were fewer than a dozen guests, including Ahmet and Nesuhi Ertegun, sons of the Turkish Ambassador (and eventual founders of Atlantic Records). The music, though containing stars from disparate styles, came off smoothly. As it turned out, a now legendary event was created!

(william) count basie

Basie became associated with the Southwest band tradition and continued to lead his band until his death. The band that originally used the riffing style of the Moten band later became known for its tight ensemble capable of the most tailored dynamic control. Basie was pianist for the group that helped establish the contemporary swing style.

1927   Basie toured on the Keith and TOBA vaudeville circuits as a pianist and accompanist

and got stranded in Kansas City, where he remained. He played for silent films and joined Walter Page's band in 1928.

1929   He joined Bennie Moten's band, Kansas City Orchestra.

1935   Shortly after Moten's death he left the band and organized his own nine-piece group with several of Moten's players. His new group included Lester Young.

1936   His band officially became the Count Basie Orchestra and began to gain international acclaim. After Lester Young left the group, the band began to move toward written arrangements that later characterized the controlled ensemble for which the band is famous.

1950   The group disbanded for financial reasons and Basie worked with a small six- to nine-piece group.

1952   He reorganized the band and traveled internationally.

1985   After his death the band continued under the leadership of Thad Jones and finally under Frank Foster (1986).

that, after Hawkins left Henderson's band, he was replaced by Young in 1934. Young's approach was different enough from Hawkins's that Henderson and the members of the saxophone section did not like his playing.

This incompatibility may have been more than just the lightness of Young's tone when compared to that of Hawkins. Within the riff-style format, the soloist has a great deal more room to expand ideas. In the Harlem bands, the solo areas tended to be more formalized and punctuated by stylized ensemble passages. Young's sense of line may have outranged the solo areas allotted for him in the Henderson style of arrangements. The energy of the riff bands was certainly intended to be as hot as that of the Harlem bands, and Young was more than successful in the best-known Southwest band. In Basie's riff-based band, Young's cooler sound had room to shape energetic solo lines not appropriate in the Henderson style. This is not to say that Hawkins was incapable of extended solos ("Body and Soul," "Picasso") but that his vitality as a soloist was more effective within Henderson's arrangements than was Young's more lyric style.

listening guide

(CD 1, track 15)
Count Basie and His Orchestra
"Taxi War Dance"

:00 Introduction consists of 4 measures of piano solo (Basie) in a boogie-woogie pattern followed by 4 measures of brass.

:09 First chorus: tenor sax solo (Lester Young) for 16 measures (rhythm plays $\frac{4}{4}$ except piano plays accents throughout the record).

:26 Eight measures as bridge of chorus, still tenor sax solo.

:35 Eight measures to finish up the chorus, same as first 8 measures of this first chorus.

:44 Second chorus: trombone solo (Dickie Wells), 32-measure chorus with the same chords for the bridge that were used in the first chorus.

1:23 Third chorus: 4 measures of brass.

1:27 Four measures of tenor sax solo (Buddy Tate).

1:32 Repeat of the above 8 measures.

1:41 Eight measures of piano solo on the bridge chords.

1:50 Four measures of brass.

1:55 Four measures of tenor sax solo.

1:59 Fourth chorus: 4 measures of full ensemble (piano playing boogie-woogie pattern).

2:04 Four measures of tenor sax solo (Lester Young).

2:09 Repeat of above 8 measures.

2:16 Eight measures of piano solo on bridge chords.

2:26 Four measures of full ensemble.

2:31 Four measures of tenor sax solo.

2:36 Two measures of piano, 2 measures of tenor sax (Buddy Tate), 2 measures of bass solo (Walter Page), 2 measures of drums (Jo Jones).

2:45 Full ensemble ending.

2:48 End.

Even if it were only a matter of personal sound, the fact that the replacement of Hawkins by Young was such an issue supports the notion that the arrangements, to whatever degree they were stylized, were subject to a further stylization by individual performers. Despite the gradual development of sectionally defined ensembles in the Henderson band's arrangements, the role of the improviser remained a key factor to their successful performance.

PROFILES IN

lester young

Lester Young was the model for all cool tenor saxophonists, and his playing led to a freeing-up of the language of jazz. He matured during the 1930s in Kansas City where jam sessions prepared him for all future competition. He first attracted attention with the Count Basie band, but there was some opposition to his playing, at first. Compared to Coleman Hawkins, Young's tone seemed light and airy. However, the younger players, and especially Basie himself, were more than impressed. His linear phrases carried melodic thoughts to their conclusion regardless of bar lines.

He recorded many solos with the Count Basie band that are still available in re-pressings. But those that are most cherished by his army of admirers are the small combo records, including those backing Billie Holiday. Young's playing naturally matched his personality—soft-spoken and understated.

1909	Born in Woodville, Mississippi, on August 27.
1909–19	Lived in New Orleans and was trained by his father.
1929–30	Worked with a touring band called the Bostonians.
1930s	Played with Joe "King" Oliver and Walter Page's Blue Devils.
1936–40	Worked for Count Basie, recording 105 selections.
1941–44	Played with his own combo.
1946–59	With Norman Granz's *Jazz at the Philharmonic*.
1959	Died in New York City on March 15.

The success of the riff approach to band arrangement and performance was even more directly dependent on the personnel in the ensemble. Without outstanding soloists, the otherwise energetic riffs might easily become nothing more than empty structures. Consequently, this dependence did not easily accommodate a regular change in key personnel. In fact, as we will see later, Basie eventually abandoned this approach of performer-centered arrangements after he lost Lester Young. Young essentially took with him a significant part of the Basie book. If a qualified replacement had been found, he potentially might have redefined the arrangements to such an extent that the band's identity itself might have changed.

The manner in which the sections operated within the ensemble also distinguished the Kansas City riff approach from the Harlem bands and later bands, like

listening guide

Count Basie and His Orchestra
"Doggin' Around"*

This selection offers a good example of how riffing can be used to shape an arrangement and give it a varying energy curve. Listen for the contrast in style and sound of the last soloist, Lester Young.

:00   Introduction, Basie on piano.

:07   Head of arrangement, saxes have main riff with a responding riff in the brass.

:22   Solo, Earle Warren on alto sax, brass punches riffing in background.

:30   Head returns.

:38   Solo, Herschel Evans on tenor saxophone. His tone is closer to Coleman Hawkins's sound. Light brass riffs in background.

:53   Brass lay out.

1:01   Brass back in with riff.

1:10   Solo, Harry Edison on trumpet, saxes riff in background.

1:24   Solo, Jack Washington on baritone saxophone, no riffing in background.

1:39   Solo, Basie on piano.

2:10   Solo, Lester Young on tenor saxophone. Notice his lighter tone and the way he floats his phrases over the meter. Brass and saxes riff in background.

2:26   Riffing drops out.

2:34   Riffing returns.

2:42   Drum solo.

2:49   Head returns with sectional riffing.

2:57   End.

*Smithsonian Collection, CD 1, track 20.

Ellington's, which were more compositionally based. Dickey Wells describes the riff approach with Basie as beginning with Basie's piano and rhythm until the time had been established. The saxes would then introduce a riff against the rhythm section. After that settled, then would follow the trombones and finally the trumpets. Wells goes on to say that, although it was a big band (expanded for its trip to New York in the late 1930s), Basie "handled it as though it were six pieces."[16]

This type of ensemble condensation is, perhaps, the most streamlined approach to big-band orchestration possible. The Harlem bands' arrangements made a much larger use of orchestration in their sectionalization, primarily because the sections themselves were just developing their classical shape. The instrumental lines— not yet so highly formalized as Basie's approach—often cut across the sections to create various instrumental colors. Basie's approach, like most of the other Southwest bands, seemed to view the big band as a higher-energy extension of small-group polyphony. The band's bigness restricted the extemporaneous offerings by the sectionalized voices, but the improvisatory structuring more typical of small groups was still at work. The Southwest riff approach placed the sections in contrapuntal relationships not typically heard in the Harlem bands. The riffs used by each section worked much more horizontally than the more carefully scored *tutti* ensemble areas we find in Henderson's arrangements. These ensemble areas, because they were written out in advance, allowed for some complex interchanges between sections that were unlikely to develop improvisationally. However, even these juxtapositions were more a tutti ensemble statement than contrapuntal melodies along sectional lines.

SWING BECOMES ACCEPTED

The depression came in 1929, and a few musicians, including Armstrong and Ellington, left for Europe. Some hotel-type bands, such as Guy Lombardo's, survived, and many of the better jazz players, such as Benny Goodman, were able to find employment in staff radio jobs. But, in general, the entire business suddenly failed. Music was a luxury that most of the public simply had to do without.

Many jazz authorities believe that the swing era was launched in 1934 when Benny Goodman left the radio studios and formed his own band, using arrangements scored mainly by Fletcher Henderson. However, swing was certainly well on its way before 1934. In 1932, Glen Gray and his Casa Loma Orchestra, with many reputable jazz performers, was playing weekly radio shows for Camel cigarettes. (This was a large band featuring precise arrangements laden with riffs often played with a call-and-response format between brass and saxes.) They first recorded as early as 1929 as the Orange Blossoms, then changed their name to that of a Toronto club, Casa Loma, also in 1929. Their first big hit, "Casa Loma Stomp,"[17] was recorded in 1930.

As stated earlier, before 1932 the Fletcher Henderson band was already well established, as was Duke Ellington's, and good, large swing bands were playing in the Kansas City area. The fact that large jazz bands developed in two such diverse areas as New York and Kansas City is another unusual phenomenon, like the diverse origins of the music itself, that surrounds jazz.

The public was trying to forget the stock market crash and the ensuing depression, and one logical manifestation was the great upsurge in dancing. The jazz players of the swing era became highly sought after for their dance music. The speakeasies of the 1920s were fairly small and could not house large bands. But with the repeal of the Volstead Act in 1933, social life so changed that large ballrooms were needed for the thousands who wanted to dance every night, and large bands seemed to be the answer to the dance halls. The country was covered with large ballrooms. Bands often played in towns so small that there would be only one house with an indoor bathroom. Yet there would be a ballroom large enough to hold the six or seven thousand people who would come from miles around to hear their favorite swing bands.

The bands of the swing era produced a fuller sound than that of the Dixieland bands mainly because they used two or three times as many players. Because of the number of instrumentalists, the music was organized in a homophonic construction (for notational examples, see Appendix B, example 22), making the musical sounds more organized in their effect. At times, the music of the large bands even sounded less complex than the polyphonically conceived Dixieland music. The **block chords** used by the swing bands are the obvious clues to the homophonic construction of this type of jazz. Most of the orchestras of the swing era returned to the use of a flat-four rhythm to give their music a rhythm distinct from that which immediately preceded it. During the 1920s, the widely imitated Chicago Style Dixieland was played in $\frac{2}{4}$, but the Kansas City musicians at this same time played mainly in $\frac{4}{4}$; swing jazz was usually in $\frac{4}{4}$.

Paul Whiteman

The Original Dixieland Jazz Band had played in New York in 1917, but even more people were made aware of the possibilities of jazz elements when Paul Whiteman introduced George Gershwin's "Rhapsody in Blue" in Aeolian Hall in 1924. This work can hardly be considered jazz as it is considered in this book, but it pointed out some of the idioms of this music to the public and helped focus attention in the general direction of jazz. "Rhapsody in Blue" could conceivably be construed as the first third-stream music effort. (This direction is discussed in Chapter 9.)

Obviously, Whiteman's title, the King of Jazz, was a misnomer, merely a publicity name, but Whiteman was an influential man and a great supporter of jazz players. He hired many name jazz musicians and paid the top salary of the day. Jazz players and critics are too quick to degrade Whiteman's position when they fail to consider that the jazz players joined Whiteman's orchestra of their own free will, often when they were not busy enough to maintain financial stability.

Whiteman had great admiration for these players. Consider, for example, that Bix Beiderbecke was away from the orchestra for nearly a year trying to recover from alcoholism and related problems. During that time, Whiteman retained him on full salary and, it is also reported, paid Beiderbecke's medical bills. During some of that time, Beiderbecke played one-night engagements with competing orchestras.

A look at some of the personnel from Whiteman's roster establishes his regard for, and financial support of, the jazz players of the day: Bix Beiderbecke, Frankie Trumbauer, Red Norvo, Tommy and Jimmy Dorsey, Jack and Charlie Teagarden, Eddie Lang, and Joe Venuti. Most of the recordings of the Whiteman orchestra show little influence of jazz as it is considered in this book. However, there are noteworthy recordings by jazz players made while they were members of Whiteman's band. For example, Whiteman established a group within his larger organization called the Swing Wing. Jack Teagarden and others were featured in this "band within a band."[18]

Among early jazz trombonists, Jack Teagarden is *the* outstanding performer. His easygoing manner fostered a style of playing jazz on the trombone that was unique among his predecessors and peers. His playing and his wonderful jazz singing became a lyric style to be imitated for years. He died in 1964, having recorded about a thousand sides (songs) during his lifetime. His long musical lines, flexible technique, and beautiful tone will probably never be equaled.

THE SWING BANDS

By the late 1930s, records and radio became extremely important in publicizing jazz. As a consequence, for the first time a segment of jazz was the most-listened-to music in the world, and more excellent musicians were working in this field than during any previous period. During 1937, eighteen thousand musicians were on the road, and the number continued to increase. After frequently having been considered a fairly tawdry occupation, jazz, with the rise of swing, became a respectable, remunerative profession with the "public's embrace of swing as its national music."[19]

The first jazz concert took place in 1936 at New York's Onyx Club. It was called a "Swing Music Concert." The next year, "Hollywood's Second Swing Concert" was held at the famous Palomar Ballroom, featuring Benny Goodman, Louis Prima, Les Hite, Ben Pollack, and a fine all-female big band under the direction of Peggy Gilbert. The Benny Goodman jazz concerts, presented for the first time in Carnegie Hall in 1938, were milestones in the acceptance of jazz.[20]

At this time, Benny Goodman was considered the King of Swing. It was understood that, if a clarinet player did not play the instrument in the Goodman manner, he was not playing clarinet correctly. This put great pressure on talented clarinet players who wanted to play in their own style instead of copying Goodman.

By the time Goodman became a success, large black orchestras had already established the format for this size of organization. These were the orchestras of Moten, Kirk, and Trent from the Midwest and those of Henderson, Ellington, McKinney, and Lunceford from the East. Goodman's success was not assured at all until he opened at the Palomar Ballroom in Los Angeles in 1935 after a discouraging tour across the country. But, from that moment on, there was no doubt that this next style of jazz was extremely well received by the public.[21]

The Dorsey Brothers started with a large-band version of Dixieland[22] with singer Bob Crosby. When Crosby developed his own band with the help of ex-Pollack saxophonist Gil Rodin, it was only natural that Crosby's band would be Dixieland oriented—that was the style he had been weaned on in the early Dorsey Brothers orchestra.

Occasionally, cooperative bands allowed all the members to share in the profits and woes. Glen Gray and the Casa Loma Orchestra operated in this manner[23] ("Casa Loma Stomp"). In the beginning, the Woody Herman Herds was cooperative, but later it ended this means of operating and went through several distinct changes. At first it was a mixture of an overgrown Dixieland band and a Kansas City blues-type swing band. Later it shifted toward the Goodman approach to swing, and later still it became progressive.[24]

Glenn Miller

The public decided that the most popular of all the swing bands was that of Glenn Miller. Miller had been involved with jazz in its truest sense since

listening guide

(CD 1, track 16)
Glenn Miller Band
"In the Mood"

:00   Saxophone intro with brass response.

:11   Opening chorus with saxophone riff and brass accented chords.

:28   Repeat of opening chorus.

:46   New chorus. New saxophone riff with continued brass accented chords.

:57   Repeat of previous chorus.

1:08   Alternating solo phrases by alto and tenor saxophones.

1:32   Brass play a transition to the next solo chorus. Saxophones join in at the end.

1:38   Trumpet solo over saxophone section.

2:01   Transition to a return to the first section.

2:04   Return to opening theme. Notice the long notes in the trombones. The phrase ends with no rhythm and just a long note in the trombones.

2:25   A repeat of the last phrase, softer.

2:46   Another repeat, even softer.

3:03   Another repeat, louder.

3:16   Extended brass fanfare ending with a final ascending high trumpet.

3:33   End.

childhood. He had worked with Red Nichols, Ben Pollack, and others in earlier styles and had organized and worked with the Dorsey Brothers, Ray Noble, and others heading toward swing. Miller was a brilliant arranger, an outstanding businessman, and a fine trombone player. When he started his band, he went deeply in debt but within two years he was a millionaire. One of the authors found him to be an exemplary employer. The band worked only the best jobs in the country, had a commercial radio program three nights a week, recorded often, and even made motion pictures. It was an ideal job for a young sideman. Today there are Glenn Miller societies all over the world, and at this writing Miller albums still have extremely high sales.[25]

It was only natural that new bands continually developed, being fronted by musicians who had been featured as solo artists in someone else's band. For example, from the Benny Goodman band came Harry James, Gene Krupa, Lionel Hampton, Teddy Wilson, and others who became leaders in their own right.

The first recording of a new band would often sound similar to the band that the new leader had just left, because the new leader would hire friends from the band from which he had resigned. Because the musician's union had an established minimum salary that had to be paid to the musicians for

recordings, new leaders would often hire more capable musicians outside the band for recording purposes.

The overall contributions of different swing bands to the development and future of jazz were varied. Benny Goodman's contribution was drive with an intense $\frac{4}{4}$ rhythmic feeling. The Casa Loma Band featured ensemble arrangements specializing in the call-and-response pattern. Duke Ellington offered new sounds and colors built around the individual talents of his musicians and introduced larger forms into jazz. Glenn Miller proved that unerring precision was a possibility in jazz. Lionel Hampton played with chaotic swing and uninhibited showmanship plus superior improvisation. Bob Crosby preserved and expanded Chicago Style Dixieland music. Stan Kenton used more complex harmonies and brought recognition to such innovators as Shelly Manne, Shorty Rogers, Gerry Mulligan, and many others. Count Basie contributed a type of relaxed ensemble setting with longer solo opportunities. Woody Herman aided the growth of jazz by continually adapting each new trend, and his bands were always proving grounds for rising young instrumentalists. Herman surprised many people by adding a woman trumpet player in the 1940s, Billie Rogers, who played with as much strength and swung as hard as anyone else in the band.

In the swing era, the role of composer/arranger became important. Such excellent style-setting musicians as Fletcher and Horace Henderson, Don Redman, Duke Ellington, and many others shifted the timbre of jazz from the early Paul Whiteman sounds to the sophisticated, swinging music of the large bands. Today, fine textbooks by Bill Russo, Henry Mancini, George Russell, Russ Garcia, Van Alexander, and others deal with this art.

Glenn Miller and his orchestra. Trombones (left to right): Paul Tanner, Jimmy Priddy, Frank D'Anolfo, Miller; trumpets: John Best, Steve Lipkin, Dale McMickle, Billy May; saxophones: Will Schwartz, Al Klink, Skip Martin, Ernie Caceres, Tex Beneke; drums: Moe Purtill; guitar: Bobby Hackett; bass: Doc Goldberg; piano: Chummy MacGregor; singers: Bill Conway, Hal Dickinson, Marion Hutton, Ray Eberle, Chuck Goldstein, Ralph Brewster.

BIG-BAND SOLOISTS

One of the oddities of big-band jazz was that soloists gained importance also. Critic Joachim Berendt wrote of this situation:

> Thus, the thirties also became the era of great soloists: the tenor saxists Coleman Hawkins and Chu Berry; the clarinetist Benny Goodman; the drummers Gene Krupa, Cozy Cole, and Sid Catlett; the pianists Fats Waller and Teddy Wilson;

Benny Goodman and his orchestra. Trumpets (left to right): Harry James, Ziggy Elman, Chris Griffin, Johnny Davis; trombones: Murray McEachern, Red Ballard; saxophones: Vido Musso, Hymie Schertzer, Art Rollini, George Koenig; piano: Jess Stacy; bass: Harry Goodman; guitar: Allan Reuss; drums: Gene Krupa.

the alto saxists Benny Carter and Johnny Hodges; the trumpeters Roy Eldridge, Bunny Berigan, and Rex Stewart.

Often these two tendencies—the orchestral and the soloistic—merged. Benny Goodman's clarinet seemed all the more glamorous against the backdrop of his big band, Louis Armstrong's trumpet stood out in bold relief when accompanied by Louis Russell's orchestra, and the voluminous tone of Coleman Hawkins's or Chu Berry's tenor seemed to gain from the contrast to the "hard" sound of Fletcher Henderson's band.[26]

Benny Goodman

Rave reviews for an artist (who was probably the universal symbol of jazz thirty-five years earlier) dominated the media in 1975. Although it is true that when Benny Goodman played a concert many of his listeners experienced a great deal of nostalgia, some who thoroughly enjoyed his mastery of the clarinet, his vibrant rhythm feel, and his effervescent improvisations were too young to feel any nostalgia for his music. He was truly a master of his art.

Benny Goodman was born on May 30, 1909, in Chicago, the eighth of eleven children of an immigrant tailor. Just as jazz is a product of America, Benny Goodman's rise from poverty to global fame is a typical American story.

His early musical training was in a synagogue orchestra and at Hull House in Chicago. He next studied privately with Franz Schoepp of the Chicago Symphony Orchestra. By the time Goodman was sixteen, word of his excellent musicianship had spread even to California, and Ben Pollack asked him to join his band. He had built a considerable reputation by the time he left the Pollack

Benny Goodman

band in 1929 at the age of twenty. For the next five years, he played on the radio and for recording companies in New York.

In 1934, Goodman organized his first band for a theater restaurant, the Music Hall, owned by Billy Rose. At the same time, Goodman played on a series of Saturday night, three-hour radio shows. The two jobs coincided with his association with Fletcher Henderson, who created most of the musical arrangements that were such an integral part of Goodman's success.

In the winter of 1934–35 Goodman began a tour across the United States that seemed to consist of one failure after another. No one appeared to know or care about his band. The farther the band traveled from New York, the more worried became Goodman, the band, his bookers, and the manager of the Palomar Ballroom in Los Angeles—their destination. In fact, it has often been rumored that had the manager been able to locate Goodman during that tour he would have canceled the booking. Fortunately, the booking was not canceled. Goodman opened at the Palomar Ballroom in May 1935 and was an immediate success. Whether the swing type of jazz started earlier than this is beside the point. Goodman's engagement at the Palomar is designated by most jazz writers as the beginning of the swing era.

Goodman's band played a hard-driving type of swing in comparison to other bands at that time. He often rehearsed the band without the rhythm section, reasoning that, if an arrangement could swing well and have momentum without the rhythm section, the music would offer much more when the rhythm section was added. The band also played a soft, more subtle jazz—a chamber music sort of jazz—by using trios, quartets, quintets, and so on.

vamping

Benny Goodman

Goodman was the first bandleader to force the issue of integration. Black and white musicians jammed together in after-hours clubs and recorded together, but neither the white nor the black public would go to see a "mixed" band. In 1936, when Goodman hired Teddy Wilson and Lionel Hampton, he had to pretend that they were not regular members of his band but only an act. Finally, he simply acknowledged that these musicians were part of his band and gave notice that the public would have to see and hear his music on his terms. He stated very simply in a nonpolitical way that he was selling not prejudice or integration but music.

Dave Dexter wrote glowingly of Goodman:

Goodman often did generous things, and his courage in mixing Negroes with what was essentially an all-white orchestra and touring the Southern states can never be underestimated. He achieved as much in smashing segregation in the arts as anybody in history.

Through the years, Goodman's clarinet remained the model for all beginners. Shaw could play "prettier" notes at times, Barney Bigard added an elusive coloring to Ellington's ensemble and big Irving Prestopnik wove glorious improvisations above the Dixieland blowings of the Bob Crosbyites, but Goodman had a sound all his own, a technique no other could top and a swinging, rhythmic approach that was irresistible.[27]

In 1938, the Benny Goodman band became the first swing band to play a concert in Carnegie Hall. Record sales of his Carnegie Hall concerts alone grossed more than a million dollars and continue to sell today.

Mention should also be made of Goodman's classical solo work. He commissioned and recorded a composition by Béla Bartók, commissioned clarinet concertos by Aaron Copland and Paul Hindemith, and performed works by Mozart, Debussy, Brahms, and other composers with such distinguished orchestras as the Boston Symphony, the Rochester Symphony, the NBC Symphony, the Cleveland Symphony, the Budapest String Quartet, and the American Art Quartet. Goodman was one of the few musicians who moved easily between classical music and jazz, becoming distinguished in each field. In 1955, Universal-International Studios made a motion picture based on his life, and Goodman himself recorded the music and acted as musical director.

Goodman toured in many parts of the world on behalf of the U.S. State Department. In 1956, he played to sellout audiences in Hong Kong, Singapore, Tokyo, and Bangkok. In 1958 and 1959, his overseas tours took him to Belgium, Germany, Sweden, Denmark, France, Switzerland, Austria, England, Australia, Central America, South America, and Alaska, and his reception was as great as ever each time. The Goodman band was chosen to be the first band to make a State Department tour of Russia. His triumph there was proof of his artistry, the durability of the swing style, and the worldwide popularity of this American music. Benny Goodman enjoyed truly international popularity. The mere announcement that he was to perform in a country caused great excitement among the jazz enthusiasts there, a fact probably more true about Goodman than about any other living musician.

In the mid-1960s, Goodman appeared regularly at jazz festivals and even at some of the more plush night spots. At the end of the 1960s, he toured the

United States with both jazz and classical groups and recorded in the United States and England. Through the 1970s, Goodman continued to tour Europe, the United States, and Canada. Sometimes he appeared with a full band, sometimes with a sextet, and sometimes with members of his original quartet. The reception was the same: he was the King of Swing, a jazz immortal, and an international celebrity to jazz fans of all ages.

Goodman continued to play jazz in a most exemplary manner and led the world on clarinet. He performed a concert at Carnegie Hall in 1974, thirty-six years and eight months after his first concert there. The authors saw and heard Goodman in 1975 at a jazz festival where he received a standing ovation as he walked on stage. As he played, he proved conclusively that he truly deserved the applause.

Besides being the King of Swing, and besides almost single-handedly cutting through racial barriers in music, Goodman was instrumental in making it possible for jazz musicians to earn a decent wage. He brought jazz out of back rooms into the best night spots and into the greatest theaters where young people screamed and danced in the aisles. Still, for a man whose name is synonymous with the big-band era, Goodman was extremely low key, never flamboyant. His playing was a combination of great wit, precise musicianship, beautiful subtleties, and never-ending swing. "In the 1930s he brought American jazz to the attention of his countrymen and to the world in a way that had previously not been accomplished."[28]

Down Beat magazine nominated Goodman to its All Time Jazz Hall of Fame, and the National Academy of Recording Arts and Sciences placed his recording of "Sing Sing Sing" in its hall of fame. He collaborated on four books: *The Kingdom of Swing, BG—Off the Record, BG—On the Record,* and *Benny: King of Swing.*[29] Goodman inspired musicians when he was only sixteen years old, and until he died in June 1986 he continued to inspire them. He did not follow the changing fads in jazz, so he was unusual. He attributed his continued overwhelming success to the fact that he simply played "good" music.

Coleman Hawkins

The epitome of swing tenor saxophonists was Coleman Hawkins with his full tone, flowing lines, and heavy vibrato[30] ("The Man I Love"). A good example of Hawkins's impeccable taste as an improviser is his recording of "Body and Soul."[31] "Hawkins' mesmerizing hold on all who followed—except for Lester Young—was overwhelming, permanent, and unquestioned."[32]

Hawkins had played with blues singer Mamie Smith's Jazz Hounds in 1922–23 but first gained recognition in the Fletcher Henderson Orchestra, where he played the clarinet and the bass and baritone saxes along with tenor sax, on which he really excelled. In 1923, Hawkins made his first recording with Henderson on "Dicty Blues," demonstrating a great rhythmic feel while playing a slap-tongue solo (considered strictly a comic approach today).

Eventually, his rich tone became one of the most impressive aspects of his playing, as did his long, flowing lines. His

Coleman Hawkins

listening guide

(CD 1, track 17)
Coleman Hawkins (playing)
"The Man I Love"

:00   Hawkins enters on tenor sax. He plays for two 32-bar choruses. Notice the long melodic phrases he uses that tend to span each 8-measure subdivision of each chorus.

:19   Second 8-bar phrase of the first chorus. Notice that Hawkins tends to overlap his melodic phrases with the beginning of each 8-bar phrase of the song.

:38   Third 8-bar phrase.

:57   Last 8-bar phrase. Notice how he melodically sets up the next 32-bar chorus.

1:15   Hawkins solos another complete chorus; the activity in the rhythm section increases.

1:34   Second 8-bar phrase.

1:53   Third 8-bar phrase. Listen for the flat-four feel in the rhythm section.

2:11   Last phrase of this chorus; back to a swing feel.

2:31   End.

solo on "Body and Soul," recorded in 1939, never seems to pause—it just flows on and on. Hawkins is the first figure in jazz to establish the saxophone as the dominant voice of jazz. The trumpet had already claimed a leading role as a significant solo instrument, but Hawkins established a new saxophone legacy that would equal or even exceed that held by the trumpet. Later great players like Parker and Coltrane would cement that image in the public's eye.

Lester Young

Of all the great tenor saxophonists competing with Hawkins, only one seemed to be going in a direction all his own: talented player Lester Young.

Don Heckman compared the early learning environments of two famous tenor saxophone players—Coleman Hawkins with Fletcher Henderson and Lester Young with Count Basie:[33]

> Hawkins predated Young as an active participant in the jazz scene. As a member of the Fletcher Henderson Orchestra for ten years (1923–33), he was intimately involved with what was probably the most famous jazz ensemble of the time. Henderson's orchestra typified the Eastern approach.
>
> The Henderson, Duke Ellington, and Charles Johnson orchestras all played for a variety of musical events before audiences that frequently were all white.

listening guide

(CD 1, track 18)
Count Basie's Kansas City Six
"Lester Leaps In"

This selection uses the same harmonic chord changes as the Gershwin "I've Got Rhythm," a practice that became standard in the bop period.

:00   Four-measure piano introduction.

:04   Eight measures, then repeated: tenor sax, trombone, and trumpet in cup mute in 3-part harmony.

:19   Bass and piano: 8-measure bridge.

:27   First theme repeated.

:35   Second chorus: Lester Young solos on tenor sax for 32 measures.

1:06   Third chorus: piano and sax interplay for 8 measures.

1:15   Sax solos alone for 8 measures.

1:22   Eight-measure bridge: sax solo.

1:30   Sax alone for 6 measures, rhythm comes in on next 2.

1:38   On fourth chorus, piano and sax trade fours, first the piano for 4 measures.

1:42   Sax for 4 measures.

1:46   Piano for 4 measures.

1:50   Sax for 4 measures.

1:53   Piano for 4 measures.

1:58   Sax for 4 measures.

2:01   Piano for 4 measures.

2:05   Sax for 4 measures.

2:09   Fifth chorus is still different—ensemble for 4 measures.

2:13   Sax for 4 measures.

2:18   Ensemble for 4 measures.

2:21   Piano for 4 measures.

2:23   Piano for the 8-measure bridge.

2:33   Ensemble for 4 measures.

2:37   Sax for 4 measures.

2:42   Sixth chorus starts with ensemble for 4 measures.

2:47   Bass solo for 4 measures.

2:49   Ensemble for 4 measures.

2:52   Bass for 4 measures.

2:58   Bass and piano for 8 measures.

3:04   Ensemble for 4 measures.

3:08   Ensemble plays the last 4 measures out in jam-session style.

3:17   End.

Although they were considered (with the exception of Ellington at the Cotton Club) to be primarily dance bands, the type of dance music they played was considerably more diverse than that played by the bands further west. The Henderson group might be expected on any given night to play popular hits, tangos, Irish waltzes, and original jazz tunes. The music was usually written in complex arrangements, and the bands were carefully rehearsed. With some groups, in fact, well-drilled performances became more important than either improvisation or solos. Fortunately, this never happened with Henderson, who realized the importance of good soloists when Louis Armstrong joined the band in 1924. It was only logical that Hawkins's artistic growth would have been affected by such a musical environment.

Young came into prominence in a completely different milieu. The Count Basie Band was the pinnacle of Kansas City and Southwestern jazz. Its music was blues-oriented, filled with riffing backgrounds, and frequently based on spontaneous head arrangements. The soloists had more opportunity to stretch out than the soloists in the more heavily orchestrated New York bands. Few of the Basie arrangements were very complicated; good intonation and well-drilled performances were not nearly as important as was the creation of a rolling, surging rhythmic swing. Kansas City jazz was dancing jazz, and the beat was the most important element. The revolutionary work of the Basie rhythm section made the Basie band something special. Their ability to generate a free-flowing, almost-alive pulse undoubtedly helped Young develop a rangy horizontal, that is, melodic, playing style.[34]

But even in the high-energy Basie band, Young was known for a personal sound that ultimately predicted the later cool sound. This sound was often at its best when he worked with Billie Holiday in smaller, more intimate, settings.

Lester Young, the model for cool tenor saxophonists, played softer than Coleman Hawkins and was more subtle and abstract. His improvisations offered a melodic cohesiveness that differed from the more harmonic approach taken by most other players at the time. This "led directly to a harmonic freeing-up of the language of jazz without which Bop, Modern Jazz, George Russell's Lydian Concept and eventually musicians like Ornette Coleman, John Coltrane, and Eric Dolphy could not have evolved."[35] Young was influenced the most by Rudy Wiedoeft (a nonjazz concert artist), Frankie Trumbauer, and Jimmy Dorsey. Oddly enough, all were white alto saxophone or C melody saxophone players instead of black tenor saxophone players. Young's playing naturally matched his personality—soft-spoken and understated.

Young joined the Basie band for the second time in 1936 and stayed with him through 1940, during which time he recorded 105 sides (songs) with Basie and many others with various small groups. His first job as a leader was in 1941 on Fifty-second Street in New York. However, he did return to the Basie band for a few months in 1943 and 1944 and in the latter year was drafted into the army. Young was associated with Norman Granz's *Jazz at the Philharmonic* from 1946 until his death on March 15, 1959. Young had a beautiful, light, pure sound, but his greatest asset was his phrasing—his linear playing anticipating cool in still another way. He would carry melodic thoughts to their conclusion regardless of the bar lines. Although he recorded many solos with the Basie band that are available in re-pressings, those most cherished by his army of admirers are the small combo records, including those backing Billie Holiday vocals.[36]

Sometimes it is hard for young jazz enthusiasts to see how older players have influenced contemporary favorites, but the influences are there. Both Young's lines and Hawkins's tone can be heard in Coltrane's recordings. Young's rhythmic and melodic outlooks can be heard on Ornette Coleman and Eric Dolphy records. In fact, it would not be an overstatement to say that every contemporary saxophonist is indebted to Young, Hawkins, and Parker.

Some good bands pursued the showmanship aspect of the business with great energy, a typical example being Cab Calloway.[37] Scat singing was advanced to an art form by his truly inventive singing in the 1930s. The showmanship aspect of performance was at low ebb in jazz at one time, causing record executive Irving Townsend to proclaim, "For some reason, jazz thinks it doesn't need showmanship; it couldn't be more wrong."[38]

Charlie Christian

Charlie Christian became a national figure on the jazz scene late in 1939. In the short span between 1939 and 1942 (he died of tuberculosis in 1942), Christian entirely changed the concept of playing the guitar.

listening guide

(CD 1, track 19)
Benny Goodman Quartet
"I Got Rhythm"
Benny Goodman, clarinet
Teddy Wilson, piano
Lionel Hampton, vibraphone
Gene Krupa, drums

:00	Piano solo: 2 measures.
:01	Clarinet solo: 2 measures.
:02	Vibraphone solo: 2 measures.
:04	Ensemble (all four): 2 measures.
:05	Ensemble: 34 measures (standard 32-bar chorus plus 2-bar extension).
:34	Piano solo: 34 measures.
1:01	Another chorus for piano solo: 34 measures.
1:29	Clarinet solo: 34 measures.
1:58	Another chorus for clarinet solo: 34 measures.
2:25	Vibraphone solo: 34 measures.
2:54	Another chorus for vibraphone solo: 34 measures.
3:22	Six measures of ensemble.
3:26	Two measures, complete break.
3:28	Same as last 8 measures.
3:34	Ensemble for 18 measures.
3:48	Six measures of ensemble.
3:53	Two measures, complete break.
3:55	Six measures of ensemble.
4:00	Two measures, complete break.
4:02	Ensemble for 18 measures.
4:17	Ensemble for 34 measures, becoming more exciting.
4:43	Ensemble for 34 measures, even more exciting.
5:10	End.

Charlie Christian played mostly around Oklahoma City, Kansas City, and St. Louis before joining Benny Goodman when he was only nineteen years old. Although Christian was influential, speculation remains as to what he would have contributed had he not died prematurely. His guitar playing influenced all subsequent jazz, and he must be placed in the same category as Gillespie, Parker, Lester Young, and Blanton. He elevated the guitar from a strictly rhythm instrument to

listening guide

(CD 1, track 20)
Billie Holiday (singing)
"Fine and Mellow"

:00 Unison instrumental introduction: 4 measures.

:12 First vocal chorus, which starts with the first lyric phrase.

:22 Second lyric phrase of the first chorus.

:34 Final lyric phrase, which responds to the first repeated lyric phrase.

:46 Second vocal chorus. Listen for the piano fill-ins. Long notes are played by the other instrumentalists.

1:22 Third vocal chorus. The alto sax begins to offer fill-ins with the piano.

1:58 Fourth vocal chorus opens with stop time, in which the band stops playing. As the chorus continues, listen for the increasing fill-in activity in the band.

2:33 Fifth vocal chorus.

3:09 End.

a solo melody instrument equal to other instruments. This is not to say that other guitarists did not play extremely capable solos, but Christian, who came along about the same time as the introduction of the amplifier, was by far the strongest influence. Although he was involved in a new extension of chords, Christian's main innovation was that he played solos with long lines like those for a saxophone.

Most guitarists possibly felt that the big moving chords of Eddie Lang, George Van Epps, and other earlier players were beyond them. Also, the most perfect listening conditions were necessary for hearing guitar solos. Christian's single-note lines and the advent of the amplifier opened the door for many talented players such as Wes Montgomery, Barney Kessel, George Benson, and Pat Metheny. It should be understood, however, that Christian's approach to solos—single-note lines instead of great moving chords—had been played earlier by the talented Belgian player Django Reinhardt. (There were few Reinhardt recordings at that time to document his technique.)

Even in Christian's original and modern guitar playing, the blues influence was the main feature. But, unlike other blues guitarists, Christian pioneered the use of the amplifier as early as 1937 in Oklahoma City. He joined the Benny Goodman band in 1939 in New York, at which time, after his performances every evening with Goodman, he became a regular performer at Minton's. The fact that he died in 1942 meant that he had little time to develop his impressive legacy. The most mentioned of his recordings today are "Solo Flight" with the Benny Goodman orchestra, "Gone with What Wind" with the Benny Goodman sextet, and "Profoundly Blue" with the Edmond Hall quartet[39] (Benny Goodman with Charlie Christian, "Breakfast Feud").

SWING SINGERS

Billie Holiday

Billie Holiday must be considered apart from others in the jazz field. It is true that many artists defy categorization, a fact to be applauded, but Holiday crossed musical lines while sticking with her individual singing style. She sang many blues tunes, such as "Fine and Mellow," and could compete most admirably with this one vehicle. If the blues is a feeling, then she used the blues on most of her songs. In addition, Holiday was deeply into the popular field with beautiful renditions of songs like "Lover Man" and "Travelin' Light." But if popular music means selling a great number of records, she never really entered the popular field. There can never be any doubt, however, that she was a singer of jazz.

There is a kind of jazz song style that is neither all improvised nor all embellishment but a little of each. The French jazz critic André Hodeir uses the term *paraphrase* to describe this song style. Holiday excelled at both paraphrase and invention. She is aptly described by the cliché "a legend in her own time." Whereas early instrumentalists copied singers (or at least oral stylings), Holiday's singing style seemed to stem mainly from her favorite instrumentalist, tenor saxophonist Lester Young, whom she dubbed "The Prez."

Besides Young, Holiday was undoubtedly influenced by Bessie Smith and Louis Armstrong. Singers are influenced by their background, but this background does not always lead to a predictable conclusion. Leonard Feather speaks of this unpredictability:

> It would be a gigantic oversimplification to pretend that social conditions alone shaped her life, formed her vocal style, led to her death. Ella Fitzgerald had to endure a family background and childhood not greatly different from Billie's. Each was a product of a breaking or broken family; both suffered through years of poverty; both were at the mercy of Jim Crow. In Ella's case these conditions led to a career that started her on an upward curve at the age of 16, to a success story that has never been touched by scandal, and to the achievement of economic security and creature comforts far beyond her most optimistic childhood aspirations. Yet during the same time span, these conditions in Billie's case led to marijuana at 14, a jail term as a prostitute at 15, and heroin addiction from her middle 20s.[40]

One of the most frustrating aspects of Holiday's career must have been that the public was unwilling to accept black and white musicians performing together on the same bandstand, even though musicians *en masse* were her fans. Because of this attitude, some of her best employment situations were short-lived. Musicians enjoyed hearing her sing blues, lovely ballads, novelty tunes, and gripping stories of lynching such as "Strange Fruit," written by a poet named Lewis Allen. This stark, graphic song deservedly attracted attention even after being rejected and banned in some important circles.

It is said that Holiday matured while listening to recordings of Bessie Smith and Ethel Waters. But, as stated before, the instrumentalists she seemed to admire most—Louis Armstrong and Lester Young—definitely influenced her through their simplicity and economy. To these wonderful models she added her own feelings, her own lifestyle, and the results were truly most intimate and personal.

Holiday did not record as many blues tunes as many fans think. Her style and her conceptions often led listeners to feel that she was singing blues when the

WITNESS TO jazz

billie holiday

Photo and text Courtesy William P. Gottlieb/Library of Congress

In 1948, Billie Holiday was at her peak, musically and physically. Ironically, her splendid condition was largely due to her having spent most of the previous year in a federal reformatory, serving time for the possession of narcotics. While incarcerated, she did not have access to drugs or alcohol and had

lost her previous pudginess to become a strikingly beautiful woman. Her incomparable voice, instead of having declined from lack of use, had retained its rich but bittersweet tone. If anything, it had become more wrenching than ever.

Unable to work nightclubs in New York City because of police restrictions on performers with criminal records, she marked time until some well-financed fans arranged a concert for her in Carnegie Hall (which was not subject to nightclub limitations). Her appearance was a sold-out triumph.

Eventually, she was able to resume performing in clubs. It was at one of these performances that I took a photograph often cited as the most widely used picture ever taken of a jazz person. Whether or not so, I believe it captured the beauty of her face and the anguish of her voice.

Regrettably, Billie regressed. The last time I planned to see her, the word on the street was that she often didn't show up for jobs on time, if at all. Hopefully, I nonetheless went to catch her current act. Sure enough, she wasn't at the microphone when she should have been. The audience waited . . . and waited. Playing a hunch, I went backstage and found her, half dressed, sitting on the edge of a dressing room cot, pretty much "out of it."

I helped her finish dressing, then led her to the microphone. She looked horrible. She sounded worse. I replaced my notebook in my pocket, put a lens cap on my camera, and walked away, choosing to remember this remarkable woman as she once was.

song was some fairly banal pop tune. Most successful female singers, knowingly or unknowingly, have been influenced by the jazz singing of Billie Holiday[41] ("He's Funny That Way," "I Can't Get Started," "The End of a Love Affair").

Ella Fitzgerald

There is certainly no question about the jazz credentials of Billie Holiday and Ella Fitzgerald. Their styles are different, but their singing helped to shape the

definition of the pure jazz singer. Both came to the popular forefront during the swing era. Although Holiday sang with big bands, her most memorable performances were in small-group settings.

Unlike Holiday, Ella Fitzgerald is best defined by her big-band singing. As a young woman she toured with the great Chick Webb Band. In those early performances one could find traces of the scat singing that she perfected in her later career. A blend of both popular and jazz singing can be heard in "A-Tisket A-Tasket," which she recorded with the Chick Webb Band.

The first recorded example of the wordless vocal jazz style, called **scat singing,** was by Louis Armstrong in his recording of "Heebie Jeebies" in 1926. Dispensing with the lyrics completely, the singer substitutes either nonsense or real syllables for the words. Bridging the gap between Armstrong and Fitzgerald is Leo Watson (and his vocal-instrumental group, the Spirits of Rhythm). Fitzgerald, inspired by Watson's wordless improvisations, developed a style that places her among the few singers, like Mel Torme and Anita O'Day, who could successfully and convincingly sing scat.

Ella Fitzgerald carried her scatting across the swing-to-bop transition and found a perfect place for high-paced vocalizations. She was one of the few successful swing musicians (and the only singer) to support bop. Her scatting can be heard on her classic 1947 performance of "How High the Moon." Although Fitzgerald gained tremendous popular success, she was never at risk of losing her jazz singer status. Clearly, Fitzgerald's embrace of the instrumental idioms of both swing and bop in her scat singing set her apart from other popular singers.

It was the interpretive style of Holiday and Fitzgerald that began to define the jazz singer. Although most of the melodies they performed were precomposed, the manner in which these women interpreted those melodies bordered on improvisation. They both could sing with a spontaneous interpretive skill that was manifested only by leading jazz players of the day. Songs were never sung the same, and these improvised subtle nuances assured Holiday and

listening guide

(CD 1, track 21)
Ella Fitzgerald and Nelson Riddle
"All of Me"

:00   First phrase sung a cappella.

:01   Big band chord punch.

:02   Second phrase.

:05   Band chord punch.

:06   Vocal continues with the rhythm section and accented chords between phrases.

:17   Notice the counterpoint line in the saxophones.

:26   Second verse. Ella begins to embellish the melody.

:49   Band picks up the energy to introduce the next verse.

:51   Third verse. Greater liberties are taken melodically with the addition of wider vocal intervals.

1:17   Fourth verse. More and more of the words give way to scat singing.

1:43   Fifth verse. Full scat chorus. Notice how Ella feeds on the energy created by the band backup.

1:56   Ella anticipates a melodic phrase in the band that is a familiar musical quotation.

2:09   New chorus with continued scat and increased energy. Notice how the accents in the solo line up with those in the band.

2:21   Stop time where the band falls out leaving the vocalist alone with only sparse accent chords played behind her.

2:27   Band returns.

2:31   Second stop time as Ella sets up the final ending.

2:40   Band returns.

2:45   Ella sings a common instrumental ending.

2:48   Drums enter to extend the ending.

2:51   Stop time ending.

2:57   Band returns for a big ending as Ella returns to final phrase, "Come on take, take all of me."

3:02   A signature Basie piano tag.

3:04   Ella improvises over the final chord.

3:20   End.

vamping

OTHER JAZZ VOCALISTS

Vocal jazz flowered during the swing era. Singers had to be well versed in a wide range of styles to hold their positions as soloists with the big bands. They had to be able to realize the earthy sounds of the blues, the dreamy sounds of love ballads, and that indefinable swing technique. Many of the jazz singers who first became popular during the swing era went on to have long careers that often extended into the 1990s. Carmen McRae most often performed with smaller jazz ensembles like Dave Brubeck and George Shearing. McRae cut a live album with another jazz singer, Betty Carter, *The Carmen McRae–Betty Carter Duets*. Carter also had a long career and is considered one of the early scat singers. The big band vocal tradition was extended by Joe Williams and the extremely popular Frank Sinatra. Their work with the Count Basie band is particularly notable.

Connee Boswell is deserving of mention here, as she and her sisters opened the door for many other vocal groups. Boswell wrote not only the vocal arrangements but also the instrumental parts, making her, with Mary Lou Williams, one of the first women arrangers/composers in jazz.

It is interesting that many of the better jazz singers are known primarily for their instrumental prowess. Obvious examples are Louis Armstrong, Jack Teagarden, and Clark Terry, with his style of scat singing. Conversely, some excellent instrumentalists are known primarily for their singing. For example, much of the listening public is not even aware of the talented piano work of Sarah Vaughan or Nat Cole.

Fitzgerald their membership in the jazz community. Fitzgerald's breadth of jazz musicality can be heard in her collaboration with Ellington on *Daydream: The Best of the Duke Ellington Songbook*.

Fitzgerald's long career offers a large body of recorded works that spans a broad field of musical compositions. By 1982 she had won ten Grammy Awards and twenty-two *Down Beat* readers' polls. Despite her success in the popular music market, she remained until her death the epitome of a jazz singer (S, "You'd Be So Nice to Come Home To").

SWING COMBOS

The small-combo idea was never entirely discarded. Most large bands also had a small group made up of the better jazz players in the band. The smaller combo played during intermissions of the large band, and sometimes the small group built up its own following. In his band, Goodman had a trio, quartet, quintet, sextet, and even septet, depending on the personnel in his band[42] (Benny

Goodman Sextet, "I Found a New Baby" and "Breakfast Feud" with Charlie Christian; Benny Goodman Trio, "Body and Soul," "I Found a New Baby").

The Goodman trio, which started in 1935, consisted of Teddy Wilson on piano, Gene Krupa on drums, and Goodman on clarinet. The group was enlarged to a quartet in 1936 with the addition of the exuberant Lionel Hampton on vibraphone; and, in 1939, it became a sextet when Charlie Christian on guitar and a bass player were added. These smaller groups also included at various times Red Norvo, Cootie Williams, Roy Eldridge, and Georgie Auld. The small units played during the intermissions of performances by the large band and also recorded separately. Some fans consider these recordings to be as important as those of the large band.

Artie Shaw's small "band within a band" was called the Gramercy Five and featured Johnny Guarnieri on harpsichord. Woody Herman had the Woodchoppers, Tommy Dorsey had the Clambake Seven, and so on. Throughout the swing years, Fifty-second Street in New York, with its numerous night clubs, was a real gathering place for small combos.

In July 1944, Norman Granz organized a jazz concert at the Los Angeles Philharmonic Auditorium to aid a fund for the defense of some Mexican Americans who had been sent to San Quentin after a killing in Los Angeles. This concert was recorded and was the first commercial recording made in a public place instead of in a studio. It was a **jam session** recorded live, and it started a whole new phase in recording history. Jazz at the Philharmonic, as Granz's recording and touring package became known, was an extremely successful venture.

THE DEMISE OF SWING

Because of the military draft, problems of transportation, and the American Federation of Musicians (AFM) recording ban, the swing era came to an abrupt end at the beginning of World War II. Swing bands could not function unless they could play one-night stands. Although the bands took a financial loss on location jobs, they fostered the popularity necessary for radio time and gave musicians a chance to record (and a chance to rest from the rigors of traveling). Then the bands went on the road again to recoup their losses. But World War II meant no gasoline and no automobile tires for civilians, so all unessential travel came to a halt in the United States. One other event that contributed to the shutdown of employment for musicians was that the federal government levied a 30 percent cabaret tax, and most cabarets simply closed their doors.

Just as the rise of soloists like Louis Armstrong moved the interest in Chicago Dixieland from the ensemble to the soloists, the swing bands were challenged by the rising popularity of the singers that fronted the bands. The compositional or arranging skills could not ultimately match the promoted personalities of the singers.

An even stronger musical challenger was on the horizon for swing and the big bands and even jazz itself—the emergence of rock and roll. Just as swing had become the music of the world, rock and roll would capture the attention of the media—and ultimately—the world. With the demise of swing, jazz was soon to enter a new phase in its evolution that demanded a more elite audience, but, in return, it had to forsake its immense popularity.

summary

Swing is still with us, and much of the jazz we hear today stems directly from the developments of this eight- or ten-year period. The swing era must also be credited with two beneficial side effects: It absolutely rescued the record industry, and it allowed the musical instrument industry to grow to its present strength.

To reiterate, no style ever really dies out. For years, Eddie Condon ran a nightclub that featured nothing but Chicago Style Dixieland.[43] The Early New Orleans Dixieland revival of the late 1930s was mentioned in Chapter 5.[44] Swing is still played all over the world. Not only does the nostalgia of swing contribute salable product, but swing itself is a most communicative style of jazz.[45]

Books can be found on the market today that are written solely about the swing era,[46] and these are generally both interesting and informative. Even books on the activities of just the Glenn Miller band during the swing era can be found,[47] and other books about the band are being written at this time. Bands such as those of Basie, Ellington, and Herman have certainly proven that the big bands can swing as hard as, and maintain all the vitality demonstrated by, the smaller groups of the day. The organized, written arrangements are capable of creating an energy all their own. The controversy that began with Henderson's band—that one ensemble was superior to another—is no longer appropriate.

The big band is the expression of a long ensemble tradition. From the earliest jazz ensembles, a balance between improvisation and composition has been carefully maintained. The big band represents the fullest expression of jazz composition and arrangement. As jazz has evolved, it has tread a delicate line between the improvised flights of individual players and their collective performances as ensembles. Early ensembles, such as the marching bands of New Orleans, were themselves improvised, each player adding what, at the moment, seemed necessary for a complete sound.

Players, in effect, created an extemporaneous arrangement. These ensembles later became the voice of composers and arrangers who found great subtleties in the instrumental groupings. Like the individual players of each stylistic period, the larger ensembles reflected the attitudes and musical sensibilities of the time. Marching jazz bands developed into the early society and swing bands, which were followed by the bop bands and, later, the current compositionally based jazz ensembles.

Throughout these periods, the bands have offered a vehicle of jazz expression for both the player and the writer. This band tradition represents the melding of two vital aspects of jazz performance: expression of individuals and ensembles and expressions engineered by the imagination of jazz composer/arrangers and implemented through the creativity of individual performers.

FOR FURTHER STUDY

1. In what ways did Fletcher Henderson influence the development of jazz in the swing era?

2. Describe the role of the music arranger in this era.

3. Explain why swing bands produced a fuller sound.

4. What jazz trombonist is considered the outstanding trombone virtuoso of the era?

5. Certain limitations were placed on the recordings of swing bands by the record industry. What were these limitations?

6. Identify the band that was the most popular as well as the most successful.

7. What were some factors that resulted in the end of the swing era?

8. Was swing music primarily for listening or for dancing?

9. To enhance your aural perception of the big-band sound, listen to several recordings of thirty-seven top bands playing ten years of top tunes from the album *The Great Band Era* manufactured especially for *Readers Digest* by RCA.

10. Now listen to the swing band recordings in the album *Jazz* and compare the arrangements of these earlier bands with the band sounds in the *Readers Digest* album.

11. The swing era produced many outstanding soloists, among them Benny Goodman and his clarinet. Listen to his sextet playing "I Found a New Baby" and identify the instrument that follows Benny Goodman's clarinet solo.

12. In what ways do the contemporary large bands differ from the large swing bands?

SUGGESTED ADDITIONAL LISTENING

Akiyoshi, Toshiko, and Lew Tabackin Big Band. *Insights*. RCA Records, AFL 1-2678.
Calloway, Cab. *Sixteen Calloway Classics*. Columbia Records, J-10.
Casa Loma Band. *Glen Gray's Greatest Hits*. MCA Records, 122.
Goodman, Benny. *All Time Greatest Hits*. Columbia Records, PG-31547.
———. *Benny Goodman*. Archive of Folk and Jazz Music Records, 277.
———. *Carnegie Hall Concert*. Columbia Records, OSL-160.
———. *The Complete Benny Goodman*. Bluebird Records, AXM 2-5515.
———. *From Spirituals to Swing*. Vanguard Records, VRS-8523/4.
———. *Great Benny Goodman*. Columbia Records, CS-8643.
———. *Greatest Hits*. Columbia Records, CS 9283.
———. *Small Groups*. RCA Victor Records, LPV 521.
———. *Smithsonian Collection of Classic Jazz*, vols. 4 and 6.
———. *This Is Benny Goodman*. RCA Victor Records, VPM 6040.
Herman, Woody. *Giant Steps*. Fantasy Records, 9477.
———. *Thundering Herd*. Fantasy Records, 9452.
Jammin' for the Jackpot. New World Records, 217.
Jive at Five. New World Records, 274.
Little Club Jazz. New World Records, 250.
Severinsen, Doc. *Doc Severinsen's Closet*. Command Records, RSSD-950-S.

Vig, Tommy. *The Sound of the Seventies.* Milestone Records, 9007.
The World of Swing. Columbia Records, F6-32945.

ADDITIONAL READING RESOURCES

Allen, Walter C. *Hendersonia: The Music of Fletcher Henderson and His Musicians.*
Basie, Count. *Good Morning Blues: The Autobiography of Count Basie, as Told to Albert Murray.*
Berger, Morroe; Patrick, Edward; and Patrick, James. *Benny Carter, A Life in American Music.*
Charters, Samuel B., and Kunstadt, Leonard. *Jazz: A History of the New York Scene.*
Dance, Stanley. *The World of Count Basie.*
———. *The World of Swing.*
Dexter, Dave. *The Jazz Story,* 56–87, 105–20.
Feather, Leonard. *The Book of Jazz,* 174–91.
Harris, Rex. *Jazz,* 168–74.
McCarthy, Albert. *Big Band Jazz.*
Russell, Ross. *Jazz Styles in Kansas City and the Southwest.*
Schuller, Gunther. *Early Jazz: Its Roots and Musical Development,* 242–317.
———. *The Swing Era.*
Shapiro, Nat, and Hentoff, Nat, eds. *The Jazz Makers,* 175–86, 218–26.
Simon, George T. *The Big Bands.*
———. *Glenn Miller.*
———. *Simon Says.*
Stearns, Marshall. *The Story of Jazz,* 120–54.
Ulanov, Barry. *Handbook of Jazz,* 15–26.
Walker, Leo. *The Wonderful Era of the Great Dance Bands.*

Note: Complete information, including name of publisher and date of publication, is provided in this book's bibliography.

NOTES

1. Gunther Schuller, *The Swing Era* (London: Oxford University Press, 1989), 845.
2. Benny Goodman, "Good-bye," *The Great Band Era.*
3. Tommy Dorsey, "I'm Gettin' Sentimental Over You," *The Great Band Era.*
4. Glenn Miller, "Moonlight Serenade," *The Great Band Era.*
5. Nat Shapiro and Nat Hentoff, eds., *The Jazz Makers* (New York: Grove Press, 1957), 118.
6. Fletcher Henderson, *A Study in Frustration,* Columbia Records, C4L-19; *Fletcher Henderson,* vols. 1 and 2, Decca Records, 79227-8; Fletcher Henderson, *Developing an American Orchestra, 1927–1947,* Smithsonian Collection, R-006; *Big Band Jazz,* Smithsonian Collection of Recordings.
7. Chick Webb, "Let's Get Together," *Jazz Odyssey,* vol. 3; *King of Savoy,* Decca Records, DL 9223; *Big Band Jazz,* Smithsonian Collection of Recordings.
8. Schuller, *The Swing Era,* 49.

9. Fletcher Henderson, vol. 8; "Nagasaki" and "It's the Talk of the Town," *The Jazz Story,* vol. 3; "Hop Off," *History of Classic Jazz,* vol. 8; Duke Ellington, *The Ellington Era,* Columbia Records, C3L 27; *Historically Speaking—the Duke,* Bethlehem Records, BCP 60; "Hot and Bothered," *Folkways Jazz,* vol. 8; "Sophisticated Lady," *The Jazz Story,* vol. 3; "Happy-Go-Lucky Local," *The Jazz Story,* vol. 4; "Rainy Night," *History of Classic Jazz,* vol. 8; *Big Band Jazz,* Smithsonian Collection of Recordings.

10. Schuller, *The Swing Era,* 5.

11. Bennie Moten, *Big Band Jazz,* Smithsonian Collection of Recordings.

12. Andy Kirk, *Instrumentally Speaking,* MCA Records, 1308; *My Mamma Pinned a Rose,* Pablo Records, 2310819.

13. *Big Band Jazz,* Smithsonian Collection of Recordings.

14. Schuller, *The Swing Era,* 261.

15. Count Basie, *The Best of Basie,* Columbia Records, C3L-33; *E = MC²,* Roulette Records, ST 52003; *The Best of Count Basie,* MCA Records, 4050; *Big Band Jazz,* Smithsonian Collection of Recordings.

16. *The Best of Count Basie,* Decca DXSB-7170.

17. "Casa Loma Stomp," *Big Band Jazz,* Smithsonian Collection of Recordings, cassette 1, band 13.

18. Jack Teagarden (Paul Whiteman's Orchestra), "Aunt Hagar's Blues," Decca Records, 2145; Jack Teagarden, "Giants of Jazz," Time-Life Records, STL-J08.

19. Schuller, *The Swing Era,* 100.

20. *From Spirituals to Swing,* Vanguard Records, VRS-8523/4.

21. Benny Goodman, *The Great Benny Goodman,* Columbia Records, CL-820; *Benny Goodman Carnegie Concert, The Great Band Era,* and *Big Band Jazz,* Smithsonian Collection of Recordings.

22. Dorsey Brothers, *The Fabulous Dorseys Play Dixieland Jazz,* Decca Records, DL8631.

23. The Casa Loma Band, "Casa Loma Stomp," *The Jazz Story,* vol. 4; *Big Band Jazz,* Smithsonian Collection of Recordings, cassette 1, band 13.

24. Woody Herman, *The Thundering Herds,* Columbia Records, C3L-25; "Misty Morning," *The Jazz Story,* vol. 5; *Big Band Jazz,* Smithsonian Collection of Recordings.

25. *Glenn Miller—a Memorial,* RCA Victor Records, VPM 6019; *The Great Band Era* and *Big Band Jazz,* Smithsonian Collection of Recordings.

26. Joachim Berendt, *Jazz Book: From New Orleans to Rock and Free Jazz,* trans. Dan Morgenstern (Westport, Conn.: Lawrence Hill, 1975).

27. Dave Dexter, *The Jazz Story: From the Nineties to the Sixties,* 1964. Reprinted by permission of Prentice-Hall, Inc., Englewood Cliffs, N.J., 114–15.

28. Schuller, *The Swing Era,* 45.

29. Benny Goodman and Irving Kolodin, *The Kingdom of Swing* (New York: Frederick Ungar, 1939); Benny Goodman and D. R. Connor, *BG—Off the Record* (Fairless Hills, Pa.: Gaildonna Publishers, 1969); Benny Goodman, D. R. Connor, and W. W. Hicks, *BG—On the Record* (New Rochelle, N.Y.: Arlington House, 1969); Stanley Baron, *Benny: King of Swing* (New York: William Morrow, 1979).

30. Coleman Hawkins, *The Hawk and the Hunter,* Mira Records, LPS-3003; *Coleman Hawkins,* Everest Records, FS-252; *Bean and the Boys,* Prestige Records, S-7824; *The Real Thing,* Prestige Records, 24083.

31. Coleman Hawkins, "Body and Soul," *The Greatest Names in Jazz.*

32. Schuller, *The Swing Era,* 426.

33. Coleman Hawkins (the Fletcher Henderson Orchestra), *A Study in Frustration,* Columbia Records, C4L-19; Lester Young (with the Count Basie Orchestra), *Lester Young Memorial,* Epic Records, SN 6031.

34. Don Heckman, "Pres and Hawk, Saxophone Fountainheads," *Down Beat* 30, no. 1 (January 1963): 20.

35. Schuller, *The Swing Era,* 233.

36. *The Essential Lester Young,* Verve Records, V-8398; *Giant of Jazz,* Sunset Records, SUM-1181.

37. Cab Calloway Orchestra, "Pickin' the Cabbage," *Jammin' for the Jackpot,* New World Records, 217; *Singers and Soloists of the Swing Bands,* Smithsonian Collection of Recordings.

38. Irving Townsend, "The Trouble with Jazz," *Down Beat* 29, no. 7 (March 1962): 14.

39. Charlie Christian, *Charlie Christian,* Columbia Records, CL 652, G-30779; (with Edmond Hall's Quartet) "Profoundly Blue," *Three Decades of Jazz (1939–1949);* Charlie Christian, *Solo Flight,* Columbia Records, CG-30779; *The Harlem Jazz Scene,* Archive of Folk Music, 219E; "Solo Flight," *Singers and Soloists of the Swing Bands,* Smithsonian Collection of Recordings.

40. Leonard Feather, "Billie Holiday: The Voice of Jazz," *Down Beat* 29, no. 3, (February, 1962): 18.

41. *Billie Holiday, The Golden Years,* Columbia Records, C3L-21, C3L-40; *The Billie Holiday Story,* Decca Records, DXSB7161; *Lady Day,* Columbia Records, CL637; *Billie Holiday,* Mainstream Records, s/6000; *Strange Fruit,* Atlantic Records, 1614; *Singers and Soloists,* Smithsonian Collection of Recordings.

42. Benny Goodman, *The Great Benny Goodman, Benny Goodman Carnegie Concert,* and *Singers and Soloists of the Swing Bands,* Smithsonian Collection of Recordings.

43. *History of Classic Jazz,* vol. 9.

44. Ibid., vol. 10.

45. Live Concert, *Music Made Famous by Glenn Miller,* Warner Brothers Records, W 1428; *Those Swingin' Days of the Big Bands,* Pickwick Records, TMW-002; *The Great Band Era* and *The Big Bands Are Back Swinging Today's Hits,* RCA Victor Records, RD4-112 (XRIS-9501); *Big Band Jazz,* Smithsonian Collection of Recordings.

46. George Simon, *The Big Bands* (New York: Macmillan, 1967); George Simon, *Simon Says* (New Rochelle, N.Y.: Arlington House, 1971); Schuller, *The Swing Era.*

47. John Flower, *Moonlight Serenade* (New Rochelle, N.Y.: Arlington House, 1972); George T. Simon, *Glenn Miller* (New York: Thomas Y. Crowell, 1974).

7

Duke Ellington

Duke Ellington's Orchestra is a complex configuration of many spiritual and musical elements. To be sure, it was Duke Ellington's music which was created here; but it was just as much the music of each individual member of the band.[1]

Joachim Berendt

Looking back over the first century of the evolution of jazz, there are a few individuals who stand above the rest as catalysts for the developing art form. Duke Ellington is one of those individuals. He found a solution to one of jazz's most complex questions: How does one strike an effective balance between individual and group expression? One requires personal freedom, while the other restricts individual freedom for the benefit of the group. Ellington struck a model balance between the two dominant musical and cultural forces that have shaped jazz. He showed us that compositional intent more typical of Western European musical practice can partner with the spontaneous voice of improvisation more typical of the African oral tradition. This partnership became Ellington's compositional signature.

Edward Kennedy ("Duke") Ellington was born in Washington, D.C., on April 29, 1899. He did not come from a poor family, as did Armstrong, and he had educational advantages that many musicians his age lacked. Ellington received his nickname from a high school friend. He was a better-than-average young painter and won a scholarship to study at the Pratt Institute in Brooklyn, New York. His art career was superseded by music.

Ellington listened to and was influenced by ragtime piano players in the Washington area. It is possible to hear ragtime and stride in Ellington's extended piano solos, especially at the faster tempos. The influences of Fats Waller, Willie ("The Lion") Smith, and James P. Johnson are evident. Ellington played piano, but most jazz writers agree that the orchestra was his real instrument. By the age of seventeen, he had a five-piece combo called the Washingtonians. In 1919, Ellington's son Mercer was born. He became a trumpet player, composer, and arranger—a talented musician in his own right.

WASHINGTON TO NEW YORK

Ellington, with his drummer Sonny Greer and saxophonist Toby Hardwicke, made an abortive attempt to move to New York in 1922 to join the orchestra of Wilbur Sweatman. Financial problems caused Ellington to return to Washington until Fats Waller encouraged him to try to move again in 1923.

Duke Ellington and his orchestra at the Fifth Avenue Presbyterian Church in New York City on December 26, 1965.

duke ellington

Ellington, composer, band leader, and pianist, is one of the most significant compositional figures in jazz. His compositions carried the individuality of his compositional vision as well as the individual voices of the many great soloists in his band.

1923	Ellington made his first visit to New York City from his home in Washington, D.C. Later that year, he moved to the thriving city.
1923–27	His small group (quintet) played at the Hollywood and Kentucky clubs on Broadway. His group grew gradually to become a ten-piece orchestra.
1927–31	At the Cotton Club in Harlem, he became a popular figure in jazz. His group grew to twelve, and among the new players was Johnny Hodges. He made about two hundred recordings in the jungle style that he and Bubber Miley had popularized. His famous recording of "Mood Indigo" was made in 1930.
1932–42	Ellington's group now had six brass, four reeds, and four rhythm. He made European tours in 1933 and 1939. Billy Strayhorn joined the band as an additional pianist, arranger, and composer. Ellington's association with Strayhorn marked one of his most creative periods.
1946	His band now had eighteen members, and he worked on larger compositions that could be recorded on the newly developed long-playing record.
1950–63	World tours, film music.
1964	Liturgical music, many awards. Ellington directed his band until his death in 1974.

This time Ellington and his friends went to work in New York's Harlem, where Ellington began his exceptional career as a leader, pianist, and composer/arranger.

Around 1926, the Ellington personnel began to solidify, and as a consequence his style—his sound—was established. Personnel changes were rare from then on. Complete sections of the orchestra remained constant for an entire decade. It is no wonder that they worked so well together. Baritone saxophone player Harry Carney joined the band in 1926 when he was seventeen and remained in the orchestra until he died in 1974. Johnny Hodges joined the band in 1928 and, except for a period from 1951 to 1955, stayed with the band until his death in 1971.

During these early years in New York, Ellington developed skills that he would carry throughout his entire career. He moved from band member to leader and performed in a variety of clubs. He had begun to refine the writing and arranging skills that would define his compositional style. Ellington had also begun an association with Irving Mills, a music publisher, who would prove to be an important figure in his career.

THE COTTON CLUB

A move that really established the orchestra was the booking at the Cotton Club in Harlem from 1927 to 1932. Ellington's influence from that point on has always been quite definite. His musical pictures were considerably ahead of their time, and the band could swing. Ellington's band at this time featured what were called *jungle sounds*, which included much "growling" on the instruments. As a consequence, the elaborate floor shows of the Cotton Club were designed around the music that the band played. Once again, the sounds of the individuals were woven into the tonal colors of the entire group, an attribute that was evident throughout Ellington's career.

Ellington had four rather different styles that pervaded his repertoire. One was the previously mentioned *jungle style*, built around the raucous playing of Bubber Miley and then of Cootie Williams on trumpet and Tricky Sam Nanton on trombone. Ellington also had a *mood style* that is identified with the beautiful ballads played by saxophonist Johnny Hodges. Some of the selections, such as "Solitude," are well known to the public, but others, such as "Prelude to a Kiss" and "Lotus Blossom," are known and loved mostly by musicians. Another Ellington style could be called his *concerto style*, in which he featured Cootie Williams on trumpet or Jimmy Hamilton or Barney Bigard on clarinet. The fourth style was a rather *standard style*, in which he approached his arrangements in much the same manner as other large bands. However, he always sounded exactly like Ellington, something no one else could accomplish.

Ellington was always concerned about his music being called jazz or at least *merely* jazz. Does a jazz piece have to swing? What about his harmonies? His sounds? His music was often severely criticized for not being that which it was never intended to be. One of his severest critics, John Hammond, denounced Ellington's music as pretentious and not truly jazz.

During Ellington's tenure at the Cotton Club, he had moved from an aspiring New York band leader to a leading figure in the world of jazz. His reputation reached far beyond New York. In addition to the Cotton Club reviews, he had made many special performances, records, radio broadcasts, and even film appearances. He now had a national following, and it was time to begin another episode in his career that would address both his new national and international audiences.

At the end of this period Ellington recorded one of his first larger pieces, "Creole Rhapsody." It was almost six and one-half minutes (as opposed to the three-minute restriction for 78-rpm discs). This effort proved to be a signal of later larger works that Ellington was to explore.

vamping

Racial Contradiction

The Cotton Club offered a window into some racial issues at play during the Harlem Renaissance, which was a flowering of African American art, literature, music, and culture in the 1920s and early 1930s. During this explosion of outstanding creativity, a Harlem nightspot, the Cotton Club, was both a part of the Harlem Renaissance and an expression of the racial divide. The club name itself is a reference to the main commodity of slavery. It had a white-only audience policy although the performers included popular African American musicians. Most notable was Duke Ellington, who clearly was a main contributor to the Harlem Renaissance but who was also popularized by the jungle sounds of his Cotton Club orchestra. The jungle sounds played to the racial stereotype of a black, more primitive, slave culture transported to an extravagant stage show setting. Despite the racial contradiction presented by the Cotton Club, it proved to be an important place for the exchange of musical ideas across racial boundaries. African American artists found themselves in the middle of this contradiction. They found a venue for performance but also helped support a popular stereotype.

TOURING

Beginning in 1931, touring would prove to be a major part of Ellington's life. It is remarkable that years of extensive touring did not affect the stable membership of his band.

In 1933, the Depression prompted Ellington to make what turned out to be a most successful trip to Europe. He returned home a recognized international attraction. When Ellington first went to England, he was surprised to find out how well known he and other American jazz players were. He realized the importance of jazz as an American export, but he was also aware that popularity at home somewhat determined his popularity abroad.

The death of Ellington's mother in 1935 almost robbed him of his trademark ambition. The final result was a new work, "Reminiscing in Tempo," which was larger than anything he had written before. It was four record sides in length and, for Ellington, was a move away from his more commercial compositions, demonstrating his unending interest in compositional experimentation.

THE SWING PERIOD

With the rise of swing, Ellington began to face new and high-profile competition. The newly formed swing bands were built for dancing—they produced a strong driving beat, and their large instrumentation filled the enormous dance

listening guide

(CD 1, track 22)
Duke Ellington and His Famous Orchestra
"In a Mellotone"

:00   Piano solo as introduction: 8 measures with unison saxes taking pickups on last measure.

:13   First chorus: unison saxes with trombones playing an elaborate backup for 30 measures.

1:09   Two-measure piano interlude.

1:13   Second chorus: Cootie Williams on trumpet solo with plunger; saxes back him up; 32 measures with ensemble pickups in the last measure.

2:13   Third chorus: 4 measures, ensemble.

2:21   Alto sax solo by Johnny Hodges: 4 measures plus next 6.

2:40   Two-measure break by Hodges on alto sax.

2:44   Eight-measure solo by Hodges on alto sax.

2:58   Ensemble alternates measures with Hodges on sax for 6 measures.

3:12   Ensemble plays out softly.

3:17   End.

halls with sound. The instrumentation for the swing bands and their section-alization had been put into place by Fletcher Henderson. Although Ellington's band had a similar instrumentation, it could not be considered a dance band in the same sense as that of Benny Goodman or Glenn Miller. Ellington's drummer was more of a color instrument than a driving dance force (as found in the bands of Gene Krupa or Chick Webb). Ellington's band developed out of the need for stage reviews and was characterized by the many colors compositional diversity needed to support a diversity of acts. Yet, this situation provided Ellington with a great deal of room to experiment and look for new ways to use his collection of musicians that were not typical of the emerging dance bands.

The result was a slump in Ellington's activity and popularity. His music was a little too complex for the public, who wanted to dance. Ellington used this time to explore composition rather than pursue the more restrictive and commercialized swing style. He began to examine the colors of smaller subgroups in his band. He wrote for sextets, octets, and nonets that were made up of members from his larger group. It was after his recordings of these smaller groups that Benny Goodman recorded his trio, and Tommy Dorsey his Clambake Seven. In 1939 Ellington began a European tour that proved to be one of the high points of this period in his life. His European audience appreciated his refined concert approach to jazz.

listening guide

🎧 (CD 1, track 23)
Johnny Hodges (performing)
"Passion Flower"

:00	Piano introduction setting the mood, 4 measures (Ellington).
:13	Alto sax solo in the low register (Hodges) with sustained background.
:43	Second 8 bars, sax goes up an octave.
1:08	Bridge, still sax solo ending with long *glissando*.
1:34	Original strain.
2:01	Return to the bridge.
2:27	Original strain.
2:58	Ending retards with carefully selected piano notes on the end.
3:01	End.

BILLY STRAYHORN

Before Ellington left on his European tour in 1939, he met Billy Strayhorn and began one of the most creative associations in the history of jazz. Ellington first hired Strayhorn as a lyricist, but, in a very short time, Strayhorn learned almost every detail of what he called the "Ellington effect." His formal training added even more emphasis to Ellington's constant search for colorful and extended harmonies. Strayhorn composed some of the most significant selections in the Ellington library, including "Chelsea Bridge," "Passion Flower," and the band's theme song "Take the 'A' Train."

Billy Strayhorn—often called Ellington's alter ego—was a strong arranging and composing force in the band. Both Ellington and Strayhorn were pianists, composers, and arrangers who thought so much alike musically that it was often difficult to tell which musician had written a given work. Influences from the French impressionists on Strayhorn can be heard in his "Chelsea Bridge."

It is interesting to note that even with all of his original compositions, Ellington chose "Take the 'A' Train," a Strayhorn contribution, as his theme song. The lyrics for the song came from instructions Ellington gave to Strayhorn for getting to his apartment. After Strayhorn died, Ellington finished every concert by sitting at the piano and playing Strayhorn's "Lotus Blossom" as a tribute to his colleague's exceptional influence. At the end of his album *And His Mother Called Him Bill*, which was recorded right after the

Vamping

Bass Players

One of the fine bass players to follow Blanton was Oscar Pettiford, who, with Dizzy Gillespie, formed the first bop band to appear on Fifty-second Street in 1944. Although there have been many great bass players, two must be singled out: Ray Brown and Charles Mingus. Brown progressed so quickly that he had been out of high school only two years when he joined the famous Dizzy Gillespie sextet in 1946. Brown's style seems modern today, and although he sounds relaxed, he displays great technical ability and fine taste. The musicianship of Mingus was ever present as he included ostinato figures, **pedal points,** and **double stops** even during accompaniment. When Mingus soloed, you were aware that he was also a good contemporary composer.

death of Strayhorn, Ellington is caught in a very private moment playing this tune. It was at the end of the recording session and the engineer let the tape continue to record. Ellington, in a private reverie and unaware that he was being recorded, played a moving rendition of "Lotus Blossom," as if to say a personal good-bye. Afterward, he merely said that was the tune Strayhorn most liked to hear him play.

NEW ADDITIONS

Two important additions were also made to the band at this time—Jimmy Blanton on bass and Ben Webster on tenor saxophone (discussed more in the chapter on bebop). Both musicians brought a new soloistic style to the band. Blanton helped redefine the bass as a more melodic instrument. Webster's addition filled Ellington's wish to expand his saxophone section and added a new soloing virtuosity for Ellington to weave into his music. The addition of these two players to the band ultimately proved so important that the band, during this period, is sometimes referred to as the Blanton-Webster band.

Jimmy Blanton

Until Jimmy Blanton joined Duke Ellington in 1939, the bass player played either two or four notes to a bar and played very simple lines, mainly the roots and fifths of the chords. There was hardly ever a bass solo, as these demanded more technique from players as well as some entirely new techniques from recording engineers. In the Ellington band, Blanton excited the jazz world with his solo "Jack the Bear" and his duets with Ellington, "Mr. J. B. Blues" and

"Pitter Panther Patter." Blanton satisfied his listeners with the bass parts that he played, but while accomplishing this he also played tasteful, interesting lines. He used eighth notes and sixteenth notes without ever sounding clumsy on the instrument, and he also proved that he could bow well. Although he died early, Blanton laid the foundations for all bass players who followed. They would assume responsibility for keeping the pulse for the whole combo while weaving their way among the new, advanced chords. Blanton's solo on Duke Ellington's "Jack the Bear" was considered for a long time to be the greatest bass solo on record[2] ("Pitter Panther Patter").

Ben Webster

Ben Webster first joined the Ellington band in 1935. He credits the influence of lead alto saxophonist Johnny Hodges for helping him create his own sound that would ultimately add his name to the most important "swing tenor" players, the other two being Lester Young and Coleman Hawkins. His aggressive style that often included growls earned him the nickname of "The Brute."

Webster became the first major tenor soloist for the Ellington band and was featured on many of the most famous recordings made by Ellington during this period. You can hear him on Ellington's recording of "Cotton Tail." This composition is based on the rhythm changes from George Gershwin's "I Got Rhythm" and features Webster as a soloist. Webster left the Ellington band in 1943.

Lawrence Brown and Johnny Hodges

Vamping

Plunger Mute

Cootie Williams was known for his "jungle" sounds in the tradition of Bubber Miley and Joe Nanton. He was famous for his use of the plunger mute. This mute is actually the rubber bottom of a plumber's helper used to unplug stopped-up sinks. Waving it in front of the bell of a brass instrument like a trumpet causes the sound to be modified dramatically. Williams used the plunger during his solos to create a type of musical talking. Ellington used Williams's plunger technique in many of his compositions.

JOHNNY HODGES

Ellington's band remained unusually stable until about 1942. In many ways this stability allowed him to compose with specific players in mind, players around which entire compositions would revolve. However, after 1942 his band would shift dramatically, as did his fortunes. One of the most difficult losses to the band was the departure of Johnny Hodges.

Hodges was one of the signature voices for the Ellington band and influenced Ellington's compositional style immensely. Rather than merely leaving room for improvisational input during performance, Ellington accepted input from performers during the composition process itself. If the performers are active participants in the compositional process, then their solo flights must necessarily reflect the improvisationally composed ensemble areas. The delineation between solo and compositional areas becomes blurred in such a process of collective composition. One might wonder how much of Hodges's input was at work in the shaping of the compositional ideas in "Passion Flower." The continuity of compositional and improvisational activity in the performance suggests a similar continuum in the process that crafted the piece. Ellington taught this arrangement to the band verbally without providing written notation. Hearing how Hodges's line and sound grow out of the opening voicings in the band shows a continuity seldom, if ever, rivaled in big-band arrangements. The instrumental colors selected by Ellington reflect both the color and inflection so typical of Hodges; it is certainly conceivable that instrumental colors were inspired by the player they were meant to support. Such a continuity of style and arrangement would not occur if we were to place, hypothetically, either Hawkins or Young as the lead voice in this arrangement. To do so would disrupt the reciprocal compositional and improvisational relationship that was at work between Ellington and Hodges.

Johnny Hodges returned to the band in 1955. Although he was undoubtedly the most memorable of the voices in Ellington's band, there were several others who had their signatures over the course of the band's history.

PROFILES IN jazz

johnny hodges

Johnny Hodges gained renown as a swinging alto saxophonist in the 1930s. He also occasionally played soprano sax. But his fame spread through a series of very melodic solos in which he demonstrated an intimate, yet very passionate, style. His beautiful tone blended with songs written by Duke Ellington and Billy Strayhorn, and the results were lush classics.

1906	Born in Cambridge, Massachusetts, on July 25.
1920	Worked with and learned from Sidney Bechet.
1927	Played with Chick Webb's orchestra.
1928–1951	Played with Duke Ellington.
1951–1955	Directed and played with his own combo.
1955	Rejoined Duke Ellington.
1970	Died in New York City on May 11.

Ellington himself acknowledged that trumpeter James "Bubber" Miley dramatically changed the band's sound when he joined the band in 1923. His sound became a trademark of the Cotton Club years. Cootie Williams on trumpet was also important to the Ellington sound, and his long tenure in the band attracted Ellington's compositional interest. Barney Bigard on clarinet, like Williams, was the subject of one of Ellington's concertos. Ellington's trombone section, ultimately called "God's trombones," included Tricky Sam Nanton, Juan Tizol, and Lawrence Brown. Rex Stewart on cornet was known for the vocal sounds that he made by pushing the valves down only halfway. The addition to the band of Ben Webster on tenor sax and Jimmie Blanton offered Ellington a brand-new dimension to explore in his compositions. The musicians validated the wonderful balance Ellington achieved between his compositional intent and the individual expression of the members of his band.

WITNESS TO jazz

dapper duke and gunman glen

Photo and text Courtesy William P. Gottlieb/Library of Congress

Future music critics may well recognize Duke Ellington as the greatest twentieth-century figure in jazz. He may also be remembered for his dapper manner — elegant, handsome, sophisticated, and suave. That was Duke.

Once, in 1947, I interviewed and photographed him in his dressing room at the Paramount Theater in New York. He had just come off a stage performance and prepared to shower. Naked, he looked like just another sagging middle-ager. Suave? Elegant? Not quite.

But, shower finished, he applied some baby powder and various other emollients, selected one of the many suits with which he traveled, added an expensive shirt and tie, and assumed his regal bearing. Presto! He suddenly became the elegant, suave, handsome Duke. Dapper indeed.

Some months later, in the same dressing room, I got together with Glen Gray, the leader of the Casa Loma Orchestra, one of the first big white bands to play jazz. Its music had been — and still was — rather stiff; but it had helped prepare the public for Benny Goodman and the swing era.

I didn't deliberately photograph Glen and Duke to make comparisons. Note: In place of Duke's line-up of sharp suits, Glen had a scraggly shirt and a couple of tired jackets; instead of a piano and sheet music, Glen had a set of golf clubs and a brief case; and where Duke's shelf was loaded with powders and creams, Glen's was indeed loaded . . . with a gun! Go figure.

listening guide

(CD 1, track 24)
Duke Ellington and His Famous Orchestra
"Ko-Ko"

:00   Begins with baritone saxophone, trombones, and drums. The drums were meant to be reminiscent of the drums of Congo Square. This tom-tom pattern is prevalent throughout the piece. After this introduction the piece follows a blues progression.

:12   The opening chorus features trombonist Juan Tizol in an antiphonal exchange with the saxophone section.

:31   Second chorus: a new trombone soloist (Joe Nanton) is now featured with muted brass backup. Listen for Nanton's use of a plunger over his bell for interpretive effect.

:50   Third chorus: trombone solo continues.

1:08   New chorus: the saxophone section enters and takes over the exchange with the muted brass. Listen for Ellington on the piano as he plays accented chords and fill-ins.

1:27   New chorus: brass now take the lead while part of the reed section plays long notes. The rest of the section responds melodically to the brass figures. Notice the dissonant chords played by the woodwinds.

1:45   A rising chord pyramids up from the saxophones, then the trombones, the trumpets, and finally the upper woodwinds. The chorus ends on accented chords.

1:48   The bass (Jimmy Blanton) plays solo breaks with the rest of the band for the next chorus.

1:51   The band responds.

1:54   Bass solo break.

1:57   Band returns with an ascending chord.

2:00   Bass solo break.

2:03   Brass begin the next chorus with loud shout chords while the saxophones play a responding melody.

2:22   Returns to a texture like the introduction with the tom-tom beat, trombones, and baritone saxophone.

2:34   Final phrase crescendos to the end.

2:43   End.

A PERIOD OF TRANSITION

In the years from 1943 to 1951 Ellington withstood a great turnover in his band personnel, World War II, the demise of the big bands and much of their popularity, the decline of the ballroom and nightclub business, and the challenge of bebop. Ellington had garnered a reputation for being one of the experimenters in jazz, and that title was now assumed by the new bop players. However, Ellington's unique voice allowed him to continue his work and not chase after the new bop style, much as he had remained distanced from the more commercialized type of swing. By this time, he was viewed by much of the jazz community as having carefully walked the line between art and commercialization. In many ways, Ellington had become one of the major statesmen of jazz.

Still, it was a difficult time for Ellington and his band to find a place in the new musical landscape. In 1956 his chance to reclaim much of his lost prominence occurred. At the Newport Jazz Festival, his *Newport Jazz Festival Suite* proved to be the high point of the festival's program. Also performed with great success at this festival was his "Diminuendo and Crescendo in Blue," which is fourteen minutes in length. These pieces reasserted Ellington's place as the premier composer in jazz.

LATE ELLINGTON

Ellington's success at the Newport festival signaled a new period (1956–65) in his compositional life, during which he demonstrated his continued ability to address creatively the many musical influences around him, both at home and in the world. He performed and composed for players, such as Dizzy Gillespie and John Coltrane, clearly outside the swing style for which he is most known. His musical, creative, and productive strengths did not slow at all as his award-winning reputation grew.

Significant works from this period include the album *A Drum Is a Woman* (1956), which paints a history of jazz and was narrated by Ellington himself. This work was a result of another collaboration of Ellington and Strayhorn, as was *The Shakespearean Suite.* Ellington also composed a motion picture soundtrack for *Anatomy of a Murder.* At the end of this period, Ellington completed his *Concert of Sacred Music* (1965), which was performed in cathedrals and churches many times. Ellington had seen jazz rise from a somewhat unrespectable entertainment form to a style appropriate for the concert stages like Carnegie Hall and the sacred halls of cathedrals. Ironically, when he performed his second sacred concert at Washington's Constitution Hall, it was challenged for being too "worldly" by the Baptist Ministers' Conference of Washington.

In his later years (1966–74) he lost Billy Strayhorn, who composed even from his hospital bed ("Blood Count"). Ellington continued to tour, and he received awards and honors from around the world. In 1968, he recorded his *Second Sacred Concert*, which he considered to be his best achievement. He

**Duke Ellington and
Billy Strayhorn**

died on May 24, 1974. It is certainly no surprise that over 12,000 mourners attempted to attend his funeral.

INDIVIDUAL AND GROUP EXPRESSION

Like any art form, jazz has a history balanced by a variety of forces that direct its evolution. Many of those forces work in apparent opposition—individual and group expressions, improvisation and composition, and the marketplace and personal ideology. Here we look at one polarity, the balance between group and individual expressions as they are each manifested in the larger ensembles of jazz. It would be unwise to isolate these balancing influences as unrelated to the many other forces at work in emergent jazz expressions and expect to have an accurate understanding of how jazz works as a signature art form. However, the issue of the individual and the group can be viewed as a possible microcosm of the inner forces that have always been a part of the larger flow of jazz styles. Even the avant-garde work of later groups, like those that came out of the Association for the Advancement of Creative Musicians (AACM), struggled with the same issue.

> The consequences—which are still being worked with and through today—were several. One of the most crucial was the misnamed "free jazz" movement—misnamed because, in fact, it dealt with new kinds of interrelations between composition and improvisation, the dialectical engine that powers what we call jazz.[3]

Seemingly, there is no apparent limit to the number of ways in which an effective balance between the expression of a collective ensemble and a player within that collective might be struck. On one extreme would be a solo performance where only an individual expression is present and any ensemble interaction is impossible; on the other extreme is an ensemble composed of faceless performers who can be replaced at will with no recognizable change to the outcome. The former rests most heavily on the personal aesthetic of the performer, while the latter places the composer in the lead aesthetically. One might argue that the faceless ensemble must fall outside the definition of what jazz is understood to be because of the individuality inherent in the jazz tradition. However, jazz groups have successfully flirted with the notion of tight compositional direction as a guiding principle while striking some balance to accommodate individual expression.

Such groups have certainly been in a minority throughout the developing jazz tradition. Jazz composers are relatively rare and the history of jazz centers mostly on performers who have in some way influenced or redirected existing jazz styles. The dialectic between composition for an ensemble and the extemporaneous composition by an ensemble is real. It is fueled by jazz's nonliterate streetwise legacy, a legacy that can be seen as separate from—but interactive with—that of the more literature-based academy.

One of the difficulties of addressing the issue of jazz composition and improvised performance is deciding when it is appropriate to map the academic's Europeanized notions of compositional viability into a discussion of group jazz expression. The discussion embraces more than just the balance between the real-time expressions of a group as a whole and that of an individual; it also includes the Western European compositional approach for larger ensembles and the range of possibilities for real-time improvised expression within that approach.

Ellington, as noted above, greatly customized his music around the attributes of individual performers. His compositions are replete with new instrumental colors that can be found only by cutting across sectional lines and borrowing the voices of individual players. His approach, therefore, uses what might otherwise be considered paradoxical: detailed arrangements to launch the individual voices within the ensemble. Because the compositions had the improvisers woven into their fabric, a change of soloists would most likely create a musical disjuncture. Duke Ellington gave credit for his success to his famous **sidemen** who, in turn, gave all the credit to Ellington. His legacy followed him as a giant in the blending of the jazz spirit and compositional foresight as well as one of the truly noble forces of jazz.

Ellington's larger works are sometimes criticized for being too loosely bound together rather than compositionally tight. Such criticism is no doubt a risk a composer like Ellington must take if he wants to compositionally open musical areas that feature the individual voices within an ensemble.

More than any other musician in jazz, Ellington represented a successful blend of the two musical heritages that spawned the jazz idiom. While recognized as jazz's premier composer, Ellington never compromised the voice of jazz so firmly rooted in the oral tradition. He represents the truly American hybrid that sits at the center of the Western European compositional legacy and the expressive oral tradition of the African American.

INNOVATIONS

Ellington's innovations include the following: the wonderful ensemble sound (developed using individuals in the band), the larger forms in jazz (which often ignored the three-minute limit on recordings that dictated the repertoire of most bands), his more than skillful orchestration, the use of voices as instruments (as far back as 1927 with singer Adelaide Hall on "Creole Love Song"), and many innovative jazz tunes starting with "Mood Indigo" (first recorded as "Dreamy Blues" in 1930), "Sophisticated Lady" (1933), and "Solitude" (1934). Ellington's band had an instrumentation much like the other swing bands of the period. There were four primary instrumental sections, saxophones, trumpets, trombones, and rhythm. Ellington used these sections quite differently than most other big bands. Usually each of the sections played as a whole. In a riffing composition used by many of the Kansas City bands one would expect each section to have its own riff that worked against the riffs of the other sections. In a soil section the harmonies were often created within sections.

Ellington altered this practice by grouping instruments across the sections. Instead of all the saxophones playing together, a "cross-sectional" grouping (also called voicing) might include one or two saxophones, one or two trombones, and one or two trumpets. Ellington's use of **cross-sectional voicing** produced new timbres seldom heard from the standard big band. By carefully orchestrating his compositions he not only added a new level of sophistication to his work but also was able to better showcase his soloists. Ellington often changed the titles of his tunes. For example, "Rumpus in Richmond" was changed to "Harlem Air Shaft." This puts the liner notes on some albums in a suspicious light, as some record company employee tried to explain the final title as if it were Ellington's idea of daily life in New York's Harlem.

Those listeners who challenge all changes disturbed Ellington—to a point. His later music was sometimes compared unfavorably with that which he had played in the past. Ellington's answer to the "time test," in comparing jazz to other music, was that he was not interested in writing or playing music for posterity; he wanted his music to sound good at the very moment it was performed.

REPERTOIRE

The earliest Ellington recording available is an album called *The Birth of Big Band Jazz*. These sides were recorded in 1923 (some writers place the date at 1925). The album called *Early Ellington* comprises recordings made between 1927 and 1931. Most writers feel that Ellington's greatest recordings were made between 1940 and 1942, including such records as "Jack the Bear," "Warm Valley," "Cotton Tail," "Chelsea Bridge," "Take the 'A' Train," "C Jam Blues," and so on. Ellington recorded more than one hundred fifty albums, although well over half can no longer be purchased. However, the Smithsonian Institution has helped to remedy this situation with sets that fill many of the would-be gaps in collections of Ellington's music.[4]

True, Ellington did perform his standards—he was almost required to. But it cannot be said that his repertoire did not have good variety. He performed in so many different situations (dance halls, large clubs, theaters, festivals, concert halls) that he had to diversify. Before trumpeter Cootie Williams left the band to play with Benny Goodman, Ellington wrote his most famous concerto, "Concerto for Cootie." He also wrote a concerto for clarinetist Barney Bigard ("Barney's Concerto"). In 1941 Ellington composed a civil rights musical, "Jump for Joy," which is credited as the first work of its kind to present an all-African American cast in a nonstereotypical way. Another large (fifty minutes in length) composition of this period is his "Black, Brown and Beige" (1943), which Ellington intended to be a "musical evolution of the Negro race." This is his largest piece and was written for his Carnegie Hall debut. It was during his Carnegie Hall concert series that Ellington introduced and essentially established the role of larger scale works as appropriate for jazz.

It is worth noting that Ellington, while feeling that his music was always primarily black music, never felt ethnic ties to the point of using only black musicians in his band, as witnessed by the white drummer Louie Bellson.

summary

It appears that the talents and influences of Duke Ellington will always be with us. Today there are Ellington societies, the Duke Ellington Cancer Fund, and even Duke Ellington Boulevard in upper Manhattan and a Broadway play titled *Sophisticated Ladies,* which featured Mercer Ellington conducting the Duke Ellington Orchestra performing his father's music. Ellington's style of arranging and composing has been valued enough to be taught at the Berklee College of Music in Boston. In Washington, D.C., students attend Duke Ellington High School of the Arts. At the University of California, Los Angeles, guitarist Kenny Burrell has taught a course called "Ellingtonia."[5]

Ellington's band, his music, and his recordings are proof of his belief that, although jazz borrowed from any and every source available, it remained personal. His ensemble was an integrated whole, yet no one's orchestra has ever been based so much on the talents of its individuals. Some jazz writers actually credit Ellington's success to his brilliant sidemen, but these sidemen always point to Ellington's composing, arranging, piano playing, and leadership in general. In 1962, Leonard Feather wrote of Ellington, "We see him today as the most challenging, most provocative, most brilliant, and most irreplaceable paragon in the sixty-year history of jazz."[6] That statement is still true.

FOR FURTHER STUDY

1. Describe the differences in the way performers react to one another in big bands and in small ensembles.
2. Discuss the different roles played by the composer/arranger in small ensembles and in big bands.

SUGGESTED ADDITIONAL LISTENING

And His Mother Called Him Bill. RCA Victor Records, LSP-3906.
At His Very Best. RCA Victor Records, LPM-1715.
Best of Duke Ellington. Capitol Records, SM-1602.
Birth of Big Band Jazz. Riverside Records, 129.
Concert of Sacred Music. RCA Victor Records, LSP-3582.
Duke Ellington, 70th Birthday Concert. Solid State Records, SS 19000.
Duke Ellington, The Beginning. Decca Records, DL-9224.
Duke Ellington's Greatest Hits. Reprise Records, S-6234.
Duke's Big 4. Pablo Records, 2310703.
Early Ellington. Brunswick Records, 54007.
Ellington at Newport. Columbia Records, CS 8648.
Ellington Era. Columbia Records, C3L 27.
Ellington '66. Reprise Records, 6154.
Historically Speaking—The Duke. Bethlehem Records, BCP 60.
New Orleans Suite. Atlantic Records, SD 1580.
Smithsonian Collection of Classic Jazz, vols. 6 and 7.
This Is Duke Ellington. RCA Victor Records, VPM-6042.
This One's for Blanton. Pablo Records, 2310721.
Togo Brava Suite. United Artists Records, UXS-92.

ADDITIONAL READING RESOURCES

Collier, James Lincoln. *Duke Ellington.*
Dance, Stanley. *The World of Duke Ellington.*
Ellington, Edward Kennedy. *Music Is My Mistress.*
Hasse, John Edward. *Beyond Category.*
Rattenbury, Ken. *Duke Ellington Jazz Composer.*

Note: Complete information, including name of publisher and date of publication, is provided in this book's bibliography.

NOTES

1. Joachim Berendt, *Jazz Book: From New Orleans to Rock and Free Jazz,* trans. Dan Morgenstern (Westport, Conn.: Lawrence Hill, 1975), 59.
2. Jimmy Blanton (Duke Ellington's Orchestra), "Jack the Bear," *Historically Speaking—the Duke,* Bethlehem Records, BCP 60.
3. Gene Santoro, "Anthony Braxton," *Nation,* 8 May 1989, 643.
4. Duke Ellington, *Ellington '38,* Smithsonian Records, R003; *Ellington '39,* Smithsonian Records, R010.
5. Kenny Burrell, *Ellington Is Forever,* vols. 1 and 2, Fantasy Records, 79005 and 79008.
6. Leonard Feather, "The Duke's Progress," *Down Beat* 29, no. 12 (June 1962): 19.

8

Bop

When a group of bop musicians had finished with a given tune it would be unrecognizable even to the composer. The musicians acknowledged the distortion by renaming the pieces.[1]

Henry Pleasants

Bop jazz was sometimes called *bebop* or *rebop*, but common usage shortened it to *bop*. One explanation for the name is that players sang the words *bebop* and *rebop* to an early bop phrase, as shown in example 8.1.

Example 8.1

THE SHIFT TO BOP

Although the swing style may have improved the status of jazz by placing it in the ears and minds of the world, bop, its successor, ultimately claimed mainstream status. More significant changes, both musical and nonmusical, occurred in jazz with the advent of bop than at any other single time in jazz history. As we saw in Chapters 6 and 7, the demise of swing brought about the dissolution of the big bands and the rise of small combos. The country was nervous, and the music was nervous and agitated. Many well-known players were in the military, which allowed new, younger, players and their ideas to receive more exposure.

Bop was much more than a dramatic musical shift; it was a reflection of a developing African American defiance. Although swing was an African American development, it was the popular white swing bands that capitalized most on the style. There was a feeling among African American musicians that their music had been co-opted. The complexities of bop offered a way to step away from the commercialization of swing and center the musical voice of jazz squarely in the African American identity.

At the same time, the Second World War effort was being powered by African Americans drafted into the mililtary and working in defense plants.

At Bob Reisner's Open Door, Greenwich Village, New York (ca. 1953). Left to right: Charles Mingus, Roy Haynes, Thelonious Monk, and Charlie "Bird" Parker.

listening guide

Interactive Guide 6
Bop

:00   Ensemble chorus (trumpet, alto sax, and electric guitar in unison); bass and drums keep $\frac{4}{4}$ rhythm with accents on the piano. It was common practice to have the "head" played in unison by all the various horn players in the ensemble. It was meant to show the technical prowess that differentiated bebop from swing players.

:03   Second phrase of the head.

:07   Final phrase of the head.

:11   Improvised trumpet solo for two choruses in a frantic style. Notice the clipped melodic phrase endings and double-time melody that distinguished the style.

:22   Second chorus of the trumpet solo. Notice that the solo moves into the upper range for greater intensity.

:34   Ensemble chorus (same as the first chorus). A head arrangement like this closed after all the solos were taken with a repeat of the unison head melody.

:38   Second phrase of the head.

:42   Final phrase of the head with a closing tag.

:48   End.

For black musicians, bebop gave voice to the racisim they found in the military and in the defense plants. The result was a more select music that separated itself technicially from that of the popular white musicians and a nonconformist persona that was antiwar, anitcommercial, and exclusive. The late-night hours and drug habits associated with bebop helped accentuate this more defiant African American identity.[2]

There were considerable changes in techniques and attitudes toward performances. There also were changes of attitude toward audiences. Bop became the first jazz style that was not used for dancing. Consequently, there were great changes in the repertoire. There was also a shift away from the popularity that swing enjoyed to a more elite listening audience, and this elitism expanded to include the players. If you were an accomplished swing player, there was no guarantee that you would be able to survive the expectations of the bop musical world. The music took on a complexity that required players to extend their former playing knowledge and technique. A theoretical underpinning began to emerge as players stretched the harmonic boundaries of early jazz styles. Players were required to have a greater and more immediate sense of chord recognition as well as chord extensions and possible substitutions. The music was generally fast, demanding execution on individual instruments seldom required in previous styles. It is interesting that bop is today the main-stream of jazz style, yet it was not enthusiastically accepted by the jazz community at the time of its emergence.

The short, stylized solos typical of the large bands of the swing era minimized the opportunity for exploratory expression. Soloists not only desired more freedom for experimentation but also searched for a different, fresh approach to jazz. The young players were tired of reading written arrangements, tired of the clichés of swing, tired of the limited opportunities for improvisation, and so on. They also felt that many musicians with little creativity were earning more than their share of fame and wealth and that the time had come for many changes. (For an introduction to bop, listen to Interactive Guide 6 at the interactive listening site, http://www.emegill.com/listening.)

Most bop players turned naturally to small combos. A quintet seemed to be the size Charlie Parker found most comfortable. It is interesting that the combos resembled, in appearance at least, the earlier Dixieland bands, that is, a rhythm section with a sparse (by comparison to swing) front line. Without a doubt, the bop combo reflected Kansas City jam sessions. Regardless of what is claimed, bop or any other style of music surely does not begin at any one place and at any one time. It could not, for example, have been decided in October 1940, at Minton's Playhouse in New York's Harlem, that bop was to be the next jazz style.

Charlie Parker

Many unrelated events brought bop about quite natu-rally. Just as Early New Orleans Dixieland jazz solidified in New Orleans years before, bop solidified in New York in the early 1940s. Charlie Parker said that an alto saxophone player from Dallas named Buster Smith was playing the beginnings of this free style. In the South-west, Charlie Christian surely played saxophone-type lines on the guitar. In the St. Louis area, Jimmy Blanton was innovating on the bass. All this activity meant that the bop style developed not only in New York but also in Kansas City, St. Louis, Oklahoma City, and elsewhere.

THE DEVELOPING MAINSTREAM AND THE JAZZ CANON

A *canon* is a historical category of works that includes the descriptors of an evolutionary line. Many types of canons exist. There are literary canons, aca-demic canons, visual art canons, and so on. Each of these helps us interpret the historical events that led to the flowering of the art form or discipline it serves. A canon describes who the heroes of that tradition are and what values are addressed by these heroes. It also offers criteria for judging new work con-tributed to the tradition by the newest generation of artists. Conscious or not, canons exist for most all musics; however, they only become codified or for-malized historically for those that gain a general consensus as being worthy.

A transition of some magnitude occurred in the literature of jazz with the advent of bop in the late 1940s. What was so different? Was the loss of popularity necessary for achieving art status? Bop certainly did not have the same large audience enjoyed by the swing bands. If bop is the turning point in the jazz canon, how does it relate to its predecessors? Despite its lack of a large audience, how dependent was bop on the popularity of the swing period? What role did the earlier Dixieland bands play in the shaping of this canon? How did the players' understanding of jazz as a tradition differ between the early bands and the bop bands? And how did bop players' understanding of jazz differ from that of the later neoclassical players? Jazz musicians viewed their place in history differently in each stylistic period, but in no period did their view of themselves change so drastically as in the bop period.

Jazz, despite its popularity, was not viewed as an art form by the general public. Even the players were looking for an audience, responding mostly to the popular trends. They certainly knew what players preceded them, but they did not yet view them as the progenitors of an art form. Time helps us to see the codifying forces that shaped the canon and to drop the less influential ones; however, we lose the vitality of the times with many of the details.

Only in retrospect do our historical leaders emerge. If we look at the music, the heroes are more likely to be the composer/arrangers who offered us a re-performable repertoire than the individuals whose interpretation of that repertoire gave the music life. Again, we see the duality in jazz that reflects the cultural traditions that gave birth to it.

Jazz used to be music of the dance hall, the street, and the church. Today it finds itself on concert stages, in universities, and the subject of historical accounts. The players who have been remembered were players who pushed on the developing front edge of stylistic change. Their repertoires contained little of earlier jazz styles, yet they were still a part of the growing mainstream. Their work has weathered several attempts to redirect the mainstream. Today, we have many prominent players who are strong advocates of the traditional voice of jazz, placing a majority of their interest in the past and the bop style in particular. Is the neoclassical only possible because of bop?

Bop was the era from which a majority of our canon's jazz giants emerged. The musical changes that occurred in that period, although not popular by previous standards, set the framework for the developing jazz mainstream. By this time, the small-group medium that still flourishes today had been established as the vehicle of mainstream jazz. Through this medium, players could express their personal voices. Improvisation was codified as a valued component of the jazz expression within a dominantly interactive and improvised performance medium. The mouth of the mainstream had been found.

BOP ARRANGING

The shift to bop embraced the most radical changes in the development of jazz to this point. The smaller band necessary for these new experimentations was in part a result of the military draft and the transportation difficulties during World War II. In contrast to the musical arrangements of the swing era, notations for the bop bands were usually confined to **unison** lines for the melodic instruments. A standard format for performing tunes in the bop manner was to play the first chorus in unison (trumpet and saxophone usually), then the improvised choruses, followed by the unison chorus again. Therefore, if the tune had a chorus of thirty-two bars and the form AABA, the first eight bars (A) would be composed, the second eight would be a repetition of the first eight (A), the third eight would be improvised (B), and the last eight would again be a repetition of the first eight (A). This added up to thirty-two bars and constituted the first chorus and the last chorus. Therefore, only one eight-bar strain, the A part, had to be planned beforehand.[3]

MUSICAL EXPANSION

For greater freedom of expression, these players used **extended harmonies** in their improvised choruses. The development of new harmonic resources for the jazz musician followed closely on the heels of experimentations by classical composers. At the turn of the century, harmonies were enriched through the successive inclusion of higher members of the **overtone series,** resulting in an extensive use of **ninth, eleventh,** and **thirteenth chords** and beyond (see notational examples 24 and 25 in Appendix B). Use of the flatted fifth became so ordinary that from this point on it was considered another blue note, just as the third and seventh tones of the scale had been.

It was not until the bop era that the use of **higher harmonics** and their resultant complex harmonies became prevalent. Harmonic sonorities that were complex enough to be designated as polychords were used extensively. This harmonic construction can best be understood as a combination of two conventional chords. As long as these chords have a close relationship, such as common tones, they are perceived as one chord in the same key rather than in two separate keys (see notational example 25 in Appendix B). These new, more complex, chords were substituted for the simpler chords used in the standard tunes of the day. The players were greatly stimulated by fresh chords inside of old progressions. This shift to more complex harmonies was significant enough that few successful swing players were able to adopt the new requirements of bop, creating a significant shift in the continuity of jazz's evolution.

Bop playing in general employed faster tempos[4] (Dizzy Gillespie and Charlie Parker, "Shaw 'Nuff"; Charlie Parker, "KoKo"; Dizzy Gillespie, "Things to Come"). To create excitement by merely increasing the tempo would have been impractical with the large, unwieldy bands of the swing era, but it was done effectively in bop. Moreover, bop was the first style of jazz that was not specifically for dancing. Although the early jazz players used primarily quarter notes and four-tone chords or chords of the seventh, the bop players often played sixteenth-note rhythms and harmonies of greater complexity. One of the unusual phrasing idioms in bop occurred when there was a series of eighth notes:

Example 8.2

The bop players accented the note between the beats:

Example 8.3

Compare the swing style:

Example 8.4

Therefore, if the phrase were counted "one and, two and, three and, four and," the players would accent the "ands." Also, bop phrasing was at first heavily influenced by Kansas City–type short riffs, but soon the statements, both planned and improvised, became longer and less repetitive.

There was more tension in the music of this era than in the music of the swing era. The musical tension was created by **tonal clashes,** unusual harmonies, and fast tempos with complex rhythms. To play bop well, the musicians had to have a good knowledge of harmony plus great technical facility. Even with these attributes, the hectic tempos and rapidly moving chords of many of the works caused some experienced players to merely run the chords, **arpeggios,** instead of creating interesting melodic lines.

One major change that occurred during the bop era was the repertoire, the building of which was accomplished mainly by using the chords of a **standard tune** as the framework on which to compose a new melody. An example of this kind of borrowing is found in the selection "Ornithology," which is a melody improvised from the harmonies in the composition "How High the Moon."[5] Both Miles Davis and Thelonious Monk recorded tunes based on "All God's Children Got Rhythm." Davis called his "Little Willie Leaps," and Monk's is titled "Suburban Eyes." Chords from "What Is This Thing Called Love" became "Hot House," "Indiana" became "Donna Lee," "Whispering" became "Groovin' High," "I Got Rhythm" became "Anthropology," "KoKo" is from the chords to "Cherokee," "S'Wonderful" became "Stupendous," and so on. Twelve-bar blues had such titles as "Relaxin' at Camarillo," "Parker's Mood," "Now's the Time," and "Congo Blues." In previous eras, the melody was usually stated in the first chorus, and improvisation began after that. The bop innovators, however, often disregarded the initial statement of the melody and began their improvisation at the beginning of the selection. Besides changing the harmonies, melodies, and rhythms, the bop players changed the approach to phrasing from neat **symmetrical** phrases to phrases that seemed uneven and unnatural compared to earlier jazz.

THE BOP RHYTHM SECTION

The assigned parts played by individual members of the rhythm section also underwent radical changes. Instead of the regular $\frac{4}{4}$ steady rhythm heard in swing music, the drummer now used the bass and snare drums mainly for accents and punctuations. He usually maintained an overall sound by playing eighth-note rhythms on the top cymbal. If the accents were not spontaneous, they were played on either the fourth beat of the bar or the fourth beat of every other bar. The more spontaneous punctuations on the bass drum were called **bombs,** which had to be played with great discernment to aid the impetus instead of being a distraction.

The piano player changed from playing $\frac{4}{4}$ steady rhythm to syncopated chordal punctuations (Count Basie had played in this style for some time). These punctuations were played at specific moments to designate the chord changes and thus added to the overall musical excitement. With the advent of the amplifier, the guitar became a melody instrument and took its place with the trumpet, saxophone, and others. This left the sole responsibility for the steady pulse of the beat to the string bass. Although the string bass part now had a more interesting line, this line was secondary to the job of maintaining a rhythmic pulse. However, the rhythmic pulse was not the result of a series of repeated notes for each chord. Instead, the bass player now played a new note almost every beat to create a walking bass line.

The beauty of the bop rhythm section was that the individual members were freed from duplicating one another's role. In the swing style, all four players were forced mainly to keep the pulse because the bands were quite large and the public wanted to feel the pure, unornamented, uncomplicated beat in order to dance. Generally, these bop approaches were not really new, as shown by Basie's piano work, Jimmy Blanton's bass playing with Ellington, and Charlie Christian's guitar work with Benny Goodman's orchestra. The bop players also added rhythm players from Cuba who not only aided the pulse assigned to the bass player but also brought new rhythmic excitement into jazz through improvised **cross-rhythms.** This addition pointed out the fact that the more intricate aspects of the West African musical tradition had been kept alive much more in Cuba than in the United States. Of course, Latin rhythms, as they were considered, were not new to jazz. For example, there is a tango section in Handy's "St. Louis Blues," which had been written about thirty years earlier.

THE PERFORMERS

Much of the leadership of this era must be attributed to Charlie Parker's fluid alto sax, Dizzy Gillespie's virtuosic trumpet playing, Thelonious Monk's melodies, and the brilliantly accented drumming of Kenny Clarke and Max Roach. The early bop sessions at Minton's Playhouse emerged from a band led by drummer Kenny Clarke. Charlie Parker was not there at first, but he came later. Ex-bandleader Teddy Hill applied the Kansas City formula to Minton's style. As the manager, he hired a good contemporary nucleus of players with whom the performers of this advanced jazz enjoyed jamming. The musicians who played regularly at Minton's devised ways to discourage the unwanted from sitting in on the jam sessions. They would play tunes at such fast tempos, and play what at the time were such strange chords, that those musicians not really in the clique simply could not compete.

Roy Eldridge and Dizzy Gillespie

Dizzy Gillespie, as talented a trumpet player as he was a showman, combined great technique with fresh thoughts and extensive harmonic knowledge. Along

**Roy Eldridge on
the trumpet with
Kai Winding on the
trombone**

with Parker, he was a leader in the style of jazz that he and his contemporaries labeled bop. Gillespie's trumpet playing stemmed from Louis Armstrong by way of Roy Eldridge.

Not nearly enough is ever said about Roy Eldridge. He had played in a fiery style for many years before bop came along,[6] and he first became prominent during his stint with Fletcher Henderson in 1936. He was admired not only for his virtuosic technique and startling use of the extreme upper register of the trumpet, but also for his exciting and refreshingly new musical lines. Eldridge was featured with the bands of Gene Krupa (1941–43) and Artie Shaw (1944–45).

Dizzy Gillespie's playing was so modeled on the talents of Eldridge that when Eldridge left the Teddy Hill band, Gillespie was naturally hired to replace him. Gillespie's first recorded solos were with this band in 1937. "King Porter Stomp" and "Blue Rhythm Fantasy" reflect the Ellington influence most directly, but "Things to Come" was probably his most important record.

Around 1939, with Cab Calloway's band, Gillespie made his first appearance as arranger/composer. The tunes were "Paradiddle" (featuring Cozy Cole on drums) and "Pickin' the Cabbage." He was with Calloway for two years, during which time he improved considerably. "Dizzy, always a prankster and cutup, was finally fired by Calloway, who accused him of throwing spitballs on the bandstand—ironically, the *one* time Gillespie was actually blameless."[7] There is no doubt that Gillespie was the most talked-about bop musician at that time.

The reactions to Gillespie's style of playing ranged all the way from unqualified enthusiasm to pure indignation. He is highly regarded all over the world, and his contributions to modern jazz trends cannot possibly be disputed[8] (Dizzy Gillespie, "I Can't Get Started with You"; Dizzy Gillespie and Charlie Parker, "Shaw 'Nuff," "Groovin' High").

The period from 1944 to 1947 was noted for the great jazz groups that worked in the clubs on Fifty-second Street in New York, where the first actual bop band was formed by Dizzy Gillespie and bassist Oscar Pettiford in January 1944. The Earl "Fatha" Hines band had experimented in 1942 and 1943, but

WITNESS TO jazz

dizzie gillespie: "king of 52nd street"

Photo and text Courtesy William P. Gottlieb/Library of Congress

By 1947, the block in New York City on Fifty-second Street, between Fifth and Sixth Avenues, long known as Swing Street, had begun to slip. This "Center of the Jazz World" was being hit by a nationwide economic decline as well as by the streetwide growth of an unappetizing drug scene. Most severely threatening were the encroachments of Rockefeller Center, whose new skyscrapers were beginning to push out the many brownstone buildings in whose basements the jazz clubs had settled. Finally, there was the gradual replacement of swing by bebop, a style of jazz that alienated the swing fans who had supported the clubs.

But bop had a vitality of its own; and, for a while, it filled the street with a new group of musicians and new (or converted) audiences. The leader of this revolutionary movement and "The King of 52nd Street" was Dizzy Gillespie.

Earlier, John Birks "Dizzy" Gillespie had been known for his wild antics. When, in the beginning, he was hired by orchestra leader Teddy Hill, he often played rehearsals dressed in hat, gloves, and overcoat. Teddy gave him the name "Dizzy" but was quick to add that, with all his eccentricities, "he was the most stable of us all. Diz crazy? Crazy like a fox."

Diz was a joy to interview and photograph. Normally, when taking a picture, I don't move my subjects but show them while performing or in a dressing room. However, once in 1947 while Diz was working in a club on the street, I asked him to come outside and stand next to an appropriate street sign. Diz always seemed to sense what to do. Without any direction from me, he struck just the right pose. Perfect!

until the emergence of the Gillespie-Pettiford band in 1944, bop had been confined mainly to Harlem's after-hours clubs, such as Monroe's and Minton's, and to occasional improvised solos in big bands by performers such as Howard McGee, Charlie Parker, and Dizzy Gillespie. These choruses seemed out of context in the big swing bands—Cab Calloway, Andy Kirk, and so on.

listening guide

(CD 2, track 1)
Dizzy Gillespie All Star Quintette
"Shaw 'Nuff"
Charlie Parker, alto sax
Dizzy Gillespie, trumpet
Al Haig, piano
Curley Russell, bass
Sidney Catlett, drums

:00	Eight measures: drums, bass, and bass of piano.
:06	Trumpet and alto sax in thirds for 8 measures.
:13	Six measures of unison ending with famous "Salt Peanuts" phrase.
:17	Piano break for 2 measures.
:19	Unison main theme (head): 32 measures.
:47	Alto sax solo by Charlie Parker for 32 measures.
1:14	Trumpet solo by Dizzy Gillespie for 32 measures.
1:41	Piano solo for 32 measures.
2:07	Original theme in unison as first chorus.
2:34	Same as top of record: drums, bass, and bass of piano for 8 measures.
2:41	Trumpet and sax in thirds again.
2:48	Eight bars of unison as in the earlier part of the record.
2:56	End.

Charlie Parker

Charlie Parker, called "Yardbird"—or more often simply "Bird"—was born on August 29, 1921, in Kansas City, Kansas, and moved to Kansas City, Missouri, at age seven. As a youngster, he listened a great deal to saxophonists Lester Young and Buster Smith. An important predecessor of Parker, Smith was from the Kansas City school. After Bennie Moten's death, Smith was a co-leader, with Basie, of Moten's group.

As far back as 1932, Buster Smith recordings foreshadow Charlie Parker. There is no doubt about the strong influence that altoist Smith and tenor saxophonist Young had on young Parker. But it is surprising that Parker himself credited five white saxophonists with being the greatest early influences on his playing: nonjazz players Rudy Wiedoeft and Rudy Vallee and jazzmen Frank Teschemacher, Jimmy Dorsey, and Bud Freeman. He definitely surpassed all these players.

listening guide

🎧 (CD 2, track 2)
Charlie Parker's Re-Boppers
"KoKo"

:00   Introduction: unison alto sax (Charlie Parker) and muted trumpet (Dizzy Gillespie); drums with brushes using many accents (Max Roach).

:06   Muted trumpet solo, drums continue as before.

:12   Alto sax solo, drums the same.

:19   Alto sax and muted trumpet in parallel harmony, drums the same.

:25   First chorus: alto sax solo, drums on a fast $\frac{4}{4}$ rhythm plus accents, bass playing a fast walking style (Curley Russell), piano enters with chordal punctuations. If the piano seems a bit late, that is because that is also Gillespie; he had to put his trumpet down.

:50   Bridge of first chorus: change of chords.

1:04   Last part of first chorus.

1:15   Second chorus: Parker still on alto sax.

1:40   Bridge of second chorus.

1:54   Last part of second chorus.

2:07   Drum solo: intricate as far as the pulse is concerned (this gives Gillespie time to go from piano to the trumpet).

2:27   Alto sax and muted trumpet in unison, drums now on cymbals.

2:34   Muted trumpet solo, drums the same.

2:40   Alto sax solo, drummer a bit lighter on cymbals now.

2:45   Alto sax and muted trumpet in parallel harmony (a reminder of the introduction for the sake of continuity).

2:49   End.

In 1936, Parker would stand around in the alley behind the Reno Club in Kansas City and listen to the Basie band. At age fifteen, he was learning in the same way that most jazz players learned their trade: He listened and attempted to imitate. Parker was always curious about advanced harmony, and he worked for and studied with a graduate of the Boston Conservatory, Tommy Douglas, who was ahead of his time in this direction in 1935. Parker's studies with pianists and guitarists furthered this knowledge. He became intensely interested in the use of the higher harmonics of chords as structures on which to improvise new melodies. This approach became one of the mainstays of the bop movement, and many new tunes were created from old chord progressions.

When saxophonist Budd Johnson heard eighteen-year-old Parker in Chicago, he noted that Parker already had some of the elements of bop—such as double time—in his repertoire.

Parker first came to New York in 1939 to search out jam sessions and every other opportunity to listen and learn, supporting himself by washing dishes and other menial jobs. The first combo job that Parker played in New York was at Clark Monroe's Uptown House on 134th Street. He left town afterward with the Jay McShann band. The first recorded solos of Parker are on transcriptions made by the Jay McShann band in 1940 at a Wichita, Kansas, radio station. The McShann band, besides being blues-based, was also riff-oriented like Basie's. It was McShann who brought Parker back to New York in 1942, this time as a mature musician. Today it is hard to locate recordings of Parker with McShann. Folkways pressed "Hootie Blues," recorded in Dallas in 1941, and Decca pressed "Sepian Bounce," recorded in New York in 1942[9] (Jay McShann, "Hootie Blues"). By 1942, mainly because of jam sessions at Minton's Playhouse, Parker and Dizzy Gillespie had become the most talked-about musicians in the new style of jazz called bop.

In 1942, saxophonist Budd Johnson was urging Earl Hines to hire Parker from McShann's blues-oriented band. In December 1942, Johnson himself left Hines. Billy Eckstine then talked Hines into hiring Parker and buying a tenor sax for him even though Parker much preferred to play alto sax. The Hines band collapsed, but Eckstine held most of the avant-garde players together by hiring them for his band. In 1944, as this band started a tour toward St. Louis, a trumpeter became ill and was replaced temporarily by a young teenager named Miles Davis. Thus, the association between Davis and Parker began. "The key musicians each produced certain ideas independently, and when they came together in New York, they discovered their affinities and stimulated each other to further effort. Over a period of several years this produced a synthesis of new elements based on old that became known as modern jazz, or bop."[10]

Parker's first job as leader was in 1944 at the Spotlight Club on New York's Fifty-second Street after he had left Eckstine. His most mature jazz statements are generally conceded to be those recorded in 1945 under his name as leader: "KoKo," "Now's the Time," "Billie's Bounce," "Meandering," "Warming Up a Riff," and "Thriving from a Riff." On these records he shows a rich, expressive tone and unprecedented rhythmic freedom in his phrasing.

Parker's success was demonstrated by the fact that after World War II he was sometimes paid $1,200 a week by the same people who had hired him earlier for $2 a night.

In 1946, Parker spent seven months in Camarillo State Hospital in California. By 1949, because of a combination of ulcers, drugs, and alcohol, his playing began to decline. He was not considered reliable by booking offices, so employment began to be a problem. Some musicians never see the drug and alcohol problems affecting them, but Parker was very much aware that his career had been ruined by these mistakes. He constantly advised against such indulgence. Sonny Rollins tells of conversations along this line with Parker.

> Bird befriended quite a few guys. Sonny Stitt before me. With us and a few other cats, especially saxophone players, it was like a father thing. When we were hung up personally, we went just to talk to him, just to see him. The purpose of his whole existence was music and he showed me that music was the paramount

thing and anything that interfered with it I should stay away from. Later on I was able to take advantage of his advice, but he died before I had a chance to see him and tell him I had.[11]

In 1950, Parker recorded with strings (as did Gillespie). Although it was the fulfillment of a dream for Parker, his fans screamed that he had "gone commercial."

When Parker's young daughter Pree died of pneumonia, he seemed to decline for the last time both musically and physically. He died on March 12, 1955, at age thirty-three.

One of the trying aspects of Parker's career is that he knew that even among contemporary musicians only a few understood his music. Parker's abilities and contributions have, of course, been finally recognized. In fact, it would be extremely difficult to find a musician who is more recognized and so little understood.

In February 1942, one *Down Beat* reporter stated that Parker had a tendency to play too many notes. In July of that year, another reporter from the same magazine noted that Parker used a minimum of notes. To say that there was controversy and a lack of understanding of Parker's work even among his peers would be a gross understatement. Some who write and talk about jazz feel that Parker was the most important catalyst in the advancement of jazz. Surely, no one can doubt that he brought to culmination the many innovations of the 1940s and 1950s, more changes than had previously occurred in the history of jazz.

Parker was one of the rare musicians who could play slow blues very well but was also comfortable at extremely fast tempos. Most of what Parker played was based on the blues: "Now's the Time," "Cool Blues," and others.

One of Parker's most impressive assets was his use of rhythmic nuances. "Relaxin' at Camarillo" shows how beautifully these can be applied to the standard blues form. Of course, Parker had an impeccable ear and virtuosity on the alto saxophone that could be exploited unconsciously rather than being contrived. When a musician realizes what Parker was able to invent within the six-note phrase in "Embraceable You," the musician hears developments leading to Sonny Rollins and others. Parker used the phrase repeatedly, but he also changed each time, demonstrating a creativeness worthy of Mozart, Beethoven, and others who composed great music from motifs. Most musicians agree that as advanced as Parker's style was, he never seemed to lose sight of the early jazz roots. Some casual observers seem surprised that Parker could appreciate all kinds of music that were performed well—classical music as well as early jazz.

Parker thought that there must be something in jazz improvisation that had not been done before because he thought that he could hear things that he could not play. By continually working over his favorite tune, "Cherokee," he finally found that he could play what he had been hearing by developing melodic lines from the higher harmonics of the chords. Parker freed the solo aspect of jazz not only melodically and harmonically but also rhythmically. Those who follow him can benefit from this freedom, not necessarily from copying his actual phrases.

It is true that drummers Kenny Clarke and Max Roach developed new rhythmic approaches, Thelonious Monk new harmonic approaches, Dizzy Gillespie new solo directions, and so on. But it did seem to be Charlie Parker who brought all these elements to maturity in bop. Parker's playing was the realization of the potential of what was available; Parker's influence, like Armstrong's earlier, extended to all instruments.

> Parker's achievements are unique and for a continually sick man almost incredible. It is hard to imagine what he would have accomplished given a long and healthy life. In many ways his admirers got more out of his life than Parker did himself but, in the end, he is not a man to be pitied. On all but his darkest days he experienced the joy of creation that is given few men to know and he enriched the lives of all those who could respond to his work.[12]

There has never been a greater dedication to a jazz musician than *To Bird with Love* by Societo Wizlov (La Cure, 86310, Antigny, France), a 424-page epic on Parker.

Bud Powell

Bud Powell should rightfully share the honors of the bop era with such luminaries as Parker and Gillespie. Powell, who came from a musical family, won prizes as a schoolboy for his Bach recitals. He brought this advanced technique and his harmonic acuity into the bop community, where he was welcomed most openly. Powell then became an established member of the Fifty-second Street scene before he moved to France in 1959, where he received the recognition to which he was entitled.

Powell's left-hand *voicings* proved to be his major contribution to jazz piano playing. Although he used the same chords as other players, his choice of notes and how they were voiced (spaced) on the piano were so fresh and innovative that they were adopted by many players to follow. Powell was known for his ability to play accurately at fast tempos. His improvisations might be considered classic bebop—high energy, well-defined, and inspired.

Powell's early death did not deprive jazz listeners of a worthwhile legacy. He recorded solo albums and was well represented on many recordings in his chosen style. Powell, a seemingly logical piano heir to Art Tatum's reign, was truly a pioneer in bop piano. He played with the John Kirby and Dizzy Gillespie groups, as well as others, but was constantly plagued by mental illnesses, which began when he was only twenty-one. In spite of this, re-pressings by both Verve and Blue Note record companies, as well as recordings with Parker and Gillespie, attest to his contributions[13] ("Un Poco Loco").

Thelonious Monk

Thelonious Sphere Monk's importance to the development of jazz, and bebop in particular, was not readily recognized. He studied piano from a young age and won amateur competitions at the Apollo Theater, proving his mastery of the instrument. His mature piano style developed into one of the most recognizable (and at times controversial) of any jazz pianist before him. He is credited along with Parker and Gillespie with developing the bop style.

Monk was situated right at the front edge of bop's development. He joined the house band at Minton's Playhouse in Harlem at age nineteen. There he worked with the two major figures of bop, Charlie Parker and Dizzy Gillespie. In 1947 he made his first recordings for Blue Note, which documented his unique style of melody and composition.

vamping

Thelonious Monk

Monk's piano style tended to be both sparse and disjunct. He often played dissonant intervals and chord clusters that one might at first think were simply mistakes. However, this fragmented style proved to be out of a sense of play and compositional intent and became his improvisational signature. His playing style was not always appreciated. When playing on "Swing Spring" with Milt Jackson, Miles Davis, Percy Heath, and Kenny Clarke, Monk *lays out* (does not play) behind Davis's solos. It is believed that Miles didn't like Monk's unique comping style and had him lay out until his solo was over.

Monk spent sixty days in jail on a narcotics charge, which resulted in his loss of his Cabaret Card. Without the card he could not work in New York City. However, he could still record. Monk played with Miles Davis and Sonny Rollins as well as Charlie Parker for Prestige Records in the years that followed.

Two of his most memorable recordings were for Riverside Records, *Brilliant Corners* and *Thelonious Monk with John Coltrane*, which placed him on the world map as both a pianist and composer. In 1957 the Thelonious Monk Quartet, which included John Coltrane, gained critical acclaim when they played regularly at the Five Spot. Monk went on to tour the United States and Europe until the 1970s, when he played only on occasion.

When Monk improvised, he did not simply play variations; sometimes he fragmented lines and at other times elaborated on them. He often started with a basic phrase and, like Sonny Rollins on the tenor sax, played the phrase in

listening guide

(CD 2, track 3)
Thelonious Monk with the Miles Davis All Stars
"Bags' Groove"

This excerpt features the piano solo of Thelonious Monk. Listen for the overall shape of the solo created from a single melodic idea. Monk takes an amazingly economical approach to the use of melody throughout the solo but still creates an effective solo structure.

:00   Notice the simple beginning motive and how it begins to be transformed.

:18   Second chorus: motive becomes more angular.

:37   Third chorus: motive takes a new shape that is maintained throughout the chorus with scattered chordal support.

:55   Fourth chorus: motive takes on a harmonic shape developed from the chordal shapes used in the previous chorus.

1:15   Fourth chorus: open melody with silence between the short motivic statements. He begins to introduce some dissonant notes as part of the motive.

1:33   Fifth chorus: sparse melodic approach continues with the use of unexpected ending notes in the motive, which proves to be very dramatic.

1:51   Sixth chorus: dissonant intervals (2 notes close together) to accent the motivic statements. This type of melodic activity became a trademark of Monk's style.

2:10   Seventh chorus: the motive is reduced even further in size.

2:29   Eighth chorus: simple chord punctuations that are separated by a lot of silence; notice the open quality of the chords and how sparsely they are voiced.

2:48   End.

almost every conceivable manner. However, he received recognition for his composing before he was accepted as an innovating pianist.

Works written by Monk are more compositional than other newly composed bop tunes of the day. Bop tunes were often a melody (head) written over familiar bop chords. Monk tended to blend the melodic lines with his harmonies, which were often more dissonant and inventive that the standard harmonies. Both the melodies and harmonies were often fragmented and economical—fewer notes but more distinctive ones. His improvisational style followed this same compostitional appraoch.

An example of Monk's strong influence is the effect he had on John Coltrane. Already a proven player, when he joined Monk's combo, he had to struggle with the repertoire. But after his experience in the group, Monk's influence on Coltrane was firmly imprinted. It was as if Monk were able to open Coltrane's ears and point out possible directions as yet unconceived by the saxophonist[14] (Thelonious Monk, "Misterioso," "Evidence," "Criss Cross," and "I Should Care"; Miles Davis's All Stars, "Bags' Groove," "Misterioso").

Thelonious Sphere Monk died in February 1982.

J. J. Johnson

Trombone playing did not contribute to the beginning of the bop style. Trombone players who had the virtuosity to play this style were not sufficiently interested at first, as it required a highly developed technique as well as understanding. J. J. Johnson proved to trombonists that the style was possible on the instrument.

Johnson's smooth and clean style of playing proved perfect for the bop style, and listeners often thought that he was not playing a slide trombone but one with valves like a trumpet, which would make it much easier to play fast melodic lines. He says that his early influences were Parker and Gillespie. Johnson, in turn, became the leading influence for all trombonists that would follow. Kai Winding, Frank Rosolino, and many others followed his lead.

BOP AND PROGRESSIVE BIG BANDS

When large bands used bop harmonic and melodic developments, the jazz was labeled *progressive*. At first, the only contributions in this direction were solos in big bands by such musicians as Gillespie and Parker, but soon entire bands were dedicated to these new directions. The progressive bandleaders included Stan Kenton (who even adopted the label "progressive"),[15] Woody Herman, Earl Hines, Billy Eckstine, Boyd Raeburn, and Gillespie himself. The Boyd Raeburn band played music as far removed from the earlier swing bands as could be envisioned.

Billy Eckstine

Billy Eckstine, having built a following as a ballad singer with Earl Hines, formed a band including almost every leading bop player at one time[16] (Billy Eckstine, "Good Jelly Blues"). Between 1944 and 1946, his female singer was Sarah Vaughan. The Earl Hines and Billy Eckstine bands of this type reached their peak during a record ban, so there is not much recorded documentation of them. (Record bans occur when the musicians' union strikes against the record companies.) Eckstine's band dates from June 1944 to February 1947. Some of the consequences of the ban included limited audience appeal for the new music, bans on recording by the musicians' union, and lack of sympathy, cooperation, and encouragement from record companies when there was no ban.

At times Eckstine's band was a financial success, but when the orchestra disbanded, Eckstine was left somewhat in debt. Gillespie was the musical director of Eckstine's band. Their first records sold mainly because of Eckstine's fine vocals. In fact, his vocals, along with those of Sarah Vaughan, were the band's best means of communication with both the public and the recording executives. In 1944, when Gillespie left the Billy Eckstine band, he was first replaced by Fats Navarro and then by Miles Davis, who remained with the band until

vamping

Sarah Vaughan

Sarah Vaughan played piano with the Earl Hines orchestra and later became a featured vocalist. As a pianist, her knowledge of harmony greatly influenced her ability to sing scat as well as ballads. Vaughan sang for presidents and toured the world with rhythm sections, a cappella choirs, jazz combos, large jazz bands, and symphony orchestras. One of her best albums—*I Love Brazil*— was recorded in Brazil in 1977[17] ("All Alone," "My Funny Valentine," "Key Largo").

Vaughan has influenced many singers, and she was considerably influenced by those musicians with whom she worked. This most impressive list includes Dizzy Gillespie, Earl Hines, Charlie Parker, Miles Davis, Clifford Brown, Herbie Mann, Cannonball Adderley, the Count Basie Band, Thad Jones, Jimmy Rowles, Michel Legrand, and Bob James. It is no wonder that her creative vocalizing was so steeped in jazz. Sarah Vaughan died in 1990.

it disbanded in 1947. George Hoefer of *Down Beat* described what happened when Davis first joined the band for a short stay in 1944:

> Trumpeter Anderson was taken seriously ill shortly after the band's arrival in St. Louis and was hospitalized. On the night the band opened at the Riviera, the first customer was a high school student with a trumpet under his arm. Gillespie asked him if he had a union card, and Miles Davis, 16, of East St. Louis, said that he did. The music director told him to go up on the stand and see what he could do.
>
> "Miles," Eckstine later said, "he sounded terrible." Davis recalled, "I couldn't read the book, I was so busy listening to Bird and Dizzy." He played a few nights with the band and then headed for Juilliard in New York.[18]

The band eventually recorded a variety of jazz for National Records, including up-tempo works, ballads, and blues. Eckstine can even be heard on valve trombone solos. The trend was for vocalists to be more successful attractions than bands, and Eckstine surely must be considered one of the finest singers to come out of jazz or any other background.

Stan Kenton

Stan Kenton, who was continually an influential pioneer in jazz, had been working as a pianist in Los Angeles before organizing his first band in Balboa, California, in 1941. Kenton stated that he soon became aware of the adventurous excitement of jazz players and began to base his repertoire on the talents of the excellent musicians who passed through his band. Great credit should be accorded Kenton for having never compromised what to him was art for the comfort and safety of more commercial aspects of big bands. Kenton added Jack Costanzo to play Latin rhythms in 1948, furthering this direction in contemporary jazz.[19]

Gillespie's Bop Band

In 1945, Gillespie organized his first big band, preferring the larger band at a time when all other bop advocates were performing in combos. His first big

Stan Kenton

Dizzy Gillespie

listening guide

(CD 2, track 4)
**Dizzy Gillespie and His Big Band
in Concert with Chano Pozo**
"Manteca"

:00   Count off.

:04   Bass enters followed by other members
of the rhythm section.

:11   Saxophones sneak into rhythmic mix and
crescendo with the rest of the rhythm
section.

:18   Trumpets join in.

:21   Trumpet accent chords punctuate a rapid
trumpet solo.

:31   Brass shout ends the intro with a falling
glissando.

:36   Rhythm section lead into the opening
chorus, which has the saxophones with
the lead melodic motive with responding
brass punches.

:50   Repeat.

1:01   New section with more melodic saxophone lines. Notice the active bass line.

1:09   Brass response.

1:11   Trumpet solo.

1:21   Saxophones return with brass punches.

1:32   Rhythm section interlude. Notice the
entrance of the low trombone and the
syncopated sax accents as a crescendo
builds, ending in high-energy brass
chords that launch the tenor saxophone
solo in the background.

1:50   Saxophone solo. Notice the rhythm section has changed to a more traditional
swing feel.

2:05   Brass enter again as a transition to the
trumpet solo.

2:14   Trumpet solo. Notice the bebop style
used during this solo.

2:26   Return to the opening section with the
return to a more Latin feel.

2:37   Rhythm section alone with shouts from
the band. Notice the clave in the rhythm
section (an important element of the Latin
rhythm section).

3:07   Conga solo begins.

3:48   Soloist stops suddenly.

3:51   Conga returns with cross rhythms.

3:57   Solo moves to other lower drums.

4:11   A steady beat is established.

4:38   Decrescendo.

4:44   Crescendo with the addition of cymbals.

5:00   Big accents on drums and cymbals.

5:17   Sudden stop.

5:19   Latin rhythm begins as in the intro with a
call and response among members of the
band.

5:52   New rhythm in the bass drum.

6:08   Return to the opening chorus with saxophones and brass punches.

6:22   Rhythm section interlude.

6:48   Low heavy drum beat returns.

7:03   Return to the opening chorus.

7:20   End of brass glissando waiting for the
final chord.

7:22   Final chord.

7:32   End.

band, called Hep-Sations, was short-lived. Gillespie became interested in African-Cuban rhythms after having performed with Cuban orchestras around New York. In 1947, he added Chano Pozo to his band to bring Latin American and West African rhythms to jazz. With the addition of Pozo, the gap between bop and the $\frac{4}{4}$ meter of swing became more apparent. The followers of Gillespie's trumpet excursions included Fats Navarro, Kenny Dorham, Miles Davis (early in his career), Clifford Brown, Thad Jones, Donald Byrd, Pete and Conte Condoli, Freddie Hubbard, Wynton Marsalis, and Jon Faddis.

It should also be noted that Gillespie was the first to take a jazz band on tour for the U.S. State Department. His band, composed of both black and white musicians, helped to relieve diplomatic tension in some parts of the world.

SWING TO CUBOP

By the late 1940s, most all of the big swing bands had Latin numbers in their repertoires. As the bands became more progressive in scope, Latin jazz found a fertile connection with the jazz mainstream. A signature composition of this time is Dizzy Gillespie's "A Night in Tunisia" for the Earl Hines big band. Gillespie is clearly the most important figure in the effort to import Latin music into the developing jazz mainstream. His work in Calloway's band and his association with Mario Bauzá offered a fertile ground for Latin jazz to take hold. Stan Kenton also developed a new band at this time and issued three recordings that were clearly Latin-influenced—"Taboo," "Adios," and "The Nango."

One of the most important Latin jazz groups at this time was Machito's Afro-Cubans. It was this group's musical director, Mario Bauzá, who found the formula for shaping future Latin jazz orchestras. First, he enlarged Machito's group to better parallel the American orchestras. Then, he hired arrangers from the Calloway and Chick Webb bands to write for the new group. The result was a blend that included the Cuban repertoire and rhythm section with a trumpet and sax front line more typical of the African American bands. This Afro-Cuban blend is still a vital musical stream in Latin jazz.

As the progressive big bands like that of Gillespie adopted the music of these early Afro-Cuban bands, the new bop style of the Latin jazz movement was clearly under way. At the same time, the slang term *cubop* began surfacing to describe this fusion. The seminal moment for this style may well have been in 1947, when Cuban conga player Chano Pozo played with Dizzy Gillespie's bebop big band, which produced a true blend of authentic Afro-Cuban percussion with an established jazz ensemble.

Similar to the collaboration of Gillespie and Bauzá was the experimental work shared by Stan Kenton and Machito. Kenton's commitment to and interest in Latin music resulted in a number of compositions that helped place him in the forefront of progressive jazz. Throughout the 1940s, Machito and his brother-in-law, Bauzá, were continually in the center of the cubop and Latin jazz movement. It was in their work that the partnership between the two parallel musical streams was inextricably merged.

THE MAMBO AND CUBOP

As cubop matured, another dance rhythm—the mambo—captured the attention of the jazz and Latin communities. A young timbalero and vibraphone player, Tito Puente, began to enjoy the success of leading Latin musicians Machito and Tito Rodriguez. In Puente's playing one could find Latin versions of jazz material as well as mambos that had a clear jazz swing. Jazz material was traditionally more harmonically complex than Latin material, while Latin rhythms were more complex than those of jazz. Puente would borrow the more complex harmonies of jazz for his Latin arrangements and, conversely, infuse his jazz performances with complex Latin rhythms. This fusion generated great excitement and variation in his performances.

Cubop and Latin jazz also continued to have a West Coast presence, primarily through the ongoing work of Kenton. Bassist Howard Rumsey, an alumnus of Kenton's band, also carried cubop and Latin jazz into his work with his Lighthouse All-Stars. Players like Shorty Rogers and Shelly Manne successfully combined straight jazz with Latin rhythms.

The influence of cubop began to appear in the compositions of bandleaders like Ellington ("Caravan") and Woody Herman (*Herman's Heat & Puente's Beat*, Evidence Music). The small-group format also embraced Latin influences. Puente's introduction of the vibraphone into the mambo surfaced in George Shearing's

listening guide

(CD 2, track 5)
Tito Puente
"Donna Lee"

This is an arrangement of the Charlie Parker classic "Donna Lee."

:00   Drum introduction; notice the interlocking drum patterns.

:24   Horn players enter with an introductory section that will appear again later as interludes between solos. Notice the cross-rhythms between the trombones (and bass player) and the other horn players (alto saxophone, trumpet, and piccolo).

:32   The melody (head) is played in unison by the saxophone, trumpet, and piccolo while the trombones and bass play an accompanying cross-rhythm.

:46   The second part of the head over the same chords.

:57   Alto saxophone lead-in to a solo over the same chords as the head. Notice the change in the rhythmic backup characterized by heavily syncopated cross-rhythms.

1:11   Second part of the solo chorus.

1:24   Second chorus with a new stop-time backup by the other horn players.

1:37   Horn players drop out, and solo continues for the second part of the second chorus.

1:50   Trumpet solo begins. Same backup is maintained.

2:02   Second part of first chorus.

2:15   Flügelhorn solo with the stop-time backup.

2:28   Second part of flügelhorn chorus.

2:40   Interlude similar to the introduction. Complex cross-rhythms are used.

2:50   Piccolo lead-in to solo.

2:53   Solo actually begins. Notice the bop phrasing and accents.

3:06   Second part of solo chorus.

3:19   Second chorus begins with the addition of the stop-time backup.

3:31   Second section of the second chorus.

3:44   Repeat of introduction.

3:50   Repeat of the opening head.

4:03   Second part of the head.

4:14   Drums alone to end the performance.

4:30   End.

quintet with Cal Tjader, and later in Tjader's Modern Mambo Quintet. Billy Taylor also recorded numbers like "I Love to Mambo" and "Candido Mambo." Charles Mingus found his personal approach in his 1957 "Tijuana Moods."

Gillespie continued his work with Latin jazz in a large-scale piece, *Manteca Suite,* which was performed by an ensemble typical of many Latin jazz groups. The horn players were well-known jazz players Ernie Royal and Quincy Jones, while the percussion section included Latin conga players Candido Camero and Mongo Santamaria. By the late 1950s, however, large-scale compositions like those of Gillespie and Kenton had given way to the works of smaller Latin jazz ensembles.

summary

By 1946, bop was being heard even in some commercial dance bands. Today, most good amateur players improvise in the bop style. Even most name jazz players perform in a manner directly related to the bop school. Some more than others show the effects of having worked through the cool and funky styles since bop, but the phrases, the harmonies, and the approach still seem to be quite clearly derived from bop.

Bop did not have a chance to emerge gradually for public listening as the other styles had. By the time the differences between the union and the record industry were resolved, bop was well advanced. One reason for its slow acceptance by listeners was that the public was saturated with bad publicity about bop that made the music appear more like a passing fad than an advance in the development of jazz. An example is the way in which the followers of Gillespie imitated his dark glasses, goatee, and beret. Fan magazines even began advertising "bebop ties."

After World War II, when bop started to be heard by more of the public, its radical departure from swing caused great consternation. Some of the older jazz players accepted the advance, but most rejected bop, feeling that it lacked the more desirable jazz characteristics: the emphasis on pulse, the theme-and-variations approach, and so on. However, the real opposition appeared to stem from jazz critics, which seems to be the case as each new innovation arrives on the jazz scene. The adverse reaction to bop resulted in the revival of simpler forms of jazz, such as Early New Orleans Dixieland. Oddly enough, Parker and Gillespie were not terribly far from the early roots of jazz. Parker's earliest recordings were blues numbers; Gillespie's earliest recording was "King Porter Stomp," written by Jelly Roll Morton.

These changes in jazz were a result of musicians constantly searching for new means of expression. The absence of an easily recognizable melody has been one of the main obstacles to the acceptance of bop by the general public. The complexities of the style of jazz demand deeper concentration and more attentive listening. Rex Harris suggests that bop should not be dismissed at first hearing: "No worthwhile form of music will yield its secret so readily as that."[20]

Bop music included some vocals, but bop players primarily thought instrumentally. Earlier players played as they would have sung, seeming to work over a melody. Bop players were much more involved with working over the chord progressions.

FOR FURTHER STUDY

1. Explain the term *bop*.

2. In what ways was this direction in the development of jazz a change from the swing era?

3. Compare the arrangements of bop music with those of the swing era.

4. What is meant by "extended harmonies"?

5. Why were bop ensembles able to employ a faster tempo than swing bands?

6. Why is the word *tension* most appropriate in describing the feeling of bop music?

7. In what manner did the percussionist obtain the effect of accent and punctuation?

8. Listen to Dizzy Gillespie's rendition of "Things to Come," and describe your reactions to the music.

9. An excellent example of the true bop sound is found on the album *Jazz at Massey Hall* in the selection "Wee" as played by Charlie Parker (credited as Charlie Chan), Dizzy Gillespie, Bud Powell, Max Roach, and Charles Mingus. Name the instrument featured in the solo spot that follows the short introduction. Do you hear the ascending and descending melodic playing of the string bass? Is the instrument bowed or plucked? Which instrument improvises next? What would you say about the range of tones this instrument realizes? What instrument is third? What instrument takes over in the wild climax?

10. Listen to Charlie Parker's Re-Boppers playing "KoKo" (not to be confused with Ellington's blues "Ko-Ko"). Parker's song borrows its chord changes from the song "Cherokee" and is a classic example of the true bop style of playing. Listen carefully to the interplay between the saxophone and trumpet as they toss the melody back and forth to the accompaniment of the exciting drummer Max Roach.

11. How does the fusion of cubop reflect both musical stylistic streams?

SUGGESTED ADDITIONAL LISTENING

Art Blakey and the Jazz Messengers. *Straight Ahead*. Concord Jazz Records, CJ-168.
Bebop. New World Records, 271.
The Be-Bop Era.
Bird and Diz. Verve Records, V6-8006.
Bird Symbols. Charlie Parker Records, PLP-407.
Bird—The Savoy Recordings (Master Takes). Savoy Records, SJL-2201.

Charlie Parker. Everest Records, FS-254.

Charlie Parker. Prestige Records, 24009.

Charlie Parker. Savoy Records, S5J5500.

Charlie Parker in Historical Recordings. Le Jazz Cool Records, JC102.

Charlie Parker Memorial Album. Savoy Records, MG-12000.

Charlie Parker Story, vols. 1–3. Verve Records, V6-8000-1-2.

Echoes of an Era. Roulette Records, RE-105.

Eckstine, Billy. *Mister B and the Band—the Savoy Sessions.* Savoy Records, SJL-2214.

Essential Charlie Parker. Verve Records, V-8409.

The Genius of Bud Powell. Verve Records, VE2-2506.

The Genius of Charlie Parker. Savoy Records, MG-12014.

Giants of Jazz. Atlantic Records, 2-905.

Gillespie, Dizzy. *Big 4.* Pablo Records, 23107.

———. *In the Beginning.* Prestige Records, 24030.

———. *The Great Dizzy Gillespie.* Counterpoint Records, 554.

Greatest Jazz Concert Ever. Prestige Records, 24024.

Jazz at Massey Hall. Fantasy Records, 6003.

Jazz in Revolution—the Big Bands in the 1940s. New World Records, 284.

Kenton, Stan. *The Kenton Era.* The Creative World of Stan Kenton, ST-1030.

Monk, Thelonious. *Genius of Thelonious Monk.* Prestige Records, 7656.

———. *Memorial Album.* Milestone Records, M-47064.

———. *Straight, No Chaser.* Columbia Records, CS-9451.

Original Recordings. Onyx Records, 221.

Smithsonian Collection of Classic Jazz, vols. 7 and 8.

Strictly Bebop. Capitol Records, ML-11059.

ADDITIONAL READING RESOURCES

Berendt, Joachim. *The New Jazz Book,* 17–19, 61–70.

Dankworth, Avril. *Jazz: An Introduction to Its Musical Basis,* 68–75.

Dexter, Dave. *The Jazz Story,* 121–31.

Feather, Leonard. *The Book of Jazz.*

———. *Inside Jazz.*

Francis, André. *Jazz,* 107–15, 124–30.

Harrison, Max. *Charlie Parker.*

———. "Thelonious Monk," *Musician and Musicians,* London, May 1982.

Hodeir, André. *Jazz: Its Evolution and Essence,* 99–115.

Keepnews, Orrin. "The Monk of Jazz: Memories of Thelonious, The Legendary Pianist," *Washington Post,* 18 February 1982.

Reisner, Robert G. *Bird: The Legend of Charlie Parker.*

Russell, Ross. *Bird Lives: The High Life and Hard Times of Charlie (Yardbird) Parker.*

Shapiro, Nat, and Hentoff, Nat, eds. *The Jazz Makers,* 332–48.

Stearns, Marshall. *The Story of Jazz,* 155–72.

Williams, Martin T. *The Jazz Tradition,* 187–213.

Wilson, John S. "Thelonious Monk, Created Wry Jazz Melodies and Harmonies," *New York Times,* 23 February 1982, D20.

Note: Complete information, including name of publisher and date of publication, is provided in this book's bibliography.

NOTES

1. From Henry Pleasants, *Serious Music and All That Jazz,* 1969. Reprinted by permission of Simon & Schuster, Inc.
2. Charlie Hore, "Jazz—A People's Music?" Issue 61 of *International Socialism Journal,* Winter 1993. Copyright © International Socialism.
3. Charlie Parker, "Yardbird Suite," *Bird Symbols,* Charlie Parker Records, PLP-407.
4. Dizzy Gillespie and Charlie Parker, "Wee," *Jazz at Massey Hall,* Fantasy Records, 6003; *Big Band Jazz,* Smithsonian Collection of Recordings.
5. Al Casey, "How High the Moon," *The History of Jazz,* vol. 4; Charlie Parker, "Ornithology," *Bird Symbols,* Charlie Parker Records, PLP-407.
6. Roy Eldridge, *Dale's Wail,* Verve Records, MGV-8089.
7. Gunther Schuller, *The Swing Era* (London: Oxford University Press, 1989), 347.
8. Dizzy Gillespie and the All Stars, "Leap Here," *Dizzy Gillespie, Jazz Story,* vol. 5; *Dizzy Gillespie,* RCA Victor Records, LPV 530; *Essential,* Verve Records, 68566; *The Greatest Names in Jazz;* "Carombola," *History of Jazz,* vol. 4; *Dizzy Gillespie: Composer's Concepts,* Mercury EmArcy Records, EMS-2-410; *Dizzy Gillespie and Stan Getz,* Verve Records, VE 2-2521; *Benny Carter and Dizzy Gillespie,* Pablo Records, 231-0781; *Bahiana,* Pablo Records, 262-5708; *Big Band Jazz,* Smithsonian Collection of Recordings.
9. Jay McShann, "Sepian Bounce," *Encyclopedia of Jazz,* vol. 3, Decca Records, DL 8400, and *Encyclopedia of Jazz on Records,* vol. 3.
10. Max Harrison, *Charlie Parker* (New York: A. S. Barnes, 1961), 17.
11. Harrison, *Charlie Parker,* 64–65.
12. Harrison, *Charlie Parker,* 74.
13. Bud Powell, *The Amazing Bud Powell,* vols. 1 and 2, Blue Note Records, 81503-4.
14. Thelonious Monk, *Thelonious Monk,* Prestige Records, 24006; *Brilliant Corners,* Riverside Records, RLP 12-226; *Monk's Dream,* Columbia Special Products, JCS-8765; *The Thelonious Monk Orchestra at Town Hall,* Riverside Records, 1138; Miles Davis, "Bags' Groove, Take 1," *Bags' Groove,* Prestige Records, 7109; *Misterioso,* Columbia Records, CS-9236.
15. Stan Kenton, *Kenton in Stereo,* The Creative World of Stan Kenton, ST 1004.
16. Billy Eckstine Orchestra, *Big Band Jazz,* Smithsonian Collection of Recordings.
17. Sarah Vaughan, *Sarah Vaughan,* Archive of Folk Music, FS-250; *Sarah Vaughan,* Trip Records, 5501; *Live in Japan,* Mainstream Records, 401; *Swings Easy,* Trip Records, 5511; *Love Brazil,* Pablo Records, 2312101.
18. George Hoefer, "The First Big Bop Band," *Down Beat* 32, no. 16 (July 1965): 21.
19. Stan Kenton, *Cuban Fire,* The Creative World of Stan Kenton, ST 1008.
20. Rex Harris, *Jazz* (Baltimore: Penguin Books, 1956), 188.

9

Cool/Third Stream

The direction of jazz is determined by three things: the men, their instruments, and the times.[1]

from *The Jazz World*

Just as the bop style of jazz offered a strong contrast to swing, the cool style of playing is markedly different from the complexities of bop.

Bop was an exciting and intense music. It reflected a new type of virtuosity that set it apart from swing. *Cool* stepped away from the fiery performance and aggressive playing style to one of understatement. The tempos relaxed and virtuosity gave way to subtle instrumental colors and a reserved tonal style. The size of the performance group also expanded from the typical bop quintet to include new instrumental colors. The individual voices in the ensemble yielded to compositional design, and players assumed an attitude of emotional detachment that helped define what it meant to be cool.

Unlike the large swing bands that were designed to fill large dance halls, the cool ensembles—while again larger than the bop groups—were designed to find new and subtle tonal colors. The swing bands can be compared to the symphonic orchestras of classical music and the cool bands more to the somewhat smaller and more delicate chamber ensembles that perform in more intimate settings. In the cool style, jazz found its chamber ensembles.

Instruments not common in jazz now found prominence in the cool ensembles, and their players often had received conservatory training. Chico Hamilton, a drummer, was surprisingly a leader in the new direction.[2] Of course, Hamilton was no ordinary drummer, as indicated by his subtle rhythmic control and use of different drum pitches and timbres. One of his surprises was that he featured Fred Katz on cello.[3] (For an introduction to cool jazz, listen to Interactive Guide 7 at the Online Learning Center or directly from http://www.emegill.com/listening.)

The bowed sounds of the violin and other stringed instruments (excepting the string bass) did not compete well in the normally percussive landscape of a jazz ensemble, but in cool they could become important voices in the composition. Despite the limited use of stringed instruments, there are several important string players who contributed to jazz, such as Jean Luc Ponty, Noel Pointer, Leroy Jenkins, Joe Venuti, Stuff Smith, Eddie South,[4] Ray Nance, and Stephane Grappelli[5] (Joe Venuti, "My Honey's Loving Arms"; Eddie South, "Hejre Kati"; Stuff Smith, "Knock Knock"). Edgar Redmond, a woodwind player, has put forth much effort to enlighten music educators along this line and has produced an excellent album to prove his point.[6]

Modern Jazz Quartet © Institute of Jazz Studies, Rutgers University

listening guide

Interactive Guide 7
Cool

:00 Ensemble chorus (flute lead and flügelhorn harmony); bass, guitar, and drums keep a relaxed $\frac{4}{4}$ rhythm while piano plays fill-ins. The use of exotic instruments (for jazz) was common in the cool style.

:09 Second phrase.

:18 Third phrase.

:27 Flute solo (one chorus); listen also for continued piano fill-ins. Notice that even in the faster melodic areas there is still a relaxed feeling important to cool.

:55 Ensemble chorus (same as first chorus). Cool ensembles were often written arrangements that tied the style to third stream at times. The written arrangements offered more complex orchestration possibilities as composers looked for new tone colors.

1:04 Second phrase.

1:14 Third phrase.

1:26 End.

The **tonal sonorities** of these conservative players could be compared to pastel colors, whereas the solos of Gillespie and his followers could be compared to fiery red colors. Marshall Stearns thought of cool as a new "kind of jazz which could be quite easily arranged . . . by conservatory-trained musicians with a real feeling for contrapuntal jazz in an extended form."[7] By the extended form, Stearns refers to the fact that this new style was not restricted to twelve-, sixteen-, and thirty-two-measure choruses. Cool players devised a way to go even further than bop players in the direction of freedom from the square-cut divisions of jazz music. For example, in playing a thirty-two-bar chorus, the soloist would play a little into the next player's chorus, causing the second soloist to play into the third soloist's chorus in order to play thirty-two bars, and so on (see example 9.1). This helped the music flow as a continuous entity and erased the conception of a block type of form. By 1950, the acceptance of the long-playing record made possible the recording of longer works and longer improvisations.

This music sacrificed excitement for subtlety, and the players underplayed their variations. André Hodeir analyzed cool music according to three principal characteristics: "First, a sonority very different from the one adopted by earlier schools; second, a special type of phrase; and finally, an orchestral conception that . . . is not its least interesting element."[8] These three characteristics deserve examination. The most pronounced difference from the preceding eras was the more delicate **attack** used by the cool players. Little or no vibrato was used,

Example 9.1

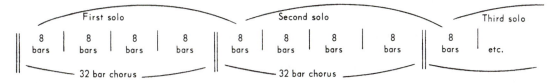

and the wind players had a tendency to use the **middle registers** rather than the extremes. The delicate attacks used in the cool era and the lack of vibrato caused the playing to resemble that of classical playing, although relaxation was more salient to this style of jazz than to the classical performances.[9] It should also be noted that increasing numbers of schooled players were entering the jazz field.

In general, cool phrasing did not permit the player to deviate far from the original line. Some critics consider this backtracking rather than an advance. Even with their melodic charm, these lines often lacked the richness and boldness of music of the bop era. The cool players conceived their harmonic parts polyphonically, an approach that gave the instrumentalist an independence of line not found in the swing era.

THE SOUNDS OF COOL

The chamber-type orchestral groups or combos were usually composed of three to eight players. The introduction of instruments not previously associated with jazz changed the overall sound: the flute became important as a jazz instrument, as did the French horn, oboe, and cello. Important flute players include Paul Horn,[10] Buddy Collette, Herbie Mann,[11] Bud Shank, Frank Wess, and others. The soft sounds of the French horn fit beautifully with the general feeling of cool jazz. Although Willie Ruff, Johnny Graas,[12] Junior Collins, and Julius Watkins deserve mention, there has nevertheless been a scarcity of jazz French horn players.

Playing jazz on double-reed instruments is still not common. Bob Cooper began playing jazz on the oboe while he was with Stan Kenton. Today, fresh blues and other jazz formats can be heard on the oboe on records by Yusef Lateef[13] and Rahsaan Roland Kirk. The oboe and other double-reed instruments, new to jazz, fit in well with the more standard instruments (trumpet, trombone, and saxophone) when the standard instruments are played in a cool manner as individual instruments instead of as parts of a section. The tuba was brought into jazz for the first time since the earliest Dixieland period and was given slow-moving melodic lines instead of the familiar bass parts of marches.

The **flügelhorn** worked its way into the jazz scene mainly through the efforts of Miles Davis, Clark Terry, and Art Farmer.[14] The flügel, as it is often called, is in the same key and pitch as the B-flat trumpet and cornet. It has a conical bore and, as a consequence, a darker, more mellow sound; it is also easier to play at a low register and harder to play at a high register than the trumpet. The most enjoyable examples are the Clark Terry–Bob Brookmeyer recordings that team flügelist Terry with the talented and tasteful valve trombonist Brookmeyer.[15]

The cool players established that jazz need not be confined to $\frac{4}{4}$ and $\frac{2}{4}$ meters and that choruses need not always be divided symmetrically. Many new meter signatures came into use in jazz, including $\frac{3}{4}$, $\frac{5}{4}$, $\frac{9}{4}$, and others. Successful jazz compositions often used an interchange of signatures within a selection. Pianist Dave Brubeck stimulated interest by laying one rhythm or more over another, creating both polyrhythms and **polymeters.**[16] Don Ellis carried the use of meters new in jazz much further (see Chapter 15).

This school of jazz moved closer to classical music, even to the point of adopting such forms as rondos and fugues.[17] The use of classical forms in jazz has sometimes been categorized as **third-stream music.** At times, however, the Modern Jazz Quartet (and other groups) used the fugue and similar forms just to play good, swinging, subtle jazz and gave no thought to third-stream music. It should also be noted that the quartet played classical forms quite precisely. For example, the fugues it played were truly baroque in form except that the exposition parts were improvised. The Modern Jazz Quartet performed from 1951 to 1974. After a hiatus, they regrouped in 1981.

The public seemed quite divided in its attitude toward cool players. Some people felt that the musicians were bored and arrogant or disdainful and cold. Others considered the cool players to be creative, hardworking, serious musicians, not clowns trying to be impressive. They understood that the players were in fact saying, "Like my music for itself."

COOL BANDS

Cool developed gradually, as did previous styles. For example, saxophonist Benny Carter underplayed his attacks. Teddy Wilson played the piano with a delicate touch, and Benny Goodman stopped using the thick vibrato of Jimmy Noone and other clarinetists. Miles Davis's solo on Charlie Parker's "Chasin' the Bird" in 1947 and John Lewis's piano solo on Dizzy Gillespie's record of "Round Midnight" in 1948 also anticipated the cool era. However, it took Lester Young to prove that great swing could be generated without using any of the aggressive performance practices typical of earlier jazz styles.

Much of the compositional interest in the cool period was presaged by the arranger/composers of the swing era. During that period, like cool, the individual performer's voice was restricted to make room for the composer's intent. Benny Carter was one of those arranger/composers who set the stage for the future composers. His work in the early swing period helped establish the format used by most swing bands to follow. He later composed for many and quite different types of groups and media, including film and television. Carter was among the few performers who played, performed, and recorded on both saxophone and trumpet.

Of all the bands in the swing period it was Ellington's that demonstrated in compositions the colors that could be extracted from a larger ensemble, an interest pursued by the later arranger/composers of the cool period.

Near the end of the 1940s, two large bands that seemed to have entirely different feelings and directions were quite influential in the beginnings of

cool: Claude Thornhill's band from about 1946 to 1949 and Woody Herman's band from 1947 to 1949. Both were instrumental in directing the trend away from the hot feel toward the cool feel.

Woody Herman

Woody Herman was the type of bandleader who always seemed to make changes in his personnel to keep the band up-to-date. He formed a band in Los Angeles in 1947 after he had disbanded for three months. This band had a saxophone section that influenced the workings of sax sections that followed. He hired Sam Marowitz on alto; Stan Getz, Zoot Sims, and Herbie Stewart on tenors; and Serge Chaloff on baritone. From this group (not using alto sax) came the famous "Four Brothers" sound. This was a tightly knit, beautifully blended section of four excellent jazz players who again disproved the theory that good improvisers are too individualistic to coordinate well. (The tune "Four Brothers," incidentally, was written by another talented reed player, Jimmy Giuffre.) Another boost for the cool advocate was the recording by the Herman band of Ralph Burns's "Early Autumn," a record that alone was enough to launch the career of Stan Getz.[18]

Claude Thornhill

The Claude Thornhill band, in addition to a tuba and a French horn player, had such talented musicians as Lee Konitz on alto sax, Gerry Mulligan on baritone sax and as arranger, and Gil Evans also as arranger[19] (Claude Thornhill, "Donna Lee"). The nucleus of this band made the first Miles Davis–Gil Evans records. One of the several recording bans was lifted in December 1948, and the way

Gerry Mulligan

was open for the three recording sessions in 1949 and 1950 for an album that was eventually called *Birth of the Cool*[20] ("Boplicity").

As for his part in these recordings, Miles Davis believed that at the time he was interested in nothing more original than playing with a lighter sound; it

vamping

Chatting with Gerry Mulligan

An excerpt of a question-and-answer session with Gerry Mulligan throws a little light on how the *Birth of the Cool* album was created. Notice the role that composition had in these recording sessions.

Question: Was the fact that so many men on the Miles Davis dates came from the Thornhill band coincidental?

Mulligan: No, the Thornhill orchestra was a tremendous influence on that small band. Because the instrumentation, when you get down to it,

was a reduced version of what Claude was using at the time.

Question: Was this an attempt to get away from the conventional bop format?

Mulligan: No, the idea was just to try to get a good little rehearsal band together. Something to write for.

Question: Then it was more or less regarded as a workshop experiment?

Mulligan: Yes. As far as the "Cool Jazz" part of it, all of that comes after the fact of what it was designed to be.[21]

was more expressive, he thought. At any rate, the recordings of this nine-man orchestra did set the tone for the cool era. Mulligan wrote "Jeru," "Venus de Milo," "Rocker," and "Godchild"; Gil Evans contributed "Boplicity" and "Moon Dreams"; John Lewis wrote "Move," "Budo," and "Rouge"; and John Carisi wrote "Israel."

The George Shearing Quintet also influenced the beginning of cool. Shearing, a classically trained pianist originally from England, can play in any style of jazz or classical music that he cares to. One of his favorite approaches is to play bop-type thoughts in a subtle manner, thus making a good transition from one era to the next.[22]

THE PERFORMERS

Miles Davis and Gil Evans

If jazz favored an oral tradition with bop, it reversed its direction as cool began to emerge. Although we often associate cool with the small-group sounds of players like Miles Davis and Chet Baker, the inspiration for much of the early cool influence came out of the experimentation of a New York group centered on the compositional talents of Gil Evans. This mostly white group was interested in finding a new sound that was not as aggressive as the bop expression. Their interest also included a wider range of instruments than was being used in small-group jazz. Gerry Mulligan brought the baritone saxophone to prominence in this medium, and the arrangements of Gil Evans made use of string instruments as well as other, nontraditional, jazz instruments.

The experimentations of these men gained more focus when Miles Davis joined the group and was able to get them into a recording studio. The result was the album *Birth of the Cool*. The sound that accompanied these arrangements was extremely underspoken with an interest in harmonic color outweighing bop's interest in harmonic complexity. The tempos of the style were relaxed as the music cooled down. Much like bop, the musicians were now making conscious decisions to move in a new direction in response to previous styles.

Unlike the music of Dixieland or bop, the music of cool was as much associated with the arranger (and Gil Evans, in particular) as it was with the players. As we saw above, in the late 1940s the Herman and Thornhill bands consciously moved away from the bop sounds to a cool jazz feel. Many of the seminal members of cool in New York came out of the Thornhill band—for example, arranger Gil Evans and saxophonists Lee Konitz and Gerry Mulligan. Gil Evans continued his relationship with Miles Davis to write other arrangement-based cool recordings, including the influential *Sketches of Spain* and *Porgy and Bess*.

The relationship between Davis and Evans proved equally beneficial to both. Evans's creative and yet subtle manner of using the orchestra effectively highlighted Davis's talent. Davis's tone, straight with little vibrato, and melodic ideas, overarching and characterized by long tones, epitomized the cool attitude. He was also instrumental in moving this experimental ensemble into the spotlight of jazz. (For a more detailed discussion of Miles Davis, see Chapter 10.)

listening guide

(CD 2, track 6)
Miles Davis
"Boplicity"*

:00   First chorus (no introduction): trumpet lead (Miles Davis), bass and drums play a relaxed $\frac{4}{4}$ rhythm throughout; piano plays gentle chordal punctuations.

:27   Bridge: change of melody and chords.

:42   Last part of first chorus.

:56   Second chorus: baritone sax solo (Gerry Mulligan), rhythm section continues as before.

1:24   Bridge: sax unison with French horn, trombone, and tuba.

1:35   Trumpet solo.

1:42   Last part of second chorus: slight variation on the original 8 measures of the tune, ensemble.

1:58   Third chorus: trumpet solo, sustained harmonic background.

2:25   Bridge: piano solo (John Lewis), sustained harmonic background for half of solo (saxes, trombone, French horn, tuba).

2:40   Ensemble with the original melody.

2:57   End.

*Smithsonian Collection, CD 4, track 1.

Lennie Tristano

Another center for the developing cool sound in New York could be found in the work of pianist Lennie Tristano. Between 1946 and 1951, Tristano led a group of musicians in his compositional efforts. This group included alto saxophonist Lee Konitz and, like the group around Miles Davis, explored a new music quite different from bop. Its intellectual approach featured long and abstract lines first suggested by swing players like Lester Young, Teddy Wilson, and Charlie Christian.

In 1951, Tristano formed a "New School of Music" in which players like Konitz taught. Tristano's influence can be heard in the performances of his students Art Pepper, Bud Freedman, Dave Brubeck, and Bill Evans. He stressed the importance of melodic structure over emotional expression. His subtle compositions reflect a complexity that proved influential in the development of cool (*Lennie Tristano/The New Lennie Tristano*).

Tristano's interest in experimentation signals several later developments in modern jazz. His explorations of collective improvisation will be more fully developed in the free jazz period ("Descent into the Maelstrom"). Also, his

technical interest in multitrack recording anticipates future experiments in jazz/rock fusion ("Turkish Mambo").

Bill Evans

In many ways, Bill Evans fulfills the piano legacy begun in the early days of jazz. It began with the early ragtime players like Scott Joplin and Jelly Roll Morton and continued with the boogie-woogie and stride playing of James P. Johnson, "Fats" Waller, Meade Lux Lewis, and Art Tatum. These early players placed the piano in the middle of the developing jazz tradition. Later players like Earl Hines, Duke Ellington, Bud Powell, Horace Silver, Oscar Peterson, and Thelonious Monk helped keep that tradition alive. Bill Evans added a new improvisational authority to this legacy. Just as the early pianists charted the early road through jazz history, Evans in his quiet way laid the foundation for future generations of jazz piano players.

Evans was born in New Jersey in 1929 and began his piano studies at the age of six. His early classical training on piano (and flute and violin) would reappear in his later works for piano and orchestra (Bill Evans Trio with Symphony Orchestra) and his short tenure with composer George Russell. His first jazz album, *New Jazz Conceptions*, was recorded in 1956 and included one of his most famous compositions, "Waltz for Debby."

He moved to the head of the jazz community when he was asked to join the Miles Davis group in 1958. This group, which included Cannonball Adderley and John Coltrane, is now recognized as one of the classic ensembles in jazz

listening guide

(CD 2, track 7)
Bill Evans with Scott Lafaro and Paul Motian
"Autumn Leaves"

This song form is made up of a verse (A) and chorus (B) section, each with two 8-bar phrases. Although not always obvious, this form is maintained through all of the solo sections. Each (A)(B) section is often referred to as a single chorus for soloing purposes. Try to listen for this form during the performance.

:00   Introduction. Syncopated version of the opening phrase of the song is used as an introduction. The bass and drums hold a steady beat while the piano plays a syncopated rhythm for the first phrase.

:05   (A) For the second phrase the bass and drums move to a more syncopated rhythm.

:09   (A) First verse. The piano plays the melody while the drums play straight time. Notice the syncopated semi-walking pattern played in the bass.

:28   (B) Chorus. The bass uses a straight walking pattern. Notice the chordal patterns used as part of the piano solo. Such chordal voicings are a trademark of Bill Evans's style.

:45   (A) Bass solo. Piano and drums lay out.

:56   Piano adds short melodic responses to the bass solo.

1:07   (B) Drums enter as a third member in the interchange of melodic ideas. This type of balance of duties among the trio members is also a feature of Bill Evans's trios.

1:25   (A) Second chorus for bass solo. The three members participate equally in the exchange of ideas.

1:45   (B) The exchange of ideas continues.

2:02   (A) The trio finally falls into a more traditional straight-time format over the verse section of the song for the first chorus of piano solo.

2:21   (B) Motivic exploration by Evans.

2:40   (A) Second chorus of piano solo. Notice the short comping chords in the left hand.

2:58   (B) Evans develops some melodic motives.

3:17   (A) Evans takes another solo chorus. Notice the balance between melodic and chordal activity.

3:35   (B) More syncopated chordal accents offset the melodic activity.

3:54   (A) Fourth chorus of piano solo. Very creative comping used to support the melodic flights.

4:12   (B) Chordal punches connected by melodic phrases.

4:30   (A) The piano and drums fade to leave the bass as the leading soloist.

4:44   The piano and bass work in counterpoint.

4:50   (B) Bass solo with short piano responses.

5:07   (A) A return to the melody highly embellished with improvisation.

5:27   (B) Notice how the melodic activity is reduced to chordal patterns as the chorus is brought to a close.

5:41   The rhythm of the final measures is repeated to create an ending.

5:56   End.

history. Evans worked with that group for about a year and participated in the landmark album *Kind of Blue.*

Following his stay with Davis, Evans formed a trio in which his personal voice was arguably best displayed. Scott LaFaro on bass and Paul Motian on drums filled out the trio. His live sessions at New York City's Village Vanguard in 1961 offer good insight into Evans's innovative offerings. Tragically, LaFaro was killed in an automobile accident in 1962, an event that clearly affected Evans personally.

Evans won a Grammy for his *Conversations with Myself* in 1963. As on his later album, *New Conversations,* Evans double- and triple-tracked his playing to create subtle improvisational interweavings. Evans returned to the small-group format in 1966 with Eddie Gomez on bass and a variety of leading jazz drummers. In the 1970s he recorded several quintet albums but in 1978 returned to the trio format with Marc Johnson on bass and Joe LaBarbera on drums. Evans himself compared this group favorably with that important earlier trio with LaFaro on bass.

Evans was an introspective musician who suffered from bouts of drug addiction that no doubt contributed to his death in 1980. His personality may have been soft, but his musical voice has proven to be quite the opposite. He created a new sound for the piano, one that took traditional chords and reshaped them with his trademark voicings. His chord vocabulary and improvisational musings are still a part of the lexicon for new and upcoming jazz players.

Piano players have always been capable of shouldering the musical responsibilities of larger ensembles. Although the piano often worked in larger groups like the big bands, its true voice was developed in solo or small-group performances. It is this small-group legacy that Bill Evans anchored in the later, more mature, mainstream of jazz.

Other Performers

Lee Konitz worked under the influence of both Miles Davis and Lennie Tristano. He credits the latter for really being the first to be labeled cool.[23] He had met Davis through his connection with Gil Evans. He and other members of the Thornhill band decided to pull together a group that was essentially that of Thornhill including the tuba and French horn. Davis offered them the voice they wanted for the ensemble, and they designated him the leader because he was able to get playing engagements. While Davis brought cool to the forefront of the jazz scene, in many ways, it was Tristano, more in the background, who helped define the cool sound.

Cool is a style of jazz that even the general public can agree is beautiful music. Few players contributed more to this beauty than tenor saxophonist Stan Getz. Getz was heavily influenced by Lester Young, but as time went on he was able to establish an identity of his own that is quite distinctive. His bossa nova excursions brought together a moving Brazilian rhythm with pure tone and melodic charm, a combination that was readily accepted throughout the world.[24]

As cool jazz drifted farther from bop and all other preceding styles, it reached the apex of subtlety when Jimmy Giuffre, playing low-register clarinet instead of tenor sax, decided to do away entirely with the steady pulse of jazz. Giuffre claimed that the beat of the music could be implicit instead of explicit. But when the listener experiences Giuffre's trio (clarinet, bass, and guitar) playing "Happy Man," the pulse can be felt quite readily even though no instrument is relegated to the pulse alone.[25]

WEST COAST JAZZ

During the late 1940s, a cool style was also developing on the West Coast. Although the Miles Davis–Gil Evans collaboration in 1949 was an East Coast expression and is thought to have had a germinal influence on the development of cool, the style moved west and was brought to fruition in the writing and performing skills of players such as saxophonist Jimmy Giuffre and trumpeter Shorty Rogers. These two, joined by drummer Shelly Manne, were all former members of the Stan Kenton band and proved to be leading influences in the development of the West Coast cool movement.

Just as Minton's was a center of activity for the bop community in New York, so was the Lighthouse at Hermosa Beach for the developing West Coast jazz style. Howard Rumsey, a former bass player for Stan Kenton, organized Sunday concerts in this club in 1948. By 1950, the Lighthouse had become a part of the West Coast jazz definition.

It is difficult to draw any clear distinction between the East and West Coast cool styles. They both reflect an interest in an introverted tone and a commitment to unique instrumentations for which specialized arrangements were made. Unlike big bands, which have sections of like instruments, the cool groups tended to group unlike instruments in search of a new ensemble sound.

The fact that the cool style moved from New York to the West Coast set the two geographic locations in a competition for the attention of the jazz community. The distinction between the two schools was one more of publicity than of style. The players themselves were not restricted to just one style—cool or hot. For example, Stan Getz, who was a leader of cool jazz on the East Coast, was also capable of a spirited bop style.[26] The separation of styles and their geographic locations were not as sharply drawn as the marketing promotion of the day may have suggested. Both cool and bop players could be found on both coasts. However, the West Coast did, undeniably, offer cool players a rich center for their exchange of ideas.

The East Coast did eventually recapture the jazz mainstream as the *hard bop style* emerged in response to the more intellectual cool style popular on the West Coast. The debate between the two styles was further fueled by the fact that most of the West Coast musicians were white, whereas most of the East Coast hard bop players were African American. The white players mostly came out of the swing-band tradition, whereas the African American players usually were associated with the bop style. The development of hard bop is viewed as both a return to the hotter spirit of jazz and a reclamation of the jazz tradition by the African American community.

The writers of cool on the West Coast often worked in the tradition of Duke Ellington by writing arrangements with specific players and specific sounds in mind.[27] The compositions were further customized by the unique grouping of instruments in each ensemble.[28] Both Shorty Rogers and Jimmy Giuffre composed during their tenure with the Kenton band, and they carried these

listening guide

(CD 2, track 8)
Dave Brubeck Quartet
"Blue Rondo à la Turk"
Dave Brubeck, piano
Paul Desmond, saxophone

:00 Opening 9/8 motive with the eighth notes accented on the first, third, fifth, and seventh notes. This creates an uneven rhythmic feel of 2,2,2,3 where the final three feels like a stretched beat.

:05 Bass enters playing only on the accented notes. The cymbal plays only on the final long beat.

:11 Saxophone enters and the cymbal first plays on the final three eighth notes but eventually moves across the entire rhythm and adds more of the drum set.

:22 Piano bass, and drums only.

:33 Same rhythm but the melodic pattern is expanded.

:44 Saxophone returns in a duet with the piano.

:55 Piano again takes the lead with a repeated note in one hand and changing chords in the other.

1:07 Saxophone and piano duet returns.

1:18 Piano and saxophone introduce a new motive punctuated with piano chords.

1:38 Syncopated chords used to close the 9/8 section.

1:51 Relaxed swing section begins with a saxophone solo.

1:56 Two measures of 9/8.

1:59 Return to swing (4/4) for two measures.

2:03 Two measures of 9/8.

2:06 Return to swing.

2:10 Two measures of 9/8.

2:13 Return to swing and maintains it throughout the next chorus.

2:36 New chorus. Notice the melodic technique to set up the next solo chorus (called a turn around).

3:01 New chorus. A different turn around to set up the next chorus.

3:26 New chorus. At the end of this chorus the solo is brought to a close so the piano solo can begin.

3:52 Piano solo.

4:17 New solo chorus. More chordal than the previous chorus.

4:38 Turn around to the next chorus.

4:42 Chord solo continues.

5:08 Next chord returns to a more economical melodic soloing style.

5:33 Saxophone returns for the first two measures of a new chorus.

5:37 Two measures of 9/8.

5:41 Return to swing for two measures.

5:45 9/8 for two measures.

5:48 Final two measures of swing.

5:52 9/8 returns for the next chorus which begins with the piano.

5:57 Saxophone joins in as a duet with the piano.

6:03 Syncopated chords signal the final phrase.

6:23 Final chordal ending.

6:35 Slows.

6:40 Ends with a final drum accent.

compositional skills into their cool ensembles. Joining these two was Gerry Mulligan, who had been a part of the original "Birth of the Cool" recordings in New York. His quartet without a piano is perhaps one of the more famous ensembles illustrating the cool arranger's interest in finding new approaches. His work in this quartet, with Chet Baker on trumpet, offers some of the best examples of balance between compositional and individual expressions typical of West Coast jazz.[29]

The musicians on the West Coast often made their living by also working in Hollywood studio orchestras. The use of carefully arranged music was characteristic of their work in the studios and may have influenced their approach to their jazz. Just as many of the East Coast cool players shared a tie to the Claude Thornhill band, many of the players on the West Coast shared one to Kenton's early band; in addition to Manne, Giuffre, and Rogers were active players such as Art Pepper, Bud Shank, and Bill Holman. Gerry Mulligan bridges the two coasts by bringing his background with the Thornhill band and his work with Miles Davis and Gil Evans to the West Coast. To a certain extent, Dave Brubeck's role on the West Coast paralleled Lennie Tristano's work on the East Coast. Both brought more esoteric compositional concerns to their work, and each centered on small but dedicated groups of players and listeners.

In many cases, the ensemble writing used in the West Coast style showed influences of Western Europe, if not in actual musical content, at least in the compositional approach. Brubeck's music reflected his study with the modern classical composer Darius Milhaud. Some of Giuffre's later pieces even approached a type of experimental style not unlike the atonal work of classical composers. This move toward a type of jazz classicism stood in sharp contrast to the developing regression to hard bop on the East Coast. (For a more thorough discussion of hard bop regression, see Chapter 11.)

THIRD STREAM

Throughout jazz's history, composers have struck a balance between the fully composed pieces typical of Western European models and the more open improvisatory structures characteristic of the oral tradition. The cool era marked a move toward the more fully composed and formally defined works. The hard bop period was, in contrast, a call for a return to the more individual and spontaneous oral tradition. Third-stream jazz can be seen as an extension of the cool compositional style and can be linked to Gunther Schuller, who participated with Miles Davis on *Birth of the Cool*. In fact, the phrase *third stream* is usually attributed to Schuller, although writer John S. Wilson is also credited with inventing it.

The evolution of musical styles is often metaphorically referred to as a collection of streams that share a common source but have branched to create individual identities. However, unlike its river analogue, once a musical stream branches from its source it is still subject to the influences of all other musical streams around it. Musical streams, in essence, share a common riverbed: the cultural milieu of the day. Because they often share listeners, performers, and critics, elements of each style tend to cross over into one another, creating even newer streams.

Gunther Schuller

Musical crossovers are certainly not new to jazz. The players of jazz have always borrowed from anywhere and everywhere. The terms **crossover** and **fusion,** however, became especially prevalent during the late 1950s and into the 1970s, after rock and roll had captured the attention of the public, opening new doors for the development of jazz itself.

The fact that jazz's art status was certain led many to question whether it was foul play to assimilate the characteristics of other clearly delineated musical styles. How classical can jazz become and still remain jazz? Likewise, where does one draw the line between jazz and rock expressions? Questions such as these have unsettled, time and again, our efforts to fix a firm definition of jazz. As frustrating as this constant assimilation of other idioms is for historians, it is also the driving force behind the evolving jazz musical stream. The very fact that jazz is unique and indigenous to America demonstrates the multiplicity of cultural influences at work here and absent in the same proportions anywhere else. Jazz is a carefully blended style that depends on its past, but now it also depends on the fertile crossovers from the various musical styles around it.

The degree to which the crossover occurs and the directions in which it moves influences any newly emerging musical style. Sometimes the crossover is one-sided, as when one stream assimilates much but exports little. In contrast, a more equal fusion can occur that creates a new style capable of being claimed by each of the contributing streams. Third-stream music is more typical of the former. Jazz has continually borrowed from the European classical model, but the reverse—the classical use of jazz idioms—has been only sporadic and short-lived.

Gunther Schuller

Gunther Schuller was a French horn player with the Metropolitan Opera in New York and has composed both classical and third-stream pieces. From 1967 to 1977 he was the director of the New England Conservatory of Music in Boston. He therefore brought much of his classical training to his efforts

listening guide

(CD 2, track 9)
Modern Jazz Quartet
"Django"
Milt Jackson, vibes
John Lewis, piano
Percy Heath, bass
Kenny Clarke, drums

This composition is named in memory of the French gypsy guitarist Django Reinhardt, who died in 1953.

:00   (A) Piano and vibraphone statement of the theme on which the work is based. The first 2 measures offer the motive that generates the entire theme and piece.

:14   Second 4-bar phrase that answers the first. Still uses the same motive.

:26   Third 4-bar phrase that extends the second and leads to the second part of the opening theme, which is itself derived from the first part used in these 3 opening phrases.

:39   (B) Second section of the opening theme. The new motive is just 3 notes shared between bass, piano, and vibes.

:52   Concluding 4 bars of this second section, which slows down before solos begin.

1:06   (A) Vibe solo. Two choruses of ABA. Tempo picks up with a light swing feel. Listen for the light comping in the piano behind the solo (12 bars).

1:33   (B) Motivic use of the theme in vibe solo as a setup to the next chorus (8 bars).

1:50   (A) Return to swing feel to close the first chorus.

1:59   Motivic bass line under the soloist.

2:16   (A) Second chorus follows the same formal design as the first. Return to straight time (first of two 6-bar phrases).

2:29   Second 6-bar phrase to complete the 12-bar section.

2:42   (B) Middle phrase of the second chorus (8 bars).

2:59   (A) Return to swing feel for final 12 bars of the second chorus. Motivic bass line reappears.

3:25   A double-speed statement (diminution) of the second part of the opening theme used as an interlude between solos.

3:34   (A) Piano solo begins. The same formal structure used for the vibe solo is followed for the piano solo—2 choruses of ABA.

4:00   (B) Listen for repeated notes in the bass.

4:17   (A) Same bass motive used under solo.

4:43   (A) Of second chorus.

5:10   (B) Same repeated notes in the bass.

5:27   (A) Last 12 bars with bass motive underneath.

5:53   Opening theme is repeated at the same tempo as the beginning.

6:30   Second section of opening (now closing) theme.

7:00   Slows down and ends.

in third-stream jazz. Schuller's "Abstraction" and Larry Austin's "Improvisation for Orchestra and Jazz Soloists" are good examples of early third-stream music.

Third-stream jazz shares both the instrumental sound and the instrumental variety first employed during the cool era. The jazz musicians play their instruments in a manner closely resembling the technique used by symphonic players, which employs a precise tonal attack and a minimum of vibrato. Third stream, also like cool, introduces more exotic and typically classical instruments, such as the French horn, oboe, bassoon, and cello. The harmonies used in third-stream music are similar to those associated with contemporary jazz; however, musical forms—such as the fugue, canon, theme and variations, and other extended types—were borrowed from classical music.[30] The use of these forms by third-stream composers resulted in a return to a more polyphonic type of composition. Classical music markedly differs from jazz in its use of meter and rhythmic pulse. Although present in both, jazz has always given it great prominence. Third-stream jazz often uses a more classical notion of rhythm, which gives more weight to the melodic and harmonic activity than to a strong rhythmic pulse. For this reason, some contend that third-stream music cannot be considered jazz.[31]

Robert Freedman's "An Interlude" is an example of a third-stream composition that uses classical models of **polytonal** and **polymodal** techniques.[32] Leon Dallin defines a polytonal composition as one that clearly emphasizes two or more tonal centers at the same time.[33] Polymodal music uses two modes (major and minor) with the same tonic or two forms of the same chord simultaneously. Dallin calls it "dual modality."

Jazz as an art form has also been embraced by the classical art world through commissions of jazz works for performance by symphony orchestras, for example, Brubeck's *Dialogues for Jazz Combo and Symphony Orchestra,*[34] Rolph Lieberman's *Concerto for Jazz Band and Symphony Orchestra,* and John Graas's *Jazz Symphony No. 1.* These compositions fall into two distinct groups: (1) compositions that contain jazz elements intended for performance by large symphonic orchestras using traditional instrumentation and (2) **concerto grosso** approaches that place a small jazz group of seven or eight players within a large symphonic orchestra.

Too often, however, the concerto grosso format offers a little jazz and a little of the classical ensemble but no integrated effect. John Lewis's "Sketch" is an example of a third-stream composition that combined the Modern Jazz Quartet and the Beaux Arts String Quartet.[35] During this performance, neither of the two groups seems to lose its identity, but an integrated feeling is still created.

During the late 1950s, the Modern Jazz Quartet proved to be a pivotal group between cool and third stream. John Lewis's classical training can be seen in the composed nature of the ensemble passages and the formal compositional structures used. His use of Renaissance brass sounds and his characteristic improvisatory style offers yet another third-stream blend in his composition "Piazza Navona."[36] In a manner similar to Lewis's "Sketch," Chuck Mangione also merged his jazz quintet with a symphony orchestra as well as a full choir on the album *Land of Make Believe.*[37]

On closer inspection of third-stream techniques, particularly the use of more fully composed compositional forms, we find that composers throughout the

history of jazz have been importing classical techniques. Scott Joplin used quite strict forms for his rags, and Jelly Roll Morton was a master of the compositional concept of theme and variations. Duke Ellington's music certainly reflects the power of a classical compositional approach in a strictly jazz medium. Only during the third-stream period, however, was such a conscious effort to assimilate classical music idioms evident.

The Sauter-Finegan Orchestra was an earlier attempt to bridge the gap between jazz and classical music. The orchestra was originally organized strictly as a recording orchestra and was strongly influenced by the impressionistic music of Debussy and Ravel. Eddie Sauter was as well known an arranger for the Benny Goodman orchestra as Bill Finegan was for the Glenn Miller orchestra. Their most ambitious effort was the Lieberman work, which was extremely well received when performed and recorded with the Chicago Symphony Orchestra.

The Stan Kenton orchestra showcased several third-stream compositions. William Russo's compositions for this orchestra were often bold and adventuresome in their blend of classical, avant-garde, and jazz elements[38] ("Mirage," "Eldon Heath").

"All About Rosie" from the *Modern Jazz Concert* album demonstrates how George Russell developed an extended jazz (or third-stream) work from a children's song-game.[39]

Yet another approach to third-stream music is the actual use of classical composed music in a larger jazz work or the complete statement of a classical work with jazz interpretation. The Swingle Singers used many of Bach's pieces, and Hubert Laws effectively recorded Stravinsky's *Rite of Spring*.[40]

Jazz in Classical Composition

Classical composers were actually first in their efforts to cross over the classical/jazz line. The most lasting and popular attempt to include jazz idioms in classical music occurred in France in the 1920s. Composers such as Darius Milhaud, in his travels to the United States, actually obtained firsthand knowledge of the New Orleans jazz style as heard in Harlem.[41] As a result of his trip, he composed a work, *La Création du Monde,* about which he writes, "I adopted the same orchestra as used in Harlem, and I made wholesale use of the jazz style to convey a purely classical feeling."[42]

Rhythmic and harmonic jazz elements were consciously used in France as exotic music references to the free-spirited music of the African American. This interest in jazz was also promoted among literary leaders such as Jean Cocteau, who, in his essay *Le Coq et l'arlequin,* holds up American jazz as an example of the virtue of indigenous and more accessible music that should be assimilated by classical composers.

Ernst Krenek, an Austrian composer, looking to the success of jazz in Paris, wrote a jazz opera called *Jonny Spielt Auf* that was popular all over Europe. It was translated into eighteen languages and performed in over a hundred cities. The leading character was, appropriately, an African American jazz musician. Stravinsky's *Ragtime for Eleven Instruments* is another example of a classical composer adopting jazz idioms for use in a classical composition.

Stravinsky crossed over in the reverse direction when he wrote the *Ebony Concerto* for the Woody Herman band. This piece is unique in that it is written by a classical composer for a traditional jazz ensemble.

In the United States, composers such as George Gershwin and Morton Gould also worked in a classical medium that reflected jazz influences. These composers remained classical in their form and style but made use of the jazz idioms in a generalized sense. Claude Bolling's *Suite for Flute and Jazz Piano* serves as a clear example of this type of fully composed yet jazz-imbued composition. On his recording of this piece with the renowned classical flutist Pierre Rampal, the use of jazz inflections and idioms helps create a spirit of improvisation even though the composition is completely notated.[43]

These classical works, although greatly influenced by jazz, are not considered to be third stream because they originate from, and maintain their allegiance to, the classical idiom. The deciding feature seems to be the direction in which the crossover moves. A composer who is associated primarily with jazz but who uses classical models or idioms is considered a participant in the third stream. On the other hand, classical composers who fuse jazz expressions in their works are generally excluded, most likely because the third stream is a notion belonging primarily to jazz historians. Despite the shading in terminology, it is worth noting that the crossover between the classical and jazz worlds is a two-way street. Both stylistic streams have been enriched by their association with each other. As we saw in the previous chapters, these two musical streams will again interact as the avant-garde school of jazz emerges.

Airto Moreira, Flora Purim, and Hermeto Pascoal

1960s, THE BRAZILIAN WAVE

Brazilian music always occurred on the periphery of Latin jazz, but it claimed the spotlight in the 1960s as the jazz bossa enjoyed widespread popularity. This more subtle dance rhythm proved particularly appropriate for the West Coast style of jazz and its cooler performance manner. The bossa brought a shift in emphasis from the complex, highly charged percussion to a more complex melodic and harmonic style. After tours of Brazil by musicians like guitarist Charlie Byrd, trumpeter Dizzy Gillespie, and flutist Herbie Mann, the bossa nova was carried to the forefront of Latin jazz. These musicians led the way for many others to explore the music of Brazil. Cool players like Herbie Mann, Stan Getz, and Gerry Mulligan found the bossa to be a natural extension of their West Coast style of playing. Getz, who performed frequently and effectively with Brazilian guitarist João Gilberto, rode the crest of the bossa nova popularity, as did Charlie Byrd.

listening guide

(CD 2, track 10)
"The Girl from Ipanema"
Astrud Gilberto
João Gilberto
Stan Getz

:00 Non word vocal over bossa rhythm intro.

:07 First phrase in Portuguese, guitar and voice only.

:22 Second phrase with bass and drums added.

:37 Chorus, each phrase started with a long note on a dissonant chord tone but still sounds very relaxed.

:59 Closing phrase of the chorus.

1:07 Return to the opening phrase completing the AABA form.

1:21 Second chorus with female vocalist in English.

1:31 Second phrase.

1:51 Chorus. Notice how the rhythm section maintains a very steady rhythm even as the vocalist floats melodically above it.

2:20 Final phrase of the second chorus.

2:35 Saxophone solo for the third chorus. The solo remains very close to the melody itself with only minor embellishments.

2:49 Second phrase with a little more improvisation.

3:05 Chorus. Solo returns to the melody with embellishments.

3:28 Solo takes more liberties to close the chorus.

3:33 Final phrase. The soloist uses mostly repeated notes rather than the melody.

3:48 Piano solo begins with a chordal version of the melody.

4:17 Vocalist returns for the chorus as the saxophone fills in between the melodic phrases.

4:47 Final phrase with the saxophone playing single notes to accompany the vocalist.

5:00 The final measures of the previous phrase are used to close the performance.

5:24 End.

The bossa jazz movement also brought nonpercussion Latin musicians to prominence. The guitar claimed center stage with Laurindo Almeida and Bola Sete. Almeida approached the medium as a classical guitarist, while Sete, who came directly out of the Brazilian bossa community, was equally skilled in jazz. His album *Bossa Nova* shows the breadth of his compositional and performance attributes.

The bossa nova's popularity led in many ways to an eventual decline in the jazz circle just as much of the original jazz bossa excitement gave way to a lighter bossa pop style. However, there was a continued interest in the jazz samba as the decade wore on. The waning popularity of the bossa nova was not the end of the Brazilian influence in the 1960s. It would return in a new hybrid form as a combination of funky jazz and late cubop. The Latin-jazz-funk style took its early leadership from newly arriving Brazilians like arranger/producer Eumir Deodato, vocalist Flora Purim, and percussionist Airto Moreira.

The fusion of Brazilian bossa with funky jazz can be heard in Horace Silver's "Song for My Father," in which he expressly tried to incorporate the true bossa feeling. Cal Tjader recordings of the late 1960s also reflected this funky Latin jazz (*Soul Sauce*). Tjader also joined with pianist Eddie Palmieri to record the album *El Sonido Nuevo*, which was well received in both the Latin and jazz communities. Eddie Palmieri, with his older brother Charlie, represented a new generation of players who would develop over the next decade and help define the transition to Latin **salsa,** a term that is translated to "a hot, piquant sauce." This term came into use as the crossover of Latin jazz and soul—or funky jazz—began to develop.

R&B and soul proved to be the new fusion for Latin jazz as interest in the samba was replaced by the more funky boogaloo. A leader in the Latin-jazz-funk was Mongo Santamaria, who originally played in Cal Tjader's band but later formed his own jazz-flavored group. Several of his recordings included Chick Corea, who proved important in the later jazz fusion period. Latin funk can also be heard on Herbie Hancock's *Cantaloupe Island*.

The 1960s offered a number of fronts for the hybridization of jazz, Latin, R&B, funky jazz, and, increasingly, rock and roll. The groundwork laid in this decade would play itself out more fully in the fusion of the 1970s.

Mongo Santamaria

summary

In many ways, cool was a jazz period that reflected the compositional practice of Western European art music. Much of the music was arrangement based, and issues of orchestration and musical texture became compositional concerns. During the cool era, an intellectual and often compositional approach to jazz was a dominant force. Cool offered a response to the hot jazz of bop. The energetic performance efforts of bop performers were replaced by subtleties in both the arrangements and the playing style.

During this period, the range of suitable jazz instruments was also expanded to include those used more often in the classical music world. The flute became important as a jazz instrument, as did the French horn, oboe, and cello. However, it was not until the later third-stream and avant-garde periods that the double reeds became more prominent. Although the flügelhorn is not commonly considered a classical instrument, it also gained exposure during the cool period and underscores that style's concern with softer and more mellow sounds.

Perhaps the exaggerated movement of bop away from the compositionally based music of the big bands triggered an equally dramatic response in the style of cool. Compositional concerns had certainly returned. However, they were to recede temporarily until they again surfaced during the 1960s with third-stream jazz.

There was a period in the late 1950s and early 1960s during which a conscious effort was made by many jazz composers to blend the jazz and classical musical streams to form a third stream. As we have seen, this blend between the two streams is not new to jazz. In fact, jazz's very existence is dependent on that blend. It was only during this period that the fusion of the two music traditions was undertaken as a conscious approach toward jazz. The term *third stream* appears almost exclusively in jazz histories rather than histories of Western art music. Third stream is therefore a jazz term that describes the importation of classical music models into the working arena of jazz performance rather than an exportation of jazz to the classical model.

FOR FURTHER STUDY

1. What are some words that might be used to describe the feeling and tone of the cool era?

2. How does the cool type of tonal attack and vibrato influence the descriptive terms listed in your answer to question 1?

3. What instruments became important in this era that were not prominent previously?

4. What instrument used in early Dixieland music became more prominent and was used melodically in this era?

5. What new meters were used in place of $\frac{2}{4}$ and $\frac{4}{4}$?

6. Define the terms *polyrhythm* and *polymeter*.

7. Who were the leading exponents of cool jazz?

8. Two selections that are good examples of this jazz era are "Jeru" and "Moon Dreams" from the Miles Davis album *Birth of the Cool*. Compare and contrast these selections by answering the following:
   a. Are the instruments played mostly in the middle range, or do you hear extremely high and low pitches?
   b. Do the instrumentalists use vibrato in solo spots?
   c. Compare the percussion rhythm with that of the bop era. How do you react to the rhythmic pulse of "Moon Dreams"?

9. An example of the use of alternating meters is "Three to Get Ready" in the album *Time Out* by the Dave Brubeck Quartet. After the short waltzlike melody, the meter alternates between $\frac{3}{4}$ and $\frac{4}{4}$. Listen carefully and clap lightly two measures of three (heavy-light-light, heavy-light-light) followed by two measures of four (heavy-light-light-light, heavy-light-light-light) and continue to alternate.

10. Listen to "The Morning After" and "I Want to Be Happy" from the album *Chico Hamilton Quintet* and identify by sound two instruments used in jazz for the first time.

11. Present-day jazz is a potpourri of many years of continuous development. Name the sources and kinds of music jazz musicians adopt today.

12. What are some characteristics of third-stream music? Name the jazz era from which it stemmed.

13. Listen to the Modern Jazz Quartet playing with a string quartet to produce third-stream music in the selection "Sketch" from the album *Third Stream Music*. How would you describe the total effect? What musical elements seem to be most prominent in the string quartet's part? What jazz elements are most prominent in the Modern Jazz Quartet's part?

SUGGESTED ADDITIONAL LISTENING

Baker, Chet. *Cool Burnin'*. Prestige Records, PR 7496.

Dankworth, Johnny, and the London Philharmonic Orchestra. *Collaboration*. Roulette Records, SR 52059.

Davis, Miles. *Basic Miles*. Columbia Records, C 32025.

———. *Greatest Hits*. Columbia Records, CS-9809.

———. *Greatest Hits*. Prestige Records, S-7457.

———. *Miles Ahead*. Columbia Records, CL 1041.

———. *Miles Davis*. Prestige Records, 24001.

———. *Miles Davis at Fillmore*. Columbia Records, G 30038.

———. *Walkin'*. Prestige Records, 7608.

Desmond, Paul, and Mulligan, Gerry. *Two of a Mind*. RCA Victor Records, LSP-2624.

Evans, Bill. *Bill Evans Trio with Symphony Orchestra*. Verve Records, V6-8640.

Evans, Gil. *Out of the Cool*. Impulse Records, A-4.

Getz, Stan. *Best of Stan Getz*. Verve Records, V6-8719.

———. *Stan Getz Years*. Roost Records, RK-103.

Greatest Names in Jazz. Verve Records, PR 2-3.

Leviev, Milcho. *Music for Big Band and Symphony Orchestra*. Philippopolis Records, PH-101.

Lewis, John. *European Windows*. RCA Victor Records, LPM-1742.

Martin, Skip. *Scheherajazz*. Somerset Records, P-9700.

Modern Jazz Quintet. *European Concert*. Atlantic Records, 2-603.

———. *European Tour*. Atlantic Records, SD 20603.

———. *The Last Concert*. Atlantic Records, 909.

———. *Modern Jazz Quartet*. Prestige Records, 24005.

Mulligan, Gerry, and Baker, Chet. *Timeless*. Pacific Jazz Records, PJ-75.

New Wave in Jazz. Impulse Records, A-90.

Nica's Dream. New World Records, 242.

Orchestra. Capitol Records, ST-484.

Outstanding Jazz Compositions of the Twentieth Century. Columbia Records, C2S 831/C2L 31.

Russell, George. *Jazz in the Space Age/New York, New York*. MCA Records, 2-4017.

———. *Outer Thoughts.* Milestone Records, M-47027.
Schuller, Gunther. *Jazz Abstractions.* Atlantic Records, S-1365.
Stoltzman, Richard. *Begin Sweet World.* RCA Victor Records, 1-7124.
Young, Lester. *The Aladdin Sessions.* Blue Note Records, BN-LA456-H2.
———. *Complete Lester Young on Savoy.* Arista Records, SJL-2022.
———. *Young Lester Young.* Columbia Records, J 24.

ADDITIONAL READING RESOURCES

Berendt, Joachim. *The New Jazz Book,* 19–24.
Cole, Bill. *Miles Davis.*
Francis, André. *Jazz,* 130–49.
Hodeir, André. *Jazz: Its Evolution and Essence,* 116–38.
Megill, Donald D., and Demory, Richard S. *Introduction to Jazz History.*
Shapiro, Nat, and Hentoff, Nat, eds. *The Jazz Makers,* 243–75.
Stearns, Marshall. *The Story of Jazz,* 167–72.
Williams, Martin T. *The Jazz Tradition,* 219, 233.

Note: Complete information, including name of publisher and date of publication, is provided in this book's bibliography.

NOTES

1. Dom Cerulli, Burt Korall, and Mort Nasatir, *The Jazz World* (New York: Ballantine Books, 1960), 206.
2. Chico Hamilton, *The Best of Chico Hamilton,* Impulse Records, A-9174; *Easy Livin',* Sunset Records, SUS-5215.
3. *Chico Hamilton Quintet,* Pacific Jazz Records, PJ-1209.
4. Eddie Lang and Joe Venuti, "Farewell Blues," *Encyclopedia of Jazz on Records;* Joe Venuti, *The Daddy of the Violin,* BASF Records, BASF-MPS 2120885-0; *Stringing the Blues,* Columbia Records, C2L-24.
5. Stephane Grappelli, *Django,* Barclay Records, 820105; Django Reinhardt record, *Djangology,* RCA Victor Records, LPM-2319; *Violin Summit: 1966,* BASF Records, 10 626.
6. *Edgar Redmond and the Modern String Ensemble,* Disque Phenomenon Records, DP 2696.
7. Marshall Stearns, *The Story of Jazz* (London: Oxford University Press, 1958), 170.
8. André Hodeir, *Jazz: Its Evolution and Essence* (New York: Grove Press, 1956), 118.
9. Woody Herman, "Summer Sequence," *The Thundering Herds,* Columbia Records, C3L-25; "Early Autumn," *History of Jazz,* vol. 4; *Big Band Jazz,* Smithsonian Collection of Recordings.
10. Paul Horn, *Profile of a Jazz Musician,* Columbia Records, CL 1922.
11. Herbie Mann, *Latin Mann,* Columbia Records, CL 2388; *Today,* Atlantic Records, SD 1454; *Stone Flute,* Embryo Records, SD 18035.

12. Johnny Graas, "Mulliganesque," *Encyclopedia of Jazz on Records,* vol. 4.

13. Yusef Lateef, *Eastern Sounds,* Prestige Records, PR 7319.

14. Art Farmer, *Art,* Argo Records, 678.

15. Clark Terry, *Bobby Brookmeyer Quintet,* Mainstream Records, 320.

16. Dave Brubeck, *Time Out,* Columbia Records, CL-1397.

17. Modern Jazz Quartet, "A Fugue for Music Inn," *The Modern Jazz Quartet at Music Inn,* Atlantic Records, 1247.

18. Woody Herman, *The Thundering Herds;* "Early Autumn," *Singers and Soloists of the Swing Bands,* Smithsonian Collection of Recordings.

19. Claude Thornhill, "Snowfall," *The Great Band Era;* Claude Thornhill Orchestra, "Donna Lee," *Jazz in Revolution—the Big Bands in the 1940s,* New World Records, 284; *The Memorable Claude Thornhill,* Columbia Records, KG-32906; *Big Band Jazz,* Smithsonian Collection of Recordings.

20. Miles Davis, *Birth of the Cool,* Capitol Records, DT 1974.

21. Leonard Feather, "Cool," in *Jazz* (Los Angeles: Pacific Press, 1959), 26.

22. George Shearing, *Best of George Shearing,* Capitol Records, ST 2104; *Touch of Genius,* MGM Records, E 90.

23. "When Jazz Was Cool," *Village Voice,* 25 June 1996.

24. Stan Getz, *Jazz Samba,* Verve Records, V-8432; *Jazz Samba Encore,* Verve Records, 68523.

25. Jimmy Giuffre, "Happy Man," *Seven Pieces,* Verve Records, MG V-8307.

26. *Stan Getz Plays,* Clef Records, MGC-137.

27. Jimmy Giuffre, *Four Brothers,* Capitol, LP KPL102.

28. *Shorty Rogers Giants,* Capitol, LP LC6549.

29. *Gerry Mulligan Quartet,* vol. 1, Pacific Jazz, Vogue, LP LDE029.

30. Harold Shapero, "On Green Mountain," *Modern Jazz Concert,* Columbia Records, WL 127.

31. Gunther Schuller, "Transformation," *Modern Jazz Concert.*

32. Robert Freedman, "An Interlude," *Jazz in the Classroom,* Berklee Records, BLPIA.

33. Leon Dallin, *Techniques of Twentieth Century Composition* (Dubuque, Iowa: Wm. C. Brown, 1974), 132.

34. The New York Philharmonic Orchestra with the Dave Brubeck Quartet, conducted by Leonard Bernstein, *Bernstein Plays Brubeck Plays Bernstein,* Columbia Records, CL 1466.

35. The Modern Jazz Quartet, *Third Stream Music,* Atlantic Records, 1345.

36. The Modern Jazz Quartet, "Piazza Navona," New World Records, 216.

37. Chuck Mangione, *Land of Make Believe,* Mercury Records, SRM 1-684.

38. William Russo, "Mirage" and "Eldon Heath," New World Records, 216.

39. George Russell, "All About Rosie," *Modern Jazz Concert.*

40. Swingle Singers, *Bach's Greatest Hits,* Philips Records, 200-097; Metropolitan Pops Choir with Robert Mandel, *More of the Greatest Hits of Bach,* Laurie Records, LLP 2023; The Jacques Loussier Trio, *Play Bach Jazz,* London Records, 3289; Hubert Laws, *Rite of Spring,* CTI Records, 6012; Nina Simone, "Love Me or Leave Me," *Little Girl Blue,* Bethlehem Records, 6028.

41. Darius Milhaud, *Notes without Music* (New York: Knopf, 1953), 136.

42. Ibid., 148.

43. Claude Bolling, *Suite for Flute and Jazz Piano,* Columbia Records, M33233.

10

Miles Davis

When one steps back to gain a more global view of the history of jazz, several figures loom large above all the rest. Miles Davis can easily be argued as the leading historical personality among the giants of jazz. There are many jazz musicians who nourished the developing jazz canon, but none were as consistently influential over their entire career. As we have seen, jazz can be viewed as a series of overlapping stylistic shifts. Davis can be found at the inception of, not one, but several of the significant stylistic periods—cool, modal, jazz/rock fusion (and, to a lesser extent, free), and even a short experiment with jazz/pop.

Davis's persona was also unique. It was at times aloof, penetrating, and aesthetically confident. As a result, he was capable of marshaling the talents of marquee players to explore new jazz frontiers. At the same time, Davis developed his signature trumpet sound, which is immediately recognized by jazz listeners.

Davis's prominence in the jazz scene was not paralleled by the stereotypical attributes, poverty, and prodigious talent normally associated with leading jazz players. He was born of a relatively affluent family in 1926 and was even able to attend Juilliard for a short time in 1944. He was never a highly polished trumpet player in technical terms, but he had an aggressive nature that continually pushed him to the forefront of jazz developments. He reigned there despite dramatic musical changes inside and outside the jazz world.

BOP

The forthright approach that characterized Davis throughout much of his career began as early as 1944, when he convinced Billy Eckstine to allow him to sit in with Earl Hines during a tour through St. Louis.[2] At that time, Hines's band, later Eckstine's band, represented the front edge of the big-band bop style and no doubt captured Davis's attention.

Miles Davis first came to New York in 1944 to study at Juilliard. He said that when he began playing he tried to imitate anyone he could but that Clark Terry was his main influence. It seems that no matter what Davis played on his

vamping

Miles Davis Chronology

1926	Born into a relatively affluent family in Alton, Illinois, on May 25.
1944	Sat in with the Earl Hines band.
1945	Attended Juilliard Conservatory for a short period of time.
1946	Rejoined the Earl Hines band.
1947–1949	Played with Charlie Parker.
1949–1950	Recorded *Birth of the Cool* with members of the Claude Thornhill band. Began his association with Gil Evans.
1954	Began playing more scale-oriented rather than chord-oriented improvisations.
1958	Important association with Gil Evans on recordings—*Sketches of Spain, Porgy and Bess,* "Summertime," *Miles Ahead.*
1958	Developed the use of modal-type solos with slow-moving harmonies.
1969	Recorded *Bitches Brew.*
1985	Recorded *You're Under Arrest,* which blended pop and jazz.
1991	Died in New York City of a stroke on September 28.

**Gil Evans and
Miles Davis**

listening guide

(CD 2, track 11)
Miles Davis with the Gil Evans Orchestra
"Summertime" from Porgy and Bess

:00   Begins with Davis playing the melody with a light, cool backup in the orchestra. Listen for the orchestral colors pulled from the unusual instrumentation, which includes French horns, tuba, and flutes as well as saxes, trumpets, and trombones.

:35   First solo chorus taken by Davis. Motivic response continues in the orchestra.

1:10   Second chorus by Davis. Orchestral colors expand somewhat as the gentle peak of the arrangement is reached.

1:46   Third chorus by Davis.

2:22   Davis returns to the melody for the final chorus.

3:03   Slows down.

3:16   End.

horn, it had a rather sad feeling to it. There is no doubt that he played with the sound he desired and that he simply would not trust his personal thoughts to any other type of sound. He seemed to have a highly developed sense of communicative simplicity. At first, Davis could not play high, loud, or very fast. When he arrived on the New York scene, he was young enough to be in the process of developing strength in his lip muscles, but he felt that he could think better if he were playing with a light sound; he was more relaxed with that approach. The critics of his bop playing with Charlie Parker in 1945 should remember that eighteen-year-old Davis was only in his formative years.

Davis was not destined to be known only for his contribution to the development of cool jazz. As we will see, he continued to be an innovative force in the evolution of jazz. It is true that the only real constant in his career was his unpredictability. Davis was a musician who was always searching for a new, fresh, exciting way to play his music. He did not feel obligated to older fans; after all, they could buy his previous albums and thereby preserve the style that they prefer. Fans of the cool era feel that the collaboration of the talents of Davis and Gil Evans is one of the highlights of music history. For interesting contrasts, compare the feelings on such Davis albums as *Sketches of Spain,* done with Gil Evans, and *Bitches Brew,* done with an electrified rhythm section as well as with an **amplification** of Davis's trumpet[3] ("Summertime").

In 1945, after his short stay at Juilliard, Davis sought out Charlie Parker, the leading bop player of the day, and actually roomed with him. His association with Parker gave him an unusually early (for his age) start in the top echelons of the jazz community. He even took over Fats Navarro's prestigious chair in Eckstine's band when he was only twenty. Before Navarro, this chair was defined by Gillespie himself as the showplace for trumpet virtuosity. Although following in the Gillespie tradition, Davis was not the technician necessary for the bravura bop style. Whether this incongruity between style and ability had anything to do with Davis's later, more fragmented and slower, melodic style has been much debated.

COOL

Davis left Eckstine to play with Parker from 1947 to 1949, at which time he began working with members of the Claude Thornhill band. The instrumentation of the Thornhill band, which already included the French horn and tuba, was carried over to this first cool nonet. The nonet grew out of a dialogue among the Thornhill players who wanted to write arrangements and compositions that eventually would define the cool sound. Although the main writers were Gil Evans and Gerry Mulligan, the group's leadership came from Davis. He established the final instrumentation and secured the group's one engagement, a two-week club date. But it was the recording of the twelve sides that collectively formed *Birth of the Cool* that would launch the cool sound.

The membership of the nonet included saxophonists Gerry Mulligan and Lee Konitz, trombonists J. J. Johnson and Kai Winding, and bassist Al McKibbon. The French horn and tuba players included Gunther Schuller. John Lewis also participated in this group and in 1952 organized the long-tenured Modern Jazz Quartet. At the same time, Mulligan formed his pianoless quartet with Chet Baker. Schuller coined the phrase *third stream,* while Winding and Johnson formed a quintet that became a landmark for future trombonists.

Of all the stylistic periods contributed to or initiated by Davis, it was clearly the cool period with which the Miles Davis persona is most connected. He had an aloof performance style that at times seemed to have a disregard, if not disdain, for the audience. Sometimes he would even stand with his back to the audience while playing solos. This persona remained with him throughout his career. At this point, Davis joined those few performing personalities that need no last name. Davis and his dominating persona simply became "Miles."

SMALL GROUPS

The West Coast cool sound that grew out of the membership of the Kenton orchestra can be viewed as a derivative of the East Coast cool movement. However, even as the West Coast groups were gaining momentum, Davis had begun to look elsewhere for his creative efforts. At the same time that the West Coast sound reached its peak, the hard bop style was beginning to define the East Coast sound. Davis contributed to this rising counter to the cool sound in

listening guide

(CD 2, track 12)
Miles Davis Quintet
"Footprints"

:00   Performance begins with piano and bass. Notice the signature motive played by the bass. The piano plays chords above the bass.

:20   Head is played by the trumpet and saxophone. This is the first of three phrases that make up the head. The head uses a basic blues harmonic structure, but it has a modal feel because of the repeating bass motive.

:25   Notice how the piano answers each phrase with chords similar to the introduction. In contrast to the slow melody, the drummer maintains a double-time feel.

:28   Second phrase.

:36   Third phrase.

:45   Head is repeated. Notice the static harmony that is a trademark of modal jazz. You can hear this best in the bass, which only breaks its motivic pattern in the third phrase of each chorus.

1:09   Trumpet solo begins. The solos follow the same harmonic and phrase structure as the head. The fragmented melodic style is a trademark of Davis's playing.

1:17   Second phrase.

1:26   Third phrase. Notice the bass still uses the same motive but occasionally breaks it up to play a double-time feel in the third phrase in each chorus.

1:34   Second chorus: trumpet solo.

1:59   Third chorus: trumpet solo. It begins with the trumpet picking up the short notes the piano played at the end of the previous chorus. After a short interchange, the trumpet begins to raise the energy of the solo by moving into the upper range.

2:23   Fourth chorus: solo takes on a double-time melodic style.

2:44   Fifth chorus: energy is increased with trills and continued faster melodic phrases.

3:08   Sixth chorus: Davis continues to build energy with faster melodic phrases. Notice the building support in the drums.

3:28   Seventh chorus: Davis now uses short fragments to build his melody.

3:49   Eighth chorus: long slurred notes contrast with the earlier choruses. Notice the responses in the piano. The energy is relaxed as the solo is brought to a close.

4:00   CD selection cuts to 8:30

4:12   Solo ends with a 4-bar extension to pass the solo to the saxophone.

4:20   Saxophone solo begins slowly with slower notes. Double time used on the final phrases.

4:42   Second chorus: increasingly faster melodic lines.

5:04   Third chorus: more angular and dissonant solo lines. Listen for the increased activity in the drums. Notice the references to the head in the melody.

5:26   Fourth chorus: fragmented lines passed between the saxophone and piano. Saxophone explores and works a single motive into longer melodic phrases.

5:46   Fifth chorus: saxophone moves to the higher range to build energy. Chromatic chords played by the piano in openings in the melody.

6:09   Saxophone solo ends and is passed to the piano. Solo is primarily harmonic. Notice the chromatic chord passages.

6:31   Second piano solo chorus: short staccato chords.

6:52   Third chorus: notice the dissonant and extended chords.

7:07   The bass and drummer fall into a swing style for the third phrase.

7:14   Head returns with piano chords between the phrases.

7:29   Swing returns in the bass and drums.

7:37   Head is repeated. Notice the responses between the horn phrases by the drummer.

7:59   Head is repeated.

8:21   Light swing feel in the drums as a drum solo begins. The bass player maintains the motive with only sparse chords by the piano. This is the only point that the shape of the blues chorus is not used.

8:30   CD selection resumes.

8:56   4:23 Head is repeated.

9:18   4:45 Texture thins as the performance comes to a close. Notice how the bass motive straightens out anticipating the ending.

9:49   5:14 End.

vamping

Gil Evans Chronology

1912   Born in Toronto, Canada, on May 13.
1943–46 In U.S. Army.
1941–48 Arranged for the Claude Thornhill orchestra.
1949   Orchestrated "Boplicity"* and "Moondreams" for *Birth of the Cool*.
1952   Began playing piano professionally.
1957–60 Reunion with Miles Davis on *Miles Ahead* (1957), *Porgy and Bess* (1959), and *Sketches of Spain* (1960).
1958   Became a recording bandleader in his own right.
1960–87 Involved primarily in composing for recordings and films.
1988   Died in Cuernavaca, Mexico, on March 20.

*"Boplicity" listening guide can be found in Chapter 9.

recordings like "Walkin'" (1954), which revealed a definite move to the more emotionally direct sound of the hard bop group of players.

Although Davis backed away from cool as his stylistic center, his sound would remain through his career as closely reminiscent of the detached and underspoken cool approach. His next effort centered on a quintet that had an intermittent life for about two years and ultimately led to his sextet. From these groups came many songs that are now today's standards. His quintet is often called the "Classic Quintet" and may be one of the most influential small ensembles in jazz. This quintet redefined the role of the rhythm section, which included Red Garland on keyboard, Paul Chambers on bass, and Philly Joe Jones on drums. It also included John Coltrane, who was to become one of the dominant voices of later jazz styles. The quintet became a sextet when Davis recruited Cannonball Adderley in 1958. The sextet recorded *Milestones* before Garland and Jones were replaced with Bill Evans on piano and Jimmy Cobb on drums. Coltrane was to carry the initial stirrings of Davis's modal jazz to new heights as his playing grew more and more free. Both Davis and Coltrane could be the musical center of gravity in any ensemble. To have both in one ensemble gave the quintet unusual artistic weight.

By 1954, Davis had begun to develop the playing style that characterizes much of his later work. Rather than the high-energy, note-filled melodic lines typical of the bop era, Davis borrowed the softer tone of the cool era and slowed down the melodic activity. His phrasing became fragmented, leaving open spaces for just the rhythm section. He set himself apart from the rhythm section by playing scale-oriented rather than chord-oriented long notes. When responses are made to the energy of the rhythm section, they are usually in the form of short motivic fragments.

vamping

1950s Rhythm Section

Previous rhythm sections worked to support the soloists' improvisational curves. This rhythm section took a much more active role in shaping the rising and falling energy curves charted by the soloists. The rhythm section also created a different and shared sense of rhythmic time. It was no longer the role of the bass player to play only the primary notes of the chord; the drummer was freed from a strict role as timekeeper. Chambers played more melodic bass lines, and Jones now interacted more directly with soloists, offering melodic accents and changing rhythmic patterns on the ride cymbal. Garland moved his left hand higher up the piano and played punctuated chords to add to the complex rhythmic fabric. No one player was solely responsible for the time but, instead, it was shared across the rhythm section. Time had become a dynamic composite that would redefine future rhythm sections.

MODAL

By 1958 Davis's playing style was freed further by his use of modal scales and slower-moving harmonies. Rather than weave a melody through complex bop or blues-based funk harmonies, he suspended his melodies, based on early modes, above the harmony. The lack of harmonic movement and the scalar concept of improvisation seemed to disassociate the melody from whatever rhythmic underpinning there might be. His *Milestones* recording demonstrates this modal and almost arrhythmic melodic approach.[4] Davis's collaboration with Gil Evans on "Summertime" produced a particularly effective demonstration of the fragmented and plaintive style that was to be Davis's trademark. The backup riffs from the rest of the group plug the open spaces in Davis's solo, and Gershwin's slow melody could not be more appropriate for Davis's penchant for long tones.

The "Summertime" arrangement from the *Miles Ahead* album signaled two more important collaborations with Gil Evans, *Porgy and Bess* and *Sketches of Spain.* The latter not only further explored the colors of a large group juxtaposed against the plaintive voice of Davis but was an effort to incorporate the sounds of world music.

Davis's 1959 landmark album *Kind of Blue* and the selection "So What" clearly demonstrate his new modal approach toward improvisation. There are really only two different harmonies in the entire piece. During the solos, the first harmony lasts sixteen measures (approximately twenty-five seconds), and the second harmony is a half step higher and lasts eight measures. The solo chorus is completed with a return to the first chord for another eight measures. The fact that the two harmonies are related by only a half step is itself a move

away from tradition, which would more properly dictate a move of four or five scale tones away from the contrasting harmony. The solos above this almost frozen chord progression are usually marked by an introspective and motivic melodic style.

JAZZ/ROCK FUSION

Davis had successfully carried music through the transition from bop to cool and again on to a modal jazz that would launch players like John Coltrane (heard on the "So What" recording). He was to face yet another turn in music with the advent of rock. As rock began to dominate the popular music culture, Davis faced the dilemma confronted by most leaders in jazz: that of maintaining leadership as styles change. Just as Davis was not held to his bop heritage or trapped in the cool idiom, he would not blindly hold to his modal jazz expression and ignore the growing activity in the rock world.

listening guide

(CD 2, track 13)
Miles Davis
"So What"
Miles Davis, trumpet
Julian "Cannonball" Adderley, alto sax
John Coltrane, tenor sax
Bill Evans, piano
James Cobb, drums
Paul Chambers, bass

:00 Introduction: An out-of-time call and response between the piano and bass. This interplay is a preview of the head itself, which also has a call and response between the bass and the ensemble.

:33 (A) The bass introduces the defining motive for the piece and establishes time. Notice how the interplay in the introduction is formalized here as first the drums and then the horns join in.

1:02 (B) The chord (mode) changes. Typical of modal jazz, the harmonies move slowly. This creates a major structural point in the piece.

1:18 (A) The chord (mode) switches back to the original.

1:30 (A) Trumpet solo begins. The bass begins to walk here. Miles plays in his signature relaxed cool style made up of melodic fragments.

2:00 Chord (mode) change.

2:14 (A) Return to the original mode.

2:29 (A) Trumpet solo continues on to a second chorus. Notice the economical comping by the piano.

2:58 (B) Change of chord (mode). Notice how the whole ensemble has increased the energy level throughout the solo.

3:11 (A) Return to original mode.

3:26 (A) Tenor sax solo begins. Notice how Coltrane's style differs from Miles's in both

the length of phrases and the pace of the melodic activity.

3:53 (B) Chord change. Sax begins to use a higher range.

4:06 (A) Return to original mode. Notice how Coltrane explores a melodic motive and carries from the low to high register as he develops it.

4:21 (A) Tenor solo continues on to a second chorus.

4:35 (B) Chord change.

4:49 (A) Return to original mode. Notice the increase in melodic activity.

5:17 (A) Alto sax solo begins. Adderley's style is more bebop. He makes use of some blues idioms as well.

5:45 (B) Notice the blend of both bop and blues as this section concludes.

5:57 (A)

6:12 Adderley begins a second solo chorus. The form remains the same: A (repeated), B, A.

7:06 The horns play the 2-note motive from the head to signal the beginning of the piano solo. Notice the harmonically based solo. The rich chords used here are an Evans signature.

7:20 Solo becomes more melodic.

7:36 Returns to chordal punctuations.

8:03 Bass animates his walking pattern briefly as a transition back to the head.

8:18 (A) Return to original bass motive with horn responses.

8:31 (B)

8:44 (A)

8:57 Bass and piano repeat the motive and fade out.

9:19 End.

vamping

Betty Mabry

Miles's interest in rock might be attributed to Betty Davis (née Betty Mabry), who met him in 1967 and married him in 1968. She was Davis's second wife. She was a model and a funk and soul singer. In Miles's autobiography she is credited with introducing Miles to rock guitarist Jimi Hendrix and funk performer Sly Stone. The marriage only lasted one year but may be an important contribution to the character of Miles's seminal album, *Bitches Brew*.

In 1964 Davis formed what is sometimes called the "Second Great Quintet." It included Wayne Shorter on saxophone (and principle composer), Herbie Hancock on piano, Ron Carter on bass, and Tony Williams on drums. The quintet's new personnel pointed the way toward Miles's fusion period. This rhythm section proved to be the foundation for the modern rhythm section, and its personnel would take on leadership roles in later jazz/rock fusion groups. He found players who were not as closely tied to the past bop and funky traditions. His *Nefertiti* shows his early efforts at assimilating some of the rock idioms.[5] But it was his 1969 album *In a Silent Way* that first truly addressed the rock issue.[6] He took on John McLaughlin, a guitarist known also to the rock world, to grant a greater integrity to his jazz/rock approach. In 1970 his next album, *Bitches Brew,* brought his effort into focus and, with the aid of a Grammy, gained him much popularity. His rhythm section, which was characterized by rock patterns and electronic instruments, supported his already well-defined modal jazz approach[7] (see Chapter 14 for a more detailed discussion and a listening guide for this selection). The cuts on this album even show a relationship to the other quickly developing jazz style: free jazz. The title cut alternates between a free, arrhythmic opening theme and hard-driving rock solo areas. Davis had again discovered a musical forefront and aggressively placed himself in the middle of it. Jazz/rock fusions were already at hand in other bands—Gary Burton, Billy Cobham (Dreams), Larry Coryell, and others—but Davis had created the dominant statement for the developing genre.

Again Davis proved to be the seminal force in the developing fusion movement. All one has to do is look at the personnel in the *Bitches Brew* album to find leading figures of the mature fusion style: John McLaughlin (Mahavishnu Orchestra), Chick Corea (Return to Forever and Elektric Band), Joe Zawinul and Wayne Shorter (Weather Report).

JAZZ/POP

Performers of Davis's stature do not make major stylistic moves without generating controversy. Those who hold to previous styles once led by Davis might find his flirtations with newly developing styles somewhat disconcerting. In a career as dynamic as Davis's, not all musical efforts carry the same weight in his stylistic evolution. Many albums fall between the gaps of the giant steps made by *Birth of the Cool* and *Bitches Brew*. These other albums might often lack the surprise and power of the giants, but they show a musician who continues to experiment while maintaining an individual identity. His 1985 album *You're Under Arrest* shows a new interest in commercial music and its allied recording studio sound.[8] The musical mix is more commercial, and some of the musical material is even drawn from the popular music scene ("Time After Time" by pop singer Cyndi Lauper). Despite the new format, Davis is still recognizable through his melodic style: plaintive, fragmented, and somewhat isolated from its musical underpinning.

LEGACY

Davis was unique in his ability to sense new directions, assimilate their attributes, and then popularize the newly fused style. As a personality, his out-spoken nature was sometimes as strident as his music was definitive. In many ways, he was a maverick among jazz musicians. His intensely introspective, if not melancholy, playing style was characterized by expressions that can be perceived as technical blunders when contrasted to the lineage of trumpet virtuosos such as Armstrong and Gillespie. Yet these same flaws in technique offered Davis a personalized style that was conducive to his intimate expression. His half-valved notes and broken pitches supported the glimpse he often gave us of the raw emotional world emanating from his music.

Davis's legacy is one of melodic phrasing that breaks holes in the solo fabric while freeing the soloist from the bondage of harmonic movement. Rather than long, unbroken lines, the detail of short melodic motives took center stage. The melodic lines born of these motives then floated above the static harmonic support.

summary

The legacy of Miles Davis is imprinted on jazz more than that of any other musician. Unlike the other giants of jazz, he is not associated with a single stylistic period but actually served as the seminal force of several. Davis entered the jazz community in the bop period as a performer but left it as a leader who had found his signature jazz voice. He was the center of gravity for the developing cool style, then left it to explore a modal jazz of his own making and one that supported his unique playing style.

Within the small-group format his explorations led him to another stylistic breakthrough—fusion. He was the first to meet the new popular American music to find a hybrid musical style that preserved jazz's identity but imported the energy of rock. This exploration even carried him into areas more fully explored by the free jazz musicians who followed.

His ongoing partnership with Gil Evans fostered a sound that set the free and plaintive sound of Davis against colorfully orchestrated arrangements. Davis was at all times the stylistic explorer, an attribute that fed both his growing persona and consequent notoriety. Even before his death, his status in the rank of jazz progenitors was fixed.

SUGGESTED ADDITIONAL LISTENING

Adderley, Cannonball. *Cannonball Adderley Quintet and Amandia.* Warner
    Brothers Records, 25873-2.
Aura. Columbia Records, CK 45332.
Basic Miles. Columbia Records, PC-32025.
Best of Miles Davis (2 vols.). PDL Records, 2-1095E.
Birth of the Cool. Capitol Records, N-16168.
Bitches Brew (2 vols.). Columbia Records, GP 26.
Collector's Items (with Parker and Mingus) (2 vols.). Prestige Records, 24022E.
In a Silent Way. Columbia Records, PC-9875.
Kind of Blue (with Coltrane and Evans). Columbia Records, PC-8163.
Miles Ahead (with Gil Evans Orchestra). Columbia Records, PC-8633E.
Miles Ahead (with Parker, Lewis, and Silver). Prestige Records, 7822E.
Milestones (with Coltrane and Adderley). Columbia Records, PC-9428E.
My Funny Valentine (with Hancock). Columbia Records, PC-9106.
Nefertiti (with Shorter et al.). Columbia Records, PC-9594.
Porgy and Bess (with Gil Evans Orchestra). Columbia Records, PC-8085.
Quiet Nights (with Gil Evans Orchestra). Columbia Records, PC-8906.
Sketches of Spain (with Gil Evans Orchestra). Columbia Records, PC-8271.
Some Day My Prince Will Come. Columbia Records, PC-8456.
Tutu. Warner Brothers Records, 25490-1.
You're Under Arrest. Columbia Records, FCT 40023.

ADDITIONAL READING RESOURCES

Carr, Ian. *Miles Davis.*
Cole, Bill. *Miles Davis.*
Coryell, Julie, and Friedman, Laura. *Jazz-Rock Fusion.*
Courlander, Harold. *Miles Davis: A Musical Biography.*
Davis, Miles, and Troupe, Quincy. *Miles.*

Note: Complete information, including name of publisher and date of publication, is provided in this book's bibliography.

NOTES

1. Arranger Gil Evans; cited from Joachim E. Berendt, *The Jazz Book* (Westport, Connecticut: 1981), 80.
2. James Lincoln Collier, *The Making of Jazz* (New York: Dell, 1978), 427.
3. Miles Davis, *Sketches of Spain,* Columbia Records CL 1480; *Bitches Brew,* Columbia Records GP 26.
4. Miles Davis, *Milestones,* Columbia Records, PC-9428E.
5. Miles Davis, *Nefertiti,* Columbia Records, PC 9594.
6. Miles Davis, *In a Silent Way,* Columbia Records, PC 9875.
7. Miles Davis, *Bitches Brew.*
8. Miles Davis, *You're Under Arrest,* Columbia Records, FCT 40023; *Tutu,* Warner Brothers Records, 25490-1.

The funky idiom represented an attempt by the jazzman to rediscover his emotional roots.[1]

Martin T. Williams

Hard Bop, Funky, Gospel Jazz

This style was first called funky hard bop regression, but as the style changed considerably the title was shortened to funky. *Funky* refers to the rollicking, rhythmic feeling of the style. *Hard* means a performance that is more driving and less relaxed than cool jazz. *Bop regression* implies a return to the elements of the bop style.

It may well be true that musical styles swing back and forth like a pendulum, but the swinging of that pendulum is not smooth. The swing has been toward more complexity, and it occurs fairly gradually. For example, the players of the swing era added more musicians, the bop players played with extended harmonies and complicated melodies, and the cool players brought in new instruments, time signatures, and extended forms. But the funky style that followed seemed to revert quite suddenly to the most basic of music elements, for example, the *amen chords* from religious services. (For an introduction to the funky style, listen to Interactive Guide 8 at the Online Learning Center or directly at http://www.emcgill.com/listening.)

The term *funky* was often used interchangeably with *soul* during this period. Both the funky and the soul styles are also associated with the music prevalent in African American churches. *Soul* certainly has a connection to the church and perhaps speaks of the intended emotional content of the music. On the other hand, *funky* has a more earthy association. "Emotional" and "earthy" are both appropriate descriptions of this music.

Funky was a raw-boned type of playing that used highly rhythmical melodies and less complex harmonies than were used in the preceding era. The music had a happy sound and lacked tension and frustration. Performers of this music, having passed through the cool era, used bop elements that were generally simplified. Today, the simplification has gone even further. Most of the bop sounds have been dropped in favor of elements that tend toward gospel jazz.

The new, growing African American awareness in the United States contributed to the development of the funky and gospel styles. During this time African Americans found that their churches, with their use of harmonies and blues inflections, provided a link to their roots.

Charles Mingus

listening guide

Interactive Guide 8
Hard Bop/Funky

:00   Introduction (piano solo and bass solo alternate measures); makes use of the amen chords popular with funky players.

:06   Ensemble chorus (flügelhorn lead and alto sax harmony); piano, bass, guitar, and drums play $\frac{2}{4}$ rhythm.

:14   Second phrase.

:21   Third phrase.

:28   Flügelhorn solo (one chorus); listen for drums accenting second and fourth beats.

:50   Ensemble chorus (same as first chorus). Funky players made heavy use of the blue tones (flatted 3 and flatted 7) in their melodies. These same blue tones can be heard in the ensemble melody heard here.

:57   Second phrase.

1:05   Third phrase.

1:16   End.

Some historians even suggest that the funky style was an effort among African Americans to recapture jazz as their expression.[2] It may have been an effort by some to reclaim jazz, but the funky idiom quickly spread throughout the jazz world and was soon played by everyone, from school bands to professional ensembles, regardless of race.

Perhaps even more than an ethnic reaction, the funky idiom can be seen as a reaction to the cool intellectualism that many found in music of the cool period. The lively and emotionally exuberant nature of the funky players stands in strong contrast to the measured and controlled expression of the cool players. Unlike the cool style, which looked to European compositional techniques, the funky style adopted the truly American, and oral, idioms found in gospel and blues.

The distinction between cool and hard bop was also geographical. The cool style was often called West Coast jazz because it seemed centered in California. Shelly Manne even suggested that a more relaxed lifestyle in California might have been a factor in the development of the relaxed cool jazz style in contrast to the more driving bop style he found typical of New York jazz.[3]

THE MUSIC

Funky music borrowed elements from African American church music of the day. The loose style and the manner in which the melodies were harmonized were quite similar to the manner of performance in the church. The scale used in funky is reminiscent of the scale used in early blues but is now refined by its use in the church. The result is a gospel blues sound typified by a consistent use of blue notes.

Although these blue notes are not really the same as the original blue notes heard by church singers, their prevalent use in this style is meant to create the same effect. The original blue notes were slightly mistuned notes (often the third and seventh of the scale) in a major key. This mistuning created a disagreement between the major key and the almost minor blue notes sung against it. In an effort to re-create the earlier blues sound, players in this period actually played many pieces in minor keys (for notational examples 26, 27A, see Appendix B).

GOSPEL JAZZ

Gospel jazz is an extension of the funky style. If a distinction can be made between funky and gospel, it is in gospel's more triadic use of harmonies, much like those associated with the improvisational singing of hymns. As the name implies, gospel jazz uses elements from, and has a definite feeling of, early gospel music.[4] A primary example of these elements is the constant use of the amen chord progression (I, IV, I), or **plagal cadence.** Amen chords were used extensively in Les McCann's "Fish This Week."[5] Although this style represents a return to prejazz music, gospel jazz has also been influenced by all preceding jazz styles, including their harmonies, forms, and advanced musical techniques.[6] Rhythm, as well as emotional intensity, is highlighted in gospel jazz.

Many selections of this form of jazz can be performed in a church as easily as in a nightclub. One is Les McCann's "A Little 3/4 for God and Company."[7] Big gospel bands sometimes perform in a handclapping, shouting Baptist, manner as they enact a scene of baptism in a work such as "Wade in the Water."[8]

Originally, gospel jazz was also called *soul jazz,* but that term began to have some racial and revolutionary connotations. As the music reverted to church roots, it became known as *gospel jazz.*

THE PERFORMERS

The funky style was introduced by pianists but was quickly adopted by all instrumentalists. It was brought to public notice by pianist Horace Silver and a group led by drummer Art Blakey called the Jazz Messengers.[9] Silver also made many records with his own combo.[10] Most pianists who play funky music admit that Silver was its progenitor.

Horace Silver

Joachim Berendt mentions Horace Silver as the beginning:

> The pianist-composer Horace Silver—and along with him a few others—has broken through with a manner of playing known as "funky": slow or medium blues, played hard on the beat, with all of the heavy feeling and expression characteristic of the old blues. Jazz musicians of all persuasions and on both coasts have thrown themselves into funk with notable enthusiasm.[11]

A good example of a big band playing in a funky manner is "Hey, Pete" on Dizzy Gillespie's album *Dizzy in Greece*.[12] This album contains part of the music that Gillespie performed on the first State Department–sponsored tour in jazz history. It is also excellent proof that the talented Quincy Jones could write good funky blues works for big bands. In addition, the album demonstrates that the funky melodies were more rifflike and both rhythmically and melodically more simple than bop.

Critic Don Heckman has some different insights into these changes as he writes about the jazz of the 1960s:

listening guide

(CD 2, track 14)
Horace Silver
"The Preacher"

:00 Begins without an introduction with a trumpet (Kenny Dorham) and tenor saxophone (Hank Mobley) duet. Notice the bounce-type beat created by the syncopated chords in the piano and the simple syncopation in the melody.

:23 Head repeats. Notice the church chords and especially the amen harmonies that close many of the phrases.

:44 Trumpet solo. The comping used on the piano grows more syncopated and uses chords that are reminiscent of church harmonies. Notice that the trumpet lays back behind the beat to give the solo a relaxed feeling.

1:06 Second chorus of the trumpet solo. The solo pushes the upper range to gain more energy.

1:27 Saxophone solo begins. Comping in the piano continues.

1:48 Second chorus of the saxophone solo begins with an increase in melodic complexity, but the style still has a relaxed, laid-back feel.

2:04 Chorus closes with syncopated repeated notes over the rising harmonies of the last phrase.

2:09 Piano solo opens with simple melodic figures.

2:31 Piano solo continues with a cascading melodic motive.

2:43 Notice the cross-accents between the two hands of the piano on this final phrase.

2:50 The saxophone and trumpet enter with a unison melodic figure that interchanges with the piano solo riffs.

3:11 New chorus continues in the same style.

3:31 The group returns to the original duet that opened the piece.

3:51 The duet is repeated for the final chorus.

4:13 Final chord.

4:16 End.

Perhaps the most significant was the music that was called, variously funk, soul, etc. Its roots in modern jazz could be traced to Horace Silver's efforts to translate the blues-based forms, riffs, and rhythms of the Midwestern and Southwestern bands of the late '20s and early '30s into the idiom of the contemporary small group. Its roots in Negro society were less well defined but also important.

listening guide

Horace Silver Quintet (with Art Blakey)
"Stop Time"*
Kenny Dorham, trumpet
Hank Mobley, tenor saxophone
Horace Silver, piano
Doug Watkins, bass
Art Blakey, drums

:00   Introductory theme with one repeat at a lower range.

:08   Head melody with trumpet and saxophone in unison.

:24   Trumpet solo.

1:11   Tenor saxophone solo.

1:58   Piano solo; listen to the left-hand-punctuated comping patterns as Silver solos with his right hand.

2:55   Just as his solo ends, listen for the blues (funky) melodic references.

2:58   Trumpet solo, at which point the band begins to trade fours; each player solos for 4 measures with 4-bar drum solos in between.

3:02   Four-bar drum solo.

3:06   Four-bar tenor solo.

3:10   Four-bar drum solo.

3:14   Four-bar trumpet solo.

3:18   Four-bar drum solo.

3:21   Four-bar tenor solo.

3:25   Extended drum solo.

3:44   Introductory theme restated.

4:03   End.

*Bebop, New World Records, 271 (originally Blue Note, 45–1631).

Silver's work, however, was soon modified, simplified, and repeated—over and over. And few of the imitators understood the delicate balance of elements that was crucial to the music's artistic success. As often happens, the values Silver was seeking to express were discarded by most of his imitators in favor of the superficialities—the simple rhythms, the reduction of blues changes to their most simple form, and the distortion of Gospel-derived techniques. The relationship between this music, which was considered by many to be a genuine expression of the Negro past, and the growing Civil Rights movement was very close.[13]

vamping

Hammond B3 Organ

The Hammond organ had been used only rarely before 1951 (by Fats Waller and Count Basie) when Wild Bill Davis surprised everyone by performing real blues-oriented works on it. Later, Jimmy Smith proved the potential of the instrument by using a larger variety of organ stops (effects) than any other player in the jazz field and by using incredible technique. The instrument was accepted wholeheartedly in the funky era. A parallel, if not the root of this style of organ playing, can be found in the African American church service. This association with the church is not new to the historical development of jazz.

The return to jazz roots indicated by the less complex harmonies, excessive use of blue notes, and simpler rhythmic feeling emphasized communication between players and listeners and led away from the compositional or technical complexities of cool or bop. It is interesting that on early Horace Silver recordings the bop concept is prominent and the afterbeat accent hardly discernible. In the funky style, the bop elements faded gradually as the accented afterbeat developed.

Cannonball Adderley

Cannonball Adderley was a signature alto saxophone player of the hard bop period. His playing style was blues based, no doubt influenced by his early work with Ray Charles. He was sought after by Miles Davis and finally joined his quintet in 1957. With John Coltrane's return to the band a few months later the quintet contained two of the leading saxophone players of the day. While with Davis, Cannonball recorded *Milestones* and *Kind of Blue*. Bill Evans later joined Miles and recorded *Portrait of Cannonball*.

After his stay with Davis, Cannonball formed his own quintet with his brother Nat. By the end of the 1960s his work developed more of a crossover style that maintained his original blues-rooted playing. He gained a new popularity in the 1970s with songs like "Mercy, Mercy, Mercy," written by Joe Zawinul. Although Cannonball's career spanned the transition to both the avant-garde and jazz rock styles his own music remained accessible to the general listener.

ART BLAKEY AND THE DEVELOPING MAINSTREAM

On the tail of the hard bop movement, with its close relationship to bop itself, emerged a jazz legacy that soon came to be recognized as the jazz mainstream. Eventually, jazz would be viewed by later players as having an artistic beginning in the bop movement with its move away from popular following to one of

more elite listeners. The players that define the mainstream either were prominent performers in the bop era or played in a derivative fashion. The hard bop players carried the bop style into a more accessible format that retained the allegiance to the personal voices of the jazz improvisers.

Many of the key personnel found at the mouth of the mainstream could also be found under the tutelage of drummer Art Blakey. The membership of his ensembles boasts some of the most important players at this time: Horace Silver, Freddie Hubbard, Wayne Shorter, Lee Morgan, Hank Mobley, Kenny Dorham, and both Marsalis brothers, Branford and Wynton. Blakey described his efforts to pass on the jazz tradition by saying, "I look for the new guys, and I just give them a place to hone their art and they grow. They do it themselves. I just give them a chance. All they need is a little guidance, a little direction, and they're gone. When they get big enough, I let them go and get their own thing. Then I find some more."[14] Blakey died in 1990.

Clifford Brown

Clifford Brown had a very short performance career but left an important mark on the bop to hard bop transition. He died in a car crash at the young age of 25, and his recordings spanned only four years. His own influences were boppers Dizzy Gillespie and Fats Navarro. Like these two players, Brown was capable of fast-tempo solos that charted their way through the complex harmonies typical of bop standards. Brown was equally expressive in ballads.

Like so many of the hard bop players Brown played with Art Blakey before forming his own group with Max Roach. The Clifford Brown and Max Roach Quintet proved to be important in the refinement of the hard bop style. In addition to Brown and Roach, the group included Harold Land on tenor saxophone, who was briefly replaced by Teddy Edwards and ultimately Sonny Rollins.

listening guide

(CD 3, track 1)
Art Blakey and the Jazz Messengers
"E.T.A."
Art Blakey, drums
Wynton Marsalis, trumpet
Charles Fambrough, bass
Bobby Watson, alto saxophone
James Williams, piano

Each chorus of this piece is 32 measures long with four 8-bar phrases, making an AABA structure that can be heard most clearly when the theme is played at the beginning and end of the performance.

:00   Drum solo sets up the head.

:26   (A) Band enters playing the head in harmony; (A) repeat of first 8 bars of the head.

:37   (B) Middle 8 bars, or bridge.

:42   (A) Return to first 8 bars.

:48   Alto sax solo; notice bop phrasing and driving walking bass.

:58   (B) Section of the chorus.

1:04   (A) Return to the A section.

1:10   Second chorus of alto sax solo.

1:32   Third chorus of solo.

1:54   Trumpet solo, also three choruses.

2:15   Second chorus.

2:37   Third chorus.

2:59   Tenor sax solo, only two choruses.

3:19   Second chorus.

3:41   Piano solo, again only two choruses.

4:25   All the horn players play a single chorus in unison, similar to the unison chorus used in the bop era.

4:47   Drum solo.

5:32   Head returns with the two A sections.

5:43   (B) Bridge.

5:48   (A) Return to last A.

5:54   Slows down with an ending phrase.

6:09   End.

Despite his short career, Brown's legacy is reflected in the number of recordings and events honoring his work. Benny Golson's "I Remember Clifford," which has become a jazz standard, and the Clifford Brown Jazz Festival held in Wilmington, Delaware, are just two examples of his remaining influence.

Sonny Rollins

Tenor saxophonist Sonny Rollins exercised much influence during the late 1950s. He captured the attention of many of the day's players with his melodic style of improvisation in which he often improvised from a melodic line with apparent disregard for chord structure.[15] As previously stated, an improvising player in the swing era usually had only a few measures in which to express his ideas. Rollins often improvises for twenty or thirty minutes to develop his musical thoughts, inventing a short phrase, elaborating on it, and expanding the idea in every conceivable direction, much as Mozart, Haydn, and Beethoven did. The concept is at least five hundred years old.

Rollins's playing shows cool and bop influences repeatedly. For two choruses of "Limehouse Blues" he shows great economy of notes, playing only what he thinks the listener needs to hear. Then the bop influences become apparent, and an occasional funky phrase is added.[16] On his recording of "St. Thomas," his solo flows extremely well as he establishes a short melodic thought and elaborates on it, changing it in every way he can.[17] By little phrases he continually brings the listener back to thoughts that he has played earlier. Listen to "Doxy" to hear this approach.[18]

Sonny Rollins

listening guide

(CD 3, track 2)
Sonny Rollins Quartet
"Blue 7"

:00 Bass (Doug Watkins) plays a walking solo.

:15 Drums (Max Roach) enter lightly, with mainly second and fourth beats on the hi hat.

:43 Tenor sax (Sonny Rollins) enters, establishing the theme.

1:06 Piano (Tommy Flannagan) enters, solving any key problem listeners may have had because of Rollins's angular solo lines.

2:57 Piano solo; the I, IV, and V chords can be detected quite easily.

3:57 Tenor sax returns; short interlude, just a clue to designate that the piano solo is over and that the drum solo should start.

4:07 Drum solo; lightly and steadily on the hi hat (on beats 2 and 4) while playing intricate syncopated work on the snare drum, bass drum, and tom-toms.

6:23 Drummer splashes a definite clue that he has finished his solo.

6:23 Tenor sax solos again.

7:05 Tenor sax softens to accentuate the walking bass as in the beginning.

8:09 Piano and drums soften to feature the bass (demonstration tape fades out here).

8:30 Piano drops out, leaving just the walking bass and afterbeats on the foot cymbals.

9:19 Tenor sax solo reenters; 4 bars, starting a series of trading fours with the drums.

9:26 Four-bar drum solo.

9:33 Four-bar tenor sax solo.

9:40 Four-bar drum solo.

9:47 Four-bar tenor sax solo.

9:55 Four-bar drum solo.

10:02 Four-bar tenor sax solo.

10:44 Tenor sax softens and plays sustained notes.

11:11 End.

The key in Rollins's advancement is thematic improvisation rather than either improvisation on a chord progression or variations on an established melody. Rollins is more concerned with fragments of a piece than with the whole melody itself, and he uses these fragments for his personal expression. Many musicians use this approach, but Rollins seems to have brought it to a recognizable, viable level.

This thematic, or motivic, approach can be heard in the way Rollins works the theme of "St. Thomas."[19] His recording of "Blue 7" is a clear example of how he, sometimes humorously, dissects a melodic line.[20] It is sometimes noted that this approach stems from the piano playing of Thelonious Monk, at least as far as Rollins is concerned. Therefore, another example of the thematic approach is Monk's development of a little three-note motif in "Bags' Groove."[21] Most musicians who had observed Monk's approach considered it valid but pianistic. After Rollins demonstrated that playing such a motif was feasible and logical on a saxophone (which can be played only one note at a time), an entire school of wind players followed his lead.

Rollins demonstrated his commitment to his improvisational skills when he stepped away from a successful performing career because he was dissatisfied with his playing. He retired for two years, from the summer of 1959 to the fall of 1961 (and again in 1969), to practice. (The story goes that much of this practicing took place on top of the Williamsburg Bridge in New York.)

Charles Mingus

Charles Mingus is perhaps the most difficult player/composer of the bop and post-bop eras to categorize. His musical output covers a wide berth of idioms and styles, from his earliest work with Armstrong and Kid Ory to the later,

listening guide

(CD 3, track 3)
Charles Mingus
"Eclipse"

:00   Cello solo; loose arrhythmic support and atonal horn statements.

:30   Vocal enters; more metric feel; cello plays a countermelody to the vocal; more traditional chordal support but still extended harmonies.

1:32   Instrumental interlude, faster tempo with loose-sounding counterpoint.

1:47   Bass and cello play counterpoint lines that build as other instruments enter; atonal feeling results from the counterpoint.

2:30   Vocal enters with cello obligato; more traditional harmonic support.

2:55   End.

Charles Mingus

almost free compositions such as "Pithecanthropus Erectus,"[22] and his efforts became centrally important during the hard bop days. His connection to that idiom may not at first be stylistically apparent. However, his compositional intent was to create a direct, immediate emotional statement. His legacy to this jazz tradition lies in the manner in which he tried to convey the emotion.

Mingus attempted to channel the creative energies of his players into a unified statement. Although he relied on the individual strengths of his players, he also expected them to work toward a common emotional statement during a performance. This approach differs from the traditional bop approach, which encourages players to seek individual statements during their improvisations.

An example of Mingus's emotional intent can be heard in his recording of "Haitian Fight Song."[23] He has been quoted that it could also have been called "Afro-American Fight Song."[24] He goes on to say that to play it successfully, he must think about prejudice, hate, and persecution. In this regard, Mingus shows his tie to the funky movement and its relationship to the developing civil rights activities.

listening guide

Charles Mingus
"Haitian Fight Song"*

:00 Bass solo: listen for thematic material to be quoted later.

:50 Mingus sets up a rhythmic pattern that establishes time.

1:05 Tambourine enters.

1:10 Drums enter with time.

1:18 Trombone enters softly in background with one of the two main motives.

1:32 Alto saxophone enters softly in background and gets louder.

1:35 Listen for the sax and trombone as they exchange motives back and forth.

1:54 Mingus adds vocal line.

2:07 Trombone solo; first of 5 blues choruses.

2:25 Second chorus.

2:30 Saxophone softly in background.

2:44 Double-time feel in both rhythm section and soloist; third chorus.

3:02 Marchlike beat in whole ensemble under the trombone solo; fourth chorus.

3:19 Drum fill.

3:22 Return to original tempo, still trombone solo; fifth chorus.

3:41 Piano solo begins; first of 5 blues choruses.

3:55 Piano solo uses motive from opening section.

4:00 Second chorus.

4:20 March feel returns; third chorus.

4:40 Return to original tempo, still piano solo; fourth chorus.

5:00 Fifth chorus.

5:19 Saxophone solo begins; first of 5 blues choruses.

5:39 Second chorus.

5:58 Double-time chorus as in trombone solo; third chorus.

6:16 March feel under sax solo; fourth chorus.

6:33 Drum fill.

6:36 Return to original tempo, still saxophone solo; fifth chorus.

6:55 Bass solo with light piano comping underneath and straight time in drums; first of 9 blues choruses.

7:14 Second chorus.

7:34 Third chorus.

7:53 Fourth chorus.

7:58 Gospel chords in piano.

8:13 Fifth chorus: listen for motive in bass solo.

8:27 Drums drop out.

8:32 Sixth chorus.

8:50 Seventh chorus.

9:08 Eighth chorus, freer style and time.

9:30 Ninth chorus.

9:33 Mingus hints at time with response from drums.

9:52 Mingus again begins rhythmic time pattern used at the beginning.

10:50 Horns again exchange motives back and forth.

11:03 Mingus vocalizes.

11:25 Ensemble slows down.

11:40 Mingus uses bow on bass.

11:55 End.

---

*Smithsonian Collection, CD 4, track 13.

A more direct tie to the gospel idiom can be found in his 1959 recording of "Better Git It in Your Soul" from his album *Mingus Ah Um*.[25] In this recording, the reference to the gospel church is made clear.

Mingus's ties to both the swing and the bop traditions can be heard in his composition "Hora Decubitus."[26] The 1963 recording of this piece shows the balance between individual statement and collective intent that Mingus was able to inspire in his players. The emotional level is high from the beginning to the end of the performance. Only an ensemble that is both loose and secure could successfully support the different solo styles of Booker Ervin (tenor saxophone) and Eric Dolphy (alto saxophone). Also listen to his quintet playing "Haitian Fight Song" for an example of his bass playing and his compositional approach.[27]

Charles Mingus approached his composition and performance with an intensity seldom matched in jazz. His emotional style spanned the gap between composition and improvisation. To maintain the intensity and accuracy of his ideas, he would sometimes recite the composition to the group rather than limit his ideas by writing them down. He would even stop performances to correct compositional ideas or to scold the audience for not listening. His constant experimentation seldom placed him in the mainstream of jazz's evolution, but he exerted a constant influence on that evolution.

summary

The hard bop school often explained its development as a return to the basics of jazz. It saw the new instrumentation and compositional devices used by cool musicians as gimmicks rather than valid developments of the jazz tradition. Their call was therefore back to a *straight-ahead* jazz that was more improvisational and emotionally based. In essence, they were charting a traditional line of development for jazz that did not veer from the *mainstream,* another expression often applied to this return-to-basics movement. This was more than a mere revival of an older tradition; it was also a recognition by jazz musicians that they had a guiding jazz tradition that was worth preserving.

The funky hard bop era has proved to be more than merely a return to the bop style. In many ways, it demonstrates the development of an emerging tradition that begins to define itself as a maturing art form. An apparent paradox exists as the players look back to move forward. When looking back they saw the vitality that has always been a part of the jazz tradition and that seemed to come into focus somewhat during the bop period. The Civil Rights movement, with its search for African American roots, no doubt strongly influenced the development of this music. The gospel sound of the black church merged with the energy remembered from the bop period to generate this new style.

This era also offers a window to a continuing jazz tradition. The mainstream has continued to flow and coexist with the many styles that have developed since that time. To many players such as Wynton Marsalis, this straight-ahead style represents the true tradition of jazz. Whether it is the purest form of jazz is certainly debatable; however, it must be recognized as perhaps the style most associated with the present jazz community's notion of what is meant by the jazz tradition.

This period, therefore, represents an important time in the history of jazz as a developing art form. As proven jazz performers passed on their attitudes and abilities to a new generation of performers, they also passed on a respect for the tradition from which they all came.

FOR FURTHER STUDY

1. In terms of rhythmic feeling, what does the word *funky* mean?
2. How would one describe the emotion or feeling of the music of the funky era?
3. What electronic instrument became popular in this era?
4. Listen to the excellent example of the funky style, "The Preacher," by Horace Silver. Give your reactions to the total sound. Is the melody recognizable? Do you hear the amen chord progression? Which of the two solo instruments, trumpet or saxophone, plays blue notes? Do you hear the musical conversation between the piano and ensemble near the end?

SUGGESTED ADDITIONAL LISTENING

Adderley, Cannonball. *The Best of Cannonball Adderley*. Capitol Records, SN 16002.
———. *Cannonball Adderley Quintet and Amandia*. Warner Brothers Records, 25873-2.
———. *The Cannonball Adderley Quintet Plus*. Riverside Records, 9388.
———. *Mercy, Mercy, Mercy*. Capitol Records, T 2663.
Brown, Clifford. *Brown and Roach Incorporated*. EmArcy, 1954.
———. *Clifford Brown and Max Roach*. EmArcy, 1955.
Evans, Bill. *Bill Evans Trio with Symphony Orchestra*. Verve Records, V6-8540.
———. *Conversations with Myself*. Verve Records, A-68526.
———. *New Conversations*. Warner Brothers Records, BSK 3177.
———. *Waltz for Debby*. Original Jazz Classics, OJC 210.
Lewis, Ramsey. *The Best of Ramsey Lewis*. Cadet Records, S-839.
———. *The In Crowd*. Cadet Records, S-757.
Morgan, Lee. "The Sidewinder," *Three Decades of Jazz (1959–1969)*.
Rollins, Sonny. "Blue 7," *Saxophone Colossus*. Prestige Records, LP 7079.
———. *Sonny Rollins* (2 vols.). Blue Note Records, 1542, 1558.
———. *Taking Care of Business*. Prestige Records, 24082.
Silver, Horace. *Best of Horace Silver*. Blue Note Records, 84325.
Smith, Jimmy. "Back at the Chicken Shack," *Three Decades of Jazz (1959–1969)*.
———. *Jimmy Smith's Greatest Hits*. Blue Note Records, BST 89901.

ADDITIONAL READING RESOURCES

Blancq, Charles. *Sonny Rollins: The Journey of a Jazzman*.
Mingus, Charles. *Beneath the Underdog*.

Priestley, Brian. *Mingus: A Critical Biography.*
Williams, Martin T., ed. *The Art of Jazz,* 233–38.

_____

Note: Complete information, including name of publisher and date of publication, is provided in this book's bibliography.

NOTES

1. Martin T. Williams, "Bebop and After: A Report," in *Jazz,* ed. Nat Hentoff and Albert McCarthy (New York: Holt, Rinehart & Winston, 1959), 297.
2. James Lincoln Collier, *The Making of Jazz* (New York: Dell, 1978), 435–53.
3. Shelly Manne, from an interview with Reginald Buckner, *Jazz: American Classic,* videotape no. 7.
4. Les McCann, *Les McCann Plays the Truth.*
5. Ibid.
6. Jazz Brothers, "Something Different," *The Soul of Jazz.*
7. Les McCann, *Les McCann Plays the Truth.*
8. Johnny Griffin, "Wade in the Water," *The Soul of Jazz.*
9. Horace Silver (Art Blakey), *A Night at Birdland,* Blue Note Records, vol. 1, 1521; *Horace Silver and the Jazz Messengers,* Blue Note Records, BLP1518.
10. Horace Silver, *Blowing the Blues Away,* Blue Note Records, 4017; *Song for My Father,* Blue Note Records, 4185.
11. Joachim Berendt, *Jazz Book: From New Orleans to Rock and Free Jazz,* trans. by Dan Morgenstern (Westport, Conn.: Lawrence Hill, 1975).
12. Dizzy Gillespie, "Hey Pete," *Dizzy in Greece,* Verve Records, MEV-8017.
13. Don Heckman, "Ornette and the Sixties," *Down Beat* 31, no. 20 (July 1964): 59.
14. Art Blakey, "Art Blakey in His Prime," *Down Beat* 52, no. 7 (July 1985): 21.
15. Sonny Rollins, *Sonny Rollins at Music Inn,* Metro Jazz Records, E 1011.
16. Sonny Rollins, "Limehouse Blues," *Sonny Rollins at Music Inn.*
17. Sonny Rollins, "St. Thomas," *Saxophone Colossus,* Prestige Records, LP 7079.
18. Sonny Rollins, "Doxy," *Sonny Rollins at Music Inn* and *One Man in Jazz,* RCA Victor Records, LPM/LSP-2612.
19. Sonny Rollins, "St. Thomas," *Saxophone Colossus.*
20. Sonny Rollins, "Blue 7," *Saxophone Colossus* and *Smithsonian Collection of Classic Jazz.*
21. Thelonious Monk (Miles Davis record), "Bags' Groove (Take 1)," *Bags Groove,* Prestige Records, 7109.
22. Charles Mingus, *The Best of Charles Mingus,* Atlantic, SD 1555.
23. Ibid.
24. Collier, *The Making of Jazz,* 446.
25. Charles Mingus, *Mingus Ah Um,* Columbus, CS 8171.
26. Charles Mingus, "Hora Decubitus," *Smithsonian Collection of Classic Jazz* (1st ed.)
27. Charles Mingus, "Haitian Fight Song," *Smithsonian Collection of Classic Jazz.*

12

John Coltrane

"My goal is to live the truly religious life, and express it in my music. If you live it, when you play there's no problem because the music is part of the whole thing. To be a musician is really something. It goes very, very deep. My music is the spiritual expression of what I am—my faith, my knowledge, my being."[1]

John Coltrane

Saxophonist John Coltrane combined great emotion with excellent musicianship and discipline with freedom. Like Parker, he did not have an extensive career (compared to Armstrong and Ellington). It lasted about twelve years, from 1955 to 1967. His influence however proved far reaching. Through his short career he charted a unique musical course through a variety of jazz styles, contributing to each along the way.

Musicians may disagree about the validity of avant-garde jazz as expressed by contemporary players such as Ornette Coleman (see chapter 13), but there are few disagreements about John Coltrane's place in jazz history and his contribution to avant-garde jazz. He took his place among the most renowned saxophone players in jazz. Coltrane produced a large, dark, lush sound from his instrument (on both tenor and soprano). A brief listen to "Ogunde" verifies this.[2] On the album *Giant Steps* (Coltrane's first Atlantic album under his name), his beautiful, solid tone is most evident in "Naima."[3] This recording shows his confidence at this time in his career and reveals deeper feeling and conviction than when he worked for Davis. His drive is especially apparent on "Cousin Mary."

Coltrane's legacy includes his beautiful tone, harmonic manipulation, and technical proficiency on the saxophone, particularly his control of the upper register. (He had equal strength in all registers of the instrument—an unusual trait.) Wayne Shorter, Charles Lloyd, Pharaoh Sanders, and Eddie Harris all show traces of this legacy. The influence of Coltrane's passionate approach appears in unlikely places, as in an occasional near scream from cool saxophonist Stan Getz. Coltrane said that Sidney Bechet, an early soprano saxophone player, was an important influence on his playing. Coltrane advanced jazz improvisation harmonically through long excursions into the higher harmonics of chords on an instrument (tenor saxophone) that is sounded where a trombone, or a man's voice, is pitched. Coltrane had great coordination between his fingering of the saxophone and his tonguing (the manner in which you touch the reed with your tongue to begin and end notes). This coordination allowed him a fast technique, and he played arpeggios so rapidly that they are referred to by jazz critic Ira Gitler as Coltrane's "sheets of sound." These can be heard as early in his career as "All Blues" with Miles Davis as well as in "Cousin Mary" with his own quartet. Coltrane's

vamping

John Coltrane Chronology

September 23, 1926	Born in Hamlet, North Carolina; as a boy played E-flat horn and clarinet.
1938–1939	Aunt, grandparents and father all died.
ca. 1941	Switched to alto saxophone.
1943	Moved to Philadelphia, studied at Granoff Studios and the Ornstein School of Music.
1945–46	Enlisted in the Navy, played in the Navy jazz band when in Hawaii.
1947–48	Played alto saxophone with bands led by Joe Webb and King Kolax and later tenor saxophone with the Eddie Vinson Band.
Late 1940s	Played with Jimmy Heath, Dizzy Gillespie and Earl Bostic.
1951	Joined Gillespie's sextet and played at Birdland in New York and in Detroit.
1955–57	Replaced Sonny Rollins in Miles Davis' "First Great Quintet".
1956 (October) and 1957 (April)	Replaced by either Rollins, Bobby Jaspar, or Cannonball Adderley because of addiction to drugs and alcoholism. However Coltrane is heard on all the most famous albums during this time.
1957	Worked with Thelonious Monk's quartet in New York and began to develop his "sheets of sound" style.
1957	Recorded a hard bop album for Blue Note, *Blue Train*, first use of his new harmonic approach, "Coltrane Changes".
1958–60	Rejoined Davis with alto saxophonist Cannonball Adderley.
1959	Formed his own group and recorded *Giant Steps* for Atlantic Records, extending his new melodic and harmonic language.
1960	Formed his own group with McCoy Tyner (pianist), Steve Davis (bass) and Elvin Jones (drums). Debuted on soprano saxophone.
1961–1965	Coltrane's Classic Quartet with Jimmy Garrison now on bass.
1961	Eric Dolphy on bass clarinet, alto saxophone and flute joined Coltrane's group. When on the West Coast Wes Montgomery worked with the quintet.
1963	Roy Haynes was a regular replacement for Elvin Jones.
1964	*A Love Supreme* is recorded. His work was becoming more and more spiritually based.
1965–1967	Avant-garde quintet with Pharaoh Sanders (tenor saxophone), Jimmy Garrison (bass), Rashied Ali (a second drummer until Jones leaves) and his second wife Alice Coltrane (piano). This group was Coltrane's most experimental and controversial to date but still attracted large audiences.
July 17, 1967	Died of liver cancer on Long Island. His funeral was opened by the Albert Ayler Quartet and closed by the Ornette Coleman Quartet.

creativity with his sheets of sound was actually homophonically constructed music that had been carried to a higher level. He thought of these runs as if they were chords on top of chords. His fast arpeggios have great emotional impact, and he was an expert in the use of **sequences.**

COLTRANE'S MUSICAL EVOLUTION

Throughout his career Coltrane continued to explore increasingly experimental music to ultimately become jazz's leading avant-garde performer. He began this evolution from a bop/hard bop and modal context and ended in the free experimental setting of his late quartet. A logical starting place for those uninitiated in Coltrane's music is Miles Davis's recording of *Kind of Blue*.[4] On "All Blues," "So What," and "Freddie Freeloader," the listener can hear Coltrane when he was working for a fairly conservative leader. Therefore, he had not greatly expanded his directions and is quite easy to understand and appreciate immediately. It is interesting to compare the Coltrane of this album with Cannonball Adderley, a consummate hard bop performer. On both "So What" and "Freddie Freeloader," Adderley shows a more direct association with Parker while playing some very funky phrases not to be found in Coltrane's playing. In "Freddie Freeloader," Coltrane is blowing aggressively and melodically at the same time. See the listening guide for Miles' sextet with Cannonball Adderley and John Coltrane, *So What,* in Chapter 10.

Coltrane played rhythmically but his relationship to the rhythm section was extended even becoming somewhat **arrhythmic.** He often seemed free of the metric underpinning of the rhythm section. This freed the rhythm players to respond to the melodic thoughts they were hearing from the soloists. Coltrane could play "on top of the beat" whenever he wanted to, but he liked to play differently from the rhythm players with the idea that this freed them from having to play exclusively with him. This is an important concept for his later avant-garde experiments. His counter rhythms can be heard in later recordings on both "Countdown" and "Spiral" on *Giant Steps.* He also seemed to fuse melody and rhythm in "The Father and the Son and the Holy Ghost."[5] In the bebop tradition Coltrane was capable of improvising rapid bop melodies over the fast moving changes of the bop standards. Like Charlie Parker, he had an impressive high-speed technical facility which seemed to increase throughout his career. To this facility he would add his own harmonic scheme, referred to as "Coltrane Changes," that would come to fruition in the performance of his own composition, "Giant Steps" (1959).

Eventually, Coltrane turned toward emphasizing the melodic line above all else. Chords were used only as they related to the melody. Instead of melody being improvised out of harmony, melody was improvised from melody, an approach used by classical composers quite early in the history of music, but seldom by jazz performers. Coltrane had the advantage of working with Thelonious Monk, from whom he learned to establish a mature, consistent relationship between the chords and his melodic thoughts. Monk stimulated Coltrane's interest in wide intervals, although it is possible that his interest in various types of scales came from his time with the Miles Davis group. Coltrane continued to push the range and tone of the saxophone by using what are called "false fingerings" (new fingerings for notes that change the tonal color of a note) and extreme changes at extreme speeds from one range on the saxophone to another.

Coltrane broke away from the format of theme, solos, theme. His recording of "The Father and the Son and the Holy Ghost" has no real theme before his solo, and the ensemble portion has no theme at all. This can be disturbing to jazz listeners who expect only traditional approaches to jazz. In "Countdown," Coltrane shows his great coordination. The work sounds free, yet when chords are brought in under his solo, he is exactly where he should be harmonically. An example of Coltrane's innovation is a selection called "India," recorded before the Beatles received credit for "discovering" Ravi Shankar. On this recording, one hears influences such as Indian scales and rhythms. Coltrane's interest in new complex harmonies is reminiscent of the first generation of bop and offered an alternative to the funky/soul side of hard bop. His work on *Giant Steps* is hard driving like hard bop, but his melodic flights explored new harmonic relationships that would ultimately mature into a new freedom more in line with the avant-garde side of jazz.

Just as Coltrane continued to develop his own sound he also continued to develop the sound and texture of his groups, especially in the later quartet. The roles of all the players were given more improvisational freedom that allowed for more interaction among members. Also the intensity increased especially with the addition of Pharaoh Sanders's high energy and at times overblown tone and Eric Dolphy's melodic flights. The addition of multiple drummers and a second double bass also added to the textual intensity. The group moved naturally into a dense and increasingly dissonant collective improvisation that was free structurally and tonally.

vamping

Alice Coltrane, jazz pianist and composer

Alice Coltrane (née McLeod) was an active jazz player before she first met John Coltrane. She had her own trio and worked as a duo with vibist Terry Pollard. She had a daughter with her first husband Kenny Hagood after they were married in 1960. While she was playing with Terry Gibbs's quartet she met John Coltrane. In 1965 she married Coltrane and ultimately replaced McCoy Tyner in John Coltrane's group. They had three children together, drummer John Jr. in 1964, Ravi in 1965 and saxophonist Oranyan in 1967. She played with John Coltrane until his death in 1967. She continued to play with her own groups after Coltrane's death until about 1975 when she established and became the swamini for the Vedantic Center in California. She recorded a comeback album, *Translinear Light*, in 2004 as interest in her music returned. She died January 12, 2007 and was buried alongside her late husband John Coltrane.

listening guide

(CD 3, Track 4)
Trinkle, Tinkle
The Definitive John Coltrane On
Prestige and Riverside
Thelonious Monk with John Coltrane

:00 Piano intro opens with a reference to the head. Notice the short trill at the end which will become an important melodic element through the performance.

:09 Drum fill introduces the next saxophone statement which starts with a flourish and the descending piano scale pattern and finally then the angular head motive. All these elements will be exploited during the following solos.

:20 Repeat of the short drum statement and the head motive.

:33 Saxophone plays a melodic trills which responses from the piano.

:40 The saxophone plays a melodic motive with accompanying piano punches.

:48 Head motive closes this section.

:56 Saxophone solo begins. Listen for the short melodic references to the head motive.

1:02 Fast scale-like runs.

1:13 A reference to the head is followed by bop-like melodic patterns.

1:30 Notice how the solo moves between the more disjunct melodic motives and more traditional bebop patterns. At times you can hear fast melodic areas with big melodic leaps that signal the developing sheets of sound which characterized Coltrane's later style.

2:33 The fast melodic passages give way to a more melodic style.

2:40 A return the rapid melodic work.

3:06 Notice the overblown notes and wide intervals.

3:21 A return to a more melodic style to close the solo.

3:25 Piano solo begins. Notice the signature Monk style with the economy of notes and the dissonant tone clusters.

3:48 The chordal trills come from the end of the opening head.

3:55 Dissonant chord punctuations.

4:05 Cites the head motive.

4:12 Syncopated dissonant chords.

4:24 Solo works with variations of the head rhythm and chords.

4:44 Notice how the chord punches are reinforced by the rhythm section.

5:00 Bass solo begins.

5:25 Piano offers backup responses to the bass.

5:42 Bass sets up a return to the head.

5:50 Return to the head.

5:59 Drum interlude and repeat of the head.

6:10 Drum lead into the ending phrase built on the harmonic trill from the end of the head.

6:27 Final statement of the end of the head motive.

6:35 End.

INNOVATIONS

Coltrane had two important influences on his musical development, bebop and modal jazz.

An Extension of Bebop

Of all the big name bebop players Gillespie was the most theoretical. Performing with Gillespie may have been important to Coltrane's own theoretical development. His interest in extended harmonic changes and the melodic patterns needed to weave through them was only a starting point for Coltrane. Bebop was characterized by high-speed performance and technical prowess, also two characteristics of Coltrane's personal style. He was to elevate all these bop elements as he matured. His "sheets of sound" were only possible because of outstanding technical skill. The fact that he is known for developing his own harmonic approach, Coltrane Changes, shows his continued interest in the harmonic complexity rooted in bebop. Coltrane's evolving harmonic style became more complex and extended and as a result created a more dissonant sound. Also, he actually increased the number of chords used in traditional harmonic sequences. Where a bebop standard might have two chords in a musical phrase Coltrane would extend the harmonic sequence by adding substitute chords that had a more dissonant relationship to the key. He would then create new complex melodic patterns that worked with the new harmonic sequence. Coltrane had the unique technical ability to perform at blistering speeds weaving his own melodic patterns through his own complex harmonic changes. The culmination of this process can be heard in his landmark performance of "Giant Steps."

An Extension of Modal

Modal jazz is the harmonic flip side to bebop jazz. Whereas bebop harmonies are frequent and numerous (most often two chords per measure), modal jazz is characterized by infrequent chord changes. How fast the chords change is

vamping

Coltrane Changes

Coltrane's approach to harmony was so unique it earned its own name, "Coltrane Changes." As early as the *Blue Train* album he began to use substitute chords over more traditional jazz harmonic progression to ultimately define his style. A substitute chord is a chord different from the one usually used at that point in a song. Although the rhythm section may still use the original chord, Coltrane would use this substitute chord as the foundation for his melodic solo. The result is a more dissonant sounding solo heard as an extension of the original harmony. The process became more definitely defined on his *Giant Steps* album. The title cut, "Giant Steps," is actually built on the Coltrane Changes. The harmonic progression is very difficult to solo over and has become a measuring stick for aspiring jazz players.

referred to as "**harmonic rhythm**." Bebop has a very fast harmonic rhythm that requires fast melodic patterns to navigate the fast moving chords. The slow harmonic rhythm of modal jazz has chords that may not change for many measures. The harmonies seem frozen and encourage a more melodic and motivic approach to soloing. When the chord finally does change, it creates a significant harmonic and structural event. Coltrane's penchant for harmonic patterns so effective in high speed bebop playing now found a new freedom. Melodic motives now proved more useful than harmonic patterns.

Despite Coltrane's relatively short career, he charted one of the most direct, continuous courses from the **modal jazz** of the Miles Davis quintet to his own late albums, rich with free improvisation. Rather than declare independence from traditional form and harmonic practice as Coleman did, Coltrane extended the traditional harmonic chords until they no longer functioned tonally. The resulting **atonal** medium offered Coltrane a free environment in which he could develop his melodic ideas. Coltrane used the modal jazz approach as a springboard for his characteristic melodic extensions. His melodies were often based on modes played over slow-moving harmonies. Rather than using the lower notes of a chord (i.e., the root, third, or fifth), Coltrane centered his melodies on higher **harmonics** such as the ninth, eleventh, and thirteenth. The result was a more complex harmonic sound that could, when pushed harder, develop into atonal passages characteristic of free-form jazz.

The slow-moving harmonies of modal jazz actually contained the seeds of atonality because they fostered a melodic approach toward improvisation and allowed time for the player to explore more complex harmonic extensions. Coltrane uses this modal jazz approach on his recording of "Alabama." Notice the relationship of his melody to the harmonic underpinning. He is able to consistently maintain an extended distance from the basic harmony. The opening and closing statements use only one chord, over which Coltrane plays a modal melodic line. Coltrane's sense of melody is displayed in one of his most celebrated performances on a Rodgers and Hammerstein tune, "My Favorite Things," performed with his quartet.[6] His solo on this recording shows how he applied his modal and extended harmonic techniques to the more traditional song form. As his solo develops, it becomes so extended harmonically that it seems only vaguely related to the ongoing and apparently frozen harmonic center below it. At several points the quartet collectively weaves musical textures not dissimilar to those heard in Ornette Coleman's free expressions. Coltrane completes his transition toward free form in performances like "Manifestation," in which his later quartet operates in a free interchange.[7]

Just as Coltrane's extension of bebop culminated in "Giant Steps," his modal/free landmark performance (still reflecting his unique bebop development) is his recording of "A Love Supreme."

LEGACY

Even with the freedom allowed the players, Coltrane's guiding influence can be heard. The long but disjunct melodic lines, frozen harmonic centers, and emotional intensity characterize the later Coltrane performances. Coltrane opened the path for others such as Archie Shepp through his conviction that improvisation could continue past all existing melodic considerations, harmonic considerations, and rhythmic flow. Free form seemed to need another leader besides Ornette Coleman.

listening guide

John Coltrane
"A Love Supreme,
Part 1—Acknowledgment" *
John Coltrane, tenor sax
McCoy Tyner, piano
Jimmy Garrison, bass
Elvin Jones, drums

:00   Saxophone fanfare with cymbal accompaniment.

:30   Melody of 4 notes played by bass.

:41   Drums start making time.

:49   Piano enters.

1:04   Sax enters with new melodic material (still motivic in nature); piano generally keeps 2-note movement taken from opening bass motive as the **comping** pattern.

1:32   Example of ascending and descending chromatic chord patterns used by the piano; listen for constant motivic variation by the saxophonists.

2:01   Bass begins to move toward 4-beat patterns instead of variations of the motive; loose references to the motive are maintained most of the time and passed between the various players. Saxophone works gradually up to the extreme top range of the instrument.

3:08   Example of bass 4-beat pattern that still reflects motive. Notice how the saxophone gradually brings the energy down only to take it back up again.

4:14   Example of soloists using short, fragmented statements of a motive.

4:28   Melodic activity simplifi es and decreases in intensity.

4:55   A return to the simple melodic motive, continually repeated.

6:07   Players sing the motive, "A Love Supreme."

6:36   Motive moves down a step.

6:44   Singing drops out and ensemble begins to fade.

7:08   Piano drops out, only bass and drums remain.

7:24   Only bass remains, playing the motive with very short solo excursions.

7:45   End.

* *A Love Supreme*, Impulse Records, AS-77.

Coltrane became this leader with his long improvisations (sometimes forty minutes), his sheets of sound, his tone, and his technique. He was looked on as a spiritual leader. Coltrane and his followers have often been criticized for playing solos that were too long, but their answer was that they needed the time to explore the music in depth. At first, Coltrane was admired more as a technically complete musician than as a creative artist. He showed speed as he cascaded chords with his powerful moving tone. But his recording "A Love Supreme" seemed to change the attitude toward his playing,[8] as it is an emotional recording that does away with some earlier excesses and is more a work of art than an exhibition. Coltrane tried to explain (in his music) the wonderful things that the universe meant to him. Playing jazz was a spiritual experience to Coltrane, and he always felt that he should share his feelings with his listeners. There is no doubt about his strong religious motivation seen in both the playing and the liner notes of his later albums.

Coltrane continually experimented. Even when listeners were well acquainted with Coltrane's recordings, they would still be constantly surprised and amazed at each live performance. His fans learned to expect only the unexpected. In 1965, Coltrane won four *Down Beat* polls: Record of the Year (*A Love Supreme*), Jazzman of the Year, Hall of Fame, and Number One Tenor Saxophonist. "Coltrane came, and he made music. He built on existing foundations. He and his music lived in inexorable relation to other lives, other ideas, other musics. But how he built! The musical structures are changed forever because of him."[9]

Summary

Coltrane's influence created an alternative to the neoclassical mainstream that developed in the 1990s and 2000s. Neoclassicism looked back to the bebop period for its inspiration while the new avant-garde looked back to the particular brand of avant-garde exhibited by Coltrane, a more affective and performance rooted avant-garde rather than a more cerebral one. A new mainstream may be developing with players who seem to look back to Coltrane and the avant-garde players more than to the straight-ahead hard boppers. Coltrane certainly established himself in the hard bop style, but his voice led him to a new free style of his own. The new players in this evolving mainstream are involved in a fusion of historical and even world styles. We see elements of avant-garde and fusion finding their way into the small-group jazz ensemble inherited from earlier straight-ahead groups.

SUGGESTED ADDITIONAL LISTENING

Green Haze (with Coltrane) (2 vols.). Prestige Records, 24064.
Jazz Classics (with Coltrane). Prestige Records, 7373E.
Kind of Blue (with Coltrane and Evans). Columbia Records, PC-8163.

NOTES

1. Taken from www.johncoltrane.com.
2. John Coltrane, "Ogunde," *Expression,* Impulse Records, A-9120.
3. John Coltrane, *Giant Steps,* Atlantic Records, 1311.
4. Miles Davis album, *Kind of Blue,* Columbia Records, CL 1355.
5. John Coltrane, "The Father and the Son and the Holy Ghost," *Meditations,* Impulse Records, A-9110.
6. John Coltrane, *The Best of John Coltrane,* Impulse Records, AS-9200-2.
7. John Coltrane, *The Best of John Coltrane: His Greatest Years,* Impulse Records, AS-9223-2.
8. John Coltrane, *A Love Supreme,* Impulse Records, A-77.
9. Gordon Kopulus, "John Coltrane: Retrospective Perspective," *Down Beat* 38, no. 14 (July 1971): 40.

13

Free Form, Avant-Garde

Most new developments in jazz have been extensions of earlier traditions and only modify the musical structures and idioms defined by preceding styles. The **avant-garde** of a developing art form implies a conscious breaking away from the tradition established by that art form. Free jazz was such a movement. *Free form,* also known as **free improvisation** or even the "new thing," breaks sharply with its musical predecessors. It is actually easier to describe what free form is not than to find descriptors for the limitless number of expressions of which it is capable. Most free-form efforts operate in a medium that is not defined by the harmonic and rhythmic forms prescribed by earlier jazz practices.

Even with the new approach taken by bop, the song structure, with its repeating harmonic form, was maintained. The songs were characterized by a steady rhythmic meter that varied little throughout the course of the performance. If a tune were in $\frac{4}{4}$, it would likely remain that throughout. Although the melody to the tune was often absent during the improvised solos, the harmonies remained the same. There was therefore a formal, unchanging structure that supported each player's improvisation.

Free-form improvisation sheds these structures of harmonic repetition and rhythmic regularity to allow players to react to one another without restrictions. The musical material for the improvisation comes extemporaneously from the players rather than from a commonly known tune. The greatest empathy possible is necessary for this means of performance to be successful. Also, the old axiom "The more freedom allowed, the more discipline necessary" is pertinent to this style. Without discipline, a performer might merely make unusual, unrelated sounds instead of reacting in a musical way to the other players. (For an example of how two players might interact in a free music environment, listen to Interactive Guide 9 at the Online Learning Center or directly at the interactive listening site, http://www.emcgill.com/listening.)

In an age when the finished product is the only criterion for judgment, it is refreshing to have a situation in which the process, not the product, is really important. However, this one fact makes free-form jazz difficult to understand—at first. The listener must conscientiously observe, and then attempt to empathize with, the players to appreciate the excitement of this process. It is often easier to understand this style first in a live performance, where the listener can more readily become involved with the players.

Eric Dolphy

Part I

Part II

Part III

Part IV

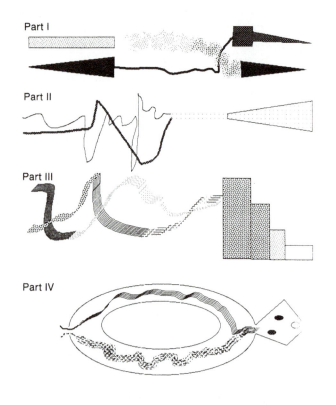

This type of music can be compared to action or nonrepresentational painting, such as a Jackson Pollock work. Listen to Red Mitchell (bass) and Shelly Manne (drums) as they attempt to communicate with Ornette Coleman (and vice versa) on "Lorraine."[2] Alto saxophonist Joe Harriott, sometimes called an abstractionist, claims to have worked in this idiom before there could have been any of the seminal influence of Ornette Coleman.

It would not be illogical to feel that the seeds of free-form jazz existed from the beginnings of jazz itself. The very nature of improvisation places great emphasis on spontaneous musical creativity. To some degree, every jazz performance contains an element of improvisation, if only in the rhythm section, where the specific notes are left to the players' discretion. The balance between fixed compositions and improvisatory development has shifted throughout jazz's history. Free-form jazz proves to be the fullest expression of spontaneous composition, and improvisation takes the dominant role.

The leading players and composers in this medium come to it from different musical and philosophical backgrounds that add a distinctive stamp to each of their efforts. As we will see, the traditional musical structures of harmony and rhythm are only two of the many possible glues available to musicians. The effectiveness of free-form performance rests in the individual and collective compositional strengths of the players. The individual musical characteristics of the players carry over into the performance itself, instilling it with a unique expression. The dominant musical voice in an ensemble helps establish the trademarks that unify and narrow the infinite possibilities of a free-form composition. These trademarks, in turn, help distinguish the performances of Cecil Taylor from those of Ornette Coleman or John Coltrane.

listening guide

Interactive Guide 9
Free Form
"Dialogue"
Ann LaBerge, flute
David Megill, alto saxophone

:00   Part 1: the sax player is singing and growling while playing and the flute player is hissing and playing at the same time as the performance begins.

:06   Flute player uses breath articulations while the saxophone plays soft melodic fragments.

:17   Flute player sings while playing.

:25   Part 2: interchange of repeated notes. Listen for special extended performance effects like rolled r's by the flute (called flutter tonguing) and the use of large intervals and extended range (sax). More important, notice the interplay between the two players and how they interpret the score.

:39   Exchange of short punctuated notes between players.

:55   Part 3: the players take a more lyric approach to this part and experiment with extremes in tone variation (sax) and lip slurs (flute, sax). Notice the glissando in the flute and how the players musically signal when to move on in the score.

1:10   Gradually picks up more melodic speed as short melodic motives are passed back and forth.

1:26   Sharp change from soft, low tones to louder, less lyric sound.

1:36   Soft consonant ending.

1:41   Part 4: begins very quietly but actively. Soft, rapid exchange of melodic ideas that grow in intensity and volume.

2:02   Short, very loud, and overblown notes exchanged as piece ends.

2:08   End.

Free-form jazz did not just suddenly appear with Ornette Coleman's "Free Jazz" recording. Composers such as Lennie Tristano and Charles Mingus had already pushed hard on the musical fabric, forcing it into a freer expression. As early as 1956, Mingus had recorded "Pithecanthropus Erectus" and shocked the listening world with his daring use of some free playing. In much the same way, Coltrane broke into a style as a natural result of his harmonic and melodic extensions.

It was Ornette Coleman, however, who drew the sharpest line between the traditional jazz idiom and his new expression as he coined a name: free jazz.

ORNETTE COLEMAN

Saxophonist Ornette Coleman was one of the most controversial free jazz players. Critics who have examined his work fall into one of two distinct groups. One group is composed of staunch admirers, whereas the other group views his work as unworthy of any consideration. These adverse opinions are due to Coleman's apparent disregard for tradition[3] ("Lonely Woman," "Congeniality," "Free Jazz"). It is said that Coleman refuses to comply with restrictions normally imposed by rhythm and meter, chord progressions, and melodic continuity and that he desires the freedom to play any thought that occurs to him at any time, regardless of context.

There are many misunderstandings concerning Coleman's playing. One is that he turned to free form because he was incapable of anything else. To say that Coleman "doesn't sound good" is too loose a statement. Questions immediately arise: Good compared to what? Compared to other saxophonists? Compared to European scales and harmony?

Coleman shows on "Part 1" that he can play both melodically and rhythmically.[4] Despite the free playing in this cut, many of the melodic rhythms are consistent with those used by traditional jazz players. The melodic lines still

listening guide

Ornette Coleman
"Free Jazz"*

:00 Introduction.

:10 Melody (from which to improvise later) played in unison at this point.

:22 Alto sax solo (Ornette Coleman); listen for 2 basses and the accenting on the drums.

1:10 Backup horns enter.

3:33 Horns play independently.

4:10 Alto sax plays faster, one bass is bowing.

4:45 Ensemble players now playing very independently.

5:05 Peak.

5:30 Alto sax solos again.

5:40 Everybody is improvising.

6:10 Alto sax solos again.

6:43 Everybody is improvising.

7:45 Everybody plays fast for a moment.

9:46 Original motive played here in unison.

10:00 Fade.

10:03 End.

*Smithsonian Collection, CD 5, track 9 (excerpt), Atlantic, S-1364.

swing in a hard bop fashion, but their relationship to the independent bass line is harmonically vague. The steady meter in this cut is not necessarily typical of free jazz performances, but it works well as a support for Coleman's solo and the responses by the other horn players.

In fact, Coleman is very melody oriented. He also phrases freely. He feels no obligation to contain or extend his musical thoughts so that they fit neatly into a certain number of measures, which is logical because he does not use defined chord progressions. Also, he is not involved in keeping a certain pulse; after all, his music is not for dancing. Coleman's melodies have pitch relationships even for the uninitiated, but his metrically invented phrases are placed over a free rhythm with no identifiable chord progressions, an approach that tends to lose those who have not listened to free form. The shift from a steady pulse to a free-flowing rhythm can be traced first to Lester Young and then to Gerry Mulligan and others as they attempted to avoid constraint within the **bar lines.**

vamping

Ornette Coleman

Ornette Coleman has had a career of controversy. As the first popularly known leader of the jazz avant-garde with his 1960 performance of free jazz, he initiated a controversy of strong, opposing opinions from many of the other established jazz leaders, including Miles Davis and Charles Mingus, who themselves were innovators of jazz styles. Coleman's influence on the development of jazz was rekindled in 1985 with his recording *Song X* with Pat Metheny as well as his introduction of what he calls the "harmolodic theory" that he now employs. This theory centers on the melodic activity of the ensemble that collectively establishes the harmonic texture. "I mean, when you hear my band, you know that everybody is soloing, harmolodically."[5]

Because there is no chord progression, some players feel free enough to avoid a key center and play with an atonal feel. This sense of not being in a key is not quite the same as **Schoenberg's twelve-tone system,** where each tone has equal importance and no key center is implied. Rather, these players seem to have no home base, which many listeners evidently need. However, atonality in jazz is not necessarily new. Remember that many of the roots of jazz, such as the field holler, were in no specific key. Some authorities consider the lack of a steady pulse or beat to be a new rhythmic concept, whereas others consider it no concept at all. One of the more appreciated concepts of this new music is the way in which musical thoughts and attitudes from the entire world are incorporated. Obviously, these young musicians feel that older musical concepts are too rigid, too predictable, and certainly too laden with clichés.

Coleman was the first player to move all the way into harmonic freedom. This idea had been examined earlier by classical composers but in an entirely different way. Although Coleman approached it through improvisation, to say that he was the first is only partially true. Actually, he was only the first to receive widespread recognition. When Coleman organized a quartet in 1957 in Los Angeles, Cecil Taylor was playing in a free manner at the Newport Jazz Festival. Charles Mingus had played free sounds even earlier. It was only the term *free form* that first appeared on a Coleman album with Eric Dolphy titled *Free Jazz*.

Faulty intonation has been one of the criticisms leveled at Coleman, but perhaps the fault lies in the well-tempered scale of European classical music. Reference could be made to the blue areas or blue notes and questions raised about the cultures that do not subscribe to the European concept. Possibly, there is faulty intonation in any emotional music in which notes are constantly pushed this way or that way to intensify the expression.

Martin Williams quotes Coleman on this issue: "You can play sharp in tune and flat in tune," pointing out that the intonation for any note depends on the musical context.[6]

In the late 1980s, Coleman continued to push into new theoretical and philosophical areas with his proposed *harmolodic theory*. This theory strikes

listening guide

🎧 (CD 3, track 5)
Ornette Coleman Trio
"Faces and Places"
Ornette Coleman, alto saxophone
David Izenzon, bass
Charles Moffett, drums

It is particularly useful to listen to the entire recording (as well as the free-form excerpt on Interactive Guide 9) to hear the energy curve at work in this performance. Throughout the piece, the trio plays very clear hard-driving sections referred to as *straight time.* Contrasted with these sections are those with less metric focus. The bass generally maintains a straight four-beat pattern, but the drums use accents that sometimes conflict with the meter. As Coleman moves in and out of time in his solo, he is sometimes supported by a similar move in the drums and at other times by a clear meter. Also listen for how Coleman's solo strikes varying amounts of independence from the harmonic areas implied by the bass. The performance shows the trio's ability both to control the traditional jazz language and to move outside that language as they shape their energy curve.

Complete Original

:00	Saxophone introduction with intermittent time in bass and drums.
:18	Short use of time in the drums but not yet in the bass.
:26	Time established under saxophone solo.
:33	Bass uses a repeating pattern, establishing an ostinato feel with straight time in drums (with accents).
:47	Bass walks.
1:05	Melodic variation, shifting the whole motive chromatically for each statement.
1:32	Drums fall into a straight-time feeling with walking bass pattern.
1:55	Backup again moves away from straight time, creating a contrast for the harder-swinging straight-time areas.
2:13	Walking feeling as time returns.
2:31	Drummer syncopates meter with cross-accents.
2:42	Straight time returns.
2:49	Accents in drums.
3:13	Straight time returns.
3:30	Cross-accents on saxophone.
3:50	Coleman uses more traditional melodic language here.

4:01	:00	(Student CD track begins here.) Coleman begins moving further from the harmonic area established by the bass. He also begins moving at an accelerated pace. His solo at this point has moved to a higher energy level, which he began to set up during the first part of the solo.
4:20	:23	Some vocalization?
4:35	:34	Double-time saxophone solo leading to more fragmented solo lines.
5:20	1:19	Listen for the exchange of rhythmic ideas between the saxophone and the drums.
5:25	1:22	Chromatically shifting lines that are more independent harmonically.
5:30	1:29	Rhythmic and harmonic independence in the saxophone.
5:55	1:54	Short double-time saxophone section.
6:26	2:25	Motivic exchange between saxophone and drums.
6:40	2:39	Rhythmic line passed between Coleman and the drums; steady, fast tempo maintained by drums (with accents) and bass.
6:53	2:52	Rhythmic and metric cross-accents to set up return to time.
7:05	3:04	Returns to straight time.
7:15	3:14	Listen for rhythmic exchange between the saxophone and drums.
7:35	3:34	Cross-accents on drums setting up drum solo and bringing the saxophone solo to a climax. Polymetric feel.
8:00	3:59	Return to straight time.
8:10	4:09	Drum solo begins. Time is maintained throughout solo.
8:37	4:36	Notice how time is maintained with the hi hat.
9:10	5:09	Coleman enters with a double-time saxophone break followed by a fast metric support. Saxophone motivic lines even more independent of the harmonic area suggested by the bass. Drumming also gradually becomes more accented.
9:50	5:49	Double-time melodic lines.
10:07	6:06	Half-time melody; melodic lines become more chromatic and developmental.
10:45	6:44	Solo breaks with drum responses; melodic material is the same as at the beginning.
11:11	7:10	End.

a new balance between the traditional musical elements of melody and harmony. The distinctions between the two are relaxed to form a more blended definition that creates a more melodic sense of chords and, conversely, a more harmonic context for melodies. His pursuit of such new ideas is a trademark of his continuing career.

CECIL TAYLOR

Unlike Coleman, pianist Cecil Taylor did not have an extensive background in blues bands. Rather, his contribution was an integration of a conservatory technical facility and European-based compositional practices. However, like Coleman, he is interested in a free improvisatory arena for the players. Taylor is often considered an avant-garde expression of third-stream jazz. His music is perhaps a more effective fusion of classical compositional practices and jazz improvisations than is the traditional third stream itself. Taylor was able to blend his conservatory background and the raw energy typical of the freest improvisation into a seamless whole. He found an intersection in which his music can be heard as either classical or jazz, depending on the vantage point of the listener.

Unlike Coleman's music, Taylor's does not usually reveal traditional jazz idioms, although the spirit of jazz improvisation is clearly evident. "Enter Evening," recorded in 1966, is an example of Taylor's free-form style. Notice how the players react to one another in a manner not only free of harmony and meter but also free from many of the usual melodic jazz idioms.[7] Taylor's use of an oboe and a bass clarinet in the ensemble is consistent with the third stream's earlier use of traditionally classical instruments.

The variety of musical textures used in Taylor's music can be heard on "Idut" and "Serdab."[8] "Idut" is a high-energy composition made up of fragmented and punctuated statements that are characteristic of much of Taylor's percussive style. He often approaches his piano as a drummer might, striking clusters of notes for their percussive effect. The sequence of musical textures leads the listener through a series of energy levels that are shaped by Taylor's compositional skill. Throughout these pieces, the interchange between musicians is the propelling force. What any one player does at any one time is seldom as important as the composite musical statement. It is often helpful when listening to this type of free-form music to step back from the detail of individual players and listen to the whole musical fabric that the players weave collectively. Notice that many of the transitions between musical areas are carried by Taylor himself as he sets up each new collective effort.

"Serdab" offers the listener some contrasting musical textures, although there are still several high-energy sections. In this composition, although the players have many occasions to work out melodic ideas individually, the composite sound is still dominant. In several of the more open areas, Taylor is willing to use traditional jazz idioms, only to move quickly back onto a more dense percussive style. The interchange between players is more clearly audible in the less dense areas, where the melodic fragments are given more length and often accompanied by other similar (or contrasting) melodic lines.

Taylor's music often requires stamina from listeners and players alike. His concerts are notorious for their long, uninterrupted compositions. Holding such long compositional structures in a free-form manner attests to Taylor's strength as a composer. "3 Phasis," a single piece, runs more than fifty-seven minutes, spanning two sides of a record.[9] The fact that this recording was the last of six efforts made that day to record this piece demonstrates the ensemble's intensity and stamina. Perhaps more than any other trait, Taylor's intensity is the hallmark of his music, an intensity more typical of jazz than the European counterpart with which it was fused. Few composers have been as successful as Taylor at blending the two musical worlds so completely.

vamping

John Coltrane

Rather than making a declaration of independence from more traditional jazz as Coleman did, Coltrane seemed to evolve naturally toward freer and freer expression throughout his career. Of all the avant-garde players Coltrane has the greatest legacy among younger players. His influence becomes an important balance to neoclassical jazz in the late 1990s and early 2000s.

See Chapter 12 for Coltrane's important contribution to the avant-garde movement.

CHICAGO STYLE OF FREE JAZZ

Sun Ra

The first popular expression of the new avant-garde school of jazz in Chicago can be found in the work of composer/pianist Sun Ra. After a somewhat mysterious childhood, Sun Ra worked as arranger/pianist for theater orchestras such as those of Jesse Miller and Fletcher Henderson. His career as leader began in 1953 with the organization of a quartet that later was expanded into a big band called Arkestra, with which Sun Ra is best known.

Sun Ra's work has been quite controversial. He is lauded by some as a great innovator, carefully balancing the musical worlds of composition and improvisation. By others he is seen as nothing more than a charlatan. Critics of Sun Ra cite his musical defense as grounds for dismissing his music.

> Music is a universal language. The intergalactic music in its present phase of presentation will be correlative to the key synopsis of the past and to the uncharted multi-potential planes outside the bounds of the limited earth-eternity future. The intergalactic music is in hieroglyphic sound: an abstract analysis and synthesis of man's relationship to the universe, visible and invisible first man and second man.[10]

Despite his controversial posture as a musical scientist, he was certainly the first composer in Chicago to employ techniques of collective improvisation

Sun Ra

listening guide

World Saxophone Quartet
"Steppin'"*

:00   Ostinato in baritone saxophone and soprano saxophone.

:10   Theme enters (A section).

:26   Extended harmonic and legato theme (B section).

:51   Theme A returns.

1:07   Repeat of B section legato theme.

1:23   Swing feel setup with variation of ostinato and collective improvisation in the other saxophones; listen for the interchange of ideas and the passing around of the ostinato.

2:32   Starts getting freer as ostinato is passed around.

2:55   Very free section; bass voice joins the collective improvisation.

3:10   Staccato bass returns; still free in upper parts.

3:35   All parts are free again.

3:58   Bass voice is temporarily featured; interchange top to bottom of ideas—very free; ostinato still referenced by several members; intensity increases.

4:43   Double-time feel in baritone saxophone while upper voices pull back rhythmically.

4:58   Free section with more space in the texture; hints at opening ostinato.

5:30   Very frenetic with fast melodic lines.

5:40   Fragmented ostinato enters in baritone saxophone.

6:06   Slow to stop, then return to opening ostinato.

6:16   Theme A.

6:32   Theme B.

6:48   Return to A section and beginning to fade with chord punctuations in upper saxophones.

7:07   Final chord.

7:14   End.

---

*Smithsonian Collection, CD 5, track 10.

in big-band compositions. Even Sun Ra's success with big-band jazz has not spawned many other groups like it. The only other such group is the Jazz Composers' Orchestra led by Carla Bley and Mike Mantler.

Sun Ra's *Heliocentric Worlds* (vols. 1 and 2) demonstrates his effectiveness with composing for a large ensemble and still maintaining an allegiance to collective improvisation. His success here is based on the nature of his compositional process, which allows the structure to emerge as a result of the extraordinary musical communication established among his players.[11]

Association for the Advancement of Creative Music

Throughout jazz history, musical styles have been associated with geographic locations, such as New Orleans and Chicago Dixieland, West Coast jazz, and East Coast hard bop. In the 1960s, Chicago was again a center for a developing jazz style. A new, more world-based, music was being explored by a group called the Association for the Advancement of Creative Music (AACM). The group was founded by composer/pianist/clarinetist Richard Abrams, whose work focused largely on a group called the Experimental Band, which was itself made up of smaller units. This band had no permanent membership; rather, it changed to meet whatever composition and performance demands were required for concerts and recordings. The personnel of the AACM included other prominent players of new music such as trumpeter Leo Smith, saxophonist Anthony Braxton, and violinist Leroy Jenkins.

Art Ensemble of Chicago

Out of the Experimental Band came many important innovators of avant-garde jazz. Saxophonist Joseph Jarman developed into a leading composer for AACM and worked often in multimedia formats. Jarman came to the AACM from a rock and blues background. Woodwind player Roscoe Mitchell came to the AACM from a bop background by way of Ornette Coleman. Trumpeter Lester Bowie also worked in the Experimental Band before joining forces with Jarman, Mitchell, and bassist Malachi Favors in 1968 to form the Art Ensemble of Chicago. In 1969, the Art Ensemble moved to Paris and recorded some of their most notable albums.[12]

The work of the Art Ensemble, like that of AACM, is difficult to describe in much detail because of the variety of compositional and performance tactics they employed. The diversity of intent is perhaps their most defining trademark, but some general descriptors can be applied across their work:

1. An emphasis on collective interaction
2. A wide range of tone colors
3. The exploration of sound structures
4. A suspension of fixed rhythmic support (no drummer)

Joseph Jarman

The Art Ensemble is capable of a wide range of musical styles that still hold to these general characteristics, ranging from the reciting of poetry to the quoting of traditional jazz idioms. Their use of tone color, instrumental technique, language, and traditional jazz styles may be presented in quite unexpected ways. They are able to suspend traditional musical elements, such as harmony or rhythm, and still maintain a cohesive performance because of their sophisticated ensemble skills. For example, because there is no drummer, the percussion is performed collectively: The equipment is spread throughout the group, and players move to equipment as needed.

Like most of the music of AACM, that of the Art Ensemble has a firm compositional base. The compositional detail describes not the notes to be played but rather the way in which the performance is to proceed. Although individual performances follow the charted composition, they also respond to the evolving collective improvisation. This balance between compositional intent and free improvisation is the foundation on which AACM operates.

vamping

AACM/M-BASE/Black Artists Group

The history of jazz centers mainly on the virtuosic expressions of individual players. Even name musical groups are most often defined by the individuals in them and most often by the leadership of just one individual. The Association for the Advancement of Creative Musicians (AACM), Macro-Basic Array of Structured Extemporizations (M-BASE), and the Black Artists Group work outside this more traditional definition.

The AACM was established in Chicago during the 1960s by Richard Abrams to act as a support group for musicians working in new and experimental music. This group influenced the avant-garde of jazz through groups such as the Art Ensemble and individuals such as Anthony Braxton.

It is difficult to characterize the nature of the music that AACM has fostered since the 1960s because it has been so experimental. However, a common consensus exists that the composers/performers should be free to explore not only traditional elements of pitch and meter but also the more general notions of sound and time. All sounds are considered appropriate musical material, and their placement in time is completely free.

The Black Artists Group, formed in 1968 in St. Louis, was organized in much the same manner as AACM. Out of this group came three saxophone players who would later develop the World Saxophone Quartet: Oliver Lake, alto sax; Julius Hemphill, alto sax; and Hamiet Bluiett, baritone sax. The quartet was complete when they added David Murray on tenor sax in 1976. Their compositions strike a balance between free improvisational textures (typical of Ornette Coleman) and more structured compositional passages. The quartet is capable of a wide range of compositional approaches and stylistic moods, from complex interweaving of lines to light, humorous pieces ("Steppin'").

During the late 1980s, another group of black musicians, M-BASE, developed in Brooklyn. Parallels have been drawn between it and AACM. Greg Osby, Geri Allen, Steve Coleman, and Robin Eubanks are among those who spearheaded the development of the organization. Although AACM and M-BASE each operate as collectives for the advancement of their ideas, the groups differ in their musical heritage. Whereas AACM has a strong alliance with the avant-garde (normally associated with classical and world music), M-BASE works at an experimental intersection between jazz and popular music forms such as rhythm and blues and soul. And, whereas AACM represents a search for new music that is often free from traditional forms and practice, M-BASE explores possible musical blends between various jazz and popular traditions.

Anthony Braxton

The jazz and classical avant-garde streams are in many ways practically indistinguishable. The **chance music** promoted by John Cage, although free in terms of harmony, timbre, and meter, finds its cohesion in the intellectual restrictions imposed by the composer. Without containing the traditional musical idioms to support the free use of sound and rhythm, compositions are based on the composer's ability to creatively mold the musical elements into an understandable whole. As in the highly emotional music of Mingus, Coleman, and Coltrane, the emotional theme and the players' collective understanding of that theme can be used to hold large expanses of music together. The classical approach toward new music is often based not on emotional unity as such but on an intellectual premise that explores and develops new musical areas.

Cecil Taylor maintained a careful balance between emotional and intellectual composition. Multifaceted woodwind player Anthony Braxton also maintains this kind of balance. His compositions are based on well-crafted notions about timbre and time relationships yet develop freely in an improvisational environment.

Braxton spent the mid-1960s in Chicago with AACM. He has been productive as both an author and a composer, writing a great deal about his view of creativity in music and basing his musical compositions on well-developed theories. His 1974 album *Anthony Braxton, New York, Fall 1974* offers several examples of his compositional approach.[13] Each cut from the album is represented with an enigmatic geometric design that guided the performance. Contrast the almost boplike idiom of "Side One, Cut One" with the much freer "Side Two, Cut Three." The first side clearly reflects a jazz heritage in its use of meter and melodic inflection, but the second has few obvious ties to traditional jazz.

Although similar to Taylor's more classical approach, Braxton's music presents a more specifically composed image than that of Taylor. This is not to say that Braxton's music lacks the improvisational energy that is characteristic of Taylor's or Coleman's. Braxton has often performed fully improvised solo concerts that would be difficult to match in technique or intensity. His music, however, tends to show the more measured qualities associated with more fully composed music. "Side Two, Cut One" demonstrates his ability to maintain such a controlled yet free-sounding environment. His clarinet lines are effectively intertwined with the timbres produced by Richard Teitelbaum on the Moog synthesizer.

CONTEMPORARY AVANT-GARDE

Greg Osby

Although the avant-garde school of jazz reached its zenith during the 1960s, its legacy is played out today by contemporary jazz performers. Many of these composers and performers were also connected to the Chicago school and to AACM and M-BASE in particular. Prominent among this new generation of free-thinking jazz players is saxophonist Greg Osby, who has played with Lester Bowie, David Murray, and the World Saxophone Quartet.

Osby, like previous avant-garde players, challenges the neoclassical jazz school as having lost the true spirit of jazz by looking back at previous styles and possibly sacrificing the chance to find an individual voice. In this regard, Osby proves to be truly connected to the original avant-garde school of the 1960s. By definition, *avant-garde* means to stand against the status quo. Ornette Coleman did this when he introduced free jazz, and Greg Osby does this today in both his playing and his reasoning.[14]

Henry Threadgill

Perhaps even more of an iconoclast than Greg Osby is composer Henry Threadgill, who also came from the experience of the AACM in Chicago. He sees the world as his venue, has a musical palette wider than jazz, and like Osby takes issue with the emerging neoclassical school of jazz: "There's an incestuous esthetic in jazz right now, and the ramifications come through in neoclassicism and all of these things that are retro. . . . When one starts thinking on the basis of culture, and then to justify an esthetic that is retro and anti-evolutionary inside of that idea of culture, I think that's very destructive."[15]

**Greg Osby (right)
and Jon Faddis**

Like the first generation of avant-garde jazz players and composers, Threadgill approaches his music from a philosophical approach that values the change in jazz's evolution and looks to external influences for fresh material. The avant-garde jazz musician looks back in history to embrace the context of jazz but not necessarily the content. Threadgill's work with Very Very Circus, one of his ensembles, shows his interest in pushing jazz's front edge by asserting his individualism and interest in global music.[16]

THE FREE JAZZ CONTROVERSY

Some performers who gain recognition today make no pretense of any connection with past musical styles. They specify that they play "emotion," which is entirely different from playing lines, keys, modes, and rhythms.[17] Players of free form are considered the most radical musicians since the bop era. They feel that music in general and jazz in particular should show the emotion of the player, something they believe was not adequately done with the older types of jazz. Coleman and other free-form players think that jazz should also express feelings not previously reflected. After an interview with Archie Shepp, Leonard Feather wrote, "Shepp's music—impassioned, fierce, often atonal, almost totally free of rules of harmony, melody and tone that have governed most music of this century—reflects the turmoil and frustrations that bedevil him."[18] Whether free form is "hate music," "love music," or something else, it is still a means of expression.

Left to right: Steve McCall, Henry Threadgill, and Fred Hopkins.

We suspect that it is mainly the critics and musicians who simply cannot go along with these new expansions who call free-form jazz hate music. Some of the music on Coltrane's recordings is in fact quite religious. There were many jazz critics who would neither support nor condemn free form for fear of eventually being proven wrong or at least foolish. No matter what it is called, and although many claim that it is chaotic, this music has found an audience.

Free-form players thrive on controversy. Free-form advocates who acknowledge that this style has not developed a large following argue that a person should have the right to fail. But failure is not always the result for free-form players. There are even those who are financially successful—witness Ornette Coleman's Guggenheim Foundation grant.

Because free-form jazz does not adhere to established rules, the question is often asked whether free form is jazz and, indeed, whether it is music. Each listener must decide. When free form was still fairly new in jazz (in comparison to most styles), Dan Morgenstern took a perceptive look at the controversy:

> But is it jazz? Some of the main elements are lacking. There is little of what we have come to know as "swing." There is often none of the formal organization found in most jazz—rhythm section and melody instruments, solo versus ensemble, strict time, and so forth. Yet, the sound and feeling is often of a kind peculiar to jazz as we have become accustomed to it, and it is certainly not "classical" music in any sense of that ill-defined word. Whatever it may be—and one often

has the feeling that even the musicians don't quite know what they have hold of; it is a music in flux, if anything—it must not be burdened with comparisons that are unwarranted.

To accuse a drummer of not swinging when he doesn't want to achieve swing in the sense that his critic has in mind is unfair and pointless. To demand adherence to formal patterns that the musicians are obviously rejecting is as foolish as taking a painter of geometric abstractions to task for being nonrepresentational.[19]

summary

In spite of the debate as to whether the performance is jazz, the free-form manner of expression proves to be the ultimate in improvisation. Coleman was the leader in this direction, but followers—notably Eric Dolphy and Ken McIntyre—extended this experimentation much further.[20]

Coltrane was a tremendous help in furthering the careers of other contemporary free jazz players such as Archie Shepp and Pharaoh Sanders. Coltrane and Coleman were at the top of most musicians' polls in the mid-1960s, especially in Europe.

McCoy Tyner played piano for Coltrane for almost six years (1960–65), and it took him almost eight years after that to free himself to the point where he was an individual expressing his own thoughts. When he started his group, they played set forms but later became much more flexible and free.[21]

Some contemporary groups deserve special mention because of their highly experimental nature: the Archie Shepp Quintet, the New York Art Quintet, the Albert Ayler Quintet, and the Jazz Composers Workshop (later Jazz Composers Orchestra) with Carla Bley and Mike Mantler. There is also much of this type of activity in Europe. There have been innovators of avant-garde jazz in Los Angeles, but the main strongholds are New York and Europe. However, there is a catch-22 in that the club owners will not hire these musicians until they have recordings, and record companies are reluctant to give them a recording date until they have proven that their music is commercial enough to appeal to the expanding jazz audience.

Most successful recording artists today have stepped back somewhat from the compositional freedom of the 1960s. They are more likely to shape their works by beginning with a strain with which listeners can relate, following with an entirely free portion, and then returning to the recognizable strain. The pattern may occur several times in a long selection, giving listeners pivotal points to cling to. At this time, listeners accept this: They can recognize the selection while appreciating the freedom of the player in other portions. Players, meanwhile, are tending toward retaining a key center for the seemingly free parts. It is as if the musician has learned that entire freedom is not an answer to expression—that the player needs boundaries, or bases, from which to explore. Some players with this attitude are Miles Davis, Cecil Taylor, John Klemmer, Keith Jarrett, Chick Corea, Pharaoh Sanders, McCoy Tyner, Alice Coltrane, Wayne Shorter, Anthony Braxton, Don Cherry, and Sun Ra.

The free-form player places the importance of individuality of self-expression considerably ahead of popularity or acceptance by general audiences. His or her claim to musical artistry is often through music unrelated to any previous approach to music.

FOR FURTHER STUDY

1. What relationship exists between the attitude one has toward free-form jazz and one's understanding of the way the musical elements are used by the performer in expressing musical thoughts?

2. Explain two variations of free-form technique used by performers playing this type of jazz.

3. Describe the fundamental difference between John Coltrane and Anthony Braxton in terms of their approaches to free jazz.

SUGGESTED ADDITIONAL LISTENING

Art Ensemble of Chicago. *The Third Decade*. ECM/Warner Brothers Records, 25014-1.
———. *Urban Bushman*. ECM/Warner Brothers Records, ECM 2-1211.
Ayler, Albert. *Vibrations*. Arista Freedom Records, AL 1000.
Bowie, Lester. *Numbers 1 and 2*. Nessa, n-1.
Braxton, Anthony. *New York, Fall 1974*.
Cherry, Don. *El Corazon*. ECM/Warner Brothers Records, ECM 1-1230.
———. *Old and New Dreams*. Black Saint Records, BSR-0013.
Coleman, Ornette. *At the "Golden Circle" Stockholm*. Blue Note Records, 842242.
———. *Science Fiction*. Columbia Records, KC 31061.
Handy, John, III. *Quote, Unquote*. Roulette Records, R 52124.
Jarman, Joseph. *Song For*. Delmark, 410.
Jazz Composers Orchestra. JCOA Records, 1001/2.
Mitchell, Roscoe. *Sound*. Delmark, 408.
Murray, David. *Morning Song*. Black Saint Records, BSR-0075.
Sanders, Pharaoh. *Deaf Dumb Blind*. Impulse Records, AS 9199.
———. *Journey to the One*. Theresa Records, TR 108/109.
Shepp, Archie. *Four for Trane*. Impulse Records, A-71.
———. *On This Night*. Impulse Records, A-97.
Sun Ra. *The Futuristic Sounds of Sun Ra*. Savoy, MG 12138.
———. *Sun Song*. Delmark, 411.
Taylor, Cecil. *Silent Tongues*. Unit Core Records, 30551.
———. *Unit Structures*. Blue Note Records, 84237.
World Saxophone Quartet, *W.S.Q.* Black Saint Records, BSR-0027.

ADDITIONAL READING RESOURCES

Budds, Michael J. *Jazz in the Sixties*.
Jost, Ekkehard. *Free Jazz*.

Litweiler, John. *The Freedom Principle of Jazz after 1958.*

_____

Note: Complete information, including name of publisher and date of publication, is provided in this book's bibliography.

NOTES

1. Dan Morgenstern, "The October Revolution—Two Views of the Avant Garde in Action," *Down Beat* 34, no. 30 (November 1964): 33.
2. Ornette Coleman, "Lorraine," *Tomorrow Is the Question,* Contemporary Records, M3569.
3. Ornette Coleman, *Tomorrow Is the Question.*
4. Ornette Coleman, *Free Jazz,* Atlantic Records, 1364.
5. Howard Mandel, "Ornette Coleman," *Down Beat* 54, no. 8 (August 1987): 17.
6. Ornette Coleman, *Smithsonian Collection of Classic Jazz,* liner notes, 1973: 43.
7. Cecil Taylor, "Enter Evening," *Smithsonian Collection of Classic Jazz.*
8. Cecil Taylor, "Idut" and "Serdab," New World Records, 201.
9. Cecil Taylor, *3 Phasis,* New World Records, 303.
10. Ekkehard Jost, *Free Jazz* (New York: Da Capo Press, 1981), 181.
11. *Heliocentric Worlds of Sun Ra,* vol. 1, ESP 1014 (vol. 2, ESP 1017).
12. Art Ensemble, *A Jackson in Your House,* Affinity, AFF 9; *People in Sorrow,* Nessa, 3.
13. Anthony Braxton, *Anthony Braxton, New York, Fall 1974,* Arista Records, AL 4032.
14. Greg Osby, *3-D Lifestyles,* Blue Note, 98635; *Man Talk for Moderns,* vol. 10, Blue Note, 95414.
15. *Down Beat* 62, no. 3 (March 1995): 18.
16. Henry Threadgill, *Carry the Day,* Columbia, 66995.
17. Albert Ayler, *Bells,* E.S.P. Disk, 1011.
18. Leonard Feather, "Archie Shepp Jazz: Portrait in Passion," *Los Angeles Times,* 10 April 1966, 23.
19. Dan Morgenstern, "The October Revolution—Two Views of the Avant Garde in Action," *Down Beat* 34, no. 30 (November 1964): 33.
20. Eric Dolphy, "Out to Lunch," *Three Decades of Jazz (1959–1969);* Ken McIntyre and Eric Dolphy, *Looking Ahead,* Prestige Records, 8247.
21. McCoy Tyner, *Sama Layuca,* Milestone Records, M-9056; *Together,* Milestone Records, M-9087; *Reflections,* Milestone Records, M-47062.

14

Jazz/Rock Fusion

EARLY JAZZ ROCK

By the late 1960s, rock had captured the attention of America's listeners. It was quickly becoming the most influential musical style in the United States, perhaps even the Western world. Jazz found in this popular music yet another opportunity for the assimilation of new musical idioms, sounds, and concepts. This crossover with rock is most commonly referred to as *jazz/rock fusion* or just *fusion.* Although fusion is not new to jazz's development, it became a popularized notion during the 1960s, and the term itself became specifically associated with groups that crossed over the jazz/rock line.

Miles Davis proved to be a central figure in the development of jazz/rock fusion. After his impact with the album *Birth of the Cool,* he continued to effect change in the development of jazz. His albums *In a Silent Way* (1969) and *Bitches Brew* (1970) added an impetus to the jazz/rock crossover movement that is still being felt. The list of personnel who worked with Davis during these years reads like a Who's Who of jazz/rock fusion for the 1970s and 1980s: Herbie Hancock, Chick Corea, Wayne Shorter, John McLaughlin, Joe Zawinul, Tony Williams, and Lenny White. These musicians later formed or participated in the most influential fusion groups of the 1970s and early 1980s, particularly Chick Corea with Return to Forever, Joe Zawinul and Wayne Shorter with Weather Report, and John McLaughlin with the Mahavishnu Orchestra.

Jazz, throughout its history, has always cut a careful course between an orally developed tradition and the more schooled, literate tradition characteristic of European classical music. As third-stream jazz was a move toward the literate classical tradition, jazz/rock fusion at first offered a balancing gesture toward the more improvised oral tradition. Rock in the 1950s and 1960s had a raw energy that offered a new rhythmic backdrop for jazz improvisation. Although the harmonic activity in rock was somewhat primitive with respect to jazz, its rhythmic intensity offered a different type of cohesion for extended jazz improvisation.

In addition to the newer electronic instruments and greater amplification, jazz also borrowed the new and increasingly complex rock rhythms. These rock patterns make use of straight eighth notes instead of the uneven eighth

Herbie Hancock

notes more typical of swing or bop. It is not uncommon for fusion groups to use both straight and swing eighths simultaneously, with rock patterns in the rhythm section as soloists play bop lines against it.

The changes in the rhythm section are as definite as those made in the bop era when the means of displaying the pulse was also revolutionized. Rock and jazz/rock bass players now usually play an electric bass or bass guitar instead of a traditional stand-up string bass. This allows them to play faster, invent more complex lines, and use electronic **effects** to alter their sound. The bass player also takes a more prominent position in the ensemble, often offering solo lines as well as basic harmonic support.

The rhythm guitar in most fusion groups plays the chordal punctuations that had been previously assigned to the piano, and the drums, like the bass, move to a more prominent position in the ensemble. Don Ellis explained the manner in which the drummer plays in this idiom:

> In the drums, whereas in bebop the sound went to the cymbals, in rock music (although the cymbals are still used) the opposite has happened, and the basic patterns have gone back to the drums. One of the reasons, I suspect, is that because of the high level of volume at which a great deal of rock is played the cymbals give no definition to the time and merely add a blanket to the overall sound. So the burden of time-keeping has now come back to the snare and bass drums. This also gives it a more solid rhythmic feel. For anyone who likes to swing hard, I think this is a definite step in the right direction.
>
> The patterns the snare drum and the bass drum are playing, instead of being sporadic, are now more regular in the sense that they are played continually.[2]

In later fusion groups, the rhythm section is further expanded with multiple keyboards and electronic effects for most all the other instruments. The commitment to a dominant rhythm section is a central feature of most jazz/rock fusion.

Miles Davis: *Bitches Brew*

Miles Davis's *In a Silent* Way and drummer Tony Williams's *Lifetime* might well be considered the first fusion albums. With *In a Silent Way* Miles moved to an electronic medium, and in *Lifetime*, Williams clearly imported strong rock influences. The move by Williams at first proved controversial but is now considered a fusion classic. Although these albums were important to the developing fusion genre, it was Davis's next album, *Bitches Brew*, that stormed the jazz world. Davis had now fully embraced the loud electronic world of rock.[3] Dave Holland shares his bass role with Harvey Brooks, who plays electric bass. John McLaughlin plays electric guitar, not necessarily new to jazz, and Joe Zawinul, Larry Young, and Chick Corea join in with electronic piano. Besides the horn players—Wayne Shorter on soprano sax, Bennie Maupin on bass clarinet, and Miles Davis on trumpet—the ensemble is completed with percussionist Jim Riley and with three drummers: Lenny White, Jack DeJohnette, and Charles Alias. As rock groups do, Davis gives the rhythm section a central role in the ensemble's activities. His use of such a large rhythm section offers the soloists wide but active expanses for their solos. The title cut from this record offers a good example of how the soloists can interact with the rhythm section. They sometimes hold sustained lines in contrast to the rhythm section's activity, and

listening guide

(CD 3, track 6)
Miles Davis
"Bitches Brew"*
Miles Davis, trumpet
Wayne Shorter, soprano sax
Lenny White, Jack DeJohnette, and
    Charles Alias, drums
Bennie Maupin, bass clarinet
Chick Corea and Joe Zawinul,
    electronic piano
Harvey Brooks (Fender) and Dave
    Holland, bass
John McLaughlin, electric guitar
Jim Riley, percussion

:00   Bass solo.

:07   Keyboard striking a chordal cluster with percussion.

:13   Bass solo.

:22   Keyboard cluster with percussion.

:28   Guitar enters.

:32   Bass solo.

:37   Keyboard cluster with percussion.

:40   Trumpet enters (Miles Davis) with much reverberation; section goes between trumpet entrances and keyboard clusters.

2:45   Bass solo.

2:50   Bass clarinet enters, establishing its motive.

3:27   :00 Steady rhythm, bass clarinet and keyboard prominent, guitar playing punctuations.

3:44   :17 Trumpet solo fully integrated with the ensemble.

5:46   2:09 Listen for chromatic comping patterns in keyboard behind soloist.

6:10   2:43 Trumpet gives way to keyboard and guitar; plenty of heavy rhythm on drums.

7:16   3:49 Softens (Davis says "Like that—nice").

7:40   4:13 Keyboard, guitar, and drums building again; keyboard and drums very rhythmic.

8:20   4:53 Softens again, showing that music should have highs and lows.

8:42   5:15 Trumpet enters.

10:20   6:53 Rhythmic feel changed to suit Davis's new explorations.

11:06   7:39 Trumpet out.

11:18   Soprano sax solo backed by forceful rhythm.

12:12   Soprano sax fades.

12:15   Only rhythm with sparse keyboard interjections but building from there.

13:05   Everyone softens to build again; keyboard featured.

14:17   Keyboard clusters and bass solo alternates several times as in the beginning of the selection.

15:22   Trumpet again with lots of reverberation, alternating with the clusters as near the beginning of the selection.

16:45   New subtle rhythmic feel to back bass solo.

17:31   Add bass clarinet; intensity building again.

18:37   Trumpet enters, driving forward.

19:27   Trumpet exits; group softens only to rebuild.

20:27   Trumpet enters, rather subdued, but quickly reaches out further.

21:15   Brass alone—joined by drums, guitar, and keyboard (soon an ensemble with these players and the bass clarinet)—a long rhythmic interlude.

23:15   Bass alone, alternating with keyboard clusters several times.

23:52   Trumpet enters forcefully, as at the top of the selection, jabbing at openings.

26:03   End.

*Bitches Brew, Columbia Records, GP 26, CS 9995.

at other times they act as just another member of the rhythm section and add only punctuated statements.

The harmonies used in this recording move slowly and function modally rather than in a more tonal fashion typical of mainstream jazz. Each harmonic center appears almost frozen as the players, both independently and collectively, pull away from it, only to return and reaffirm it. The home key is established more by insistence than by the traditional tonal chord relationships. The static harmonies and the rhythm section's collective embellishment create an open arena for improvisation. The musical result flows from basic rock patterns to hard bop textures, and at times passages are even more characteristic of free jazz. The cut entitled "Spanish Key" offers a more direct example of how a fusion rhythm section can establish a steady rhythmic drive over slowly moving harmonies. The harmonic changes occur so seldom that they create major articulation points in the composition.

FUSION

The fusion of jazz and rock took a new turn in the 1970s and 1980s as members of Miles Davis's *Bitches Brew* ensemble formed groups: Chick Corea with Return to Forever, Joe Zawinul and Wayne Shorter with Weather Report, and John McLaughlin with the Mahavishnu Orchestra. Although all these new leaders are associated with Davis, they did not necessarily receive their musical direction solely from his influence. Corea cites the formation of the Mahavishnu Orchestra and McLaughlin's use of the electric guitar as equally important to his own movement toward electric jazz fusion.[4]

These new groups were not characterized by the same modal harmonies and expansive solo areas as was characteristic of their work with Davis. They now showed a tighter compositional approach and a wholesale adoption of the new electronic technology. However, unlike some of the groups to follow, their performance was still based on a live ensemble interaction. The new stylistic shift common to these new groups also emphasized a virtuosic playing style. Much like bebop, the fusion groups demonstrated a virtuosity that was accentuated by a new but characteristic melodic angularity. The virtuosity often permeated the entire ensemble and extended the performance expectations of all the instrumentalists in the group, including the rhythm section.

The rock influence appeared most dominantly in the workings of the rhythm section. The meters and accents were often a highly developed extension of rock patterns. The volume level also moved significantly toward that common to rock groups. The soloists, however, often played bop-like lines above the fast-driving textures established by the rhythm section.

There was a certain amount of controversy surrounding these new groups. Many saw the changes being made as a commercialization of jazz and a significant move away from the jazz ideal. The rock instrumentation, the increased volume, and the rock-based rhythmic feel were sometimes viewed as denials of the jazz tradition. But there were also some undeniably jazz-rooted traditions: rhythmic complexity, commitment to improvisation, virtuosic and individual expression, and syncopated ensemble passages.

John McLaughlin: The Mahavishnu Orchestra

Guitarist John McLaughlin was perhaps most responsible for the sound of rock heard on the Miles Davis albums *In a Silent Way* and *Bitches Brew.* McLaughlin played in British rock bands as he was growing up, and the sound appropriate in those early groups can be heard in his later ensembles. In 1969 he made his first appearance in the American musical arena with The Tony Williams Lifetime. This same year he also joined Miles Davis to record *In a Silent Way* and later *Bitches Brew.* After his stay with Davis, he formed the Mahavishnu Orchestra and recorded several high-energy albums. The first few albums with this group—*Inner Mounting Flame, Birds of Fire,* and *Between Nothingness and Eternity*—clearly demonstrate the virtuosity and energetic sound associated with McLaughlin and his groups.[5]

After the second version of the Mahavishnu Orchestra disbanded, McLaughlin worked on some Indian-flavored albums with the group Shakti. Particularly notable after his work with that group was a collaboration with two other virtuoso guitarists, Paco De Lucia and Al Di Meola, and the resulting albums *Passion, Grace & Fire,* and *Friday Night in San Francisco.*[6]

In addition to his formidable acoustic guitar playing, McLaughlin embraced a newer synthesized guitar that interfaces with the Synclavier Digital Music System. His work with this high-tech instrument can be heard on his 1985 album *Mahavishnu,* a return to the earlier Mahavishnu format. When asked why he called this new group by the same name as his previous orchestra, he said, "Personally, the kind of spirit that was established in my first ensemble with that name, something I love very much, is now present in the new band."[7]

McLaughlin has always demonstrated virtuosic technique and high-energy musical flights. He contributed the sound of rock to the jazz mainstream. In addition, he was among the first to adopt the volume and metallic tone color more typical of rock performers and place them in a more traditional jazz setting. He has influenced the current generation of guitar players, both jazz and rock, in much the same way Wes Montgomery did a generation earlier.

Chick Corea: Return to Forever and Elektric Band

One of the most prominent and popular fusion groups of the 1970s and 1980s, Return to Forever, was led by Chick Corea, formerly with Miles Davis. Corea, a well-schooled piano player, began to use the electronic piano while with Davis. After working with his own avant-garde group, Circle, he formed Return to Forever in 1970. His move to electronic piano soon led to a complete involvement with synthesizers of all kinds.

Corea's music demonstrates a virtuosic skill in both technique and ensemble. His themes are often quite angular and complex rhythmically yet quite accessible to the listener. And despite their complexity, his records prove to be commercially successful. His music flows smoothly between up-tempo jazz, complex rock, and a more commercial rock style.

Return to Forever's 1977 album *Musicmagic* demonstrates Corea's ability to fuse many quite distinct musical styles into a single composition.[8] The title cut moves from a smooth commercial sound, through jazz interludes, and to funky rock passages. The fusion trademark—an active rock rhythmic underpinning

Chick Corea on piano

supporting a soloist with jazz phrasing above it—appears throughout the cut. Corea opens and closes the arrangement with acoustic piano but uses an electronic piano and synthesizers in the body of the piece.

Corea's later albums became more electronic as the instruments themselves became more accessible and more complex. With the advancing technology, outstanding keyboard players such as Corea often experimented with much smaller groups, replacing the usual complement of musicians with sophisticated electronic instruments. Unlike the seven musicians who performed for *Musicmagic,* Corea used only two or three at one time for his 1986 album *Elektric Band.*[9] The title proves to be a play on words: on the surface a reference to a poem called "Elektric City" and secondarily a reference to the heavy use of electronic instruments. Even his drummer, Dave Weckl, used an electronic drum set (Simmons) and drum synthesizer (Linn) on some of the cuts.

Corea wields this equipment quite effectively. His virtuosic keyboard technique and compositional skill showcase the potential for the new technology. His approach is still quite similar to that heard in the Return to Forever albums: rhythmically complex themes, tight ensemble, colorful orchestrations, and virtuosic display. His selection "Got a Match," from the *Elektric Band* album, offers an effective juxtaposition of jazz and rock phrasing. The solo areas again use the high-energy rock backdrop with a more typically bop solo in the foreground.

On his next album, *Light Years,*[10] Corea tried to make music that would fit the radio format, that is, four-minute songs with a consistent rhythm. This style is more characteristic of other, more commercial, groups such as Spyro-Gyra or the Yellowjackets. He moved away from that approach on his 1988 album *Eye of the Beholder*[11] and returned to a live recording process that allowed more room for performer interaction. Corea returned to his Elektric Band in 1990 after making an acoustic album, *Akoustic Band.*[12] On his later album *Inside Out,*[13] he used both acoustic piano and synthesizers. Some of the compositions are made up of several smaller parts that form structures larger than are usually found in this style. The playing

listening guide

Chick Corea

"Musicmagic"*

:00	Introduction: acoustic piano (Chick Corea).
:06	Flute enters.
:20	Piano interlude.
:31	Flute reenters.
:42	Piano alone.
1:09	Ritard and hold.
1:10	Low bass note on synthesizer and trombone.
1:17	Brass enters.
1:20	Keyboard with special effects.
1:44	Guitar featured.
2:05	Hold and introduction to newer section.
2:20	Ensemble.
2:33	Fretless bass sound.
2:50	Guitar solo.
3:21	Fender Rhodes keyboard solo.
3:30	Mellotron introduction for vocal.
3:43	Vocal duet—swinging background with ensemble.
4:35	Hammond organ solo—very funky.

5:25	Stop time plus Fender Rhodes.
5:36	Fender Rhodes (electronic piano) solo.
6:23	Brass enters.
6:30	New section.
6:41	Brass enters.
6:48	Repeat of sound from 6:30.
7:02	Fender Rhodes solo over stop time, then straight funky solo.
7:52	Brass enters.
8:24	Drum solo over stop time.
8:32	Vocal returns.
8:50	Soprano sax over vocal.
9:01	Soprano sax solo.
9:17	Acoustic piano solo.
9:28	Brass enters.
9:34	Ensemble.
9:52	Piano solo.
10:02	Ensemble.
10:20	Piano solo.
10:25	Ending.
10:48	End.

and melodic design continue in the complex, angular, and virtuosic style normally associated with fusion jazz. Listen to "Stretch It" or "Tale of Daring" (it is made up of four chapters) from this album to hear an example of the tight ensemble and virtuosic interplay that are increasingly associated with Corea's compositions.

Corea's most recent group, Origin, which began in 1997, is a fusion of an even broader type. Like his previous group, this group is also primarily acoustic and boasts a membership that brings a variety of cultural influences—Israeli, Afro-Cuban, Middle Eastern (Avishai Cohn, bass), world music (Jeff Balard, percussion), Celtic (Tim Garland, saxophone), and R & B and funk (Steve Wilson). And of course Corea brings a rich background of jazz styles from working with such groups as Mongo Santamaria, Miles Davis, and his own Return to

listening guide

Chick Corea, Elektric Band
"Stretch It, Part I"*
Chick Corea, keyboards
John Patitucci, bass
Eric Marienthal, saxophone
Frank Gambale, guitar
Dave Weckl, drums

:00   Piano lead-in joined later by the saxophone.

:05   Irregular metric feel.

:09   Return to opening motivic material.

:22   Listen for the ensemble accents during this short contrast section.

:29   Return to irregular motivic material with drum fills between the disjunct melodic fragments.

:39   Beginning of buildup to final chords with irregular accents; listen for how the melodic fragments are accented as a part of the active drumming.

:51   End of Part I.

Inside Out, GRP Records, GRD-9601.

Forever band. Steve Davis on trombone completes the group. This group is characterized by a live sound that is supported by constant touring. Even their recordings attempt to catch a live, spontaneous style (*A Week at the Blue Note*, Stretch, 9020).

Joe Zawinul and Wayne Shorter: Weather Report

Like Chick Corea, Joe Zawinul and Wayne Shorter worked with Miles Davis when *Bitches Brew* was recorded. Also like Corea, they formed one of the most commanding fusion bands of the 1970s and 1980s: Weather Report. A special chemistry seems to have existed between Zawinul and Shorter that gave their band a distinctive, popular sound. In an article by George Varga, Zawinul credits an even earlier Miles Davis recording with influencing his writing style: "The record was *Birth of the Cool*, and it had a great impact on me. I like to write in that sound-spectrum style."[14] A majority of the writing during Weather Report's fifteen-year existence was done by Zawinul; his respect for the composed approach to jazz typical on *Birth of the Cool* can be heard in his compositions.

listening guide

(CD 3, track 7)
Weather Report
"Birdland"*
Joseph Zawinul, Oberheim Polyphonic, Arp 2600 acoustic
   piano, vocal, melodica
Wayne Shorter, soprano, tenor saxophone
Jaco Pastorius, bass, mandocello, vocals
Alex Acuna, drums
Manolo Badrena, tambourine

:00   Analog synthesizer bass line.

:18   Bass guitar with introductory motive.

:43   Synthesizer melodic riff-like motive with saxophone.

:55   Interlude: long, low notes with a new riff-like motive above them.

1:02   Short motive over low synthesizer notes—builds energy.

1:31   Saxophone enters with synthesizer to increase energy.

1:45   Interlude to set up melody.

1:59   Main melody enters with saxophone and synthesizer; bass guitar plays fill-ins in answer to melody; repeat of melodic motive builds energy.

2:36   Long-held-note interlude with synthesizer line and some vocal sounds.

3:07   Descending chords with saxophone solo over them to build energy.

3:34   Return to opening bass guitar motive as synthesizer enters with opening synthesized bass line and some saxophone fills.

3:59   Saxophone and synthesizer riff as in opening section.

4:11   Interlude: long notes and riff motive.

4:15   Melody returns to begin a buildup; the melody repeats over and over with increasing interplay between players.

5:48   Fade out and end.

*Heavy Weather, Columbia Records, 34418.

Like Corea, Zawinul is an accomplished pianist who moved comfortably into the electronic medium of synthesizers.

Weather Report's 1980 album *Night Passage* offers several examples of fusion at different points along the jazz/rock line.[15] "Rockin' in Rhythm" is based on an Ellington tune and uses synthesizers to fill out a saxophone section sound under Shorter. The rhythm and style are mainly swing, and little is borrowed

Joe Zawinul and Wayne Shorter of Weather Report

from the rock idiom. "Fast City" offers the soloists an energetic arena for a type of virtuosity often associated with fusion groups. The thematic material is again rhythmically complex and punctuated with ensemble motives. Even the bass player, Jaco Pastorius, often joins the ensemble in the complex unison lines.

The song most associated with Weather Report is Zawinul's "Birdland" from the album *Heavy Weather*.[16] This composition is a beacon of 1970s fusion and reappeared later in settings by the Manhattan Transfer and Quincy Jones.[17]

Zawinul and Shorter's last record together as Weather Report, *This Is This*, came out in 1986 and showed another personnel shift.[18] Victor Bailey (bass) and Mino Cinelu (percussionist/vocalist who had been playing with Weather Report) remained, but Peter Erskine returned on drums, and, more important, John Scofield was added on guitar. Scofield replaced Shorter, and the group continued work as Weather Update.

Zawinul also came out with a solo album in 1986, *Dialects*, on which he used four synthesizers and four **drum machines.**[19] The only other performers on the album are four vocalists, one of whom is Bobby McFerrin. "All the pieces are improvised," Zawinul told George Varga. "Each sound is a personality. It's like a conversation in which I'm the focus."[20] Each piece on the album represents an exotic theme such as "6 A.M./Walking on the Nile" and "The Great Empire" (Japan). Although there is often a rhythmic rock underpinning to the pieces, the musical idiom shifts sharply from piece to piece, reflecting the exotic themes. The compositions might better be thought of as jazz/rock tone poems similar in concept to classical overtures or music for film.

On his next recording, *Black Water*,[21] Zawinul returned to material more typical of his prefusion days. He also joined forces with Quincy Jones on his popular 1989 album, *Back on the Block*, with an arrangement of his already popular composition "Birdland." This composition was performed originally by Weather

Report and later set to lyrics by Jon Hendricks and performed by Manhattan Transfer. Zawinul continues to write music for a variety of media, including film and classical ensembles. His success in diverse musical arenas allows him to say of himself, "Not jazz, not rock, just me. I am my own category."[22]

Michael Brecker

Saxophonist Michael Brecker was certainly not new to the jazz/rock fusion scene. He and his brother Randy were at the forefront of the development with their first band, Dreams, in 1970. Like many fusion players, Brecker's early musical experience includes a good deal of experience in rock bands. He later joined Steps Ahead, a group organized and led by vibist Michael Mainieri.

It was not until 1987 that he stepped out to lead his own group with the album *Michael Brecker*.[23] It was at this time that Brecker showed that the EWI (electronic wind instrument) could be a viable jazz instrument.

Brecker further established himself as a leader of a high-energy jazz strongly influenced by blues (often with a backbeat funk style) on his next album, *Don't Try This at Home*.[24] His work with Michael Stern (previously with Miles Davis on *Tutu*) resulted in high-energy virtuosic flights over driving rock as well as up-tempo jazz backups.

JAZZ: A NEW POPULARITY

The controversy in the jazz world that surrounded the new jazz/rock fusion was accentuated by the new generation of players and groups who further embraced stylistic and sound ideals often found in the popular music of the 1980s. These new groups also gained a popularity not enjoyed by jazz musicians since the swing era. This new interest in jazz does not necessarily spill over to the more traditional straight-ahead jazz groups. In fact, many listeners may have virtually no knowledge of the earlier jazz traditions from which these groups evolved. As a result, a new dichotomy has developed in the jazz community between those who hold a strong allegiance to the jazz tradition (embodied in performers like Wynton Marsalis) and those whose music is sometimes called jazz but in reality may have roots more directly tied to the rock or pop tradition.

Through it all, the players themselves apparently see the larger picture and work in their new arena with a firm respect for those who preceded them. Yet they are also excited by the new prospects available in other musical styles around them. Many of these players sport backgrounds not necessarily in jazz. Rather than jazz players importing rock attributes, we have for the first time in fusion performers with backgrounds equally, if not mainly, in rock.

David Sanborn

David Sanborn is an individual positioned between these two emerging definitions of jazz. He is viewed by many as the new saxophone sound in jazz, importing strong blues and rhythm and blues influences. Contrary to the opinion held by his followers, he continues to state, "Even when I do think in

listening guide

(CD 4, track 1)
Michael Brecker
"Itsbynne Reel"*
Michael Brecker, tenor saxophone
  and Akai EWI
Mike Stern, guitar
Don Grolnick, piano
Charlie Haden, acoustic bass
Jeff Andrews, fretless electric bass
Jack DeJohnette, drums
Mark O'Connor, violin

:00 Melody on Akai EWI controller (a section of melody).

:08 Violin enters and doubles the EWI.

:15 Piano enters.

:31 New middle section (B).

:38 Repeat of B section.

:46 Return of A section.

:54 New melodic section with a development of previous melodic material with counterpoint between the violin and EWI; a sustained note creates a drone, like the frozen harmonic areas to be used later.

2:12 Bass and drums enter with jazz/rock phrasing.

2:21 Listen for synthesized brasslike punches on normally unaccented beats.

2:31 Melody repeats.

2:47 New ensemble-like section.

3:01 More staccato and accented phrasing.

3:17 Slow ascending bass and piano; unison notes playing a cross-rhythm.

3:48 Ensemble material for transition to solo.

4:18 Saxophone enters for a solo over the slow cross-rhythm notes in bass and piano.

4:47 Saxophone line joins slow bass and piano notes for unison transition; listen to rhythmic activity in the drums.

5:00 Solo breaks free over a frozen harmony (drone).

5:21 Harmony changes slightly (first time since 5:00); bass ascends and descends by step.

6:09 Double-time melodic ideas move to climax.

6:17 Return to original melodic idea with variations.

6:30 Violin joins the saxophone in unison over the harmonic pedal (drone), very active drumming.

7:01 The two soloists play independent lines in counterpoint.

7:40 End.

*Don't Try This at Home, Impulse Records, MCAD-42229.

categories, I never think of myself as a jazz musician. I've never called myself a jazz musician in the public forum or privately."[25]

Despite this denial, Sanborn has figured prominently in the promotion of jazz's new popularity. He has hosted a jazz radio program called *The Jazz Show* and a late-night television show featuring leading jazz personalities. He also enjoys a popularity that extends beyond the traditional jazz community. His work with Bob James on *Double Vision*[26] demonstrates his improvisatory style in a more pop-sounding environment. Sanborn's use of the very high range of the saxophone, called the altissimo register, is one of the trademarks of his sound. This register, although not new to saxophonists, is now widely used by most players. Also on this album is a recording called "Since I Fell for You," with vocalist Al Jarreau, which demonstrates the type of sound and style perhaps controversially called jazz by the newest listening audience of jazz/pop. This audience has only recently moved to jazz and carries with it a pop/rock background. Sanborn, like other performers in this style, offers a stylistic bridge connecting the commercial world of pop with the jazz tradition.

Pat Metheny

Guitarist Pat Metheny has gained a great deal of popularity because of his proficiency on the instrument as well as his blend of jazz, rock, and Latin influences. His 1978 album *The Pat Metheny Group* gained him a wider audience than that enjoyed by other otherwise successful jazz musicians. Unlike McLaughlin, Metheny's early background was primarily jazz based. His sound is therefore more in keeping with the more lyrical tradition established by Wes Montgomery.

In 1986 Metheny collaborated with Ornette Coleman to create an album, *Song X,*[27] that offers a blend of the two players' backgrounds. As the title suggests, the sounds of this album were to be viewed as songs that cannot be named, only experienced for their imagination and creativity. Metheny's more recent albums include a Grammy Award winner, *Still Life (Talking),*[28] released in 1987. It was followed by *Letter from Home,*[29] in which Metheny makes use of sophisticated rhythmic settings that show strong Brazilian influences.

Metheny's later albums continue to demonstrate his wide interest in styles that fall between jazz and pop. On the album *Trio 99→00,* he teams up with bassist Larry Grenadier and drummer Bill Stewart to play a variety of selections, including original blues, bossas, and even covers like Coltrane's "Giant Steps."

Pat Metheny

Spyro-Gyra and Yellowjackets

Since the impact of Return to Forever and Weather Report, a second generation of groups has appeared that reflects many of the first generation's rhythmic and ensemble innovations. Most prominent of these groups are Spyro-Gyra and the Yellowjackets.

Spyro-Gyra, led by saxophonist Jay Beckenstein, offers a type of jazz/rock/Latin fusion. Although pianist Jeremy Wall was later replaced by Tom Schuman, he continues as producer/composer/arranger and studio pianist. Beckenstein and Wall, together with guitarist Chet Catallo, bassist David Wolford, drummer Eli Konikoff, and percussionist Gerardo Velez, created a sound that falls somewhere between the complexities of groups such as Weather Report and a more pop style. They first became popular with their

vamping

JAZZ/POP

Popular music is, without a doubt, the fastest changing of all musics today. Because of the short life of so many of the emerging styles, their impact on jazz is difficult to immediately assess. At the height of disco's popularity, it was tempting to say that no music would be free from its influence; but, now, years after its decline, little of its impact is being felt. It certainly strengthened the move toward a greater use of synthesizers and a refinement in studio techniques, but as a musical idiom it has almost entirely vanished.

Despite the unstable nature of popular music, several notable jazz musicians have taken active roles in its creation. Their jazz heritage and notoriety often carry the jazz label into the new medium even when the music incorporates little recognizable jazz. Quincy Jones and Herbie Hancock are two such figures. Both composers have worked in the most diverse musical fields—from jazz to film scores—primarily in the rock idiom.

album *Morning Dance*.[30] A Latin feel characterizes many of their performances, yet they are still quite effective at establishing a type of jazz groove with a rock underpinning. "Swing Street," from their album *Point of View*,[31] demonstrates a characteristic jazz/rock feel. Although the title implies a swing style, the meter has definite rock attributes. It begins with a straight-ahead feel but soon develops a half-time rock **backbeat,** leaving the swing feel to the smaller beat subdivisions. This rhythmic feel is often a trademark of fusion groups. Against this backup, the soloists adopt a bop-like melodic style as they improvise.

The Yellowjackets were formed in 1980 and, like Spyro-Gyra, follow the legacy established by Weather Report. The four members of the group—Russell Ferrante on piano and synthesizers, Jimmy Haslip on bass, Marc Russo on saxophones, and William Kennedy on drums—create complex, energetic arrangements that not only borrow from several previous jazz styles but also blend in sounds more accessible to the popular listening audiences.

The angularity of the melodic lines and the harmonic punches used by the Yellowjackets is particularly reminiscent of Weather Report. The harmonic accents work in much the same fashion that brass punches do in big-band ensembles. "Out of Town," from their 1987 album *Four Corners*,[32] exemplifies their use of synthesizers to give the impression of brass sections and their use of bop solo lines over the intricate jazz/rock–flavored backup. The Yellowjackets also blend Latin influences into their music, generally including a rock feel.

On a later album, *The Spin*,[33] the Yellowjackets move in a different, more acoustic, direction. This move brought them closer to the performance tradition common to earlier jazz ensembles. Their previous recordings took a studio approach in which they used sequencers to lay down the first tracks and then built the song through successive overdubs. This album not only took an acoustic approach but also used a **sequencer** on only one song. "The

listening guide

(CD 4, track 2)
Yellowjackets
"Out of Town"*
Russell Ferrante, keyboards
Jimmy Haslip, bass
Marc Russo, saxophones
William Kennedy, drums

:00 Four-beat jazz feel in the bass with slow rock feel backbeat in bass drum and hand claps.

:19 Melody enters on saxophone.

:37 Piano/synthesizer enters.

:51 Synthesizer and saxophone unison melody line.

1:33 Listen for how the drummer accents ("kicks") the melody and synthesizer harmonic accents.

1:38 Return to the melody.

1:54 Transition area, backbeat accents in bass and drums (on beats 2 and 4).

2:10 Big-band ensemble style punches with saxophone, synthesizers, and drum accents.

2:22 Extended sax fill leading to next chorus.

2:32 New chorus with piano solo (MIDI coupled?); listen to how the ensemble tightens at the start of the chorus as the bass starts to walk in four and the drums settle into straight time.

3:34 Synthesized brass-like punches with drum accents.

4:07 Transition with backbeat feel.

4:15 Saxophone and synthesizer unison line returns, with straight-time backup.

4:31 Drum solo.

4:38 Melody returns.

5:02 End.

*Four Corners, MCA Records, MCAD-5994.

---

new album required more blowing, more of a band performance." Their effort on this album was consciously directed toward "trying to keep some sort of traditional direction alive."[34]

Quincy Jones

Quincy Jones's 1989 album *Back on the Block*[35] offers a wide cross section of styles meant to represent the many diverse musical areas in which he has worked during his career. The album swings from rap to jazz fusion with singers such as Ella Fitzgerald, Sarah Vaughan, Ray Charles, and Take 6; rappers like Ice-T and Melle Mel; instrumentalists Dizzy Gillespie, Miles Davis, George Benson, Joe Zawinul, and Herbie Hancock; and on and on. The blend of individual and commercial styles is impressive and a tribute to Jones's production skills. Particularly interesting is the arrangement of Zawinul's "Birdland," which blends fusion and pop elements quite effectively. Miles Davis, Dizzy Gillespie, George Benson, and James Moody are featured soloists. The

underlying rhythm arrangement, which contains electronically generated sequences as well as programmed drum parts, is commercially consistent with the other cuts on the album.

Herbie Hancock

Herbie Hancock is particularly interesting because of his earlier association with the Miles Davis quintet. While working on his many other projects, he found time to reorganize this earlier group, with himself on piano, Ron Carter on bass, Tony Williams on drums, and Freddie Hubbard taking the place of Davis. The group called itself VSOP and featured mainstream jazz. VSOP 2 followed with the Marsalis brothers several years later.

While maintaining his jazz definition with excursions of this kind, Hancock is also producing albums with the Rockit band. He says of these efforts, "Most people who come from a jazz background and do anything in an area of electric or pop music still maintain a lot of the character of jazz in their pop stuff. So it's a true fusion kind of thing. I did that for a while, but I've been trying to take the pop stuff more into the pop area, and leave out the jazz. I think I've pretty much succeeded at that, because the last few records I don't consider jazz records at all."[36] An album important to the jazz fusion genre is Hancock's 1973 studio album, *Head Hunters*, performed by a band by the same name. This album took advantage of the many technical features only available in the

vamping

Commercial Jazz

Not all musicians have attempted to draw such clear stylistic lines in their work. George Benson was among the first to blur the lines between jazz and popular music with his record *Breezin'*, the first such record by a jazz-associated musician to go platinum and hold first place in pop, jazz, and rhythm and blues at the same time.[37] Chuck Mangione has gained a similar popularity with his fusion groups, his most popular piece being his 1978 instrumental "Feels So Good."

Miles Davis's 1985 album *You're Under Arrest* is a rather unusual blend of pop and jazz.[38] He even rearranges a song written and performed by Cyndi Lauper, a prominent pop music star at the time, for this album. Despite this more commercial sound, the musical approach is similar to Davis's earlier albums, which tend to place the soloists in sharp contrast to a steady rhythmic underpinning.

recording studio. Hancock played all the synthesizer tracks himself, obviously impossible in a live performance. All the tracks on the album except "Watermelon Man" were written specifically for this album. The album differed from those by most other jazz/rock pioneers with its strong rhythm and blues feel. The rhythm section with Paul Jackson on bass and Harvey Mason on drums created the jazz-funk sound that extended the appeal of this album to a wide rhythm and blues audience.

What Hancock does carry to these later albums is the technical skill and approach more typical of an accomplished jazz player. The music of his album *Sound System* falls more into the category of **beat** or **breaker music,** a rather specific type of music for a popular dance known as break dancing.[39] Hancock may very well have accomplished what he had intended: to clearly leave the jazz out.

LATIN JAZZ FUSION

An important collaboration for the development of jazz/rock fusion occurred when Joe Zawinul, who participated in Latin jazz jam sessions, recommended Airto Moreira to Miles Davis. Davis's legendary work on *Bitches Brew*, which signaled the success of the later jazz/rock fusion bands, enjoyed the participation of Latin jazz musicians Corea, Zawinul, and Moreira. Moreira stayed with Davis for two years and then joined Corea when he established the band Return to Forever.

Moreira formed his own band in 1973. With his wide flexibility of stylistic playing, he worked more regularly across the jazz and Latin music boundaries than most Latin jazz performers. His popularity, however, was eclipsed by Eumir Deodato's dramatically successful album, *Prelude*. Deodato's track based

on the Strauss theme "Also Sprach Zarathustra" captured the attention of the popular listening community.

Throughout the 1970s Latin jazz was becoming inextricably intertwined with diverse jazz streams. It was no longer easily identified as a new stylistic fusion but became a more subtle flavor of jazz itself. Pat Metheny's album *Watercolors* owes a great deal to Brazilian influences. George Duke explored Afro-Cuban influences on his album *Don't Let Go* (Epic, EK 35366) and played in Flora Purim and Airto Moreira's Brazilian group that featured Latin-jazz-funk. On the album *Red Hot* (Columbia, 35696), Mongo Santamaria continued to demonstrate his influence on jazz with players like Randy Brecker, Bob James, and Charlie Palmieri.

It is somewhat ironic, or more likely a self-preserving reaction, that just as Latin jazz was melding with other American musical streams it began a back-to-basics movement with a return to its Cuban roots. This more traditional music—increasingly identified as salsa—had as its leaders Ray Barretto and Eddie Palmieri. Although salsa was a return to the more typical New York Latin sound, Palmieri represented its more experimental side. Despite his constant experimentation, he remained tremendously popular because his music always maintained an earthy Cuban quality.

In a 1979 Carnegie Hall concert, an unannounced group, Irakere, played its first performance in the United States and captured the attention of the Latin jazz community. Joining Irakere at this concert were many of the crossover musicians who fostered Latin jazz—Stan Getz, Dizzy Gillespie, the Machito orchestra, Tito Puente's band, Mongo Santamaria, and Cal Tjader. This concert signaled the Latin-jazz revival in the 1980s.

Latin and jazz experimentation surfaced again in the late 1970s in the work of Charles Mingus. His album *Cumbia and Jazz Fusion* (Rhino, RK41404) features Panamanian flutist Mauricio Smith and a large percussion section that includes four conga players. The album reflects the influences of Mingus's trip to South America. And, like everything that Mingus did, *Cumbia and Jazz Fusion* is so personalized that it is unique in the field of Latin jazz.

listening guide

(CD 4, track 3)
"Watermelon Man"
Poncho Sanchez, conga
Mongo Santamaria, percussion

:00   Intro sets up the Latin beat. Notice the quire (scrapping sound).

:09   Trumpet, trombone, and tenor saxophone enter as a duet with the melody.

:26   Second phrase ends with vocalizations from the band.

:42   Second verse is a repeat of the first verse.

1:18   Saxophone solo. Notice it is a blend of bop and rock phrasing.

1:52   As the solo continues, horns enter to play backup lines.

2:26   Fourth verse is a repeat of the first verse with the addition of "Watermelon Man" sung by the band between phrases.

2:42   Second phrase is accompanied by vocalizations from the band.

2:57   Final measures are repeated.

3:05   Slowed down version of the watermelon motive.

3:08   Conga solo before the final chord.

3:24   Vocalization anticipating the final chord.

3:29   Final chords.

3:40   End.

JAZZ IN ROCK

In 1971, Irving L. Horowitz, a professor of sociology at Rutgers University, wrote the following about the merging of jazz and rock:

> Many recent bands [e.g., Blood, Sweat and Tears, Chicago, and Cold Blood] are highly reminiscent in their instrumentation of such earlier groups as Miles Davis' Tentet in the late '40s. And the loud, brassy arrangements are direct descendants of Count Basie. A promising new group, Ten Wheel Drive, provides a mixture of Big Mama Thornton blues and a tenor sax reminiscent of Coltrane, all set to tight arrangements that remind one of the Jazz Messengers with Art Blakey and Horace Silver.[40]

Rock from its beginnings shared much in common with jazz, particularly its strong commitment to rhythm. In its earlier days, rock, like jazz, based much of its music on the twelve-bar blues progression ("Shake Rattle & Roll" and "Every Hour"). However, it was not until the late 1960s that groups like Blood, Sweat and Tears and Chicago (Chicago Transit Authority) consciously incorporated jazz instrumentation and idioms into their work. By that time, the rock harmonic idiom was becoming more modal and the rhythmic patterns more complex. The jazz crossover was therefore most apparent in the added instrumentation—saxophones, trumpets, and trombones—to the more usual guitars. These horns did more than back up the traditional rock band. They were an integral part of the ensemble and were even given open areas for jazz solos.

The musicians in the group Chicago say that they incorporated jazz first but that the *Blood, Sweat and Tears* album was produced ahead of their album. Both bands used horn players and more composed ensemble practices. "Spinning Wheel," from the *Blood, Sweat and Tears* album, was a particularly popular example of their type of jazz/rock fusion. Bobby Colomby's drumming on this album proved to be a forerunner of the drumming heard in prominent fusion groups in the 1970s and 1980s. This particular piece worked its way into the jazz community when Maynard Ferguson used it as a basis for an exciting arrangement for his band.[41]

The material for the *Blood, Sweat and Tears* album shows both classical and jazz crossover. The use of traditional jazz tunes like "God Bless the Child" on the one hand and an Erik Satie theme from "Trois Gymnopédies" on the other potentially qualify this album as both fusion and third stream.[42]

Sting formed a band that attempted to fuse the worlds of rock and jazz. His approach was to import top jazz players and place them in a rock medium. The jazz players were already established jazz musicians: Branford Marsalis, formerly with Art Blakey; Daryl Jones, who worked with Miles Davis; Kenny Kirkland, keyboard player for Wynton Marsalis; and Omar Hakim, drummer for Weather Report. After working with many young jazz players, Sting picked those whom he considered to be the best young jazz musicians in the world: ". . . on the understanding that we weren't going to play jazz. What I wanted was a flavor. I didn't want to go off and give Branford 120 bars to explore a theme; I was gonna say, 'You're going to have 16 bars and you're going to burn from the first bar.'"[43]

Sting's credentials as a rock musician and songwriter were established while he was with the popular rock group Police. His new band was a hybrid counterpart to most other fusion groups, which are led by prominent jazz leaders. Whereas he imported jazz into a rock medium, bands like Weather Report and Return to Forever imported rock idioms into a jazz medium.

As Sting formed and rehearsed his new group, he recorded the process on videotape and produced a movie documentary that offers some insight into the excitement and dilemma associated with crossover bands. The concluding filmed concert shows a blend of both rock and jazz material. A couple of the numbers are blues in the traditional jazz sense, whereas other songs, written originally for Police, are adapted for the newer jazz/rock medium.[44]

Jam Bands

Jam bands were rock bands that featured extended musical improvisation over rhythmic grooves and chord patterns. Such improvisation was not the norm in rock bands, and those that did make improvisation part of their concerts were connected through that practice to the jazz tradition. The earliest bands that in retrospect were jam bands were the seminal groups like the Grateful Dead and Cream. Other early bands were the Allman Brothers Band, Hot Tuna, The Jimi Hendrix Experience, New Riders of the Purple Sage, Quicksilver Messenger Service, and Santana. Early Pink Floyd and the Greatful Dead were noted most for lengthy improvisations.

In the 1980s and 1990s Phish was the best-known of the jam bands. Other bands included Bela Fleck and the Flecktones, England's Ozric Tentacles, Aquarium Rescue Unit, and moe. Bands like Dave Matthews Band and Primus began their careers in the jam band scene but moved to more produced material over time. Keeping the jam band tradition alive are bands like moe, Umphrey's McGee, Yonder Mountain String Band, Widespread Panic, and the Disco Biscuits.

The term *jam band* is still fluid and broad arching. There is not always agreement on what bands should be included nor how the term is specifically defined. Many jam bands may not have broad exposure, but they do have dedicated fans. Jam bands in many ways help keep the improvisational spirit of jazz alive and in the forefront of contemporary listeners.

summary

The list of crossover musicians, all along the jazz/rock/pop line, is long and growing as fast as the music itself changes. To know which of these will leave legacies remains for time to decide. During the 1970s and 1980s, jazz began to import heavily from the increasingly popular rock styles. This crossover generated some controversy in the jazz community. Was the jazz tradition being forsaken? Was this new music jazz at all?

By the 1980s, a new shift had taken place within this crossover group, and a new popularity in jazz was developing. However, there were also some controversial aspects to this new popularity. By this time, previously controversial groups such as Weather Report and Return to Forever had established themselves as jazz expressions, and now the next generation of players was challenging the jazz definition. Because of the popularity that often accompanied these new groups, an accusation of commercial sellout was heard. Also, many of these new players are not protégés of the jazz art world but often come out of the rock or pop style. Although they may not be of the jazz tradition, it is obvious that the players have a great respect for it. The current controversy will no doubt be settled, but for now we must wait and listen.

FOR FURTHER STUDY

1. Select two recordings in your school record library that you think would be good examples of jazz/rock. Give reasons for your selections.
2. What is meant by the terms *crossover* and *fusion* as they relate to jazz/rock? Be specific.
3. Who led the way for a fusion of rock rhythm and free-form jazz?
4. In a jazz/rock percussion section, what rhythmic role is assigned to the snare and bass drums in contrast to the electric bass or bass guitar? Why?

5. Identify two of the earliest rock-and-roll groups that featured jazz solos.

6. Did Latin music challenge the jazz definition the same way that fusion did?

7. How is jazz/rock fusion like jazz/Latin fusion? How are they different?

8. Listen to Tito Puente's "Donna Lee" and tap out the accents of one of the syncopated rhythms maintained in the percussion. Pretend that you are a clave player and make up a syncopated rhythm to play with the percussion section.

SUGGESTED ADDITIONAL LISTENING

Aura. Columbia Records, CK 45332.
Bitches Brew (2 vols.). Columbia Records, GP 26.
Chicago Transit Authority. *Chicago.* Columbia Records, KGP24.
———. *Chicago Transit Authority.* Columbia Records, GP8.
Collector's Items (with Parker and Mingus) (2 vols.). Prestige Records, 24022E.
ESP (with Shorter, Hancock, Carter, and Williams). Columbia Records, PC-9150.
"Four" and More (with Hancock). Columbia Records, PC-9253.
In a Silent Way. Columbia Records, PC-9875.
Lewis, Ramsey. *The In Crowd.* Argo Records, LP-757.
The Man with the Horn. Columbia Records, PC-36790.
McCann, Les. *Beaux J. PooBoo.* Limelight Records, LS-8625.
'Round About Midnight (with Coltrane). Columbia Records, PC-8649E.
Seven Steps to Heaven (with Hancock). Columbia Records, PS-8851.

ADDITIONAL READING RESOURCES

Carr, Ian. *Miles Davis.*
Cole, Bill. *Miles Davis.*
Coryell, Julie, and Friedman, Laura. *Jazz-Rock Fusion.*
Courlander, Harold. *Miles Davis: A Musical Biography.*
Davis, Francis. *In the Moment: Jazz in the 1980s.*
Davis, Miles, and Troupe, Quincy. *Miles.*
Megill, Donald D., and Demory, Richard S. *Introduction to Jazz History.*
Roberts, John Storm, *Latin Jazz.*
———. *The Latin Tinge.*

Note: Complete information, including name of publisher and date of publication, is provided in this book's bibliography.

NOTES

1. Herbie Hancock, *Down Beat* 55, no. 6 (June 1988): 18.
2. Don Ellis, "Rock: The Rhythmic Revolution," *Down Beat* 36, no. 24 (1969): 32.
3. Miles Davis, *Bitches Brew,* Columbia Records, GP 26.
4. *Down Beat* 55, no. 9 (September 1988): 19.

5. Mahavishnu Orchestra, *Inner Mounting Flame,* Columbia Records, 31067; *Birds of Fire,* Columbia Records, 31996; *Between Nothingness and Eternity,* Columbia Records, 32766.
6. *Passion, Grace & Fire,* Columbia Records, 38645; *Friday Night in San Francisco,* Columbia Records, 37152.
7. *Down Beat* 52, no. 3 (March 1985): 17.
8. Return to Forever, *Musicmagic,* Columbia Records, AL 34682.
9. Chick Corea, *Elektric Band,* GRP Records, GRP-A-1026 (compact disc, GRP-D-9535).
10. Chick Corea, *Light Years,* GRP Records, GRP-1036.
11. Chick Corea, *Eye of the Beholder,* GRP Records, GRP-1053.
12. Chick Corea, *Akoustic Band,* GRP Records, GRD-9582.
13. Chick Corea, *Elektric Band,* and *Inside Out,* GRP Records, GRD-9601.
14. George Varga, *The San Diego Union,* 9 March 1986.
15. Weather Report, *Night Passage,* CBS Records, 36793.
16. Weather Report, *Heavy Weather,* Columbia Records, 34418.
17. Manhattan Transfer, *Extensions,* Atlantic Records, SD 19258; Quincy Jones, *Back on the Block,* Warner Brothers Records, 0 26020-2.
18. Weather Report, *This Is This,* CBS Records, CK-40280.
19. Joseph Zawinul, *Dialects,* Columbia Records, FCT 40081.
20. George Varga, *The San Diego Union,* 9 March 1986.
21. Joseph Zawinul, *Black Water,* Columbia Records, CK 44316.
22. Leonard Feather, *Los Angeles Times/Calendar,* 18 February 1990.
23. Michael Brecker, *Michael Brecker,* Impulse, 5980.
24. Michael Brecker, *Don't Try This at Home,* Impulse, MCAD-42229.
25. *Down Beat* 53, no. 8 (August 1986): 18.
26. *Double Vision,* Warner Brothers Records, 25393-4.
27. Pat Metheny, *Song X,* Geffen, 24096.
28. Pat Metheny, *Still Life (Talking),* Geffen, 24145.
29. Pat Metheny, *Letter from Home,* Geffen, 24245.
30. Spyro-Gyra, *Morning Dance,* Infinity Records, INF9004.
31. Spyro-Gyra, *Point of View,* MCA Records, MCAD-6309.
32. Yellowjackets, *Four Corners,* MCA Records, MCAD-5994.
33. Yellowjackets, *The Spin,* MCA Records, MCAD-6304.
34. *Down Beat* 56, no. 11 (November 1989): 22.
35. Quincy Jones, *Back on the Block,* Warner Brothers Records, 9 26020-2.
36. Howard Mandel, *Down Beat* 53, no. 7 (July 1986): 17.
37. George Benson, *Breezin',* Warner Brothers Records, BSK-3111.
38. Miles Davis, *You're Under Arrest,* Columbia Records, FCT 40023.
39. Herbie Hancock, *Sound System,* Columbia Records, 39478.
40. Irving L. Horowitz, "Rock on the Rocks Bubblegum Anyone?" Reprinted from *Psychology Today,* January 1971. Copyright 1971 by Ziff-Davis Publishing Company. All rights reserved.
41. Maynard Ferguson, "Spinning Wheel," *M. F. Horn II,* Columbia Records, KC 31709, CBS 65027.
42. Blood, Sweat and Tears, *Blood, Sweat and Tears,* Columbia Records, CS9720.
43. Art Lange, *Down Beat* 52, no. 12 (December 1985).
44. Sting, *Bring on the Night,* Karl/Lorimar Feature Films, A&M Films, a division of A&M Records Inc., 1985, YHS 344. The music can be heard on *The Dream of the Blue Turtles,* A&M Records.

Contemporary Trends: A Maturing Art Form

By the early 1990s the jazz community had found its center of gravity and had begun to consciously define its legacy. The small-group styles defined predominantly by improvisation rather than composition claimed landmark significance within the newly emerging legacy. This is particularly interesting because these styles—and bop in particular—were not necessarily popular during their time. In fact, in the case of bop, there was as much controversy as there was popularity; the major jazz audience still listened to swing music. Why is it that bebop gained later eminence when other styles that had held so much more popularity did not survive the cut? It would seem that the swing era would have garnered an equal if not greater respect because of its worldwide appeal.

THE NEOCLASSICAL SCHOOL

A neoclassical school of jazz appeared at the beginning of the 1990s, which, as its name implies, looked for "new" expressions of "classical" jazz. At the same time that jazz was looking back at bebop as its historical center, there was also a subtle shifting of importance throughout our historical understanding of the jazz legacy. The white bands that were clearly the most popular during the big-band era were losing pages in history books to their African American contemporaries. The emergence of the early 1990s neoclassical school of jazz, a historically conscious movement, traced its history fairly exclusively through a line of African American players. Although the details of history had not changed, the jazz community's understanding of it had.

Jazz has moved a long way from its earliest stirrings in the red-light districts of major urban areas to today's classrooms. Jazz as an art form was certainly not on the minds of the first jazz players, but it most certainly is on the minds of today's players and teachers. In fact, today's musicians carry the weight and responsibility of this new historical understanding. It is this historical framework that will continue to offer the criteria by which contemporary performance will be judged. Terms like *straight-ahead* and *mainstream* jazz signal such an allegiance to the past. It is perhaps ironic that such a historical perspective is basically Western European. Current consensus grants the

Wynton Marsalis

ownership of jazz clearly to the African American crosscurrent but at the same time places it in a uniquely Western European historical context, a context that grants validity to jazz as an art form. This interplay of the two crosscurrents is embodied in the term "America's classical music"—further proof that the two crosscurrents remain both healthy and distinct.

In the previous chapters we have seen the initial stirrings of jazz as a recognizable musical tradition. These stirrings were not preordained to be the birth of the art form that began to be clearly defined in the 1990s and that we now know as jazz. What were the conditions that shaped it into an American art form rather than let it wash out of control with the tides of fashion? Popular music is an artifact of the Western music tradition. How does a popular music develop a tradition that is consistent enough to be seen as unique, and how does that unique music gain public acceptance as an art form? We certainly see other popular music traditions around us that have similar developments in their tradition but have not generated a consensus about their art status. Musical lines as diverse as country, rock, even blues, have not gained art status, at least not yet; but jazz has.

The Young Lions

As jazz in the 1990s looked back to the masters and heroes of the bop period, a new generation of players emerged on the scene. These new players faced a different set of expectations than the original bop players did. Rather than lead

vamping

The Jazz Canon

As we saw in the chapter on bop, jazz was beginning to establish its canon and define its mainstream during that period. It began to identify those musicians who would define jazz in its purest form. It was at this time that jazz was becoming self-conscious. How contemporary musicians played began to be judged by the standards set by former jazz giants. An informal consensus was developing that would hold future players accountable and ward off competing intrusions or deviations from the defining mainstream.

Jazz has joined classical music as a functioning art form, but it is still recent enough historically to be confusingly pluralistic. Once the music of the dance hall, the street, and the church, jazz now finds itself on concert stages, in universities, and in historical accounts. The players who have been remembered are those who pushed on the developing front edge of stylistic change, change that ultimately defined the growing mainstream. The mainstream weathered the two dominant attempts at redirection—an overly strong interest in composition at the expense of improvisation and an excessive importation from competing musical styles such as classical and rock. Contemporary jazz has many prominent players who are strong advocates of the traditional voice of jazz, who place a majority of their interest in the past rather than the future. Today, jazz looks back more than it ever has.

jazz in a new direction, away from the cool sound of jazz, these new players supported a revival of an earlier jazz era. This revival, however, looked back to a time defined by musicians still alive and working. The new generation of lions therefore found it necessary to earn recognition within the pride of existing mature lions who still had a strong hold over straight-ahead jazz. This is demonstrated by the fact that a *Down Beat* poll in 1995 still listed established players such as Sonny Rollins ahead of young lions such as Joe Lovano and Joshua Redman.

The young lions differed somewhat from the original straight-ahead players in that they were generally products of formal training at schools such as Berklee. Consequently, their knowledge of jazz, both theoretical and historical, factored into their work and gave them a perspective not shared by the original players of bop. However, a complaint of neoclassical musicians was that in their reverence for a past jazz style they had been robbed of their individual voices, the very attribute that defined the earlier jazz figures being emulated.

As the historical link from bop to hard bop stretches over the cool period, a similar arch from hard bop spans later stylistic periods, such as free and fusion, to land again in the work of players like trumpeter Wynton Marsalis, who has become one of the dominant voices of neoclassicism.

THE TRUMPET LEGACY

Wynton Marsalis

Trumpeter Wynton Marsalis speaks quite strongly about the legacy of past jazz styles and is, himself, a critically acclaimed performer of the straight-ahead style. The source of Marsalis's historical respect for jazz can be attributed to his father, Ellis, an established player and teacher of traditional jazz. Wynton's brothers, saxophonist Branford and trombonist Delfayeo, are also outspoken heralds of traditional jazz. The Marsalis jazz perspective tends to be fairly exclusive: Excluded are those styles not properly respectful of the jazz originators as defined by the neoclassical tradition. This perspective tends to jump from early New Orleans music to the bop period, overlooking the contributions of the more commercialized jazz periods.

Wynton Marsalis brings the bop to hard bop period full circle. Like so many other strong players in this tradition, Marsalis worked in his youth under the tutelage of Art Blakey in the Jazz Messengers. The straight-ahead legacy can be heard in Art Blakey and the Jazz Messengers, *Album of the Year*.

A certain amount of controversy surrounds Wynton Marsalis as he speaks out for the acceptance of jazz as America's "classical music." He has worked effectively for jazz's place in the traditional strongholds of Western European classical music, such as Lincoln Center in New York. However, in his quest to legitimize jazz, he also blasts those jazz styles that do not fit his mainstream definition, a definition of jazz couched in authenticity that proves to be the dominant viewpoint in the reshaping of the jazz legacy. In this viewpoint, fusion jazz, which enjoyed great popularity, is suspect as a jazz style. The legitimization his argument offers jazz is welcomed by the traditional classical music audience. Marsalis certainly has helped this legitimization by his stellar classical trumpet playing; however, this victorious entrance into the classical music

listening guide

(CD 4, track 4)
Wynton Marsalis
"Hackensack"*

:00   This composition follows a standard AABA form. It begins with the horns (trumpet, trombone, tenor saxophone, and alto saxophone) playing the first A section. Notice how the head is contributed to collectively as each instrument is responsible for different melodic details.

:11   Head repeats (second A).

:23   The **bridge** (B section) makes use of some accented chord dissonances typical of Monk's playing. Notice how this bridge section prepares for the return to the head.

:34   Return to the head (final A).

:45   Bass solo with light piano and drum support. Listen for the same AABA structure, which is maintained during this solo.

:58   Second A section.

1:08   Bridge (B section).

1:19   Final A section of the bass solo.

1:30   New AABA chorus features a duet between Wynton Marsalis on trumpet and Wessell Anderson on alto saxophone. The soloists improvise collectively, responding to one another's melodic statements and trading off between the leading melody and a supporting countermelody.

1:42   Second A section.

1:53   Bridge (B section). Notice the saxophone's use of a short melodic motive to support Marsalis's solo.

2:04   Final A section returns to collective improvisation.

2:16   Return to the head. Notice the dissonance of the head, which is a trademark of Monk's style.

2:27   Repeat of A. Monk also had an angular sense of melody, which is evident in this theme.

2:39   Bridge (B section), which has an even more elevated level of dissonance.

2:50   Final repeat of the A section to close the piece.

3:01   Final chord and end.

*Marsalis Plays Monk: Standard Time, vol. 4.

world may require a compromise in other traditional jazz values, values that have always tolerated musical fusions. A consistent hold to classical jazz values may rob future jazz evolution of its energy. Jazz has traditionally been rough, malleable, and open-ended, yet the move toward classical art status is more exclusive than inclusive of new jazz expressions.

Terence Blanchard

Terence Blanchard represents the breadth of the young lions. Although an accomplished trumpet player, he has also crossed over into film writing, working on several films with Spike Lee. His academic knowledge of music places him in the legacy of other performer/composer/arrangers such as Herbie Hancock and Quincy Jones.

Blanchard's performance is firmly rooted in the practice of former legends such as Clifford Brown and the tutelage of mentors such as Art Blakey. Even his repertoire reflects his interest in the traditions laid down by earlier jazz figures such as Billie Holiday.[2]

Nicholas Payton and Roy Hargrove

Another young trumpet player, Nicholas Payton, also looks back for stylistic inspiration—beyond the bop period to Louis Armstrong himself. He has

Terence Blanchard

participated in many Jazz at the Lincoln Center events directed by Wynton Marsalis. His interest in early trumpet players was also demonstrated in his participation in a 1997 JVC Jazz Festival that was devoted to the music of Armstrong and Bix Beiderbecke. Payton's interest in Armstrong sets him apart from most of the other younger "repertory" players who look more to the bop players as their stylistic sources.

Although Roy Hargrove is most often connected to the hard bop tradition, his work can include Cuban influences ("Salima's Dance") and funk/jazz elements. His Cuban-based band, Crisol, included pianist Jesus "Chucho" Valdes and drummer Horatio "El Negro" Hernandez. It won the Best Latin Jazz Performance Grammy for the album *Habana*. He earned the young lion title early in his career and has played with many of the straight-ahead players, but he also shows another creative hip hop/jazz collective, The RH Factor. His work in such different musical streams has created a more forward-looking musical repertoire than his young lion title might suggest.

Jon Faddis and Wallace Roney

A central figure among the bop-inspired players is certainly Jon Faddis, who is clearly the first in line to carry on Dizzy Gillespie's trumpet tradition. He is known for an agile high range and fast execution of complex bop melodic lines.

Wallace Roney is another trumpet player directly associated with the legacy of a single musician. His introspective style and melodic approach is reminiscent of Miles Davis.

THE SAXOPHONE LEGACY

The saxophone legacy is one of the richest in jazz and is often considered to represent the instrumental voice of jazz. The dominant saxophone voice in bebop was clearly Charlie Parker's. Excursions from the mainstream such as fusion and popular jazz have offered us some newer saxophone voices like those of Wayne Shorter and Michael Brecker on the fusion front and Tom Scott, David Sanborn, Chris Patton, and Grover Washington Jr. on the more popular fronts. However, the line that connects bebop with the current mainstream includes the voices of Joe Henderson, Dave Liebman, and Phil Woods. These players have consistently carried the stylistic mainstream established by the bebop players into present-day performance. They bridged the gap to current mainstream players like Joe Lovano, Jane Ira Bloom, Kenny Garrett, Joshua Redman, and James Carter.

Joe Lovano

Saxophonist Joe Lovano is not as young as the other lions, but his solo playing only gained notice in the 1990s. He was active in the 1970s as a member of the Woody Herman band and in the 1980s with Mel Lewis and the Vanguard Jazz Orchestra. It was not until the late 1980s, when he began working with smaller groups, that the jazz community began to take notice. Lovano sits stylistically in bop but is capable of free excursions that reflect an interest in Ornette Coleman. His influences are apparently wide, including Sonny Rollins, Ben Webster, and Sonny Stitt.

Lovano is responsible for many of the compositions on his small-group recordings, but it is his playing that defines him. It is appropriate that he selected "Body and Soul," made famous by tenor saxophonist Coleman Hawkins, to display his own improvisational strengths.[3]

Jane Ira Bloom and Kenny Garrett

Jane Ira Bloom extends the soprano saxophone legacy begun by Sidney Bechet. She not only brings this instrument back to the forefront of jazz but also changes the gender expectations for the saxophone, which has been primarily advanced by men. Bloom has performed around the world and bridges the jazz, art, and world music worlds. Her compositions are often adventurous hybrids of jazz and other media with inspirations from other artists like Jackson Pollock.

Her album *Sometimes the Magic* features her as leader and producer with Mark Dresser on bass, Bobby Previte on drums, and Vincent Bourgeyx on piano. This album is her tenth recording as leader.

Kenny Garrett is clearly rooted in the straight-ahead tradition, but at the same time he may be bringing neoclassical style to the new mainstream. His spiritual playing looks more to Miles and Coltrane for inspiration. His playing

Jane Ira Bloom

can move outside (more avant-garde and free) in a way reminiscent of Coltrane. His album *Beyond the Wall* includes saxophonist Pharoah Sanders and vibraphonist Bobby Hutcherson, both stalwarts of jazz. This album is more experimental than one might expect from the neoclassical school. Garrett shows that the developing new mainstream, while still connected to the hard-driving bebop style, also includes elements of avant-garde and fusion ("November 15").

Joshua Redman and James Carter

Joshua Redman was often associated with the young lions who helped define the maturing mainstream in the 1990s. At an unusually young age, Redman began finding a personal stylistic voice that set him apart from other players. He looked back to the 1960s for his inspiration and John Coltrane in particular. Other influences that can be found in his playing come from Sonny Rollins, Joe Henderson, and Wayne Shorter. His interest in Coltrane is most evident in his performance of "Sublimation."[4]

James Carter was perhaps the most versatile young saxophone player in the 1990s. He seems to have taken in the widest range of the saxophone legacy and to have pulled from any part of it as needed. Carter also seems at home on

Joshua Redman

any member of the saxophone family. His seemingly unlimited technique and flexibility are matched by his broad understanding of his jazz predecessors. He has a strong admiration for Don Byas, but he also shows a studied knowledge of Rollins and Coltrane as well as nonsaxophonists Thelonious Monk, Clifford Brown, and Duke Ellington.[5]

THE PIANO LEGACY

Piano players established themselves as important contributors to jazz early in its evolution. Because the piano can simultaneously be both a melodic and a harmonic instrument, jazz players were able to generate a rich solo and small-group history. Even in prejazz ragtime, the piano started to shape its future role in the development of jazz as a solo instrument, leading to expansive players of boogie-woogie and blues like Art Tatum. The piano has often been featured in the intimate trio setting supported only by a drummer and bass player. The voice of the piano player was also clearly heard in the bebop ensembles as both comping support and improvisational solos.

listening guide

(CD 4, track 5)
Jane Ira Bloom
"Cagney"
Ratzo Harris, bass
Fred Hersch, piano
David Friedman, vibes
Isidro Bobadilla, percussion

:00   Begins with a bass solo with no clear meter yet but hints of an underlying time.

:42   Bass starts to set up time.

:46   Drums enter.

:51   Saxophone and vibes enter with an angular unison melody.

1:22   The saxophone and vibes take separate melodic paths in a playful counterpoint.

1:40   Saxophone begins a solo with a melodic flourish that is repeated with an electronic coupled sound. Notice that the bass maintains the same bass pattern as used in the opening section.

1:58   Bass falls into a walking pattern as the solo takes on a more straight-ahead feel.

2:00   Piano enters with punctuated dissonant chords (comping).

2:09   Piano lays out.

2:20   Listen for the motivic development in the solo.

2:29   Piano reenters and exchanges short rhythmic patterns with the saxophone.

2:33   Electronic flourish reappears.

2:34   Saxophone plays short multiphonic notes (more than one simultaneous pitch).

2:49   Vibes join the saxophone on a very fast unison closing tag to conclude the saxophone solo.

2:58   Piano solo begins with the bass again playing the original pattern set up at the beginning. The solo immediately begins to explore a motivic idea.

3:14   Very angular melody with chord punctuations in the left hand.

3:18   The bass starts walking and the solo takes on a more straight-ahead type of melody and comping.

3:29   Return to a more angular type of melodic solo. Notice how the melody is constantly interrupted by chordal statements. The bass moves between the previous motive and a walking pattern.

3:50   A return to a more straight-ahead style. Notice the staccato rhythm patterns on the snare drum.

4:01   Return to the motivic bass and disjunctive piano as the solo ends.

4:10   Return of the saxophone and vibe tag used to also close the saxophone solo.

4:15   Short drum fill before the piano comes in as the group begins to trade measures.

4:31   Bass and drum interchange before the vibes takes its turn.

4:41   Vibes enters with its part of the chorus.

4:47   Return to drum fill.

4:51   An electronic flourish from the saxophone opens the final statement before a return to the opening counterpoint between the saxophone and vibes.

5:01   Return to the counterpoint as in the opening head theme.

5:17   Drums join in with the bass playing the recurring bass motive.

5:32   The selection ends with the same closing tag used for the solos.

5:46   End.

Bop players like Thelonius Monk, Bud Powell, and Erroll Garner anchored the piano in mainstream jazz and guaranteed the legacy to be played out as the mainstream matured. Bill Evans certainly championed this legacy with his trio work as did Oscar Peterson, Dave Brubeck, and Lennie Tristano. More contemporary players contributing to the mainstream piano legacy include Ahmad Jamal, Herbie Hancock, and Keith Jarrett.

Ahmad Jamal

Like Bill Evans, Ahmad Jamal connects the bop mainstream players with the more contemporary pianists. His dominant format was the trio, which offered an intimate setting for his colorful harmonic offerings and compositional interest. Jamal's first recording, *Ahmad's Blues* (Okeh Records), was made in 1951, and his early albums were influential on the work of others at that time, in particular Miles Davis and Gil Evans.

In 1958, his success on the album *But Not For Me* later afforded him the opportunity to open his own restaurant and club at which his trio could perform. Ahmad is probably best known for the cut "Poinciana" from that same album. Jamal's work has earned him many awards for both his performance and composition.

Herbie Hancock

Herbie Hancock has not only participated in the mainstream but has been one of its leading champions. He has struck an enviable balance between the center of the jazz mainstream and the commercial music world. Throughout his career he has been able to move freely between the two worlds and not sacrifice his artistic integrity as a leading jazz figure.

Hancock's initial commercial success came in 1963 with his recording of "Watermelon Man." He also began his jazz career that same year when he was invited to join one of the most historic ensembles in jazz, the Miles Davis Quintet. He worked with that group for five years and made lasting relationships that would connect him with later Miles Davis recordings *In A Silent Way* and *Bitches Brew,* harbingers of the jazz fusion movement.

At the same time, Hancock continued his commercial work on film and television. He performed to large audiences and influenced a number of stylistic trends, including the emerging jazz funk and the soon-to-emerge hip hop scenes. Although these excursions from jazz might work against other players, Hancock continued to play important mainstream jazz roles with his work with VSOP, which was a return to the 1960s Miles Davis Quintet with Freddie Hubbard on trumpet in place of Davis. Hancock also performed duets with Oscar Peterson and Chick Corea, as well as in various trios and quartets under his name.

In 1998 Hancock's innovation brought him again to the commercial area with his R&B *Future Shock* album. His "Rockit" from that album moved him again to the front of the R&B dance world. He carried work from this stylistic effort back to jazz with his album *The New Jazz Standard*. He brought his commercial music interest into the center of the mainstream jazz world, as he adapted rock and R&B material into the straight-ahead jazz format.

Hancock's membership on the board of the Thelonious Monk Institute of Jazz demonstrates his commitment to the development and education of jazz worldwide. This and his continued performance in small-group jazz ensembles place him firmly in the current mainstream of jazz and the piano legacy in particular.

Keith Jarrett and Brad Mehldau

Although Keith Jarrett is one of the most notable standard-bearers of the small-group mainstream piano legacy, he is probably at his best in a solo setting, which offers him the free improvisational platform for his technical speed, dynamics, and strong emotional statements. In this regard, he draws a direct historical connection to the solo work of Art Tatum, who also was comfortable as a soloist and seemed to have an unlimited technical reservoir from which to draw.

Jarrett studied at Berklee College of Music in the 1960s and was invited to join Art Blakey's band, which was a clear connection to the jazz mainstream. He quickly moved to Charles Lloyd's quartet and gained an international reputation. In this quartet he worked with Jack DeJohnette on drums, a collaboration that would prove important throughout his career. In 1969 Jarrett joined Miles Davis and played organ and electronic piano as he explored the developing jazz-fusion style.

In addition to his work with Davis, he recorded his own albums working with leading players like Charlie Haden and Paul Motian. Jarrett later returned to the acoustic piano and recorded his solo album, *Facing You.* Throughout his career he has recorded with many musicians but often returned to work with DeJohnette and bassist Gary Peacock. The group came to be known as the "standards trio." Notable recordings for this group are *Changes, Standards Vol. 1 and Vol. 2, Live Standards,* and *The Cure,* which clearly extend the legacy of mainstream piano.

His solo work gave birth to expansive performances typified by his 1975 Koln Concert (Tribute). Despite not feeling well and fighting a badly tuned piano, Jarrett established himself here as a master of large-scale improvisations. Jarrett's improvisational and compositional strength draws from his flawless technique and stylistic breadth, which includes a thorough understanding of Western European classical music. Like Hancock, Jarrett enjoys both a secure place in the jazz mainstream as well as popular commercial recognition.

Brad Mehldau is probably the most direct extension of Bill Evans's introspective style and harmonic constructions. He prefers the format of the piano trio, where his subtle style is best displayed. He produced a series of "Art of the Trio" albums that were all set in his trio. He later worked with other groups outside of his usual format, which led to significant changes from his previous work (*Largo*).

EVOLVING MAINSTREAM

As the young lions mature, they develop personal voices that create new frontiers for jazz exploration. A new mainstream may be developing with these players who seem to look back to Coltrane and the avant-garde players more

listening guide

(CD 4, track 6)
Keith Jarrett
"Bop-Be (Take 2)"

This is a head tune that has the traditional AABA form of the bop style. Each phrase is made up of eight bars, creating a thirty-two bar chorus.

:00   (A) Opening phrase. Notice the 2-beat bass pattern.

:10   (A) Repeat of chords with new melody.

:21   (B) New chords. The bass begins more of 4-beat pattern.

:30   (A) Return to the chords of the original (A) and the 2-beat bass pattern.

:40   (A) Piano solo chorus. Listen to the light comping in the left hand.

:50   (A) Repeat of the chords from the previous eight bars.

:59   (B) New chords that serve as a contrasting section.

1:09   (A) Return to the initial chords of the first phrase.

1:18   Second solo piano chorus. The same

AABA form continues through the performance.

1:57   Third solo piano chorus. Soloist uses more double-time phrases.

2:35   Fourth solo piano chorus. Another motive is developed. The solo also begins to use a wider range.

3:12   Fifth solo piano chorus. More double-time melodic phrases are used.

3:50   Sixth solo piano chorus. More chordal accents are used.

4:26   The piano makes way for a bass solo. The drums make steady time while the piano comps softly in the background.

5:04   Second bass solo chorus. Thematic material from the head is used in the improvisation.

5:41   Piano again takes the lead for another solo chorus. Listen for the half-time bass pattern under the solo to help set up the final chorus.

6:16   Original head returns for the final chorus.

7:01   End.

than to the straight-ahead hard boppers. Coltrane certainly established himself in the hard bop style, but his voice led him to a new free style of his own. The new players in this evolving mainstream are involved in a fusion of historical styles. We see elements of avant-garde and fusion finding their way into the small-group jazz ensemble inherited from earlier straight-ahead groups.

John Zorn

Performers like John Zorn cut across the mainstream and reflect a truly avant-garde and more compositional approach to jazz performance. His tenor saxophone solo performance on "The Fire Book: One (Live)" demonstrates an extended technique on saxophone clearly in the tradition of Anthony Braxton. Yet he has formed tribute bands to play the music of Coleman (*Spy vs. Spy*), Hank Mobley, and Lee Morgan. In a quintet setting Zorn explores seventeen Coleman tunes within his own high-energy performance style ("Zig Zag").

Dave Douglas

Dave Douglas offers a new hybrid of electronic sounds that connect him to the fusion bands, but there is also an avant-garde crosscurrent to his music. It can be hard-driving ("Freak In"), ambient ("Argo"), or electronic avant-garde ("Wild Blue"). Douglas's trumpet style and the sound scapes he creates are sometimes reminiscent of Miles during his early fusion period. Douglas also makes use of more modern electronic technologies and effects that suggest influence from groups like Weather Report but updated for the twenty-first century ("Traveler There Is No Road").

The Bad Plus

The Bad Plus redefines the trio jazz setting. Reid Anderson on bass, David King on drums, and pianist Ethan Iverson are all highly technical players that create, at the same time, an independence from one another but an allegiance to a complex musical structure. On "Street Woman" listen to how the three musicians all seem to be simultaneously improvising yet come together at key structural points in the performance. The drumming is very high energy, and placed against it are the block chords on the piano that sound arrhythmic in reference to the meter in the bass and drums. The ending of the piece shows how tightly they work as an ensemble despite their apparent independence. It may be difficult to categorize this group because they can be viewed on the one hand as a power trio extension of the hard bop school with free elements and on the other as a pop- and rock-influenced trio in a jazz setting ("Iron Man").

This type of hybridization is becoming more typical of new ensembles that are infusing the mainstream with a renewed interest in both freer jazz styles and fusion. In a way, this is a new type of neoclassicism in which the classic styles are shifting. While the small-group setting remains the same, the classic bop and hard bop underpinnings are now infused with elements of avant-garde and fusion.

BIG-BAND LEGACY

"I call myself a coach more than a bandleader, and my teams win."[6]

The big band has often been compared to classical music's symphonic orchestra. Like the orchestra, the big band has offered jazz musicians an ensemble of relatively fixed instrumentation for which to compose. The characteristic common to most large ensembles is the carefully composed arrangements that hold the many players together. Because of the immense popularity of the big bands during the swing era, the grouping of those ensembles—saxophone, trumpet, and trombone sections with a rhythm section—became the established instrumentation for large jazz groups. Although the instrumentation was more or less standardized, the music for those ensembles was not. The most successful bands often had identifiable leaders who placed their individual stamps on the musical product.

vamping

Ghost Bands

Because the big bands spanned such a long period, from the early bands of the 1920s to contemporary big bands of the 1990s, their development reflects much of jazz's history. The bands of the swing era enjoyed a prominence and popularity in America seldom if ever felt by other jazz styles. As a result of this popularity, a nostalgia for that style still exists today and has helped keep several bands actively playing and recording even after the deaths of their leaders. Central among these bands are the contemporary Miller and Dorsey bands, which most often perform the original arrangements that made them popular during the swing era. When new arrangements are written, they are generally restricted to the same stylistic trademarks typical of the original bands. Critics and historians have often referred to these groups as "ghost bands" because of the absence of their leaders and, in most cases, completely new personnel.[7]

Transition Bands

Several of the big bands that began working in the twenties, thirties, or forties performed successfully into the seventies and eighties. These bands vary as to how much stylistic change they have undergone throughout their long careers. Prominent among these bands are those of Duke Ellington (directed after his death by his son Mercer), Count Basie (continued under the direction of Frank Foster), Woody Herman (continued under the direction of Frank Tiberi), Stan Kenton, Maynard Ferguson, Gil Evans, Ray Charles, Dizzy Gillespie, Les Brown, Harry James, Buddy Rich, and Tex Beneke. Not all these bands are still playing, and those that are, even without their original leaders, cannot properly be called ghost bands. They constantly introduce new material and are not as tightly bound to the nostalgic expectations of their listeners.

Count Basie's band, which had a long playing career with Basie at the helm, moved from the riffing sounds of Southwest bands to the tight ensemble of his later band due largely to a shift in available soloists. Basie felt that the responsibility for innovation rested with the writers, not the performers. After Basie's death, his band was led briefly by Thad Jones and then by Frank Foster, both former members of the band. The new arrangements written by both these men were not necessarily restricted to the original Basie style.

Like Basie's band, Woody Herman's retained a hard, swinging style; however, Herman flirted somewhat with newer musical styles.[8] Maynard Ferguson's band strongly embraced the rock idiom and maintained a large audience.[9] Buddy Rich's band, like Ferguson's and Herman's, spent most of its time touring, which proved to be both expensive and extremely taxing on the musicians because of the size of the groups. Despite these difficulties, the fact that these bands continue to be so active attests to the interest that audiences still have for the big-band medium.

The most varied musical styles during this transition period for big bands were heard in the Kenton and Ellington bands. Kenton explored a more expanded instrumentation with French horns and often took on a truly symphonic sound during the late 1950s and early 1960s ("Mirage"). It is noteworthy that he specified in his will that there be no ghost band under his name after his death.[10] Ellington used the big-band medium to experiment with new compositional structures not before associated with big bands.

A word should be said at this time about pianist Stan Kenton's varied career. In 1940, he organized and wrote arrangements for a band to compete with the stylings of other swing bands. His second stage, from 1945 to 1949, featured a series of "Artistry" motifs, or a large band that used harmonic and melodic advancements of the bop era, labeled progressive. Pete Rugolo was the chief arranger. Next, Kenton had a large orchestra that included classical woodwinds, horns, and a full string section. Kenton called this phase "Innovations in Modern Music." His next band, in 1954, was a traditionally sized swing jazz band, but he featured the modern writing of Bill Holman, Shorty Rogers, Gerry Mulligan, and others. The 1960s saw Kenton in front of what he called his "Neophonic Orchestra," a most interesting experiment involving many talented contemporary arranger/composers. For several more years, Kenton remained one of the most energetic, exciting personalities in jazz, with an exceptional band that toured the world. He died at age 67 on August 25, 1979.[11]

Modern Bands

Not all of the later big bands were carried over from earlier periods. The medium has remained vital enough to support the development of new bands by leaders like Thad Jones and Mel Lewis, Toshiko Akiyoshi and Lew Tabackin, Don Ellis, Doc Severinsen, Quincy Jones, Louis Bellson, and Ed Shaunessy, and, more recently, Bob Mintzer, Maria Schneider, and Gerald Wilson. Although several of these bands exhibit new and individualized styles, many of them maintain a close tie to the swinging style of the Basie and Herman bands.

Particularly interesting are the compositions by pianist Toshiko Akiyoshi, which feature both a modern and a culture-crossing style.[12] She often rates among the top jazz composers in each year's *Down Beat* critics' poll. The Thad Jones–Mel Lewis orchestra, an East Coast ensemble, began as a rehearsal band that offered musicians a chance to play arrangements for their own enjoyment.[13] It was not long, however, before the freshness of the arrangements and competent playing brought the band to national prominence. Both the Akiyoshi and the Thad Jones–Mel Lewis bands are characterized by carefully crafted arrangements that helped expand the big-band idiom. Although the musicians are of the highest caliber, they play supporting roles to the more dominant statements of the composers themselves.

Don Ellis

Trumpeter Don Ellis offered one of the most radical yet captivating approaches for big bands. While at the University of California, Los Angeles, he studied with talented Indian musicians like Ravi Shankar, who taught at the university in 1965. Ellis and Harihar Rao (from India) formed what they called the Hindustani Jazz Sextet.

Toshiko Akiyoshi

It should be noted here that possibly the most intricate rhythmic system is that from India. The amalgam of jazz elements, the **raga,** and certain Eastern rhythms produced truly extraordinary jazz music. A raga is a melodic form, a succession of notes, of which there are thousands. Ellis was also intrigued by the Indian tala, a rhythmic series that contains 3 to 108 beats. The particular tala to be played at a given moment is predetermined, but the rhythmic possibilities are almost endless. (Keep in mind that these Indian musical fragments derive from speech patterns. This is also true in the African musical culture.)

Ellis believed that young children in some countries sing and dance in meters unnatural to jazz. This would imply that meter is a matter of conditioning that differs between cultures. Ellis directed a successful large band that featured many unusual meters such as $\frac{19}{4}$ and $\frac{11}{8}$.[14] He then subdivided the measures; for example, the very title of the selection in $\frac{19}{4}$ meter is the subdivision "332221222." Ellis also recorded a number called "New Nine," in which the subdivision (the manner in which the measures are counted and played) varies: 2223, 2232, 2322, 3222, and 333.[15] His "Blues in Elf" (in $\frac{11}{4}$) is counted 3332.[16] "Indian Lady" is in $\frac{5}{4}$ and touches on gospel, rock, and free improvisation.[17]

Don Ellis was an excellent trumpet player, and he also soloed well on drums. Not only did Ellis advance rhythmic techniques, become an educated and acknowledged performer of jazz/rock, and introduce interesting uses for electronic devices, but he also devised a trumpet with an extra valve that allowed

Don Ellis

him to play quarter tones. Such pitches may seem odd when compared to the well-tempered twelve-tone European scale, but in Eastern cultures they are quite suitable. Ellis died in 1978.

Maria Schneider

Although improvisation is a key element in the evolution of jazz, composition has always been its partner. Large ensembles often require more of a compositional approach than small ensembles merely because there are so many musicians to organize. Large groups are also attractive to composers because they offer a larger musical palette from which to pull as they shape their compositions. From the early days of Jelly Roll Morton's arrangements to the more current commissioned compositions of Maria Schneider, large ensembles have attracted jazz composers and added a compositional balance to the improvisational context of jazz.

Maria Schneider is classically trained in theory and composition and best known for her work as a composer and bandleader. She first joined the jazz legacy of composers as an assistant to Gil Evans. She has written for the Woody Herman and Mel Lewis bands and conducted jazz orchestras around the world. Her work also includes a variety of commissioned works including a premier of "El Viento" with the Carnegie Hall Jazz Orchestra. Her debut album,

listening guide

(CD 4, track 7)
Maria Schneider
"Wyrgly"
Soloists: Rick Margitza, tenor saxophone; John Fedchock, trombone; Ben Monder, guitar

As you listen to this selection, notice how the composed structure allows for complex ensemble playing as well as well-crafted support for the solo sections.

:00   Drum solo establishes the tempo.

:07   Ensemble with muted brass enters, with a fragmented type of theme interspersed with light drum fills.

1:08   Lower instruments enter with a legato theme punctuated by the muted brass ensemble. This theme will appear throughout most of the composition.

1:40   Notice a third melodic line in the trombones.

1:45   A gradual shift from the straight time to a more swing style is becoming increasingly apparent. The brass lines are becoming more legato as the three melodic voices march toward a peak.

2:18   The gradual crescendo comes to an end with a dramatic shift in texture as sustained chords are played over subtle cymbal activity in the drums.

2:38   Brass reenter with legato chords and piano fills.

2:54   Saxophones enter with a countermelody.

3:10   Muted brass enter with soft punctuations.

3:42   Tenor saxophone soloist appears out of the ensemble texture. The solo continues with just the rhythm section supporting it.

4:30   Very soft sustained chords are played by various horns in the background. Notice the regular rhythm played by the background chords as well as the repeated motivic ideas presented by the soloist.

5:00   The soloist begins to pick up more energy with short double-time passages and excursions into the higher range of the saxophone. The basic format remains small group throughout.

5:44   The trombones enter playing the rhythmic chord pattern signaling the end of the solo.

5:59   Trumpets enter with an additional countermelody as the soloist increases the melodic energy.

6:14   Trumpets join the trombones on the rhythmic chordal riff.

6:28   The solo comes to a climax as it ends with a single ensemble chord.

6:30   Another shift in the rhythmic underpinning with a slight increase in tempo. This interlude again has a counterpoint between the melodic lines of the lower instruments, trombones and the trumpets. This sets up the next section.

6:48   The swing feel returns as the trombone solo begins. Notice the bass pattern under the solo that keeps repeating. The trombone slips into and out of a double-time feel.

7:20   Notice the repeated chords played briefly by the piano. They will return later and be picked up by the rest of the rhythm section.

7:38   The soloist explores motivic ideas here.

7:53   The rhythm section now picks up the rhythm played earlier by the piano. It then evaporates as quickly as it appeared.

8:00   Soft chords appear in the horns and become increasingly louder.

8:21   Trumpets join in as the solo continues to increase in energy and reaches its final peak.

8:28   A guitar soloist takes over. The punctuated chords in the background step back some but again build to support the high-energy guitar solo.

9:04   The guitar is left completely alone on a dissonant chord. The band joins back in immediately as the solo continues and builds to another high point with a driving ensemble behind it.

9:35   The ensemble takes the lead again as the guitar solo ends. The ensemble quickly brings this section to a close.

9:41   The rhythm section is left with the repeating motive.

9:48   The rhythm stops suddenly leaving only two sustained ensemble chords. The composition ends with an alteration between the rhythm section motive and sustained chords until it finally fades out.

10:25   End.

Evanescence, received Grammy nominations in 1995 as did her jazz ensemble. Her next album, *Coming About,* was released the following year and was again nominated for Grammys.

THE VOCAL LEGACY
Betty Carter

An important straight-ahead vocalist was Betty Carter, formerly with the Lionel Hampton band. She was an excellent scat singer, and with her rapid execution of nonsense syllables interspersed with the actual lyrics she almost sounds like an instrumentalist playing rapid sixteenth-note patterns.

Carter felt that she was the keeper of a dying flame—the true jazz singer. She agreed that the great jazz singer is linked to the instrumental approach to performing; the lyrics seem to become mere vehicles. Carter was profoundly influenced by Charlie Parker and Sonny Rollins, and these influences probably account for her rhythmic daring and virtuosity. These bop artists are easily detected in her highly creative scat singing[18] ("Moonlight in Vermont," "Thou Swell," and "Can't We Be Friends?").

Betty Carter died of pancreatic cancer in 1998.

Sheila Jordan

Like Carter, Sheila Jordan traces her influence back to the early bebop days. Unlike most of the previous singers who worked primarily with the leading African American musicians of the day, Jordan often sang with the prominent white jazz musicians, such as Lennie Tristano and George Russell. Her association with these theorist/composers exhibits itself in the way she reinterprets melodies and lyrics.

Jordan's collaborations with bassist Steve Swallow and, later, Harvie Swartz are particularly memorable because these artists performed only as a duet.

Sheila Jordan

listening guide

(CD 4, track 8)
Betty Carter
"You're Driving Me Crazy (What Did I Do?)"

The form for this song at the highest level is two 16-bar sections. The first 16 bars form two 8-bar phrases. The second phrase is basically a repeat of the first, so it is designated as AA. The second section is also two 8-bar phrases. The first is new material (the chorus), which is followed by a repeat of the initial phrase. The complete form is then labeled as AABA. This entire form is often referred to as a chorus for soloing purposes.

:00   Big band introduction.

:05   (A) First chorus. The band closes the phrase and helps transition to the next phrase.

:13   (A) The band helps launch this phrase and then lays out.

:22   (B) Notice how the melody here is similar to the scat singing that will be used on the next chorus.

:31   (A) This phrase ends sharply to leave room for the vocal solo lead in.

:38   (A) Solo scat chorus.

:48   (A) Notice how syllables are used to help create the jazz accents typical of swing horn soloists.

:57   (B) More interesting syllables used to mimic horn accents.

1:06   (A) Legato scat syllables parallel the style of those used by the ensemble. The scat solo is extended by a couple of bars to set up the return to the next sung chorus.

1:18   (A) Return to sung words.

1:26   (A) Notice the interplay and accents between the vocalist and the ensemble as an ending is set up.

1:32   This phrase serves as the ending by repeating the final phrase to close the arrangement. The final sung phrase is embellished with a scat melodic phrase.

1:49   End.

Without a piano or guitar player to support them harmonically, their improvisational interchanges proved to be rich with nuance. The bassist was required to cover several of the ensemble roles normally supplied by other instrumentalists. He had to expand the normal bass line for the song to suggest the harmonies that would normally be played by the piano. At the same time, he participated in a melodic dialogue with Jordan.

Cassandra Wilson

Cassandra Wilson

A more recent vocalist in the legacy of jazz singers is Cassandra Wilson. She follows in the Betty Carter tradition and, at times, is responsible for new original material. Her career began on the edge between the popular and jazz worlds (*Blue Light 'Til Dawn* and *New Moon Daughter,* Blue Note). She explored a great breadth of musical material from blues to rock as she began to develop a personal vocal style. The recognition she gained as a jazz singer slowly emerged as she imaginatively reworked the standard repertoire.

Wilson's 1996 release of *New Moon Daughter* established her as a leader among the new generation of jazz singer/writers. Her interpretative style began to show its depth in her 1988 *Blue Skies* album, in which she displayed her developing command of the jazz idiom with her performance of repertory standards. Wilson began to demonstrate that she could reclaim songs by placing a unique stamp on them with her maturing interpretative skills. Her 1999 release, *Traveling Miles* (Emd/Blue Note), assures her role in the jazz mainstream as well as the enduring legacy of jazz singers.

Bobby McFerrin

Bobby McFerrin has proven to be a singer of unusual talent. Although he follows in the scat singing tradition of Louis Armstrong, Ella Fitzgerald, Mel Torme, and Clark Terry, his ability to scat involves more than improvised syllables with jazz inflections. He also makes percussive sounds as accompaniment to his improvisations. McFerrin is particularly effective in solo performance. He is able to re-create all the essential parts of a jazz standard by himself. By dividing his time between the melody and the bass line, he is able to give the impression that both are continually present. He complements the performance with percussive sounds created by striking his chest while he sings. His album *Spontaneous Inventions* clearly demonstrates his versatility.[19]

Al Jarreau

Al Jarreau first began singing in his father's church. His mother was the church pianist, and his whole family sang. Although born in 1940, he didn't begin his singing career until the late 1960s in the San Francisco Bay Area.

Esperanza Spalding

In the early 1960s, while still a rehabilitation counselor, he sang with the George Duke trio.

In 1975 he gained popular and critical attention with his album *We Got By*. One of his most successful albums is *Breakin' Away* from 1981. He is known for his sophisticated scat singing and his ability to imitate instrument and percussive sounds. His discography is wide and varied. He performed for television and stage and toured extensively with other artists.

Esperanza Spalding

New to the jazz vocal scene is multi-instrumentalist and singer Esperanza Spalding. While growing up she played violin, oboe, and clarinet, but she ultimately settled on the bass. Her singing was originally only secondary to her playing. After attending Berklee College of Music and touring with Joe Lovano, she was hired to teach at Berklee College of Music at the age of 20. Her first album, *Junjo*, featured her trio, but it was her second album, *Esperanza*, that showed her singing skills. Her third album, *Chamber Music Society*, reflected her early violin playing when she was concert master of the Chamber Music Society of

listening guide

"What a Friend"*
Chamber Music Society
Esperanza Spalding, bass/voice
Leo Genovese, piano/keyboards
Terri Lyne Carrington, drums
Quintino Cinalli, percussion
Entcho Todorov, violin
Lois Martin, viola
David Eggar, cello

:00 Bass and drums begin softly with slow, sustained chords in the strings and sparse notes in the piano.

:17 Pizzicato notes in the strings.

:33 Wordless chant-like vocals enter.

:49 Vocals become more active, scat-like.

1:05 Rhythm section becomes more aggressive and establishes a clear meter.

1:15 Return to original vocal lines with relaxed rhythm.

1:26 Tutti pizzicato closes this section.

1:28 The bass begins to play arco below the more melodic vocal lines.

1:42 The pizzicato bass returns with sustained vocal notes.

1:49 More animated strings transition to the next section.

1:52 The two vocal lines become independent of each other.

1:58 A double-time feel is created in the rhythm section. The vocal lines become more animated, alternating between vocal punches and sustained notes.

2:13 Vocal lines use faster, scat-like patterns.

2:21 Sudden slowdown with a return to a more sustained texture.

2:37 A more melodic bass line under the vocal lines, which at times are independent of one another.

2:52 A new, more Latin feel is established in the rhythm section.

3:06 The rhythm section transitions to a double-time Latin feel. Notice the more animated keyboard in the background.

3:22 More extended vocal scat lines are sung alternating with sustained notes. This pattern is repeated to the end of this section.

4:17 Sudden slowdown returns to the texture used at the beginning.

4:30 The musical texture thins out and fades to the end.

4:49 End.

*This track can be purchased for a nominal fee at many online music stores such as iTunes.

Oregon. On this album she added a three-piece string ensemble and percussion to her trio to perform intimate compositions that offer a delicate balance of jazz and classical writing.

JAZZ/POP DISTINCTIONS

Throughout the evolution of an art form like jazz, there are always participants who sit on the periphery of its development. These individuals often blur the definition of what it means to be a member within that art form. Because the current jazz mainstream is so close to its popular past, there are many performers who were at one time incredibly popular but have diminished in historical importance. The most obvious would be some of the big bands in the swing era that actually were responsible for mainstreaming jazz. These bands, like those of Miller, Goodman, and Dorsey, were known worldwide, but, as we look back from our current perspective of the jazz mainstream, we see other bands rising to prominence, like those of Ellington and Basie.

The popularity of these groups was essential to elevate the status of jazz so that it could ultimately become the art form it is. However, popularity must always be weighed against the evolutionary forces exerted by less popular artists. There also tends to be some mistrust of excessively popular artists within more elite art music circles. For example, many popular listeners may consider Kenny G to be a jazz artist, but there is no such consensus within the jazz community.

The line between jazz and pop remains difficult to discern and makes the task of defining jazz singers even more frustrating. Singers have always been a part of the popular music scene and offer a more accessible venue for jazz to the popular audience. Vocalists, it seems, are also more readily adopted as cultural icons than their instrumental colleagues, perhaps because the songs they sing benefit from an association with the lyrics.

For the purposes of this chapter, we will consider some of these artists who remain somewhat controversial in their relationship with mainstream jazz. The filter of historical time will ultimately settle any argument about their contributions to jazz.

Frank Sinatra

Many consider Frank Sinatra the consummate American singer. His popularity, although uneven, endured across many decades. His association with jazz began as a big-band singer in the 1940s. In many ways, he redefined the jazz singer by reversing the very feature most associated with jazz—syncopation. He sang above the meter with an elongated sense of phrasing that was free from the more traditional jazz syncopation that defined standard song phrases.

His dominant medium was big-band swing, and his singing style was particularly effective when contrasted with driving ensembles like that of Count Basie. Even the later ensembles that included strings, such as Nelson Riddle's group, functioned primarily in the same mode as the big bands. Sinatra's jazz inspiration comes from singers like Billie Holiday, who also sang with an inventive sense of phrasing.

Sinatra was one of the first popular vocalists to mine the jazz standard repertory. His legacy created for future jazz singers a responsibility to the standard jazz repertoire. And it is this repertoire that helps us draw the line between jazz and popular singers.

Unlike Fitzgerald and Carter, Sinatra remained a jazz swing stylist throughout his career. His film career added to his popularity. There may not be total consensus on

Frank Sinatra

Sinatra's role in the evolution of jazz singing, but his influence on American singing in general is irrefutable.

Harry Connick Jr.

Mainstream jazz has become popularized by another New Orleans musician, pianist/vocalist/composer Harry Connick Jr. As a young player, Connick became immersed in the musical styles of New Orleans. As he matured, his interest moved from contemporary rock and jazz to the classic piano players of jazz and the styles associated with them. As a singer, he is often compared to Frank Sinatra.

His success with the soundtrack for the movie *When Harry Met Sally* not only launched his career at age twenty-one but gave a remarkable boost to the public's interest in mainstream jazz. The soundtrack album features Connick doing the standard love songs sung by the original artists in the movie.[20] Like the Marsalis family, Connick sees his role in the revival of traditional jazz. "But jazz is becoming popular again! Wynton started it, and Branford, and I'm continuing it."[21] These neoclassical adherents, like those in the hard bop traditions, see their music as a return to the real essence of jazz—revitalized and again entertaining. "In the '40s and '50s, jazz musicians entertained. In the '60s, rock & roll entertained and jazz stopped entertaining. In the '70s, jazz got very obscure. In the '80s, jazz was dead and rock was #1. Jazz was absolutely nothing until Wynton Marsalis came along and pretty much brought it out of obscurity."[22]

Despite Connick's assertion that he is carrying on the legacy of jazz, his role in the jazz community is not certain. Like Sinatra, his popularity places him in a broader musical community than just jazz. He performs often in the same swing big-band format that surrounded Sinatra, but he writes most of the arrangements and often joins the other musicians on the piano. His solo piano albums show a great respect for traditional jazz playing from boogie-woogie to bop. Unlike Sinatra, however, Connick's singing is more reflective of earlier singers than a new stylistic map for future singers to follow.

Diana Krall

Like Connick, singer/pianist Diana Krall is a crossover from the jazz world to popular music. Her popularity outside of jazz surpassed that of any other singer in the late 1990s. Krall's musical palette, like that of Cassandra Wilson, may

Diana Krall

listening guide

(CD 4, track 9)
Diana Krall
"As Long As I Live"
Diana Krall, vocal, piano,
and arrangement
John Clayton, bass
Jeff Hamilton, drums

This song has an AABA form.

:00 Opens with piano stop-time chords with fills by the drummer.

:12 (A) Vocal begins. Notice the vocal lay back phrasing and the short punctuated piano comping.

:23 (A) Even though this phrase is a repeat of the first one, notice the small interpretive changes.

:33 (B) Bridge. Listen for how this phrase is sung to set up the return to the final A section.

:45 (A) This phrase is again stylistically reinterpreted, especially the final four bars, which sets up the following piano solo.

:56 (A) Piano solo using the same AABA form.

1:07 (A)

1:17 (B)

1:28 (A) Notice how the phrasing at the end of this phrase continues directly into the next solo chorus.

1:38 (A) Second chorus of piano solo, which increases in energy as it also climbs in range.

1:49 (A) The solo begins to swing harder and becomes more syncopated.

1:59 (B) More frequent use of chord punctuations to add energy.

2:09 (A) This phrase ends with a short melodic run as the solo is handed off to the bass player.

2:20 (A) This chorus trades solo phrases between the bass and drums. Notice that even as the bass solos, the harmonic progression is still maintained.

2:31 (A) Drum solo for this phrase.

2:40 (B) Bass solos again over the bridge chords.

2:50 (A) Return to drum solo. See if you can hear the melody in the accents used in this phrase.

3:00 (A) Piano chords set up the vocal return, which is extremely laid back. Again, notice how differently the vocal inflections and phrasing are from earlier choruses. The vocal inflections here help increase the energy as the arrangement charges toward the ending.

3:11 (A) This phrase takes great liberties with the original melody.

3:20 (B) Listen to how the melody lays back behind the rhythm section.

3:31 (A)

3:42 (A) The vocal from the previous chorus overlaps the piano solo, which is used to bring the arrangement to a close.

3:52 (A) Piano solo continues.

4:03 (B) Bridge sets up the vocal ending on the final A section.

4:13 (A) Final A section is sung to close the arrangement.

4:23 Vocal tag. Listen for the harmonic tag. This is the standard ending that signals the final phrase.

4:27 Final piano tag.

4:37 End.

embrace both popular and jazz standards. But, unlike Wilson, her jazz status is acclaimed more outside than inside the jazz community.

In 2000, Krall won the best jazz vocalist Grammy on her third nomination, and her CD *When I Look in Your Eyes* was the first jazz album to be nominated for the best album Grammy in more than a decade. She has embraced a wide range of musical interests and seems unfazed by a need to be grouped within one genre. Her potential as what Betty Carter calls a "true jazz singer" will have to wait for her career to develop and her style to mature. It is a rare singer who can maintain the balance between the demands of a popular music market and the expectations of a more elite art form. Fitzgerald was perhaps the most successful in this regard. She was appreciated by the broader popular market while remaining a defining presence in the evolution of jazz singers.

VOCAL JAZZ GROUPS

In the *Down Beat* readers' polls, vocal groups have been taking their place with instrumentalists and vocal soloists since 1944. The Pied Pipers won for the first six years, then the Mills Brothers for three years, and then the Four Freshmen and the Hi-Lo's. From 1958 through 1963, it was Lambert, Hendricks, and Ross, then three years of the Double Six of Paris. The category was then altered to include nonjazz groups.

Lambert, Hendricks, and Ross

The tradition of Lambert, Hendricks, and Ross began in the 1950s. They developed to a high degree the art of taking old jazz records and setting lyrics to just about everything on them—not only the tunes themselves but also the improvised solos. This technique is labeled *vocalese.* Annie Ross was eventually replaced by Yolande Bavan; later Hendricks used his wife, Judith; his daughter, Michelle; and Bruce Scott. Their work is a contemporary form of onomatopoeia.[23]

Manhattan Transfer

Following closely in the tradition of Lambert, Hendricks, and Ross is Manhattan Transfer. They have always employed jazz overtones and used many excellent jazz instrumentalists on their recordings. However, their *Extensions* album[24] came as a revelation with the arrangement of Joe Zawinul's "Birdland" and the lyrics by Jon Hendricks, arranged by the group's own Janis Siegal. The album also included lyricization of "Body and Soul" by the great bop singer Eddie Jefferson. This version was a harmonized transcription of Coleman Hawkins's famous 1939 improvisation.

Manhattan Transfer's 1985 album *Vocalese* marshals impressive jazz forces in the vocalese style.[25] It makes use of players like McCoy Tyner, Dizzy Gillespie, and the entire Basie band as well as singers such as Jon Hendricks and Bobby McFerrin. "To You" on this album demonstrates the vocalese art. The music comes from a Basie and Ellington session, *First Time,* and the solo is one originally played by Butter Jackson on trombone. The lyrics for the solo were written

listening guide

(CD 4, track 10)
New York Voices (Peter Eldridge, Kim Nazarian, Sara Krieger, Darmon Meader, and Caprice Fox)
"Top Secret"*

:00	Synthesized ascending melodic motive.
:09	Electric bass enters.
:19	Vocal enters with melody.
1:00	Repeat of melody; listen for choral punches in background.
1:41	Staccato vocal section.
1:52	Contrasting legato vocal section; listen for the synthesizer support.
2:01	New chorus with more developed vocal backup punches.
2:43	Legato interlude.
3:03	Time returns in rhythm section.
3:14	Scat solo begins (Caprice Fox).
3:54	Synthesizer doubles scat solo line.
4:15	Synthesized backup becomes more animated.
4:34	Staccato section returns.
4:44	Legato section returns.
4:54	Return to head.
5:34	Repeat of final phrase to end.
5:55	Synthesized chords with saxophone solo fade to end.
6:19	End.

*GRP Records, GRD-0589.

by Jon Hendricks and sung by Alan Paul, who described the technique: "It was hard, but Jon said if you're doing somebody's solo you've got to do it right . . . I really listened to Butter's solo and the certain way he shaped the sounds, and Thad Jones came up and said, 'Yeah, Butter!'"[26]

New York Voices

New York Voices, a group often compared to Manhattan Transfer, produced an album in 1989, *New York Voices*,[27] that boasts a wide range of styles and developed instrumental accompaniments. Most of the material is the work of two of the vocalists—Darmon Meader and Peter Eldridge—and the group is completed with

Take 6

Kim Nazarian, Sara Krieger, and Caprice Fox. The intricacy of the instrumental backups can be heard on the opening rock-flavored track, "National Amnesia." Both voices and the synthesizer voicings combine to offer harmonic punches much like those associated with big-band arrangements. In "Top Secret," Caprice Fox offers an effective scat solo over a funky background. The album also offers a variety of Latin arrangements and a setting of Monk's "Round Midnight."

Take 6

In 1988 a group of six men under the name of Take 6 burst on the music scene and captured the attention of the jazz community. Although they first began singing together in 1980, they did not gain national prominence until 1988, at which time their success seemed immediate. Their arrangements are **a cappella** and show a blend of traditional gospel, soul, pop, and jazz. Their arrangements and stylistic delivery reflect influences from earlier groups such as Lambert, Hendricks, and Ross; the Hi-Lo's; and the Mills Brothers. The musical director is Claude V. McKnight III, and the principal arranger, Mark Kibble. The group is completed with Mervyn Warren, Cedric Dent, David Thomas, and Alvin Chea.

The musical training of the members is demonstrated clearly in the sophistication of the arrangements. Although the arrangements are quite polished and often rich in vocal display, the presentation of the material emanates clearly from the oral gospel tradition. Listen to the sextet's recording of "Get Away, Jordan" on their album *Take 6*.[28] The performance, rooted in the gospel expression, is full of individual and ensemble vocal nuances.

summary

The critics of jazz note that the musicians in this period, in which jazz matures, are masterful technicians. Yet, following the legacy of an earlier tradition does not easily afford them the same opportunities of those who preceded them. They are measured by their ability to re-create the signature voices of their predecessors rather than by the individuality of their own voices. How they survive the historical flow that jazz will follow remains to be seen.

FOR FURTHER STUDY

1. If jazz continues to follow the same path as other art forms like classical music, will it also develop at a rate associated with larger and slower-moving cultural shifts rather than the faster-paced cultural fashions that guided it in its early years?

2. Has jazz, like classical music, lost its front edge of discovery?

3. What price has jazz paid for its ascendancy to art form status?

4. Will jazz become a history in which the names of the players change but the music does not?

5. What characteristics distinguish jazz singers from popular singers?

6. Can a popular singer enjoy an equally strong acclaim from the jazz community?

7. Does the church still play a role in the development of jazz singers?

8. Compare the musical support that singers enjoy from big bands, small ensembles, and even duos like those of Sheila Jordan.

9. Discuss the types of improvisation available to jazz vocalists.

10. Discuss how vocal jazz groups might resemble the big swing bands.

SUGGESTED ADDITIONAL LISTENING

Carter, Betty. *The Audience with Betty Carter.* Uni/Verve Records, 8356842.
———. *Ray Charles—Betty Carter.* Dcc, 39.
———. *You're Mine, I'm Yours.* Uni/Verve Records, 3145331822.
Carter, James. *JC On the Set.* Sony/Columbia, CK 66149.
———. *Jurassic Classics.* DIW, CK 67058.
———. *The Real Quietstorm.* Atlantic Records, 82742.
———. *Flying Colors.* Blue Note, 56092.
———. *Paul Motian on Broadway,* vol. 1. JMT, 834430.

Connick, Harry, Jr. *Lofty's Roach Souffle*. Columbia Records, 46223.

Fitzgerald, Ella. *Best of Ella Fitzgerald*. MCA Records, 4047.

———. *Ella and Count Basie: A Perfect Match*. Pablo Records, 2312110.

———. *Ella in Berlin*. Verve Records, 3145195642.

———. *Fine and Mellow*. Pablo Records, 2310829.

———, and Joe Pass. *Fitzgerald and Pass . . . Again*. Pablo Records, 2310772.

Jordan, Sheila. *Jazz Child*. Highnote Records, 7029.

———. *Portrait of Sheila*. Emd/Blue Note Records, 89002.

Krall, Diana. *All for You: A Dedication to the Nat King Cole Trio*. GRP, 182.

———. *Love Scenes*. GRP, 233.

Lovano, Joe. *Rush Hour*. Blue Note, 29269.

Marsalis, Wynton. *Marsalis Plays Monk: Standard Time*, vol. 4. Columbia, CK 67503.

McFerrin, Bobby. *Spontaneous Inventions*. Emd/ Blue Note Records, BT 85110.

Redman, Joshua. *Wish*. Warners, 45365.

Sinatra, Frank. *The Best of the Capitol Years*. Emd/Capitol Records, 99225.

———. *In the Wee Small Hours*. Emd/Capitol Records, 94755.

———. *Songs for Swingin' Lovers!* Emd/Capitol Records, 96226.

Vaughan, Sarah. *Crazy and Mixed Up*. Fantasy/Pablo Records, 2312137.

———. *Sarah Vaughan with Clifford Brown*. Poly Tone, 814641.

———. *Swingin' Easy*. Poly Tone, 514072.

Wilson, Cassandra. *Blue Skies*. Uni/Verve Records, 8344192.

———. *New Moon Daughter*. Emd/Blue Note Records, 32861.

ADDITIONAL READING RESOURCES

Friedwald, Will, *Jazz Singing*.

Giddens, Gary. *Visions of Jazz: The First Century*.

O'Meally, Robert G. *The Jazz Cadence of American Culture*.

Sudhalter, Richard M. *Lost Chords*.

———————————

Note: Complete information, including name of publisher and date of publication, is provided in this book's bibliography.

NOTES

1. Gary Tomlinson, "The Jazz Canon as a Monological Canon," in "Cultural Dialogics and Jazz: A White Historian Signifies," *Black Music Research Journal*, 11, 2 (1991: 245-9) (excerpt).
2. Terence Blanchard, *In My Solitude: The Billie Holiday Songbook*, Columbia Records, 57793.
3. Joe Lovano, *From the Soul*, Blue Note Records, 98636.
4. Joshua Redman, *Joshua Redman*, Warner Brothers Records, 45242.
5. James Carter, *JC on the Set*, DIW, CK 66149; *Jurassic Classics*, DWI, CK 67058; *The Real Quietstorm*, Atlantic Records, 82742.
6. Woody Herman, *Down Beat* 53, no. 11 (November 1986), 21.

7. Glenn Miller, *In the Digital Mood,* GRP Records, GRP-A-1002. This record is a rerecording of original arrangements with the new digital technology.
8. Woody Herman, *Woody Herman and His Big Band,* "50th Anniversary Tour," Concord Jazz, CF-302-C.
9. Maynard Ferguson, *Live from San Francisco,* Palo Alto, 8077.
10. From a conversation with the authors.
11. Stan Kenton, *The Kenton Era,* The Creative World of Stan Kenton, ST 1030; *Big Band Jazz,* Smithsonian Collection of Recordings.
12. Toshiko Akiyoshi and Lew Tabackin, *Kogun,* RCA Victor Records, 6246.
13. Thad Jones and Mel Lewis, *Central Park North,* Solid State Records, SS 18058; *Mel Lewis and the Jazz Orchestra,* Tel-Arc Records, 10044 (first album since Thad Jones left).
14. Don Ellis Orchestra, "332221222," *Live at Monterey,* Pacific Jazz Records, PJ-10112; "Upstart," *The Don Ellis Orchestra Live in 3 = 9/4 Time,* Pacific Jazz Records, PJ-10123.
15. Don Ellis, "New Nine," *Live at Monterey,* Pacific Jazz Records, PJ-10112.
16. Don Ellis, "Blues in Elf," *Tears of Joy,* Columbia Records, G 30927.
17. Don Ellis, "Indian Lady," *Electric Bath,* Columbia Records, CL 2785.
18. Betty Carter, *Finally,* Roulette Records, 5000; *Betty Carter,* Bet-Car Productions, MK 1001; *Betty Carter Album,* Bet-Car Productions, MK 1002; *Now It's My Turn,* Roulette Records, 5005; *Ray Charles and Betty Carter,* Dcc, 39.
19. Bobby McFerrin, *Spontaneous Inventions,* Blue Note Records, BT 85110.
20. Harry Connick, Jr., *When Harry Met Sally,* Columbia, CK 45319.
21. Harry Connick, Jr., *Down Beat* 57, no. 3 (March 1990): 18.
22. Ibid.
23. *The Best of Lambert, Hendricks, and Ross,* Columbia Records, KC-32911.
24. Manhattan Transfer, *Extensions,* Atlantic Records, SD 19258.
25. Manhattan Transfer, *Vocalese,* Atlantic Records, 7 81266-1.
26. Michael Bourne, *Down Beat* 52, no. 11 (November 1985): 24.
27. New York Voices, *New York Voices,* GRP Records, GRD-9589.
28. Take 6, *Take 6,* Reprise, 9 25670-2.

appendix A

listening suggestions

Techniques of perceptive listening improve as you develop an understanding of the musical vocabulary of jazz (and of other music). The jazz listening guides were developed to give you a systematic aid to use in identifying what to listen to and for. This identification leads to the development of effective listening habits.

A valuable aid in developing perceptive listening is to listen to a composition with other people. After the first hearing, freely exchange ideas with the other listeners about what you have heard and then replay the recording. This experience tends to improve your ability to concentrate as well as to pick up previously missed nuances.

Read the listening guide before listening to be sure that you understand what the various items in the guide mean. After the first hearing, quickly respond to the items you can identify easily. Do not labor over items about which you are unsure. After the second hearing, go back and fill in the remaining items on the guide. Obviously, some items may not apply to every listening experience. Effective listening takes practice by a listener as well as guidance by an instructor.

Passive listening will not aid in developing understanding and enjoyment of jazz. Listeners must train themselves to listen *to* and *for* the content of the music and to respond actively—not only emotionally but also intellectually. The next step is for each listener to develop a specific set of references to use in deciding whether he or she enjoys and understands jazz.

JAZZ INTERPRETATION

Jazz interpretation is illustrated by examples 1A and 1B, the first without jazz interpretation and the second with suggested jazz interpretation. Listen to the differences in the performances (Interactive Guide 10) on the Online Learning Center or directly at the interactive listening site: http://www.emegill.com/listening. Interpretation is very individual and can vary widely from minor changes in the melody to a complete reshaping of the original melody. The emotional range of an interpretation can run from subdued and underspoken to emotional and dramatic outbursts.

In contrast with interpretation, example 1C (Interactive Guide 10) is an improvisation (written out) of the same melody used in example 1A. Listen to the recording and compare examples 1A, 1B, and 1C.

WHAT TO LISTEN FOR IN JAZZ

People who can bring a fund of musical knowledge to the listening experience have an advantage in gaining insight into jazz. But *knowledge about* music and an *understanding of* music are not the same. Simply stated, the first deals primarily with information (vocabulary), whereas the second relates to direct musical experiences involving concepts and possession of the vocabulary to express understanding of the concepts. The term *concept* suggests a mental image or a complete

Example 1A Interactive Guide 10

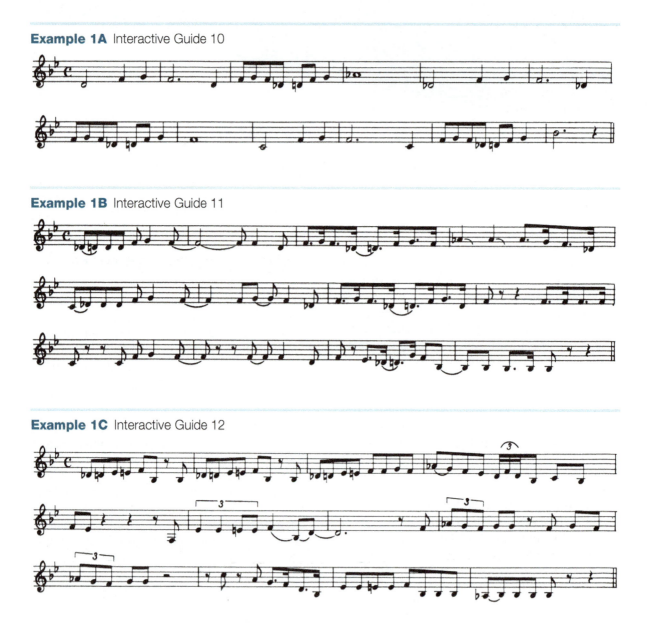

Example 1B Interactive Guide 11

Example 1C Interactive Guide 12

thought that has been acquired through the senses: hearing, seeing, touching, tasting, and smelling.

As you listen to music, you will find that the concepts of **melody,** rhythm, harmony, texture, design, and tone color are common to all music. However, some concepts of rhythm, for example, are treated differently or at least more prominently in jazz than in other types of music.

As a preparatory exercise for listening to jazz, you will find it helpful to list under each main musical element words and concepts that you identify with that musical element. For example, (1) under *melody:* high, low, smooth, jagged, **scale,** skips, **key,** diatonic, and chromatic; (2) under *texture:* thick, thin, few instruments, many instruments, homophonic, and polyphonic; (3) under *form:* repetition, contrast, theme, variations, imitation, section, part, three parts, and improvisation; (4) under *harmony:* tension, relaxation, rounds, and chords; (5) under *rhythm:* fast, slow, weak accents, strong accents, beat, **tempo,** pattern, and meter; and (6) under *tone:* piano, soprano, contralto, bass, trumpet, sax, clarinet, and bass drum.

JAZZ ENSEMBLES

An initial consideration in listening to jazz **ensembles** is the size of the instrumental group. Does it sound like a large group of more than ten players or like a small combo of instrumentalists? If the group is a large band and there is a soloist, the listener has few real clues to the size of the organization unless the soloist is supported by some other part of the band besides the rhythm section. An example is a saxophone solo backed up by a trombone section, consisting of three or four trombones, or by the entire brass section, including trumpets and trombones. While the ensemble is playing, listen for the *bigness* or *thickness* of the overall sound. Sometimes the total sound may be so full that it is almost overwhelming, such as the ensemble portion of Kenton's "Commencement."[1] Listen for complete sections of instruments: saxophone, trumpet, and trombone sections. The sections are quite easy to determine on most albums by bands such as Count Basie's.[2] Almost always, both large and small jazz groups have rhythm sections consisting of piano, **bass,** guitar, and drums. Some rhythm sections do not use all four, but rather use only piano with bass or bass and drums with piano or replace the piano with a guitar.

Another problem with listening is that sometimes a small group or combo may confuse the ear by sounding larger than a full band if the playing and recording techniques are purposefully planned to give that illusion of sound. However, in a combo, listen for the individual instruments. Instead of the saxophone section, listen for the saxophone player; do this for other instrumentalists such as the trumpet or trombone player.[3]

SOME MUSICAL CONCEPTS IN JAZZ

Melody

It is important that listeners of jazz music attend to the melodic inventiveness or improvisation on a given melody or the musical interpretation of a given melody. The emotional tone communicated by the jazz performer often reveals the temperament of the player and of society in general at the time of the playing. Usually, music is quite accurate in mirroring the temperament of the times (war, peace, and so on).

Listen as the performers create. Is the emotional tone excitement? Is it calm? (Can calm music be exciting?)[4] Performing music is extremely personal, to be sure, but so is listening. One person cannot listen for another. Sometimes big bands are very outgoing, or hot, such as Basie's in "Jumpin' at the Woodside" or "Every Tub."[5] However, this is not an exclusive element of large groups. Combos can produce the same feeling—listen to such recordings as Kenny Clarke's "Be a Good Girl."[6] The same outgoing big band can sometimes produce an extremely calm, even introverted, feeling. Such an example can be heard in Basie's "Blue and Sentimental" and "Lil' Darlin'" and in Woody Herman's "Misty Morning."[7]

A person who has little technical knowledge of music and who cannot name individual pitches on the staff still may be able to hear the differences between two melodies by feeling ascending tones as they move in steps and descending tones as they skip in varied moves.

Texture

The term *texture* as it is used in music refers to the different ways melodies and harmonies interact. Some textures may give the impression of being open and airy, whereas others may seem quite dense. Textures include not only the various ways of filling the octave and various ways of using the beat but also the many possibilities of repeating the same melody at different pitch levels, of combining two or more different melodies, or of providing a single melody with accompanying chords or harmonies.

A single melody with neither an accompanying melodic part nor harmony is known as a **monophonic** construction. The field hollers of the slaves are good examples of short melodic motives without any accompanying musical sounds.

Another way of treating a melody is to have two melodies at *different times* on the *same pitch level.* The combination of two voices singing or playing the same melody but entering at different times is called a **canon.** A canon repeated without a break is called a **round** (i.e., the melody chases itself around and around). The simultaneous sounding of one melody heard in imitation in another voice or instrument and the use of two or more different melodies of equal importance is known as **polyphonic** construction. Listening to polyphonic, or **horizontal,** texture in music is somewhat analogous to watching a three-ring circus. You realize something important is going on in each of the three rings, but it is difficult to concentrate on them simultaneously. However, it all adds to the excitement of the moment.

A third way of treating a melody is to have all the voices or instruments move together with a single melody, usually in the highest voice part. Harmony in the form of chords in the lower voices acts as an accompaniment to the single melody. This is called **homophonic,** or **vertical,** texture. Hymns and spirituals are excellent examples of this type of melodic treatment.

Form

The basic units of form in music are often compared to the basic units in written language. The individual musical note is comparable to the single alphabetical letter in written language. The musical **motive,** or *figure* (two or more tones forming a distinctive rhythmic-melodic pattern) is the equivalent of a language syllable or word. The first appearance of a **phrase** (usually four measures in length) denotes a language phrase. The extension of the phrase into two phrases, or **periods** (eight measures in length), denotes a language sentence. Sometimes language sentences are longer. In music, long phrases are called *double periods,* or *phrase groups.*

For easy identification, phrases and periods are designated by letters. The first phrase is called

A, and as each new phrase appears, it is given a different letter (B, C, D, etc.). The forms used extensively in jazz are the twelve-bar (measure) blues strain and the sixteen- and thirty-two-bar choruses that are usually designated ABAB or AABA (see example 2).

The twelve-bar blues strain has two similar phrases of four measures each and a third phrase that is different. In the blues melody given in example 3, measures 1 through 4 are the first phrases, or A part.

Since the 1940s, some jazz players have combined the AABA and blues forms. The performer does this by playing the first strain (A), repeating it (A), and following with a different strain of usually only eight measures.

Since the advent of the long-playing record, some modern jazz players have tended to adopt extended musical forms such as the **theme and variation, fugue,** and **rondo.**[8] The Modern Jazz Quartet offers several albums with examples of extended forms, such as the excellent recording *Collaboration,* in which they perform Bach's "Fugue in A Minor" with guitarist Laurindo Almeida.[9] In fact, jazz players have used the theme-and-variation form since the beginning of this art. The tune is established, and then each repetition is given a variation, whether improvised or planned, to constantly create new interest as the work progresses. This form is often compared to the **chaconne,** in which a series of improvisations is played from a predetermined chord progression.

The authors have considered the possibility that the most important element in all jazz—that of emotion—is overlooked. There is no question that emotional force has been the strongest ally of jazz throughout its history. Jazz can make one contemplate deeply, dance with joy, or weep with sadness. However, because the authors are involved in the performance of music, we are totally convinced that emotion is too necessary an element of all types of music to be considered the exclusive element of any one kind of music. Any music without emotion simply does not seem worth listening to.

The changes in emotional intensity throughout a performance can create a form of its own. As the excitement ebbs and flows, an emotional architecture develops that can be as effective as

Example 2 AABA Song

melodic change to define a form. Even when the melodic- or harmonic-based musical form is unclear, an emotional form might be what holds the form of a performance together.

Harmony

Closely related to the need to recognize the melodic line is the necessity of response to the musical element of **harmony** in jazz. Harmony is the simultaneous sounding of two or more tones. Two tones sounding together make an interval. The effect produced by the interval depends on the ratio between the vibrations created by the two tones. In general, simple ratios tend to be more harmonious and complex ratios more dissonant. For example, for most listeners the sound of three-tone chords with intervals of thirds seems pleasingly consonant and restful, whereas six-or seven-tone chords with intervals

Example 3 Blues Melody

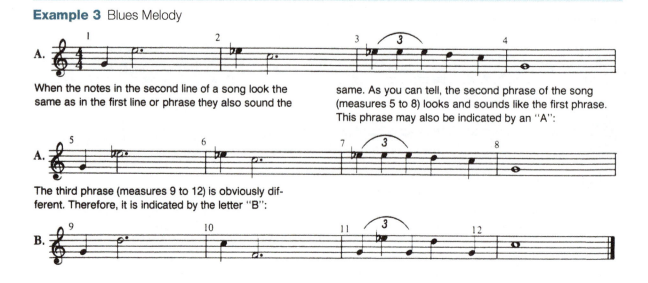

When the notes in the second line of a song look the same as in the first line or phrase they also sound the

same. As you can tell, the second phrase of the song (measures 5 to 8) looks and sounds like the first phrase. This phrase may also be indicated by an "A":

The third phrase (measures 9 to 12) is obviously different. Therefore, it is indicated by the letter "B":

of thirds having more complex ratios seem to give listeners feelings of dissonance and tension.

A listener must decide whether the harmonies are too simple, have little variety, and thus are of little interest. In more academic terms, the harmonies or chord progressions should have a sense of forward motion. Sometimes a composition has a pleasing melodic line but is quite dull harmonically. The opposite situation occurs when the composer/arranger or piano soloist is so intent on playing interesting harmonies that the music sounds contrived. This seemed to be prevalent with some large bands in the 1940s and again in the 1960s. Rather than complex harmonies with little melodic originality, a balance between the two is usually more acceptable.

Rhythm

Rhythm is the very heart of nature and of humanity. It is the pulse of life and is found in all kinds of physical activity. We unconsciously use rhythm—in walking, dancing, running, skipping, and so on. However, *rhythm* is a generic term with many meanings.

In music, one basic element of rhythm is the repetition of sound, either felt or heard, called the beat (or pulse) of the music. To feel the beat, listen and tap or clap the regular repetitions generated by the musical sound.

Although beat is a constant force in every composition, the speed of the beat varies greatly and depends on the feeling, tone, and mood of the music. In some music the beat is fast; elsewhere it is quite slow. The speed of the beat is called the tempo. Thus, to say that the rhythm is slowing is to say that the beat is moving at a slower tempo.

Occasionally, a great rhythmic pulse is felt but no melodic line is realized; the rhythm section merely sets a mood. These sections are usually called **vamps.** Some contemporary musicians play on melodic instruments but avoid the usual concept of melody. They say that they are playing a mood or an attitude. Listen to Joe Harriott's "Shadows."[10] There are many situations in which there is a definite melody, but it is subservient to the rhythmic sounds. It is primarily this rhythmic pulse, or juxtaposition of patterns, that expresses the emotion. The technique is quite common in many rock and jazz/rock recordings.[11]

One of the most important elements of rhythm is duration. The performing musician is concerned with translating the symbols on a page of music into sounds and silences (tone pauses, or rests). These sounds and silences may be of any duration. For this reason, clapping the rhythmic pattern does not accurately represent a melody, as the claps are all of equal duration.

Listen to the ticking of a clock. Do some of the ticks seem to be stronger than others? Try tapping on the table with your hand, imitating the regularity of the sound of a clock. Next, tap one beat louder than the following beat. Alternate between loud taps and soft taps. Try tapping one loud beat followed by two soft beats. You should find that in one case the beats occur in groupings of twos and in the other case in groupings of threes. The easiest approach to understanding accent, the basis of meter, is to study the grouping of louds and softs into twos, threes, fours, or more. Meter is the regular (or irregular) grouping of beats according to accent.

In musical notation, the **time signature** located at the beginning of a composition tells a player that the music moves in groupings of threes, fours, or whatever. There are complete styles of jazz that stay primarily in one meter grouping, and the listener should be able to detect these groupings fairly easily. The feeling of $\frac{4}{4}$, or flat four, is used by players of Early New Orleans Dixieland, by most swing players, and by many bop and cool players.

When $\frac{2}{4}$ meter is designated in jazz music, it denotes something different from $\frac{2}{4}$ meter in classical music, in which it means there are two beats to each measure and quarter notes receive one beat. In jazz, however, it means that there are four beats to the measure but that the second and fourth beats are accented. Thus, a jazz player never snaps the fingers or claps the hands on the first and third beats but always the second and fourth, as shown by the accents in examples 4A, 4B, and 4C. This is the only time when meter interpretation (time signature) in jazz is different than in other music.

The $\frac{2}{4}$ beat in jazz is heard most prominently in ragtime and Chicago Style Dixieland music. When funky-style jazz has four beats to the measure, the second and fourth beats are accented. Sometimes, however, funky is played in $\frac{3}{4}$ meter. Rock drummers accent the second and fourth beats, feeling that it adds interest and momentum. Very good jazz, by both small combos and large orchestras, is also performed in $\frac{3}{4}$ meter.[12]

The style of jazz called boogie-woogie is performed in $\frac{8}{8}$ meter, eight beats to each measure (see Chapter 4). In fact, it is the identifying feature of this style, whether it is a piano solo or a

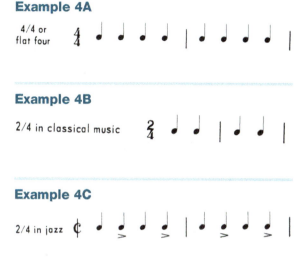

Example 4A

4/4 or flat four

Example 4B

2/4 in classical music

Example 4C

2/4 in jazz

large band[13] ("Honky Tonk Train"). Rock players make excellent use of $\frac{8}{8}$ meter without actually playing boogie-woogie, seeming to use $\frac{4}{4}$ meter in a **double-time** fashion.[14]

Syncopation

Jazz often shifts the melody so that it does not always align itself with the basic beat. This displacement of melodic and harmonic accents off the strong beats in a given meter is called syncopation. As a result of this shift, accents end up on weak beats in a measure, namely the second and fourth beats in a $\frac{4}{4}$ meter, or on the weak part of individual beats. The following two examples of the same melody illustrate this technique: example 5A has no syncopation; example 5B does.

Example 5B shows syncopated notes that have been shifted off the beats so that many of the melodic notes begin between the four metric beats in each measure. The melodic move from the third to the fourth measure shows how the first beat of the fourth measure is anticipated with a syncopation. The weight of the normally strong first beat of a measure is then out of synchronization with the last note of the melodic line. These syncopated notes are often accentuated by the performer to heighten the syncopated feel.

Example 5A

Example 5B

Certainly, there is syncopation in all musics; but, in jazz, syncopation is used often and becomes highly intricate.

There is little jazz that does not use syncopation. As a consequence, syncopation is more natural for the jazz musician and is more closely connected with jazz in the mind of the public. Of the many examples, we suggest something like Count Basie's "Jumpin' at the Woodside."[15]

Gunther Schuller has defined the syncopation of jazz as "no more than an idiomatic corruption, a flattened-out mutation of what was once the true poly-rhythmic character of African music."[16]

Tone

Another important consideration in listening to music is tone. Some listeners prefer instrumental tones to have a soft, pretty sound, whereas others consider this tone quality to lack intensity, sincerity, and even confidence. These listeners prefer to hear the type of tone made by, for example, a strong trumpet player. Listening is very personal, almost as personal as performing. Which sound do you find more interesting: a smooth, pretty tone or a rough, aggressive tone?

One of the most important points to be considered is the creativeness of individual players. Do their thoughts sound interesting and fresh, or are they playing clichés that should be forgotten? Players have been known to improvise several consecutive choruses on just one tone. This kind of playing lacks all imagination. On the other hand, some players improvise lines so far ahead of their contemporaries that acceptance and acclaim come too late to be of much satisfaction.

The real judge, of course, is the listener, who must hear the melodies, perceive the rhythm, detect the tone, and so on. Jazz observers are not particularly impressed by classical correctness. They hear enough excellent piano from Art Tatum to consider him a genius. They are not disturbed at all that Tatum's fingering is atrocious. Jazz listeners hear creativeness from Gillespie's trumpet and are not disturbed by the way he puffs out his cheeks. Present-day jazz observers actually appreciate the primitive approach to playing of many early jazz performers, most of whom had little or no musical schooling. Their lack of schooling—of knowing how to perform "correctly" by European standards—gave the early players a freedom that endears them to most jazz listeners.

One should be reminded that the "test of time" commonly used to judge music is not appropriate for jazz. It is true that there are jazz classics (Armstrong's "Savoy Blues," Hawkins's "Body and Soul," Parker's "Ornithology," and many others), but jazz players are much more concerned with immediate communication. In fact, many players do not like to compare their present playing style to works they have done in the past; they like to think that they have improved their style by fresher, more contemporary, inventiveness and creativity.

SUMMARY

Listening to music is an intimate experience. Because involvement, as opposed to passive listening, is an important key, the authors have offered guides, in this appendix and in other chapters, to help the listener appreciate and understand jazz.

One of the more obvious aspects of the recorded sound is the size of the performing group. The listener can analyze such elements as the type of melody, the texture (thick or thin), the type of form (repetition, contrast, and so on), the tempo, and the instruments. The realization of these considerations will make jazz listening more pleasurable.

FOR FURTHER STUDY

1. In your own words, define the following: melody, harmony, rhythm, design, and timbre (or tone color).
2. Skilled listeners should be able to focus on different musical elements. Listen several times to "Yancey Stomp" by Jimmy Yancey,

pianist (*Folkways Jazz Series,* vol. 10), and answer the following:
   a. Does the music have an introduction?
   b. Is the left hand at the piano (the bass part) realizing mostly harmony or a repeated melodic figure?
   c. Is the right hand realizing a distinguishable melodic line or short figures that seem almost harmonic in total effect?
   d. Is the meter in duple or triple feeling?
3. Listen to the three-part form of "Fish This Week" as played by Les McCann (*Les McCann Plays the Truth,* Pacific Jazz Records, PJ-2). Listen for the expanded improvised bridge part: A, A, B (bridge), A.
4. Name the six elements of jazz that distinguish it from other types of music.
5. Give a definition of *syncopation*.
6. Clap the following $\frac{4}{4}$ rhythm: While tapping the beat with your foot, clap an example using a syncopated pattern.
7. Sing or play the melody of the song "Swanee River." Sing or play this melody with a jazz interpretation. What did you alter or perform differently to change the style of your performance?
8. It is fun to improvise. With little musical knowledge, you can make up a melody at the piano keyboard. Using only the black keys on the piano, start with the black-key C-sharp and play any series of tones with the rhythmic patterns found in the familiar song "Twinkle, Twinkle, Little Star." Repeat the same melody you made up and vary the rhythmic patterns.
9. Listen to "The Kid from Red Bank" from $E = MC^2$. In your own words, describe some of the improvisational techniques the pianist uses. For example, does the player use primarily melodic or harmonic configurations?
10. Classical composers have frequently used the theme-and-variations form in their compositions. Listening to a number of compositions that use this form will help a listener identify the various elements of jazz and how they can be altered or changed in jazz performances.
    a. Ravel uses the theme-and-variations design in his composition *Bolero.* Listen

to this piece and discover which musical element is used most in the eighteen variations: melody, rhythm, harmony, or tone color (instrumentation).

b. Rimsky-Korsakov uses four variations in his composition *Spanish Caprice.* The theme is in a two-part form, each part being nine measures in length. How does Rimsky-Korsakov treat the variations?

c. Listen to Lucien Cailliet's *Variations on the Theme "Pop! Goes the Weasel."* You will have to be somewhat of a musical detective to follow Cailliet's musical variations on this well-known melody. In which of the variations do you hear at least two of the jazz elements described above? Name the elements.

11. Jazz performers and composers often base their variations on the themes of other composers. Compare the different ways that themes are treated in the following examples:

a. *The Great Benny Goodman,* "Let's Dance," Columbia Records, CL-820.

b. *Big Band Beat,* "Strike Up the Band," Richmond Records, B-20034.

c. *Four Freshmen and Five Trombones,* "You Stepped Out of a Dream," Capitol Records, T-683.

d. "Scheherajazz," Somerset Records, P-9700.

e. *Barney Kessel Plays "Carmen,"* Contemporary Records, 3563.

f. *Dizzy in Greece,* "Anitra's Dance," Verve Records, MEV-8017 ("Anitra's Dance," Grieg, *Peer Gynt Suite*).

NOTES

1. Stan Kenton, "Commencement," *The Jazz Story,* vol. 5; Buddy Rich, "Westside Story," *Swingin' New Band,* Pacific Jazz Records, PJ-1013.

2. Count Basie, *The Best of Basie,* Roulette Records, RE118; $E = MC^2$, Roulette Records, ST-52003.

3. Charlie Parker and Dizzy Gillespie, "Shaw 'Nuff," *Smithsonian Collection of Classic Jazz;* Charlie Parker, "KoKo," *Smithsonian Collection of Classic Jazz;* Louis Armstrong, "Struttin' with Some Barbecue," *Smithsonian Collection of Classic Jazz;* Charlie Parker, "Another Hair Do," *Charlie Parker Memorial Album,* vol. 1, Savoy Records, MG-12000; Louis Armstrong, "I Gotta Right to Sing the Blues," *The Essential Louis Armstrong,* Verve Records, V-8569; Cannonball Adderley, "I Can't Get Started with You," *The Jazz Story,* vol. 5.

4. Count Basie, "Blue and Sentimental," *The Best of Basie,* Roulette Records, RE118; Gerry Mulligan and Ben Webster, "Chelsea Bridge," *The Greatest Names in Jazz,* Verve Records, PR 2-3.

5. Count Basie, "Doggin' Around" and "Taxi War Dance," *Smithsonian Collection of Classic Jazz;* "Every Tub," *Jive at Five;* Count Basie, "Jumpin' at the Woodside" and "Every Tub," *The Best of Basie;* and "The Kid from Redbank," $E = MC^2$; "Jumpin' at the Woodside," *Big Band Jazz, Smithsonian Collection of Recordings.*

6. Kenny Clarke, "Be a Good Girl," *The Jazz Story,* vol. 5; Dizzy Gillespie and Charlie Parker, "Wee," *Jazz at Massey Hall,* Fantasy Records, 6003; "Shaw 'Nuff," *Smithsonian Collection of Classic Jazz;* Charlie Parker, "KoKo," *Smithsonian Collection of Classic Jazz;* "Little Benny," *Smithsonian Collection of Classic Jazz.*

7. Count Basie, "Blue and Sentimental," *The Best of Basie;* "Lil' Darlin'," $E = MC^2$; Woody Herman, "Misty Morning," *The Jazz Story,* vol. 5.

8. Gunther Schuller, "Variants on a Theme of Thelonious Monk," *Jazz Abstractions,* Atlantic Records, 1365; "A Fugue for Music Inn," *The Modern Jazz Quartet at Music Inn,* Atlantic Records, 1247; "On Green Mountain" (chaconne form), *Modern Jazz Concert,* Columbia Records, WL 127; Dave Brubeck Quartet, "Blue Rondo a la Turk," *Time Out,* Columbia Records, CL-1397.

9. Modern Jazz Quartet with Laurindo Almeida, "Fugue in A Minor," *Collaboration,* Atlantic Records, 1429.

10. Joe Harriott, "Shadows," *The Jazz Story,* vol. 5; Archie Shepp, "The Chased," *The*

Definitive Jazz Scene, vol. 3; "The Mac Man," *On This Night,* Impulse Records, A-97.

11. Blood, Sweat and Tears, "Spinning Wheel," *Blood, Sweat and Tears,* Columbia Records, CS9720.

12. Clark Terry, "Hammer-head Waltz," *The Definitive Jazz Scene,* vol. 1; Les McCann, "A Little 3/4 for God and Company," *Les McCann Plays the Truth,* Pacific Jazz Records, PJ-2; Tommy Vig, "Sunrise Sunset," *The Sound of the Seventies,* Milestone Records, 9007.

13. Meade Lux Lewis and Will Bradley, "Beat Me Daddy, Eight to the Bar," Columbia Records, 35530; Count Basie, "Boogie-woogie," Columbia Records, 35959; Tommy

Dorsey, "Boogie-woogie," RCA Victor Records, 26054; Benny Goodman, "Roll 'Em," RCA Victor Records, 25627.

14. Spirit, "Topanga Windows," *Spirit,* Ode 70 Records, Z18-4404.

15. Count Basie Orchestra, "Jumpin' at the Woodside," *The Best of Basie,* Roulette Records, RE118; *Big Band Jazz, Smithsonian Collection of Recordings.*

16. Gunther Schuller, *Early Jazz* (New York: Oxford University Press, 1968), 15.Early New Orleans Dixieland (no accents—flat four, or $\frac{4}{4}$).

appendix B

notational examples

CHAPTER 2

Example 6A Interactive Guide 13

Example 6C Interactive Guide 15

Example 6B Interactive Guide 14

Example 6D Interactive Guide 16

Example 7

GRUNT   GRUNT

Example 8A Polyphonic

Example 8B Homophonic

Examples 8A and 8B demonstrate the difference between polyphonic and homophonic (vertical) harmonization. Example 8A is polyphonically constructed and shows the independence of the harmonic line. Example 8B is homophonically constructed and demonstrates the extreme dependency of the harmony part on the melody.

THE BLUES FORM

Eight-bar, twelve-bar, and sixteen-bar blues forms all developed, but by the beginning of World War I the twelve-bar construction had become an accepted form.[1] The blues, like all music, has built chords from the scale tones. If a chord starts on the first note of the scale and then uses every other note (scale tones 1, 3, and 5), the roman numeral I is used to define it. A chord built up from the fourth note would be given the numeral IV, and so on. The seventh tone (or flatted seventh)

can be added and designated, such as V_7. These harmonic symbols can be used to describe the harmonic construction of various musical forms.

Most blues researchers claim that the very early blues were patterned after English ballads and often had eight, ten, or sixteen bars.[2] An example of eight-bar blues is "Trouble in Mind," sometimes called "Troubled in Mind," with the following chord progression: I, V_7, I_7, IV, I, V_7, I, I. Another eight-bar blues is "How Long Blues," using a different chord progression: I, I_7, IV, IV, I, V_7, I, I. Among the sixteen-bar blues one can find long lists of songs such as "Careless Love" (I, V_7, I, I—I, I, V_7, V_7—I, I_7, IV, IV—I, V_7, I, I), "Basin Street Blues" (I, III_7, VI_7, VI_7—II_7, I, V_7, I, V_7—I, III_7, VI_7, VI_7—II_7, V_7, I, I), and sixteen-bar blues tunes that have the standard twelve-bar progression plus a four-bar tag (I, I, I, I_7—IV, IV, I, I—V_7, V_7, I, I—and then the **tag**—II_7, V_7, I, I). Few researchers attempt to notate these early blues, perhaps because there are so many different structures.

CHAPTER 3

Example 9A Interactive Guide 17

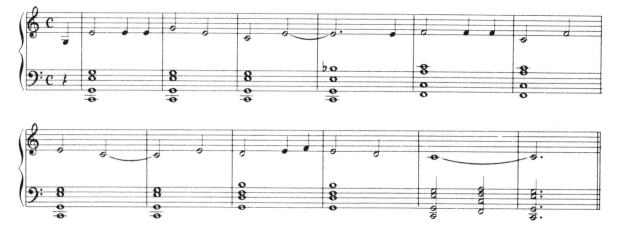

Example 9B Interactive Guide 18

THE ACCEPTED CHORD PROGRESSION

Today, the blues is a particular harmonic sequence, a definite musical form in much the same manner that the sonnet is a poetic form. The blues now contains a definite set progression of harmonies and consists of twelve measures. The harmonic progression is as follows: I, I, I, I_7, IV, IV, I, I, V_7, V_7, I, I. Each roman numeral indicates a chord built on a specific tone in the scale. Since about 1960, because of the influence of rock-and-roll artists, the chord in the tenth measure in the progression of harmonies

has been changed to IV_7. This alteration is now considered standard.

Each roman numeral specified in the foregoing harmonic progression designates a chord to be played for one measure, resulting in a **twelve-measure** chorus. Examples 10A, 10B, and 10C are in the key of C.

THE BLUES SCALE

Some theorists designate a "blues scale" as the **Dorian mode** (the white keys of the piano from D to D) or the **Mixolydian mode** (the white keys

Example 10A C Diatonic Scale

Example 10B I, IV, and V_7 Chords in the Key of C

Example 10C Basic Chords Used in the Blues in the Key of C

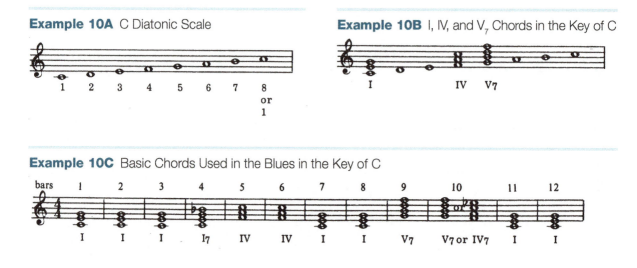

of the piano from G to G). The false logic in this theory is that the blues areas cannot be pinpointed. The Dorian implies a lowered third and lowered seventh; the Mixolydian implies a natural third and a lowered seventh. These blue tonalities are not on definite notes. The problems of analysis result from the rigidity of the **well-tempered scale** and the fluctuations of the blue tonalities themselves.

FOR FURTHER STUDY

1. Play the hymn "Lord Jesus Christ, with Us Abide" or any other hymn that contains the harmonic construction of the blues. Listen carefully and identify the blues chord progressions.

Example 11 "When to the Sessions of Sweet Silent Thought," "Lord, Lord, Lord"

2. Select a sonnet and write a blues melody to the words (see example 11: "When to the Sessions of Sweet Silent Thought," text by William Shakespeare).

3. Sing the C-major scale and note the location of the half steps. Next sing only the tones C, D, F, G, and A. You have just sung a pentatonic scale. Explain the difference between a major diatonic scale and pentatonic scale.

4. Sing the spiritual "Swing Low, Sweet Chariot" in the key of F-major. What scale does this melody use? Explain your answer.

5. Give some titles of blues melodies that do not follow the usual harmonic construction but have the word *blues* in their titles.

CHAPTER 4

In example 12A, the accompaniment consists of the bass part confined to the first and third beats and the chords played on the second and fourth beats, or off-beats. Because of the physical action of the left hand, it became the practice for pianists to accent these off-beats, a technique that led to the new rhythmic style of the following era.

Examples 13A and 13B demonstrate the use of full chords. There are various means of outlining the chords with a melodic bass line. Examples 13C, 13D, and 13E illustrate three of the most common.

Example 12A

Example 12B

Example 13A

Example 13C

Example 13B

Example 13D

In examples 13A and 13B, the bass line originally played by the third guitar is omitted; however, this is not apparent because the moving chords cause the music to sound very full and complete. In examples 13C, 13D, and 13E, the left hand plays the bass line while actually outlining the chords.

Example 13E

Boogie-woogie has also been called "8 over 4." Example 14A shows the logic of this label in printed music where the meter signature is indicated correctly as $\frac{4}{4}$. The boogie-woogie pianist superimposes eight beats in the same $\frac{4}{4}$ measure because the individual eighth notes are felt as single beats. It would be most correct to say that the pianist plays and feels the music as eight beats to the bar, or written with $\frac{8}{8}$ meter, as shown in example 14B.

Example 14A and B

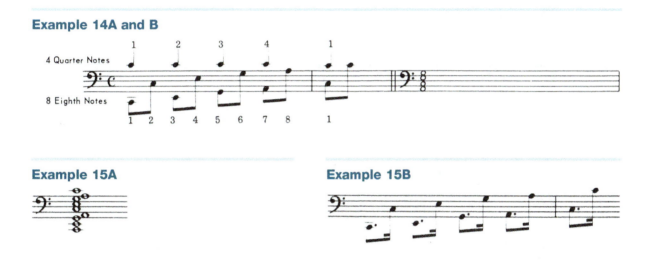

Example 15A

Example 15B

Example 16 shows the bass pattern used by the pianist on Interactive Guide 4.

Example 16

CHAPTER 5

In example 17, twelve measures are scored in
Early New Orleans Dixieland style to point out
musically the role assigned to each instrument.

Example 17

Example 18 illustrates the involved syncopation that causes the accents to shift constantly among the three lines being played by the trumpet, clarinet, and trombone.

Example 18

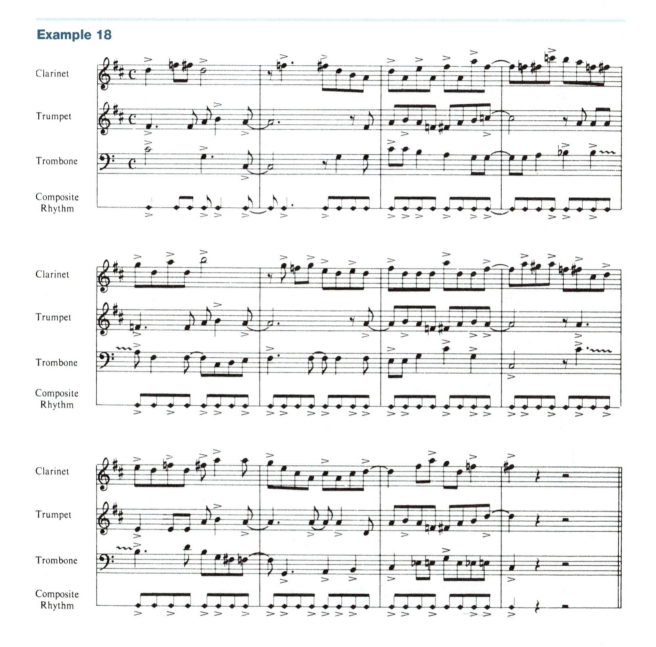

Early New Orleans Dixieland (no accents—
flat four, or $\frac{4}{4}$).

Example 19

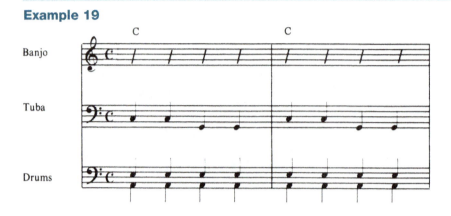

Chicago Style Dixieland (accented second
and fourth beats—$\frac{2}{4}$).

Example 20

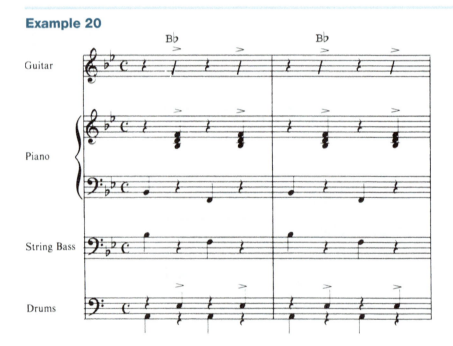

CHAPTER 6

Example 21A

Example 21B

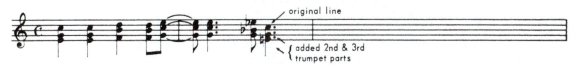

Example 22

Example 23A

Example 23B

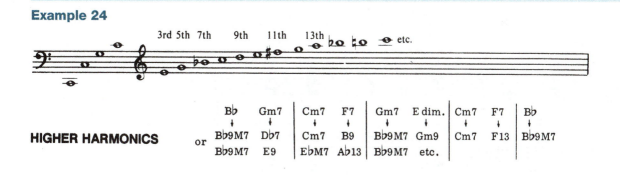

original line

added 2nd & 3rd
trumpet parts

CHAPTER 8

Example 24

3rd 5th 7th   9th   11th   13th   etc.

	Bb	Gm7	Cm7	F7	Gm7	E dim.	Cm7	F7	Bb
HIGHER HARMONICS or	Bb9M7	Db7	Cm7	B9	Bb9M7	Gm9	Cm7	F13	Bb9M7
	Bb9M7	E9	EbM7	Ab13	Bb9M7	etc.			

At the turn of the century, harmonies were enriched through the successive inclusion of higher members of the overtone series.

An A-major chord is placed directly over a G_7 chord to create an A_{13} chord.

Substitute chords also became important during the bop era. For example, C to C_7 to F could just as well be played C to Gb_7 to F, and it sounded more interesting at the time.

Example 25

A
G7

CHAPTER 11

The funky idiom embraces homophonic harmonic construction. Although the lines appear to be invented independently, as can be seen in example 26, they are actually planned homophonically. The lower note is played because of the sound of the specific interval produced when it is played against the melodic note above it. Example 26 also points up the excessive use of the fourth and fifth intervals. Another identifying feature is the use of many blue notes—the E-flats and B-flats in example 26.

Example 26

The homophonic construction of the swing era and that of the funky era are compared in examples 27A and 27B. Swing music was harmonized in a closed manner, as shown in example 27A, by the blocks of chords. The funky players, while planning their music homophonically, developed a more open, loose setting, as demonstrated in example 27B.

Example 27A

Example 27B

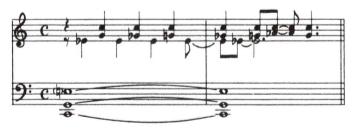

NOTES

1. Gunther Schuller, *Early Jazz* (London: Oxford University Press, 1968), 37.

2. LeRoi Jones, *Blues People* (New York: William Morrow, 1963), 62.

glossary

A

a cappella Vocal music without instrumental accompaniment.

accent To stress a melodic note, rhythm, or harmony by playing it louder and with a sharper attack.

accompaniment Performing with another performer or performers, usually in a less prominent role (e.g., playing the piano accompaniment for a trombone soloist).

amplification The process of electronically making a sound louder.

arpeggio The individual tones of a chord are not sounded simultaneously but are performed like a melody (single tones), nearly always starting at the bottom, or lowest, tone.

arrangement An adaptation of a musical composition (often called *charts* in musical slang). In a written arrangement, the musical arranger writes out the notes each performer is to play. In a head arrangement, the arrangement is made up out of someone's head, not written down.

arranger One who writes musical compositions for particular groups of performers.

arrhythmic Seemingly without meter; music that lacks a definite beat.

atonal Lacking in tonal centers; free jazz often has atonal areas that avoid the chord and melodic relationships normally associated with the major-minor system.

attack The manner in which the tone or tones are first sounded.

avant-garde A term that refers to composers and performers who break away from traditional practices and push for radical change; used primarily to describe post-bop jazz.

B

backbeat In a $\frac{4}{4}$ measure, the second and fourth beats are sometimes referred to as the backbeats; also, a song that has strong accents on those beats is said to have a backbeat.

ballad A simple song, usually romantic in nature, that uses the same melody for each stanza.

bar line A vertical line drawn down a music staff dividing it into bars or measures.

bar of music A means of dividing music, also called a *measure of music*.

bass (brass) The member of the brass family sounding the lowest tones; generally refers to the *tuba*.

bass (string) An instrument that looks like a very large violin; also called the *bass violin*. The string bass is played either by plucking the strings with the fingers (*pizzicato*) or by bowing (*arco*).

beat, or **breaker, music** A musical style characterized by electronic drum machines and a heavy beat; designed for a dancing style called *break dancing*.

block chords Usually, chords with many notes that move in parallel motion.

blue tonalities The alteration of the third and seventh tones of the major scale by a flatting inflection.

bombs Spontaneous punctuations by the drummer.

break A short interruption in the flow of the music; an interlude in which a solo player improvises or an accompanying group interpolates.

bridge Name given to the third eight-bar section in the most common construction of a thirty-two-bar chorus. In an AABA construction, the B is the bridge.

C

call-and-response pattern A musical pattern common to much jazz and African music in which a *call*, usually by a solo singer or instrumentalist, is followed by a *response* from one instrument, an ensemble, or the assembled participants in a ritual. In religious ceremonies, the congregation may respond to the call of the preacher.

canon A form of contrapuntal writing in which the melody, announced by one voice, is imitated by an answering voice.

chaconne Movement composed with a repeating bass line usually written in form of variations.

chamber music Music intended for small groups performing in intimate surroundings, as distinct from large groups performing in concert halls, theaters, and so on.

chance music Music based on chance or random relationships such as occur in the throwing of dice.

Charleston A dance form that was extremely popular during the 1920s.

chord The simultaneous sounding of three or more tones.

chord changes A series of successive chords; also called *chord progression*.

chorus   The main body or refrain of a song as distinct from the verse, which comes first. Very often an arrangement contains many choruses played by individual instrumentalists.

chromatic   Refers to the scales or the alteration of scale tones by using half steps.

collective improvisation   A situation in which all members of a small group improvise simultaneously.

combo   A small instrumental group consisting of three to eight players.

comp or **comping**   The rhythmic pattern used by keyboard or guitar players as they accompany soloists. Comping generally makes use of short rhythmic statements of the harmony, leaving room for the soloist to be heard.

concerto grosso   A composition consisting of interplay between a large body of instruments (orchestra) and a small group of instrumentalists (combo).

Congo Square   A large field in New Orleans where slaves gathered to sing and dance.

contrast   The introduction of different musical material.

Creole   A person with African and French or Spanish ancestry.

crossover   A style of music that appeals to more than one type of listener; usually refers to jazz/rock *fusion.*

cross-rhythm   Two or more rhythmic patterns played simultaneously.

cross-sectional voicing   Grouping instruments in a big band across the traditional section lines.

cutting contest   Individual musicians attempting to outplay one another, usually in a jam session situation.

D

diatonic   Pertains to the precise arrangement of tones as found in the major and minor scales.

Dorian mode   The arrangement of tones found in the scale using only the white keys of the piano from D to D.

double stop   Two tones stopped by the fingers on a stringed instrument and sounded simultaneously.

double time   When the tempo of the music becomes twice as fast.

drum machine   An electronic device used to create drum patterns similar to those played by traditional set or trap drummers.

E

effects   Electronic devices that alter electronic sounds (e.g., reverberation, delays, and distortion).

eleventh chord   A chord consisting of six different tones, each separated by an interval of a third.

embouchure   Disposition of the lips and tongue in playing wind instruments.

ensemble   Usually a small group of performers, as distinct from an orchestra or choir.

extended harmony   Tones added to a chord.

F

field hollers   A secret means of communication among slaves while they worked in the fields; sometimes called *field cries.*

fill-in   Originally, a short interlude in a song (such as a blues song) played by an instrumentalist.

flatted fifth   Lowering by a half step the fifth degree of the scale or chord.

flügelhorn   A type of brass instrument with valves, similar to a trumpet.

form   Refers to the design of a musical performance. Free jazz's lack of traditional restrictions in form and structure is called free form.

free improvisation   A descriptive term that emphasizes the complete improvisational nature of free jazz; also called *free form.*

front line   Instrumentalists who are placed along the front of an ensemble.

fugue   A type of contrapuntal composition for a given number of parts. Each part is introduced individually, and successive parts are heard in imitation.

fusion   A style of music that appeals to more than one type of listener; usually refers to jazz/rock (see *crossover*).

G

gospel song   A song whose lyrics recount passages from scripture.

H

harmonic rhythm   The rhythm that is created by the changing harmonies in a composition.

harmonics   The frequencies that collectively create a single tone; also used to refer to the higher chord tones in an extended chord.

harmony   Simultaneous sounding of two or more tones.

higher harmonics   See *extended harmony.*

homophonic   A single melody, usually in the highest voice part, with harmony in the lower voices acting as an accompaniment.

horizontal texture   Polyphonic texture; a simultaneous combination of melodies; the opposite of *homophonic texture.*

hymn   A congregational song, with words not taken directly from the Bible, sung in praise of God.

I

iambic pentameter   A type of poetry consisting of an unaccented syllable followed by an accented one, with five of these combinations in each line of poetry.

improvisation   The performing of music that is made up (created) at the moment, not performed from memory or from written music; a manner of playing extemporaneously.

instrumentation The different types of instruments that make up an ensemble.

J

jam session An informal gathering of musicians playing on their own time and improvising just for the fun of it.

K

key A classification given to a particular arrangement of tones in a scale. The first degree of the scale is the tonal center, or key name, and the necessary flats or sharps for a particular key form the key signature.

L

lay back Play slightly behind the beat established by the rhythm section.

liturgical Pertaining to the rites of a religious service.

M

measure See *bar of music.*

melody A succession of single tones varying in pitch and rhythm and having a recognizable musical shape.

meter The division of beats into accented and unaccented groupings of two, three, or more.

middle register The middle part of the complete range of the voice or instrument.

Mixolydian mode The arrangement of tones found in the scale using only the white keys of the piano from G to G.

modal jazz A jazz style that typically has slowmoving harmonies and older modal scales. The chord relationships are generally not typical of the major-minor system.

monophonic A single melody with neither accompanying melody nor harmony.

motive, or **motivic** Short melodic fragments that are used for developing a solo. Motives are often taken by soloists from the song's melody. Some entire pieces are built on short motives (e.g., *A Love Supreme* by Coltrane).

N

ninth chord A chord consisting of five different tones, each separated by an interval of a third.

O

obligato An accompanying or free melody played by a second instrument that is less prominent and secondary to the main melody played by the lead instrument.

offbeat Second or fourth beat in $\frac{4}{4}$ meter.

ostinato A clear melodic and/or rhythmic figure that is persistently repeated.

overtone series Tones that are related to the first (fundamental) tone sounded. A series of higher tones, or upper partials, that, when the first (or fundamental) is sounded, make up a complex musical tone.

P

pedal point A tone sustained below while harmonies change.

pentatonic A scale consisting of only five tones as represented by the five black keys of the piano.

period A grouping of melodic phrases to form a larger melodic section.

phrase A small unit of a melody.

pizzicato A manner of playing stringed instruments by plucking rather than by bowing.

plagal cadence A specific chord progression, namely, the IV chord resolving to the I chord (e.g., amen chords).

polymeters Simultaneous use of several meters.

polymodal The simultaneous sounding of several different modes.

polyphonic The simultaneous sounding of two or more melodies of equal importance.

polytonal The simultaneous sounding of tones in more than one key.

Q

quadrille A square dance of five figures that was popular in the nineteenth century.

R

raga A particular scale in Eastern music.

repetition Presentation of the same musical material in two or more parts of a composition.

rhythm section The section of an instrumental ensemble that provides the most prominent rhythmic feel of the music, usually consisting of drums, piano, bass, and guitar.

riff A short pattern of sounds repeated and played by a soloist or group.

rim shots Produced by striking the edge, or rim, of the drum and the drumhead simultaneously.

rondo A musical form in which one section of a composition recurs intermittently with contrasting sections coming between each repetition (e.g., ABACADA).

round A vocal canon for several voices.

S

salsa A combination of jazz and African American–Cuban rhythms.

scale A precise progression of single tones upward or downward in steps. A chromatic scale is a twelve-tone scale with intervals of a half step; a diatonic scale is an eight-tone scale with a repetition of the eighth degree, pertaining to the major and minor scales; and a pentatonic scale consists of five tones.

scat singing   The use of nonsense syllables while improvising vocally.

Schoenberg's twelve-tone system   A technique of composition in which all twelve half steps in an octave are treated as equal. A method used by Schoenberg in the form of a "tone row," in which all the twelve tones are placed in a particular order, forming the basis of a musical composition. No tone is repeated within a row. The tone row becomes a "tonal reservoir" from which the composition is drawn.

sequencer   An electronic device that stores a musical series of notes to be played back later. Sequencers can be used to build up a performance by storing several musical sequences, one after another.

sequences   A melodic phrase that is repeated several times, each time successively higher or lower.

sideman   A player in the musical ensemble as differentiated from the leader.

speakeasy   A nightclub in the 1920s.

spiritual   A name given to a type of religious folk song of African Americans, usually of a solo-and-refrain design.

standard tunes   Familiar, well-established popular or jazz tunes. Copyright can be renewed for a certain number of years after the death of the composer.

Storyville   Red-light district in New Orleans that figured in the origin of jazz.

string bass   A bass violin.

symmetrical   Exhibiting a balance of parts.

syncopation   Accenting a normally weak beat or the weak part of a beat.

T

tack piano   A piano with thumbtacks on the felts of the piano hammers to make it sound older and more authentic for playing ragtime and similar music.

tag   A short addition to the end of a musical composition.

tailgate trombone   A name deriving from the practice of early trombone players sitting on the tailgate of a wagon so that their slides could operate freely out the rear. The phrase became associated with the trombone part in a Dixieland ensemble.

tango   A dance of Spanish-American origin commonly in $\frac{4}{4}$ meter.

tempo   Refers to the speed of the underlying beat. The speed is determined by the number of beats counted over the span of sixty seconds.

theme and variation   A musical form in which the theme is introduced and successive repetitions of the theme, changed or altered in some manner, follow.

third-stream music   A combination of classical music and jazz.

thirteenth chord   A chord consisting of seven different tones, each separated by an interval of a third.

time, making time, or straight time   Often after rhythmically contrasting interludes or a rhythmically complex "head," the rhythm section will fall into a very solid metric feel to launch a solo section. A straight-time feel has very few unusual accents.

time signature   Sign at the beginning of a composition indicating the grouping of beats for each measure. The meter signature $\frac{3}{4}$ means that there are three beats in a measure and that a quarter note gets one beat.

Tin Pan Alley   The industry centered in New York that published popular music.

tonal clash   Tones played simultaneously that produce a discordant or clashing effect.

tonal sonorities   The overall effect of the juxtaposition of tonal sounds.

trading fours   Two solo instrumentalists alternating in playing four measures each.

twelve-measure chorus or **twelve-bar strain**   A composition or a part of a composition consisting of twelve measures.

twelve-tone system   A compositional system designed to avoid tonal centers, thereby creating a balanced atonal music.

U

unison   Two or more instruments or voices sounding on the same pitches (tones) or an octave apart.

up-tempo   Fast tempo.

V

vamp   A transitional chord or rhythmic progression of indefinite duration used as a filler until the soloist is ready to start or continue.

verse   The introductory section of a popular song as distinguished from the chorus. The latter consists commonly of thirty-two bars, whereas the verse may have an irregular number of bars and be sung or played in a free tempo.

vertical texture   Block chords that accompany a melodic part; opposite of horizontal thinking.

vibrato   The pulsating effect produced by small, rapid variations in pitch. Most jazz uses vibrato for warmth and interpretation in imitating the human voice.

W

walking bass   The bass part that was originally introduced in boogie-woogie in ostinato form. It concisely spells out the notes in the chords being used and is usually played in eighth notes.

well-tempered scale   Refers to the tuning system found on a keyboard.

bibliography

A

Albertson, Chris. *Bessie*. New York: Stein & Day, 1972.

Allan, William Francis; Ware, Charles Pickard; and Garrison, Lucy McKim. *Slave Songs of the United States*. New York: Peter Smith, 1867.

Allen, Walter C. *Hendersonia: The Music of Fletcher Henderson and His Musicians, Jazz Monograph no. 4*. Highland Park, N.J.: Walter C. Allen, 1973.

Allen, Walter C., and Rust, Brian. *King Joe Oliver*. London and New York: Sidgwick and Jackson, 1958.

Apel, Willi. *Harvard Dictionary of Music*. Cambridge, Mass.: Harvard University Press, 1965.

Armstrong, Louis. *Swing That Music*. New York: Longmans, Green, 1936.

———. *My Life in New Orleans*. New York: Prentice-Hall, 1954.

———. *Louis Armstrong: A Self Portrait*. New York: Eakins Press, 1971.

B

Baird, David. *From Score to Tape*. Boston: Berklee Press, 1973.

Balliett, Whitney. *The Sound of Surprise*. New York: E. P. Dutton, 1959.

———. *Dinosaurs in the Morning*. Philadelphia: J. B. Lippincott, 1962.

———. *American Musicians*. New York: Oxford University Press, 1986.

Basie, Count. *Good Morning Blues: The Autobiography of Count Basie, as Told to Albert Murray*. New York: Random House, 1986.

Bechet, Sidney. *Treat It Gentle: An Autobiography*. New York: Hill & Wang, 1960.

Berendt, Joachim. *The New Jazz Book*. Translated by Dan Morgenstern. New York: Hill & Wang, 1962.

———. *Jazz Book: From New Orleans to Rock and Free Jazz*. New York: Lawrence Hill, 1975.

Berger, Morroe; Patrick, Edward; and Patrick, James. *Benny Carter: A Life in American Music*. Metuchen, N.J.: Scarecrow Press, 1982.

Bernstein, Leonard. *The Joy of Music*. New York: Simon & Schuster, 1959.

Berton, Ralph. *Remembering Bix: A Memoir of the Jazz Age*. New York: Harper & Row, 1974.

Blancq, Charles. *Sonny Rollins: The Journey of a Jazzman*. Boston: G. K. Hall, 1983.

Blesh, Rudi. *Classic Piano Rags*. New York: Dover Publications, 1973.

Blesh, Rudi, and Janis, Harriet. *Shining Trumpets—a History of Jazz*. New York: Knopf, 1946.

———. *They All Played Ragtime*. New York: Grove Press, 1959.

Bloom, Eric, ed. *Grove's Dictionary of Music and Musicians*. 9 vols. New York: St. Martin's Press, 1959.

Brask, Ole, and Morgenstern, Dan. *Jazz People*. New York: Harry N. Abrams, 1976.

Brooks, Tilford. *America's Black Musical Heritage*. Englewood Cliffs, N.J.: Prentice-Hall, 1984.

Broonzy, William, and Bruynogle, Yannick. *Big Bill Blues*. London: Cassell, 1955.

Brown, Charles T. *The Jazz Experience*. Dubuque, Iowa: Wm. C. Brown, 1989.

Budds, Michael J. *Jazz in the Sixties*. Iowa City: University of Iowa Press, 1978.

Buerkle, Jack V., and Barker, Danny. *Bourbon Street Black*. London: Oxford University Press, 1973.

Buszin, Walter E., ed. *Anniversary Collection of Bach Chorales*. Chicago: Hall McCreary, 1935.

C

Calloway, Cab, and Rollins, Bryant. *Of Minnie the Moocher and Me*. New York: Crowell, 1976.

Carr, Ian, *Miles Davis*. New York: William Morrow, 1982.

Cerulli, Dom; Korall, Burt; and Nasatir, Mort. *The Jazz World*. New York: Ballantine Books, 1960.

Charles, Ray, and Ritz, David. *Brother Ray*. New York: Dial Press, 1978.

Charters, Samuel B. *The Country Blues*. New York: Doubleday, 1958.

———. *Jazz, New Orleans (1855–1963)*. New York: Oak Publishers, 1964.

Charters, Samuel B., and Kunstadt, Leonard. *Jazz: A History of the New York Scene*. New York: Doubleday, 1962.

Chase, Gilbert. *America's Music from the Pilgrims to the Present*. New York: McGraw-Hill, 1955.

Chilton, John. *Billie's Blues*. New York: Stein & Day, 1975.

———. *Who's Who of Jazz*. New York: Da Capo Press, 1985.

Cole, Bill. *John Coltrane*. New York: Schirmer, 1976.

————. *Miles Davis.* New York: William Morris, 1976.

Collier, Graham. *Inside Jazz.* London: Quartet Books, 1973.

Collier, James Lincoln. *The Making of Jazz.* New York: Dell, 1978.

————. *Duke Ellington.* Oxford: Oxford University Press, 1987.

Coryell, Julie, and Friedman, Laura. *Jazz-Rock Fusion.* New York: Delta Books, 1979.

Courlander, Harold. *Miles Davis: A Musical Biography.* New York: William Morrow, 1974.

D

Dahl, Linda. *Stormy Weather: The Music and Lives of a Century of Jazzwomen.* New York: Pantheon, 1984.

Dale, Rodney. *The World of Jazz.* Cambridge: Basinghall, 1980.

Dance, Stanley. *The World of Duke Ellington.* New York: Scribner, 1970.

————. *The World of Earl Hines.* New York: Scribner, 1974.

————. *The World of Swing.* New York: Scribner, 1975.

————. *The World of Count Basie.* New York: Scribner, 1980.

Dankworth, Avril. *Jazz: An Introduction to Its Musical Basis.* London: Oxford University Press, 1968.

Davis, Francis. *In the Moment: Jazz in the 1980s.* New York: Oxford University Press, 1986.

Davis, Miles, and Troupe, Quincy. *Miles.* New York: Simon & Schuster, 1989.

Davis, Nathan. *Writings in Jazz,* 3d ed. Scottsdale, Ariz.: Gorsuch Scarisbrick, 1985.

Dexter, Dave. *The Jazz Story: From the Nineties to the Sixties.* Englewood Cliffs, N.J.: Prentice-Hall, 1964.

Dineen, Janice D. *The Performing Women* (26910 Grand View Ave., Hayward, Calif. 94542).

Drake, Russell; Herder, Ronald; and Modugno, Anne D. *How to Make Electronic Music.* Pleasantville, N.Y.: EAV Inc., 1975.

E

Ellington, Duke. *Music Is My Mistress.* New York: Doubleday, 1973.

Ellington, Mercer, and Dance, Stanley. *Duke Ellington in Person: An Intimate Memoir.* New York: Houghton Mifflin, 1975.

F

Feather, Leonard. *Inside Jazz.* New York: J. J. Robbins, 1949.

————. *The New Edition of the Encyclopedia of Jazz.* New York: Horizon Press, 1960.

————. *The Book of Jazz: A Guide from Then til Now.* New York: Horizon Press, 1965.

————. *The Encyclopedia of Jazz in the Sixties.* New York: Horizon Press, 1966.

————. *From Satchmo to Miles.* New York: Stein & Day, 1974.

————. *The Encyclopedia of Jazz in the Seventies.* New York: Horizon Press, 1976.

————. *Pleasures of Jazz.* New York: Horizon Press, 1976.

————. *The Encyclopedia of Jazz.* New York: Da Capo Press, 1984.

————. *The Jazz Years: Earwitness to an Era.* New York: Da Capo Press, 1987.

Finkelstein, Sidney. *Jazz: A People's Music.* New York: Da Capo Press, 1975.

Flower, John. *Moonlight Serenade.* New Rochelle, N.Y.: Arlington House, 1972.

Francis, André. *Jazz.* Translated and revised by Martin Williams. New York: Grove Press, 1960.

Friend, David; Perlman, Alan R.; and Piggott, Thomas G. *Learning Music with Synthesizers.* Winona, Minn.: Hal Leonard, 1974.

G

Gammond, Peter, ed. *Scott Joplin and the Ragtime Era.* New York: St. Martin's Press, 1975.

————. *Duke Ellington: His Life and Music.* New York: Roy Publishers, 1977.

George, Don. *Sweet Man: The Real Duke Ellington.* New York: Putnam, 1981.

Giddins, Gary. *Satchmo.* New York: Doubleday, 1989.

————. *Visions of Jazz.* New York: Oxford University Press, 1998.

Gitler, Ira. *Jazz Masters of the Forties.* New York: Macmillan, 1966.

————. *Swing to Bop.* New York: Oxford University Press, 1986.

Gleason, Ralph. *Celebrating the Duke.* New York: Dell, 1975.

Goddard, Chris. *Jazz Away from Home.* London: Paddington Press, 1979.

Goffin, Robert. *Jazz: From the Congo to the Metropolitan.* New York: Da Capo Press, 1975.

Gold, Robert S. *A Jazz Lexicon.* New York: Knopf, 1964.

Goldberg, Joe. *Jazz Masters of the Fifties.* New York: Macmillan, 1965.

Gridley, Mark C. *Jazz Styles,* 3d ed. Englewood Cliffs, N.J.: Prentice-Hall, 1985.

H

Hadlock, Richard. *Jazz Masters of the Twenties.* New York: Macmillan, 1965.

Handy, W. C. *W. C. Handy: Father of the Blues.* New York: Collier Books, 1970.

Harris, Rex. *Jazz.* Baltimore: Penguin Books, 1956.

Harrison, Max. *Charlie Parker.* New York: A. S. Barnes, 1961.

———. *A Jazz Retrospect.* Boston: Crescendo, 1976.

Haskins, Jim. *Black Music in America.* New York: Thomas Y. Crowell, 1987.

Hasse, John Edward. *Beyond Category.* New York: Simon & Schuster, 1993.

Hentoff, Nat. *Jazz Life.* New York: Da Capo Press, 1975.

———. *Jazz Is.* New York: Random House, 1976.

———. *Boston Boy.* New York: Knopf, 1986.

Hentoff, Nat, and McCarthy, Albert, eds. *Jazz.* New York: Holt, Rinehart & Winston, 1959.

———. *Jazz: New Perspectives on the History of Jazz.* New York: Da Capo Press, 1975.

Hickok, Robert. *Exploring Music.* Dubuque, Iowa: Wm. C. Brown, 1989.

Hodeir, André. *Jazz: Its Evolution and Essence.* Translated by David Noakes. New York: Grove Press, 1956.

———. *Toward Jazz.* New York: Grove Press, 1962.

Holiday, Billie, and Duffy, William. *Lady Sings the Blues.* New York: Doubleday, 1965.

J

James, Michael. *Dizzy Gillespie.* New York: A. S. Barnes, 1959.

Jewell, Derek. *Duke: A Portrait of Duke Ellington.* New York: Norton, 1977.

Jones, LeRoi. *Blues People.* New York: William Morrow, 1963.

———. *Black Music.* New York: William Morrow, 1965.

Jones, Max. *Salute to Satchmo.* London: Longacre Press, 1970.

Jones, Max, and Chilton, John. *Louis: The Louis Armstrong Story.* New York: Little, Brown, 1971.

Jost, Ekkehard. *Free Jazz.* New York: Da Capo Press, 1981.

K

Kaminsky, Max. *My Life in Jazz.* New York: Harper & Row, 1963.

Kaufman, Frederick, and Gucklin, John P. *The African Roots of Jazz.* Sherman Oaks, Calif.: Alfred Publishing, 1979.

Keepnews, Orrin, and Grauer, Bill, Jr. *A Pictorial History of Jazz.* New York: Crown, 1955.

Keil, Charles. *Urban Blues.* Chicago: University of Chicago Press, 1966.

Kennington, Donald, and Reed, Denny L. *The Literature of Jazz,* 2d ed. Chicago: American Library Association, 1980.

Kimball, Bob, and Bolcum, Bill. *Reminiscing with Sizzle and Blake.* New York: Viking Press, 1973.

Kinkle, Roger D. *The Complete Encyclopedia of Popular Music and Jazz.* New Rochelle, N.Y.: Arlington House, 1974.

Kirkeby, Ed. *Ain't Misbehavin': The Story of Fats Waller.* New York: Da Capo Press, 1975.

L

Lee, William F. *People in Jazz: Jazz Keyboard Improvisors of the 19th and 20th Centuries.* Hialeah, Fla.: Columbia Pictures Publications, 1984.

Leonard, Neil. *Jazz and the White Americans.* Chicago: University of Chicago Press, 1962.

———. *Jazz: Myth and Religion.* New York: Oxford University Press, 1987.

Levine, Lawrence. *The Freedom Principle of Jazz after 1958.* New York: William Morrow, 1984.

Lomax, Alan. *Mr. Jelly Roll.* New York: Grosset & Dunlap, 1950.

———. *The Folk Songs of North America.* Garden City, N.J.: Doubleday, 1960.

M

McCarthy, Albert. *Louis Armstrong.* New York: A. S. Barnes, 1959.

———. *Big Band Jazz.* New York: Putnam, 1974.

Marquis, Donald. *In Search of Buddy Bolden: First Man of Jazz.* Baton Rouge: Louisiana State University Press, 1979.

Martin, Henry. *Enjoying Jazz.* New York: Schirmer, 1986.

Martin, John H., and Fritz, William F. *Listening to Jazz.* Fresno: University of California Press, 1969.

Meeker, David. *Jazz in the Movies: A Guide to Jazz Musicians, 1917–1977.* New Rochelle, N.Y.: Arlington House, 1978.

Megill, Donald D., and Demory, Richard S. *Introduction to Jazz History,* 2d ed. Englewood Cliffs, N.J.: Prentice-Hall, 1989.

Mehegan, John. *Jazz Improvisation.* New York: Watson-Guptill, 1959.

Milhaud, Darius. *Notes without Music.* New York: Knopf, 1953.

Miller, Hugh Milton. *History of Music.* New York: Barnes & Noble Books, 1957.

Mingus, Charles. *Beneath the Underdog.* New York: Knopf, 1971.

Morgenstern, Dan. *Jazz People.* New York: Abrams, 1976.

Muro, Dan. *An Introduction to Electronic Music Synthesizers.* Melville, N.Y.: Belwin-Mills, 1975.

Murray, Albert. *Stompin' the Blues.* New York: McGraw-Hill, 1976.

N

Nanry, Charles. *The Jazz Text.* New York: Van Nostrand, 1979.

O

Ogren, Kathy J. *The Jazz Revolution.* New York: Oxford University Press, 1989.

Oliver, Paul. *The Meaning of the Blues.* New York: Macmillan, 1960.

———. *Bessie Smith.* New York: A. S. Barnes, 1961.

———. *The Savannah Syncopators.* New York: Stein & Day, 1970.

O'Meally, Robert G., ed. *The Jazz Cadence of American Culture.* New York: Columbia University Press, 1998.

Ostransky, Leroy. *The Anatomy of Jazz.* Seattle: University of Washington Press, 1960.

———. *Jazz City.* Englewood Cliffs, N.J.: Prentice-Hall, 1975.

———. *Understanding Jazz.* Englewood Cliffs, N.J.: Prentice-Hall, 1977.

P

Panassie, Hughes. *The Real Jazz.* Translated by Anne Sorrelle Williams. New York: A. S. Barnes, 1960.

———. *Louis Armstrong.* New York: Scribner, 1971.

Placksin, Sally. *American Women in Jazz.* Wideview Books, 1982.

Pleasants, Henry. *The Great American Popular Singers.* New York: Oxford University Press, 1959.

———. *Serious Music and All That Jazz.* New York: Simon & Schuster, 1969.

Porter, Lewis. *Lester Young.* Boston: Twayne Press, 1985.

Priestley, Brian. *Mingus: A Critical Biography.* New York: Da Capo Press, 1984.

R

Ramsey, Frederic, Jr., and Smith, Charles Edward. *Jazzmen.* New York: Harcourt, Brace, Harvest, 1939.

Rattenbury, Ken. *Duke Ellington, Jazz Composer.* London: Yale University Press, 1990.

Reisner, Robert G. *The Jazz Titans.* New York: Doubleday, 1960.

———. *Bird: The Legend of Charlie Parker.* New York: Da Capo Press, 1975.

Roach, Hildred. *Black American Music: Past and Present.* Boston: Crescendo, 1973.

Roberts, John Storm. *Black Music of Two Worlds.* New York: William Morrow, 1974.

———. *The Latin Tinge.* New York: Oxford University Press, 1998.

———. *Latin Jazz.* New York: Schirmer Press, 1999.

Rose, Al. *Eubie Blake.* New York: Schirmer, 1979.

Russell, Ross. *Jazz Styles in Kansas City and the Southwest.* Berkeley: University of California Press, 1971.

———. *Bird Lives: The High Life and Hard Times of Charlie (Yardbird) Parker.* New York: Charterhouse Books, 1973.

Russell, Tony. *Blacks, Whites and the Blues.* New York: Stein & Day, 1970.

S

Sales, Grover. *Jazz: America's Classical Music.* Englewood Cliffs, N.J.: Prentice-Hall, 1984.

Saunders, Ruby W. *Jazz Ambassador Louis Armstrong.* Chicago: Childrens Press, 1973.

Sargeant, Winthrop. *Jazz, Hot and Hybred,* 3d ed. New York: Da Capo Press, 1975.

Schafer, William J., et al. *The Art of Ragtime.* Baton Rouge: Louisiana State University, 1983.

Schenkel, Steven M. *The Tools of Jazz.* Englewood Cliffs, N.J.: Prentice-Hall, 1983.

Schuller, Gunther. *Early Jazz: Its Roots and Musical Development.* London: Oxford University Press, 1968.

———. *The Swing Era: The Development of Jazz 1930–1945.* London: Oxford University Press, 1989.

Scott, Allen. *Jazz Educated, Man.* Silver Spring, Md.: Institute of Modern Languages, 1973.

Shapiro, Nat, and Hentoff, Nat, eds. *The Jazz Makers.* New York: Grove Press, 1957.

Simon, George T. *The Big Bands.* New York: Macmillan, 1967.

———. *Simon Says.* New Rochelle, N.Y.: Arlington House, 1971.

———. *Glenn Miller.* New York: Thomas Y. Crowell, 1974.

Simpkins, C. O. *Coltrane: A Biography.* New York: Herndon House, 1975.

Skowronski, Jo Ann. *Women in America: A Bibliography.* Metuchen, N.J.: Scarecrow Press, 1978.

Southern, Eileen. *Music of Black Americans.* New York: Norton, 1971.

Spellman, A. B. *Black Music: Four Lives in the Bebop Business.* New York: Schocken, 1970.

Standifer, James A., and Reeder, Barbara. *African and Afro-American Materials for Music Educators.* Washington, D.C.: Music Educators National Conference, 1972.

Starr, S. Frederick. *Red and Hot, the Fate of Jazz in the Soviet Union.* New York: Oxford University Press, 1983.

Stearns, Marshall. *The Story of Jazz.* London: Oxford University Press, 1958.

Stewart, Rex. *Jazz Masters of the '30s.* New York: Macmillan, 1972.

Stewart-Baxter, Derrick. *Ma Rainey.* New York: Stein & Day, 1970.

Strange, Allen. *Electronic Music: Systems, Techniques, and Controls.* Dubuque, Iowa: Wm. C. Brown, 1972.

Sudhalter, Richard M. *Lost Chords.* New York: Oxford University Press, 1999.

Sudhalter, Richard M., and Evans, Phillip R. *Bix: Man and Legend.* New York: Harper & Row, 1974.

Swenson, John. *The Rolling Stone Jazz Record Guide.* New York: Random House, 1985.

T

Tallmadge, William. *Afro-American Music.* Washington, D.C.: Music Educators National Conference, 1957.

Taylor, Billy. *Jazz and Piano: History and Development.* Dubuque, Iowa: Wm. C. Brown, 1982.

Thomas, J. C. *Chasin' the Trane.* New York: Doubleday, 1975.

Tirro, Frank. *Jazz: A History.* New York: Norton, 1977.

U

Ulanov, Barry. *Duke Ellington.* New York: Farrar, Strauss & Young, 1946.

————. *Handbook of Jazz.* New York: Viking Press, 1959.

Ulrich, Homer. *Music: A Design for Listening.* 2d ed. New York: Harcourt, Brace, & World, 1962.

Unterbrink, Mary. *Jazz Women at the Keyboard.* Jefferson, N.C.: McFarland, 1983.

W

Walker, Leo. *The Wonderful Era of the Great Dance Bands.* New York: Doubleday, 1972.

Werner, Otto. *The Origin and Development of Jazz.* Dubuque, Iowa: Kendall/Hunt, 1984.

Williams, Martin T. *King Oliver.* New York: A. S. Barnes, 1960.

————. *Jazz Masters of New Orleans.* New York: Macmillan, 1965.

————. *Jazz Masters in Transition (1957–69).* New York: Macmillan, 1970.

————. *The Jazz Tradition.* New York: Oxford University Press, 1983.

————. *Jazz Heritage.* New York: Oxford University Press, 1985.

————, ed. *The Art of Jazz.* London: Oxford University Press, 1959.

Wilson, John S. *The Collector's Jazz: Tradition and Swing.* Philadelphia: Lippincott, 1958.

————. *The Collector's Jazz: Modern.* Philadelphia: Lippincott, 1959.

————. *Jazz: The Transition Years, 1940–1960.* New York: Appleton-Century-Crofts, 1966.

credits

Chapter 12
Opener: Institute of Jazz Studies, Rutgers University

Chapter 13
Opener: Institute of Jazz Studies, Rutgers University; **p. 272:** © Allan Titmuss/ArenaPAL/Topham/Image Works; **p. 276:** © Tom Copi/Michael Ochs Archives/Getty Images; **p. 278:** © Leon Morris/Hulton Archive/Getty Images; **p. 282** & **283:** © Guy Le Querrec/Magnum Photos; **p. 285:** © Ray Avery/CTSIMAGES.COM; **p. 286:** © Frank Driggs Collection

Chapter 14
Opener: © Rick Diamond/WireImage/Getty Images; **p. 296:** © Laurent Gillieron/Corbis; **p. 300:** © Guy Le Querrec/Magnum Photos; **p. 303:** © AFP/Getty Images; **p. 306:** © AP Images/Stuart Ramson; **p. 308:** © Tad Hershorn

Chapter 15
Opener: © Lynn Goldsmith/Corbis; **p. 319:** © Rafa Rivas/AFP/Getty Images; **p. 321:** © Tom Copi/Michael Ochs Archives/Getty Images; **p. 322:** © AP Images; **p. 330:** © Tom Copi/Michael Ochs Archives/Getty Images; **p. 331:** © David Redfern/Getty; **p. 333:** © Tom Cop/Michael Ochs Archives/Getty; **p. 335:** © Javier Echezarreta/epa/Corbis; **p. 336:** © Urs Flueeler/epa/Corbis; **p. 337:** © Juan Naharro Gimenez/Getty; **p. 339:** © Ronald Startup/Hulton Archive/Getty Images; **p. 340:** © Reuters/Corbis; **p. 344:** © Shaun Heasley/Getty Images

index

Page numbers in **boldface** indicate glossary terms; page numbers in *italics* indicate photos and illustrations.

a cappella, **344**
Abrams, Richard, 279, 281
accents, **11,** 66
accompaniment, **6,** 62
active listening, 6
Adderley, Cannonball, 207, 232, 247, 261
African American church music
  categories of, 32
  funky and, 241, 243
  gospel, 35–37
  organ in, 247
  soul and, 241
  spirituals, 31–32
  and wickedness of jazz, 37
African Americans
  bop identified with, 171
  Creoles and, 26–28
  funky identified with, 241–242
  in Latin-Catholic colonies, 23–30
  in neoclassical school, 315
African music
  Ellington influenced by, 165
  importance to African culture, 21
  improvisation in, 8–9
  jazz influenced by, 19, 21–23, 315–316
  in Latin-Catholic colonies, 23–30
  rhythm in, 21–22
  scales in, 42–43
  spirituals influenced by, 33
African ritual, rhythm in, 22
Ahmad's Blues (Jamal), 324
Akiyoshi, Toshiko, 329, *330*
"Alabama" (Coltrane), 265
Albam, Manny, 23
Albert McNeil's Jubilee Singers, 36–37
Alias, Charles, 292

"All About Rosie" (Russell), 216
"All Blues" (Coltrane), 261
"All of Me" (Fitzgerald and Riddle), 142
Allen, Geri, 279
Allen, Lewis, 139
Almeida, Laurindo, 219
amen chords, 241, 243
Ammons, Albert, 71, 72
amplification, **229**
Anatomy of a Murder (film), 163
Anderson, Reid, 327
"Another Hair Do" (Parker), 41
Anthony Braxton, New York, Fall 1974 (Braxton), 284
Arkestra, 278
Armstrong, Louis, *36, 80, 92–96, 94*
  Dixieland band of, 100
  during Great Depression, 125
  Henderson (Fletcher) and, 112, 114
  Hines and, 99–100
  Holiday and, 139
  influence on Dixieland, 105
  listening guide for, 102
  oral tradition and, 84
  Payton influenced by, 319
  scat singing of, 141
  Smith (Bessie) and, 53
arpeggios, **176**
arrangements, **66**
  in bop, 174–175
  in cool, 202, 205, 212
  in Dixieland, 86–87
  of Ellington, 165
  of Morton, 65–66
  in swing, 113–115, 119–125, 129, *370, 371*
  of Take 6, 344
  of Williams (Mary Lou), 117–118
arranger, **65**
arrhythmic, **261**
Art Ensemble of Chicago, 281–282
art music, 21, 174

"As Long As I Live" (Krall), 341
Association for the Advancement of Creative Music (ACCM), 279, 281
"A-Tisket A-Tasket" (Webb), 141
atonal, **265, **274
attack, **200**
audience, in gospel performance, 33
Auld, Georgie, 144
Austin, Texas, 55
Austin High Gang, 101
"Autumn Leaves" (B. Evans), 208
avant-garde, 259, **269,** 284–285. *See also* free form

Back on the Block (Zawinul and Jones), 300, 305
backbeat, **304**
The Bad Plus, 327
"Bags' Groove" (Milt Jackson), 41
"Bags' Groove" (Monk), 186
"Bags' Groove" (Rollins), 252
Bailey, Buster, 53
Bailey, Mildred, 54
Bailey, Pearl, 54
Baker, Chet, 212, 230
ballads, 11, **111**
banjo, in Dixieland, 85, 98
bar lines, **273**
"Barney's Concerto" (Ellington), 167
"Barnyard Blues" (Original Dixieland Jazz Band), 91
Barretto, Ray, 308
Basie, (William) Count, *119, 120, 121*
  band of, 328
  in Battle of Bands, 116
  boogie-woogie of, 72
  call-and-response used by, 23
  contribution to swing, 129, 135–136
  in Kansas City swing, 117, 118–125

polytonal technique, **215**
pop, and jazz, 338–342. *See also*
    jazz/pop fusion
Powell, Bud, 74, 184
Pozo, Chano, 191
"The Preacher" (Silver), 245
"Precious Lord, Take My Hand"
    (T. A. Dorsey), 33
Prelude (Deodato), 307–308
"Prelude to a Kiss" (Ellington), 153
prison hollers, 43–44
"Profoundly Blue" (Hall), 138
progressive jazz, 187–191
Prohibition, 96, 125
Puente, Tito, 192, *192*, 193
pulse, 10
Purim, Flora, 219, 308

quadrilles, **23**
"Queer Street" (Basie), 23
Quicksell, Howdy, *103*

race
    in bebop, 171–172
    at the Cotton Club, 154
    and Ellington, 167
race records, 50
raga, **330**
ragtime
    contemporary, 66–67
    Dixieland and, 66, 84–85
    Ellington influenced by, 151
    listening guide for, 62
    origin of, 61–66
    piano in, 61–62, 364–365
Ragtime (film), 67
Ragtime for Eleven Instruments
    (Stravinsky), 217
ragtime tango, 97
Rainey, Gertrude "Ma," 50, *52*,
    53, 92
Rampal, Pierre, 217
Rao, Harihar, 329
real jazz, 105
record bans, 187
recordings
    of Armstrong, 96
    early, 90
    of Ellington, 166–167
    of Monk, 185
    of Powell, 184
    of ragtime, 66–67
    of Smith (Bessie), 53–54
The Red Back Book, 67

Red Hot (Santamaria), 308
Redd, Vi, 37
Redman, Don
    in Dixieland, 98
    Henderson (Fletcher) and,
        112, 114
    Smith (Bessie) and, 53
    in swing, 111, 112, 129
Redman, Joshua, 321, *322*
Redmond, Edgar, 199
Reese, Doc, 43
Reinhardt, Django, 138
"Relaxin' a Camarillo"
    (Parker), 183
religious music, influence on
    jazz, 30–35. *See also* African
        American church music
"Reminiscing in Tempo"
    (Ellington), 154
rent parties, 69
repetition, **12,** 44
Return to Forever, 291, 294,
    295–296, 307
"Rhapsody in Blue"
    (Gershwin), 126
rhythm, 354–355, *355. See also*
    meters
    in African music, 21–22
    on *Bitches Brew*, 292–294
    in boogie-woogie, 69–70
    in bop, 175–177, *176*
    of Coleman, 272–273
    in Dixieland, 86, 99
    experiments in, 10
    in free form, 269
    Giuffre's use of, 209–210
    in jazz, 10–11, 66
    in jazz/rock fusion, 291–292
    listening for, 12–15
    Parker's use of, 183
    in ragtime, 66
    shuffle rhythm, 72–73
    in swing, 126
    in third stream, 215
Rhythm Juggles, *103*
rhythm section, **7**
    in bop, 176–177
    Coltrane's use of, 261
    Davis's use of, 232, 233, 236
    Hancock's use of, 307
    in jazz/rock fusion,
        291–292, 294
    in swing, 113
Rich, Buddy, 328

Riddle, Nelson, 142
riff, **70**
    ensemble and, 123–125
    soloists and, 119, 121–123
    in swing, 113
Riley, Jim, 292
rim shots, **99**
ritual, in African cultures, 21, 22
Roach, Max, 248
Roaring Twenties, 96–98, 99
rock music. *See also* jazz/rock fusion
    jazz in, 309–311
    swing challenged by, 144
"Rockin' in Rhythm" (Weather
    Report), 299–300
Rockit, 306
"Rockit" (Hancock), 324
Rodin, Gil, 127
Rodriguez, Tito, 192
Rogers, Billie, 129
Rogers, Shorty, 192, 210–212
Rolfe, B. A., 92
Rollins, Sonny, *250*
    Brown and, 248
    and jazz mainstream, 250–252
    Parker and, 182–183
rondo, **352**
Roney, Wallace, 319–320
round, **352**
Royal, Ernie, 194
Rumsey, Howard, 192, 210
rural blues. *See* country blues
Rushdoony, Rousas, 68
Russell, George, 216
Russell, Louis, 95
Russell, Pee Wee, 101
Russo, Marc, 304
Russo, William, 216

St. Louis, ragtime in, 63
"St. Louis Blues" (Handy), 177
"St. Louis Blues" (Smith), 54
"St. Thomas" (Rollins), 250
salsa, **220,** 308
Sanborn, David, 301–303
Sanchez, Poncho, 309
Sanders, Pharaoh, 262
Santamaria, Mongo, 194, 220,
    221, 308, 309
Sauter, Eddie, 216
Sauter-Finegan Orchestra, 216
saxophone
    Bechet's playing of, 88
    Bloom's playing of, 320